THE
BEST
OF
Gourmet

THE
BEST
OF
Gourmet
1991 EDITION

ALL OF THE BEAUTIFULLY
ILLUSTRATED MENUS FROM 1990
PLUS OVER 500 SELECTED RECIPES

FROM THE EDITORS OF GOURMET

CONDÉ NAST BOOKS

RANDOM HOUSE

NEW YORK

LIBRARY OF CONGRESS CATALOGING-IN-PUBLICATION DATA
(Revised for vol. 6)

Main entry under title:
The Best of Gourmet.
  Includes Indexes
  1. Cookery, International. I. Gourmet.
TX725.A1B4827   1986   641.5   87-640167
ISBN 0-679-40068-0 (v. 6)
ISSN 1046-1760

Most of the recipes in this work were previously published in *Gourmet* Magazine.

Manufactured in the United States of America

98765432

Grateful acknowledgment is made to the following for permission to reprint recipes previously published in *Gourmet* Magazine.

Jayne Cohen: ''Crab-Meat Ravioli with Fennel Purée and Roasted Red Pepper Sauce'' (page 176); ''Goat Cheese Ravioli with Garlic Tomato Sauce'' (page 177); ''To Prepare Won Ton Ravioli'' (page 176). Copyright © 1990 by Jayne Cohen. Reprinted by permission of the author.

Faye Levy: ''Eggplant Stuffed with Scamorza Cheese'' (page 184); ''Grilled Eggplant Antipasto'' (page 206). Copyright © 1990 by Faye Levy. Reprinted by permission of the author.

Barbara Karoff: ''Apricot, Orange, and Carrot Soup'' (page 104); ''Cantaloupe Peach Soup'' (page 104); ''Curried Pear and Apple Soup'' (page 108); ''Pear, Pea, and Watercress Soup'' (page 107). Copyright © 1990 by Barbara Karoff. Reprinted by permission of the author.

David Rosengarten: ''Balsamic Vinegar Chicken with Wild Mushrooms'' (page 153); ''Balsamic-Marinated Lamb Chops'' (page 144); ''Fried Oysters with Radicchio and Balsamic Vinegar'' (page 123); ''Pimiento Butter'' (page 145). Copyright ©1990 by David Rosengarten. Reprinted by permission of the author.

The editors would like to thank Alexandra Schulz for her skillfully rendered illustrations for this year's ''A Gourmet Addendum,'' and the following illustrators whose work appears throughout *The Best of Gourmet—1991:* Barbara Fiore, Lauren Jarrett, Zoe Mavridis, Jeanne Meinke, Jenni Oliver, and Michael Rosen.

PROJECT STAFF

For Condé Nast Books

Jane J. Fisher, Director
Lorraine Davis, Editorial Director
Ellen Maria Bruzelius, Direct Marketing Manager
Kristine Smith-Cunningham, Advertising Promotion Manager
Mary Ellen Kelly, Fulfillment Manager
Katherine Ferrara, Assistant
Diane Pesce, Composition Production Manager
Serafino J. Cambareri, Quality Control Manager

For *Gourmet* Magazine

Jane Montant, Editor-in-Chief
Evie Righter, Senior Editor
Diane Keitt, Editor
Romulo Yanes, Staff Photographer
Irwin Glusker, Design Consultant

Produced in association with
Media Projects Incorporated

Carter Smith, Executive Editor
Judith Tropea, Project Editor
Martina D'Alton, Associate Project Editor
Patra Cogan, Indexer
Michael Shroyer, Art/Production Director

The editors would like to thank Georgia Chan Downard for her creative recipe development in ''A Gourmet Addendum,'' and Blair Brown Hoyt for her resourceful proofreading services.

Special thanks also is given to the food department and studio of *Gourmet* Magazine.

The text of this book was set in Times Roman by the Composition Department of Condé Nast Publications, Inc. and U.S. Lithograph Typographers. The four-color separations were done by The Color Company, Seiple Lithographers, and Applied Graphic Technologies—Kordet Division. The book was printed and bound at R. R. Donnelley and Sons. Text paper is Tahoe Web Gloss.

Front Jacket: ''Blackberry Sorbet'' (page 245), ''Lime Sorbet'' (page 245), ''Mango Sorbet'' (page 246), and ''Raspberry Sorbet'' (page 246).

Back Jacket: ''Grilled Chicken and Ziti Salad'' (page 199).

Frontispiece: ''Baked Pears'' (page 249).

CONTENTS

INTRODUCTION

This year *Gourmet* proudly celebrates its fiftieth year. As with all such milestones it seems an appropriate time to reflect over the years past as well as to plan for the future. Recently I spent some time looking over the early issues of the magazine and concluded that their lovely watercolor covers, black and white illustrations, and timely articles all realize our enthusiasm for the art of good living, just as our full-color photographs and up-to-date articles do today. From the beginning, a harmonious blend of imaginative food combinations and welcoming settings, as well as a meticulous eye for detail, has remained consistent.

The Best of Gourmet, a compilation of over 500 recipes from the magazine of the previous year, first appeared in 1986 and continues to be published annually. Like the magazine issues they mirror, the annuals become statements of the times in which they appear. *The Best of Gourmet, Volume Six,* for example, reflects life as we begin the 1990s. As you look through The Menu Collection, with over 70 pages of photographs and dining ideas, you will note that the style is, in general, simple: the decor has clean lines and the menus are sensible. With more and more of our time spent on careers, community involvement, travel, and so on, there is little extra time; and yet pleasures from the table, to say nothing of nutritional needs, make quick-to-prepare, light, and healthful meals more important than ever.

Because free time is scarce, relaxing in an informal setting and entertaining go hand-in-hand. You will find that many of our menus are designed for out-of-door entertaining. Zucchini Coriander Soup followed by Grilled Chicken Salad with Corn, Peppers, and Tortilla Crisps is just one of our pretty (and easy-to-prepare) Perennial Garden Luncheons. Summer picnics are numerous and locations are varied. Try our Rowboat Picnic of Ham and Münster Buns with Honey Mustard; Peperoncini Stuffed with Smoked Salmon and Dill Cream; Goat Cheese, Salami, and Tomato on Mini Bagels; and Radish Sandwiches on Zucchini Basil Muffins. Or try our Beach Picnic highlighting Shrimp, Chicken, and Pineapple Kebabs with Sweet Jalapeño Basting Sauce. A Late-Summer Dinner featuring Austrian-Style Fried Chicken and ended simply with Baked Pears and Walnut Cigarette Cookies couldn't be more appropriate for a warm evening.

And when the weather is not agreeable, we take you indoors, where many of our get-togethers are also designed for casual entertaining. A Finger-Food Buffet for Super Bowl Sunday combines such favorites as Parmesan Mustard Chicken Wings and Baked Potato Skins. We even dust off our fondue sets for A Fondue Party for the 1990s, an updated version of the informal fêtes of the 1950s and 60s. Breadsticks, potatoes, vegetables, and even tortellini are dipped into our Three-Cheese Fondue with Tomato Chutney. Individual Toblerone Mousse Fondues with Meringues and Fruit provide a simple, pleasing dessert.

While life has become more streamlined and many of the fussy extras have gone, *Gourmet* still touts the importance of elegant dining. However, special care has been made to keep the menus "do-able" for today's cook. Our Easter Dinner highlights Herbed Roast Leg of Lamb with Roasted Onions and Potatoes, Rosemary Mint Wine Jelly, Mixed Spring Vegetables, and Minted Pea Purée—traditional fare, but updated in style.

The Menu Collection is only the beginning. Many more recipes culled from the other regular food columns of the magazine—Gastronomie sans Argent, In Short Order, and The Last Touch—await you. And, three indexes make using *The Best of Gourmet* effortless.

This year our addendum addresses cooking with herbs. Nutritionists as well as traditional cooks applaud the current popularity of herbs, and *Gourmet* acknowledges their importance in today's cooking. Thirty-six original herbal recipes are just waiting to be enjoyed.

As to the future, we realize that *Gourmet* must continually evolve to meet the needs of tomorrow. As our recent Fondue Party proves, however, there is value in studying the past. Ideas of quality, however old, can and do give way to the styles of the future. *Gourmet* embarks on the next 50 years ever committed to quality and the enjoyment that it brings.

Jane Montant
Editor-in-Chief

THE MENU COLLECTION

*A*s a source of year-round entertaining ideas The Menu Collection is unique. Over 70 pages of exquisite full-color photography and menus bring together the inspirations of the *Gourmet* staff to provide the reader with a ''complete picture''—a fully realized event with wonderful food in lovely settings. As you peruse these pages, allow yourself to ''join the party'' that is about to take place. The table is set; the decor is carefully chosen; the food has been carefully prepared. As host or hostess you are about to enjoy the best part of any gathering—your guests. As a guest you are about to be pampered.

These pages represent gatherings that are both a pleasure to host and a treat to attend. In general, *Gourmet* entertaining during 1990 was more relaxed and casual. Informal events, such as our many picnics and barbecues, require minimal preparation and incorporate many make-ahead dishes. Even our more formal holiday meals, such as our Easter Dinner, provide make-ahead instructions whenever suitable. *Gourmet* allows you to spend as much time as possible with your guests!

During the year *Gourmet*'s Menus were varied in tone and scope. We begin with a choice of festive intimate fare for New Year's Eve Dinners for Two. Will it be Caviar followed by Scallops with Pink Grapefruit Beurre Blanc, with Strawberry and Banana Tartlets in Coconut Pastry Shells as a finale? Or, will it be Mozzarella in Carrozza followed by Veal Chops with Eggplant and Pepper Stuffing and Roasted Red Pepper Sauce, with a simple Champagne Orange Sorbet and Chocolate Dipped Orange Cookies for dessert? Both menus are easy to prepare with several make-ahead dishes.

Other holidays are also celebrated with flair. Thanksgiving dinner boasts Roast Turkey with Corn Bread and Kale Stuffing and Paprika Pan Gravy with all of the trimmings, while Date Pecan Pumpkin Squares, Nutmeg Ice Cream, and Bourbon Burnt Sugar Sauce complete this updated classic. The Christmas Dinner menu is one of elegance: Penne, Bell Peppers, and Smoked Salmon in Creamy Garlic Sauce is followed by Loin of Veal with Shiitake Stuffing, Buttered Haricots Verts, and Radicchio and Watercress Salad with Parmesan Curls. A heavenly Macadamia Nut and Bittersweet Chocolate Ice Cream Bombe with Macadamia Nut Praline makes this menu very celebratory indeed!

Our Cocktail Party is every bit as festive but much larger in scope. Shrimp Toast with Pickled Ginger; Oriental Stuffed Mushrooms; Tiny Rib Lamb Chops with Minted Vinegar Dipping Sauce; and Fruit Kebabs with Vanilla Mint Yogurt Sauce are just some of the enticements offered. As our photographs prove, the dishes are light and simple, the look is modern and cosmopolitan—a toast to the '90s!

Menus from the Cuisine Courante column are informal and designed for those who have only a limited amount of time to spend in the kitchen. Perhaps A Poker Party would be a fun way to gather friends. A flavorful Chicken Cacciatora with Fusilli, Arugula Salad with Carrot and Yellow Pepper, and Breadsticks can be served by colorful platefuls. Or perhaps An Informal Dinner featuring Braised Veal Shanks with White Bean Tomato Sauce and Saffron Orzo followed by a warming Apple Walnut Crisp would be a delightful way to bring together family or friends at short notice.

Throughout Part One, Gerald Asher, *Gourmet*'s wine editor, suggests appropriate beverages to complement each menu. A thirst-quenching lemonade for our Rowboat Picnic, a jubilant Edna Valley Vineyard Chardonnay '88 for our Fourth of July Dinner, a ''something new'' Pink Pony for A Santa Barbara Barbecue, a festive Veuve Clicquot ''Carte Or'' Brut '82 for New Year's—his trustworthy selections take the guesswork out of choosing libations.

Formal or informal, indoors or out, large or small, twenty-four entertaining options are now at your fingertips. The difficulty will come in trying to narrow down the choices!

NEW YEAR'S EVE DINNERS FOR TWO

Veuve Clicquot
"Carte Or"
Brut '82

Caviar with Toasts and Garnishes

Scallops with Pink Grapefruit Beurre Blanc, p. 118

Kenwood Vineyards
Sonoma Valley
Chardonnay '87

Roasted Rosemary Potato Slices, p. 192

Buttered Snow Peas, p. 194

Strawberry and Banana Tartlets
in Coconut Pastry Shells, p. 235

Iron Horse Vineyards
Brut Rosé '86

Mozzarella in Carrozza, p. 166

Veal Chops with Eggplant and Pepper Stuffing
and Roasted Red Pepper Sauce, p. 135

Santa Barbara Winery
Zinfandel '87

Sautéed Baby Artichokes, p. 180

Champagne Orange Sorbet, p. 245

Chocolate-Dipped Orange Cookies, p. 231

Scallops with Pink Grapefruit Beurre Blanc;
Roasted Rosemary Potato Slices; Buttered Snow Peas

Veal Chop with Eggplant and Pepper Stuffing and
Roasted Red Pepper Sauce; Sautéed Baby Artichokes

Champagne Orange Sorbet,
Chocolate-Dipped Orange Cookies

Gingerbread Cupcakes with Lemon Cream-Cheese Frosting

A FINGER-FOOD BUFFET FOR SUPER BOWL SUNDAY

Dill and Garlic Shrimp Skewers, p. 125

The Eyrie Vineyards
Oregon Pinot Gris '88

Herbed Zucchini Spirals, p. 93

Parmesan Mustard Chicken Wings, p. 156

Baked Potato Skins, p. 190

Rolling Rock
Extra Pale
Premium Beer

Lettuce Scoops with
Coriander Yogurt Cheese, p. 90

Gingerbread Cupcakes with
Lemon Cream-Cheese Frosting, p. 228

Dill and Garlic Shrimp Skewers, Herbed Zucchini Spirals, Parmesan Mustard
Chicken Wings, Baked Potato Skins, Lettuce Scoops with Coriander Yogurt Cheese

DINNER
FLORIDA STYLE

Chilled Curried Carrot Soup, p. 105

Grilled Red Snapper with Thyme, p. 115

*Belvedere Russian
River Valley
Chardonnay '87*   Papaya Coriander Salsa, p. 115

Grilled Marinated Zucchini, p. 197

Rice and Tomatoes, p. 179

Passion Fruit Mousses with Raspberry Swirl, p. 238

Coconut Tuiles, p. 232

White Chocolate Pecan Truffles, p. 251

Chilled Curried Carrot Soup

Grilled Red Snapper with Thyme; Papaya Coriander
Salsa; Grilled Marinated Zucchini; Rice and Tomatoes

Passion Fruit Mousses with Raspberry Swirl

Toblerone Mousse Fondues with Meringues and Fruit

A FONDUE PARTY

Three-Cheese Fondue with Tomato Onion Chutney, p. 166

Santa Barbara Winery's Paradis '88

Soft Breadsticks with Fennel Seeds, p. 95

Roasted Potatoes with Garlic, p. 192

Assorted Vegetables and Tortellini

Watercress, Endive, and Apple Salad with Cider Dressing, p. 204

Toblerone Mousse Fondues with Meringues and Fruit, p. 239

Three-Cheese Fondue with Tomato Onion Chutney; Soft Breadsticks with Fennel Seeds; Roasted Potatoes with Garlic; Assorted Vegetables and Tortellini; Watercress, Endive, and Apple Salad with Cider Dressing

DINNER IRISH STYLE

Finnan Haddie and Watercress Soup, p. 106

Brown Oatmeal Soda Bread, p. 97

Fresh Ham with Cracklings and Pan Gravy, p. 139

The Brander Vineyard
Santa Ynez Valley
Bouchet '87

Mashed Potatoes with Scallion, p. 192

Beets with Stout and Sautéed Beet Greens, p. 181

Red Onion, Apple, and Raisin Chutney, p. 217

Carrot Raisin Cake with Irish Cream Frosting, p. 222

Fresh Ham with Cracklings and Pan Gravy; Beets with Stout and
Sautéed Beet Greens; Mashed Potatoes with Scallion; Red Onion, Apple, and Raisin Chutney

**Carrot Raisin Cake
with Irish Cream Frosting**

Apple Walnut Crisp

AN INFORMAL DINNER

Braised Veal Shanks with White Bean Tomato Sauce, p. 137

Aldo Conterno
Dolcetto d'Alba '87

Saffron Orzo, p. 174

Marinated Vegetable Salad, p. 208

Parmesan Rolls, p. 96

Apple Walnut Crisp, p. 246

Braised Veal Shanks with White Bean Tomato Sauce;
Saffron Orzo; Marinated Vegetable Salad; Parmesan Rolls

EASTER DINNER

Goat Cheese and Walnut Soufflés
with Watercress and Frisée Salad, p. 169

Herbed Roast Leg of Lamb
with Roasted Onions and Potatoes, p. 146

Rosemary Mint Wine Jelly, p. 218

Château Chasse-Spleen '85   Mixed Spring Vegetables, p. 195

Minted Pea Purée, p. 189

Raspberry White Chocolate Mousse Cake, p. 225

Herbed Roast Leg of Lamb with Roasted Onions and Potatoes,
Rosemary Mint Wine Jelly, Mixed Spring Vegetables, Minted Pea Purée

Raspberry White Chocolate Mousse Cake

Miniature Tartufi

A POKER PARTY

Torre Sant' Andrea
Orvieto Secco '88

Chicken Cacciatora with Fusilli, p. 149

Arugula Salad with Carrot and Yellow Pepper, p. 201

Breadsticks

Miniature Tartufi, p. 250

Chicken Cacciatora with Fusilli; Arugula Salad with
Carrot and Yellow Pepper; Breadsticks

A MERRY
MAY LUNCHEON

Curried Crab Meat and Mushroom Salad, p. 123

*Roast Fillet of Beef with Chipotle Red Pepper Sauce
and Mustard Chive Sauce, p. 127*

Vignati de Jago   *Roasted Shallot and Sesame Asparagus, p. 194*
Valpolicella '86

Black Beans, Corn, and Tomatoes Vinaigrette, p. 205

Dilled Walnut and Cottage Cheese Cloverleaf Rolls, p. 96

Iced Cappuccino Cream Cake, p. 222

Roast Fillet of Beef with Chipotle Red
Pepper Sauce and Mustard Chive Sauce;
Roasted Shallot and Sesame Asparagus

Iced Cappuccino Cream Cake

BRUNCH ON DERBY DAY

Mint Juleps, p. 252

Ham Biscuits, p. 138

Torres Viña Sol '88   *Turkey Hash, p. 162*

Corn Cakes, p. 99

Pea Salad, p. 206

Bibb, Watercress, and Mint Salad, p. 201

Chocolate Pecan Bars, p. 250

Fresh Strawberries

Mint Juleps; Corn Cakes; Ham Biscuits;
Turkey Hash; Bibb, Watercress, and Mint Salad

A COCKTAIL PARTY

Shrimp Toast with Pickled Ginger, p. 93

Potato Samosa Tartlets, p. 91

Thai-Style Chicken Salad on Cumin Quick Bread, p. 87

Miniature Roquefort Napoleons, p. 92

Oriental Stuffed Mushrooms, p. 90

Cod Fritters with Tartar Sauce, p. 88

Tiny Rib Lamb Chops with Minted Vinegar Dipping Sauce, p. 89

Fruit Kebabs with Vanilla Mint Yogurt Sauce, p. 89

Shrimp Toast with Pickled Ginger

Top:
Miniature Roquefort Napoleons; Oriental Stuffed Mushrooms; Cod Fritters with Tartar Sauce; Fruit Kebabs with Vanilla Mint Yogurt Sauce
Bottom:
Potato Samosa Tartlets; Thai-Style Chicken Salad on Cumin Quick Bread

Pasta with Summer Vegetables, Goat Cheese Toasts

PERENNIAL GARDEN LUNCHEONS

Zucchini Coriander Soup, p. 110

Hattenheimer   *Grilled Chicken Salad with*
Nussbrunnen '88   *Corn, Peppers, and Tortilla Crisps, p. 198*

Brownie Ice-Cream Sandwiches with Caramel Sauce, p. 244

Carpaccio with Arugula and Artichoke Dressing, p. 126

Juliénas '89   *Pasta with Summer Vegetables, p. 175*

Goat Cheese Toasts, p. 101

Espresso Granita, p. 240

Grilled Chicken Salad with Corn, Peppers, and Tortilla Crisps

SUMMER PICNICS

ROWBOAT PICNIC

Ham and Münster Buns with Honey Mustard, p. 95

Lemonade   *Peperoncini Stuffed with Smoked Salmon and Dill Cream, p. 90*

Goat Cheese, Salami, and Tomato on Mini-Bagels, p. 166

Radish Sandwiches on Zucchini Basil Muffins, p. 100

MEADOW PICNIC

Grilled Chicken and Ziti Salad, p. 199

Iced Tea

Lebanese-Style Tuna Salad with Tahini Dressing, p. 201

Grgich Hills
  Napa Valley   *Green Bean, Yellow Pepper, and Bacon Salad*
    Fumé Blanc '88   *with Orégano Vinaigrette, p. 204*

Rosemount Estate   *Roast Beef and Couscous Rolls, p. 128*
  Diamond Reserve
    Hunter Valley Red '88   *Tsatsiki, p. 205*   *Cherry Tomatoes*

S'Mores Bars, p. 232

TWILIGHT DESSERT PICNIC

Chocolate Coconut Rum Cake, p. 224

Peach Wine, p. 252   *Chewy Almond Macaroons, p. 230*

Assorted Fruit

Meadow Picnic

Peach Raspberry Kuchen

CUISINE COURANTE

FOURTH OF JULY DINNER

Salmon, Scallop, and Pea Terrine, p. 116

Chive Butter Sauce, p. 116

Edna Valley Vineyard
Chardonnay '88

Dilled Potatoes Vinaigrette, p. 191

Tomato, Mint, and Red Onion Salad, p. 208

Peach Raspberry Kuchen, p. 234

Salmon, Scallop, and Pea Terrine; Chive Butter Sauce;
Dilled Potatoes Vinaigrette; Tomato, Mint, and Red Onion Salad

A SANTA BARBARA BARBECUE

Yellow Bell Pepper Salsa with
Cumin Tortilla Chips, *p. 92*

Pink Ponies, p. 252

Chili Almonds and Coconut Chips, *p. 85*

Barbecued Spareribs, *p. 143*

Sanford Winery
   Santa Barbara County
    Chardonnay '88

Southern-Style
Tomato Barbecue Sauce, *p. 143*

Okra, Squash, and Onion Kebabs, *p. 187*

Sage Butter, *p. 188*

Gainey Vineyard
   Santa Barbara County
    Merlot '87

Grilled Corn, *p. 182*

Mixed Greens and Tomatoes
with Anchovy Dressing, *p. 203*

Frozen Nectarine Mousse with Blackberry Swirl, *p. 244*

Barbecued Spareribs; Southern-Style Tomato Barbecue Sauce; Grilled Corn;
Sage Butter; Okra, Squash, and Onion Kebabs; Mixed Greens and Tomatoes with Anchovy Dressing

Shrimp, Chicken, and Pineapple Kebabs with Sweet Jalapeño
Basting Sauce; Lemon Rice Salad with Peanuts

A BEACH PICNIC

*Shrimp, Chicken, and Pineapple Kebabs
with Sweet Jalapeño Basting Sauce, p. 124*

Beer　　　　　*Lemon Rice Salad with Peanuts, p. 209*

Assorted Cheeses and Rolls

Almond Ginger Sand Tarts, p. 230

A LATE-SUMMER DINNER

Bidwell Vineyards	*Grilled Leeks with*
Long Island	*Herbed Vinaigrette, p. 186*
White Riesling '88	

Austrian-Style Fried Chicken, p. 153

Tomato Chutney, p. 217

Corn and Zucchini Timbales, p. 182

Mixed Green Salad, p. 203

Baked Pears, p. 249

Walnut Cigarette Cookies, p. 232

Austrian-Style Fried Chicken, Corn and Zucchini Timbales, Tomato Chutney

Grilled Leeks with Herbed Vinaigrette

Walnut and Wheat Germ Silver-Dollar Pancakes;
Blackberry Syrup; Melted Butter

A ROOFTOP BREAKFAST

Mango Papaya Smoothies, p. 252

Melon, Nectarine, Grape, and Plum Compote, p. 170

Walnut and Wheat Germ Silver-Dollar Pancakes, p. 172

Blackberry Syrup, p. 172

AN
AUTUMN
DINNER

*Wild Mushroom and Veal Terrine
with Roasted Yellow Pepper Coulis, p. 138*

*Spiced Venison Steaks with
Red-Cabbage Confit and Red-Wine Sauce, p. 148*

Roasted Autumn Vegetables, p. 196

*Barolo
Pio Cesare '85*

Braised Belgian Endive Gratin, p. 185

*Frisée, Radicchio, and Asian Pear Salad
with Hazelnut Vinaigrette, p. 202*

Chocolate Chestnut Torte, p. 223

Spiced Venison Steaks with Red-Cabbage Confit and Red-Wine Sauce,
Roasted Autumn Vegetables, Braised Belgian Endive Gratin

Chocolate Chestnut Torte

Prune Sherry Ice Cream with Burnt Sugar Sauce

CUISINE COURANTE

A SPANISH DINNER FOR COLUMBUS DAY

*Marquès de Riscal
Rueda '88*

Arroz con Pollo, p. 152

Escarole Salad with Tarragon, p. 202

*Prune Sherry Ice Cream
with Burnt Sugar Sauce, p. 242*

Arroz con Pollo, Escarole Salad with Tarragon

THANKSGIVING
DINNER

Spicy Almonds and Cashews, *p. 85*

*Blandy's 5-Years-Old
Dry Sercial Madeira*   Butternut Squash Soup with
Green Chili Coriander Chutney, *p. 108*

Roast Turkey with Corn Bread and Kale Stuffing
and Paprika Pan Gravy, *p. 158*

Sherried Sweet Potatoes
and Apples, *p. 193*

*ZD California
Chardonnay '88*   Mashed Potatoes, *p. 192*

Lemony Creamed Brussels Sprouts
and Celery, *p. 182*

Cranberry Sauce
with Pearl Onions and Golden Raisins, *p. 215*

Date Pecan Pumpkin Squares, *p. 227*

Nutmeg Ice Cream, *p. 227*   Bourbon Burnt Sugar Sauce, *p. 227*

Butternut Squash Soup with
Green Chili Coriander Chutney

Roast Turkey with Corn Bread and Kale Stuffing and Paprika Pan Gravy;
Cranberry Sauce with Pearl Onions and Golden Raisins;
Sherried Sweet Potatoes and Apples; Lemony Creamed Brussels Sprouts and Celery

Pumpkin Cheesecake with Bourbon Sour Cream Topping

AN ELEGANT SMALL THANKSGIVING

Mushroom and Onion Gratins, p. 186

Hanzell Vineyards
Sonoma Valley
Pinot Noir '86

Roast Quail with Cranberry Madeira Sauce, p. 158

Dauphine Potatoes, p. 191

Petits Pois, p. 188

Pumpkin Cheesecake with
Bourbon Sour Cream Topping, p. 228

Roast Quail with Cranberry Madeira Sauce;
Dauphine Potatoes; Petits Pois

CHRISTMAS DINNER

Renaissance Vineyard *North Yuba* *Sauvignon Blanc '88*	*Penne, Bell Peppers,* *and Smoked Salmon* *in Creamy Garlic Sauce, p. 175*
Robert Mondavi *Napa Valley* *Pinot Noir '88*	*Loin of Veal* *with Shiitake Stuffing, p. 136*
	Buttered Haricots Verts, p. 181
	Radicchio and Watercress Salad *with Parmesan Curls, p. 203*
Lustau's Emilin *Moscatel Sherry*	*Macadamia Nut and Bittersweet Chocolate* *Ice-Cream Bombe* *with Macadamia Nut Praline, p. 242*

Loin of Veal with Shiitake Stuffing;
Buttered Haricots Verts

Macadamia Nut and Bittersweet Chocolate
Ice-Cream Bombe with Macadamia Nut Praline

Lemon Meringue Custards

A CHRISTMAS EVE SUPPER

Arbor Crest
Columbia Valley
Chardonnay '88

Baked Oysters with Spinach Fennel Purée
and Crisp Fried Shallots, p. 123

Clams Casino, p. 120

Columbia Crest
Washington State
Cabernet Sauvignon '86

Fillet of Beef on Garlic Croutons
with Roasted Onion, Caper, and Tarragon Sauce, p. 126

Baked Olive and Mozzarella Orzo, p. 174

Yuletide Tossed Salad, p. 204

Lemon Meringue Custards, p. 237

Baked Oysters with Spinach Fennel Purée and Crisp Fried Shallots; Clams Casino; Fillet of Beef on Garlic
Croutons with Roasted Onion, Caper, and Tarragon Sauce; Olive and Mozzarella Orzo; Yuletide Tossed Salad

A RECIPE COMPENDIUM

*P*art Two of *The Best of Gourmet*, A Recipe Compendium, catalogs over 500 of the best recipes that appeared in *Gourmet* Magazine during 1990—all of the recipes from *Gourmet*'s Menus and Cuisine Courante columns in Part One, The Menu Collection, along with selections from Gastronomie sans Argent, In Short Order, The Last Touch, as well as a number of recipes from featured articles during the year. Arranged alphabetically by category, this collection of recipes is easily scanned to find a desired dish. And remember, three indexes are also provided for quick reference.

As all good cooks know, the most successful meals are those that use the freshest ingredients. Throughout the year recipes from the column Gastronomie sans Argent take inexpensive seasonal bounty and transform it into something exceptional. Now, when blueberries are freshly picked, you will have a stash of delectable ways to enjoy their goodness—Blueberry Buttermilk Tart, Blueberry Ice Cream, Blueberry Corn Muffins, Blueberry Whole-Wheat Pancakes.... Vegetables, too, receive special treatment. During the cold months the humble potato magically turns into Spiced Potato Doughnuts; Portuguese Kale and Potato Soup; Potato Rosemary Focaccia; and Sautéed Potatoes Provençale. Also, a variety of summertime stuffed vegetables show off their colors in Zucchini Boats with Tabbouleh Filling; Tomatoes with Corn and Basil Filling; and Cucumber Cups Filled with Herbed Yogurt and Smoked Salmon, to name a few. You will even find creative entrées in our ever-appealing potpies and savory shortcakes. Chicken and Dill Fricassee with Sour Cream Shortcakes; Lamb and Eggplant Potpie with Feta Potato Crust; and even Creamy Monkfish, Tomato, and Shellfish Potpie with Puff Pastry Crust—each is ideal for a light lunch or dinner and many can serve as a meal-in-one.

Life today can be hectic. It's nice to know that when there is little time to cook, a recipe from the column In Short Order will save the day. Simply turn to our Index of 45-Minute Recipes to find an extraordinary variety of recipes for two that can be made in a flash (often less than 45 minutes) *and* have panache. Perhaps a colleague is dropping in after work and there is no time to shop. Why not make our Parmesan Puffs? You probably already have the required six basic ingredients on hand. Add a glass of wine and the visit becomes warm and inviting. Or perhaps you're having a friend over for lunch. Our deceptively simple Scandinavian Vegetable Soup with Shrimp followed by our easy-to-prepare Whipped Cream Cakes with Peaches and Raspberries will turn this casual get-together into a memorable one.

If you live alone or as a twosome, In Short Order recipes were made with you in mind. You will find a host of entrées here, all quickly made flavorful dishes with flair. This week why not try our Teriyaki-Style Chicken; or Grilled Scallops with Curried Tomato Coulis; or Baked Ham with Cucumber, Tarragon, and Mushroom Sauce? A myriad of starters and desserts, all from this column, will round out your choices for speedy meals that never compromise taste.

It is also fun to use recipes from In Short Order to enliven your culinary repertoire. For example, left to your own devices would you ever have dreamed of making Curried Chili Shrimp, or Quick Cabbage and Carrot Pickle, or Microwave Chocolate Orange Raisin Cakes with Chocolate Glaze? Here is a chance to shine as a *Gourmet* cook with minimal time and effort.

The Last Touch is a thematic column that provides an assortment of both whimsical and more traditional dishes. During the year a collection of olive recipes produced Herbed Green Olive Salad; Olive Mint Quick Bread; Ripe Olive and Goat Cheese Toasts; and Lemon-Rosemary-Marinated Ripe Olives—all eye-opening

Rowboat Picnic (page 46)

dishes that add a marvelous "last touch" to an event. Even before these recipes are prepared you know that they will steal the show. Of a more traditional nature, hot sandwiches also appeared—Croques-Monsieur; Broiled Open-Faced Crab-Meat Sandwiches; Steak Sandwiches with Crispy Onions; and Hot Browns (Open-Faced Turkey Sandwiches with Mornay Sauce). The spark of creativity in each of these sandwiches sets them apart from their more classic counterparts. Recipes for dried fruits, scones, asparagus toppings, flavored butters, salad toppings, grapes… are all at hand.

A number of recipes from our feature food articles also add zest to our collection. Are you an eggplant lover? From an article on this popular vegetable by Faye Levy comes Grilled Eggplant Antipasto and Eggplant Stuffed with Scamorza Cheese. An inspired piece authored by Jayne Cohen features Won Ton Ravioli. Here exciting and unusual combinations such as Crab-Meat Ravioli with Fennel Purée and Roasted Red Pepper Sauce, and Goat Cheese Ravioli with Garlic Tomato Sauce are found. And then Barbara Karoff introduces fruit soups that will fill your tureen with color and flavor. A winning pear, pea, and watercress mixture, as well as a sensational apricot, orange, and carrot combination are sure to broaden your thoughts on soup.

Hors d'oeuvres, canapés, and spreads; breads; soups; fish and shellfish; meats; poultry; cheese, eggs, and breakfast items; pasta and grains; vegetables; salads and salad dressings; sauces; desserts; and beverages—over 500 recipes are now at your fingertips. Which one should you try first? Contemplate your mood, turn to the appropriate chapter, and indulge!

HORS D'OEUVRES, CANAPÉS, AND SPREADS

HORS D'OEUVRES

Chili Almonds and Coconut Chips

1 coconut without any cracks and
 containing liquid
1½ tablespoons fresh lemon juice
2 teaspoons chili powder
cayenne to taste
1 cup sliced almonds

With an ice pick or a skewer test the 3 eyes of the coconut to find the weakest one and pierce it to make a hole. Drain the liquid into a bowl and reserve it for another use if desired. Bake the coconut in a preheated 400° F. oven for 15 minutes, break it with a hammer on a work surface, and with the point of a strong small knife lever the flesh carefully out of the shell. With a vegetable peeler peel thin enough 1-inch-long slices of the coconut to measure 1 cup, reserving the remaining coconut for another use.

In a bowl toss the coconut slices with half the lemon juice, half the chili powder, some of the cayenne, and salt to taste until they are coated well, bake them in a jelly-roll pan in the middle of a preheated 350° F. oven, stirring occasionally, for 12 to 15 minutes, or until they are golden, and transfer them to a bowl. In another bowl toss the almonds with the remaining lemon juice, the remaining chili powder, more cayenne, and salt to taste

until they are coated well and bake them in the jelly-roll pan in the 350° F. oven, stirring occasionally, for 8 to 10 minutes, or until they are golden. Add the coconut slices, toss them with the almonds, and transfer the mixture to a serving bowl. *The chili almonds and coconut chips may be made 6 hours in advance and kept in an airtight container.* Makes about 2 cups.

Spicy Almonds and Cashews

2 tablespoons unsalted butter
1 teaspoon ground cumin
½ teaspoon chili powder
¼ teaspoon cayenne
1 teaspoon salt
1 teaspoon paprika
2 cups whole blanched almonds,
 toasted lightly
2 cups raw cashews (available at natural foods
 stores), toasted lightly

In a small heavy skillet melt the butter over moderately low heat, add the cumin, the chili powder, the cayenne, the salt, and the paprika, and cook the spices, stirring, for 30 seconds. Add the nuts and stir them to coat them well. Transfer the coated nuts to a baking pan large enough to hold them in one layer and toast them in a preheated 350° F. oven for 5 minutes. Let the nuts cool and transfer them to a serving dish. Makes about 4 cups.

Bean and Cheese Tostadas
(Flour Tortillas with Beans, Monterey Jack, and Chilies)

For the bean purée
1 small onion, minced
2 garlic cloves, minced
2 tablespoons olive oil
1 teaspoon ground cumin
a 1-pound can pinto, black, or pink beans,
    rinsed, drained, and puréed coarse

six 7- to 8-inch or four 10-inch flour tortillas
    (page 103 or store-bought)
2 tablespoons unsalted butter, melted
3 cups grated Monterey Jack (about ¾ pound)
4 fresh or pickled *jalapeño* chilies, or to taste,
    seeded and chopped (wear rubber gloves)
guacamole (page 130) and tomato *salsa*
    (page 130) as accompaniments

Make the bean purée: In a skillet cook the onion and the garlic in the oil over moderately low heat, stirring, until the onion is softened, add the cumin, the beans, ⅓ cup water, and salt and pepper to taste, and cook the mixture, stirring, for 3 to 4 minutes, or until it is heated through and thick but still spreadable. *The bean purée may be made 1 day in advance, covered and chilled.*

Arrange the tortillas in one layer on greased baking sheets, brush them lightly with the butter, and bake them in the middle of a preheated 400° F. oven for 5 minutes, or until they are crisp and golden. Divide the bean purée among the tortillas, spreading it evenly, divide the Monterey Jack and the chilies evenly among the tortillas, and bake the *tostadas* in the middle of a preheated 400° F. oven for 5 to 8 minutes, or until the cheese is melted. Serve the *tostadas*, cut into wedges, with the *guacamole* and the *salsa*. Serves 8 as an hors d'oeuvre.

Carrot Scallion Fritters

¾ cup coarsely grated carrot
½ cup thinly sliced scallion
1 large egg, beaten lightly
⅓ cup fine dry bread crumbs
vegetable oil for deep-frying

In a bowl combine well the carrot, the scallion, the egg, the bread crumbs, and salt and pepper to taste. In a large skillet heat 1 inch of the oil until it registers 375° F. on a deep-fat thermometer, in batches drop the carrot mixture into the oil by tablespoons, and fry the fritters for 1½ to 2 minutes, or until they are golden. Transfer the fritters to paper towels and let them drain. Serve the fritters as hors d'oeuvres or as a side dish. Makes about 10 fritters.

Fried Cheddar Cubes

10 ounces Cheddar, cut into ¾-inch cubes
¼ cup cornstarch
1 large egg, beaten lightly
1 cup fine fresh bread crumbs
vegetable oil for deep-frying the cubes
applesauce as an accompaniment

Dredge the Cheddar cubes in batches in the cornstarch, shaking off the excess, coat them thoroughly in the egg, and dredge them in the bread crumbs, patting and pressing the crumbs to help them adhere. Let the coated cubes stand on a sheet of wax paper for 20 minutes. In a deep fryer heat 2 inches of the oil to 350° F. on a deep-fat thermometer, in it fry the Cheddar cubes in batches, turning them, for 1½ to 2 minutes, or until they are golden, and with a slotted spoon transfer them to paper towels to drain. Serve the Cheddar cubes with the applesauce. Makes about 28 hors d'oeuvres.

Deep-Fried Chestnut Balls with
Cranberry Dipping Sauce

¾ cup finely chopped onion
1 large garlic clove, minced
1½ tablespoons unsalted butter
2 cups (about ¾ pound) canned or vacuum-
    packed whole chestnuts, rinsed, drained
    well, and patted dry if using canned
1 cup chicken broth
cayenne to taste
a pinch of ground cloves
¼ cup minced fresh parsley leaves
1½ cups fine fresh bread crumbs
    an egg wash made by beating together
    1 large egg and 1½ teaspoons water
½ cup blanched whole almonds, ground
vegetable oil for deep-frying
1 cup fresh or canned whole cranberry sauce

In a heavy saucepan cook the onion and the garlic in the butter over moderately low heat, stirring, until the onion is softened, add the chestnuts, the broth, the cayenne, the cloves, and salt and pepper to taste, and simmer the mixture, covered, stirring occasionally, for 15 minutes, or until the chestnuts are very tender. In a food processor purée the mixture until it is smooth, add the parsley and 1 cup of the bread crumbs, and process the mixture until it is combined well. Transfer the mixture to a bowl, let it cool, and chill it, covered, for at least 6 hours or overnight. Have ready in one bowl the egg wash and in another bowl the remaining ½ cup bread crumbs combined with the almonds. Form the chestnut mixture by heaping teaspoons into balls, dip the balls in the egg wash, and roll them in the almond mixture. In a deep fryer heat 2 inches of the oil until it registers 375° F. on a deep-fat thermometer, in it fry the balls in batches for 2 minutes, or until they are golden brown, and transfer them as they are fried to paper towels to drain.

In a blender or food processor purée the cranberry sauce and serve it with the chestnut balls. Makes about 40 hors d'oeuvres.

Thai-Style Chicken Salad on Cumin Quick Bread

For the chicken salad
¼ cup fresh lime juice
1 teaspoon salt
½ teaspoon chili powder
¼ cup finely chopped fresh coriander
¼ cup finely chopped fresh mint leaves
a pinch of sugar
2 poached whole skinless boneless chicken
  breasts (about 1¼ pounds), minced
  (about 3 cups)
⅓ cup finely chopped shallot
⅓ cup thinly sliced scallion
¼ cup mayonnaise, or to taste

1 loaf of cumin quick bread (recipe follows)
about ½ cup mayonnaise for garnish
finely chopped fresh parsley leaves
  for garnish

Make the chicken salad: In a large bowl whisk together the lime juice, the salt, the chili powder, the coriander, the mint, and the sugar, stir in the chicken, the shallot, and the scallion, and stir in the mayonnaise. The

chicken salad may be made 1 day in advance and kept covered and chilled.

Cut the bread into ⅓-inch-thick slices, spread each of half the slices with a scant 2 tablespoons of the chicken salad, and top the chicken salad with the remaining slices. Cut each sandwich in half. Spread a thin layer of the mayonnaise on one of the edges of each sandwich and dip it in the parsley. Makes about 34 sandwiches.

PHOTO ON PAGE 43

Cumin Quick Bread

3 cups all-purpose flour
¼ cup sugar
2 tablespoons double-acting baking powder
4 teaspoons ground cumin
1 teaspoon cuminseed, crushed lightly
½ teaspoon dry mustard
2 teaspoons salt
3 large eggs, beaten
1½ cups milk
⅓ cup vegetable oil

In a large bowl stir together the flour, the sugar, the baking powder, the ground cumin, the cuminseed, the mustard, and the salt. In a bowl whisk together the eggs, the milk, and the oil and stir the mixture into the flour mixture, stirring the batter until it is just moistened. Pour the batter into a well-buttered loaf pan, 11 by 4½ by 2¾ inches, or 9 by 5 by 3 inches, and bake it in the middle of a preheated 350° F. oven for 1 hour to 1 hour and 10 minutes, or until a tester comes out clean. Let the bread cool in the pan on a rack for 15 minutes, turn it out onto the rack, and let it cool completely. Makes 1 loaf.

Cod Fritters with
Tartar Sauce

For the tartar sauce
½ cup mayonnaise
2 tablespoons minced fresh
   parsley leaves
2 tablespoons minced sweet
   pickle relish
1 tablespoon minced onion
1 tablespoon minced celery
1½ teaspoons Dijon-style mustard
1 teaspoon fresh lemon juice
½ teaspoon minced fresh tarragon leaves or
   ¼ teaspoon dried, crumbled
a pinch of celery seeds
Tabasco to taste

1 pound cod fillet, poached
   and flaked
2 large eggs, beaten
   lightly
¼ cup thinly sliced scallion
1 tablespoon finely chopped fresh
   parsley leaves
2 tablespoons minced onion
¼ cup fine fresh bread crumbs
Tabasco to taste
1 cup finely ground Saltines seasoned
   with salt and pepper
vegetable oil for deep-frying

Make the tartar sauce: In a bowl stir together the mayonnaise, the parsley, the relish, the onion, the minced celery, the mustard, the lemon juice, the tarragon, the celery seeds, and the Tabasco until the sauce is combined well. *The tartar sauce may be made 1 day in advance and kept covered and chilled.*

In a bowl stir together the cod, the eggs, the scallion, the parsley, the onion, the bread crumbs, 2 tablespoons of the tartar sauce, the Tabasco, and salt and pepper to taste, form heaping teaspoons of the mixture into balls, and roll the balls in the ground Saltines. In a large deep skillet heat 1½ inches of the oil to 350° F. and in it fry the cod balls in batches for 1½ to 2 minutes on each side, or until they are golden. Transfer the fritters with a slotted spoon as they are fried to paper towels to drain. Serve the fritters warm with the remaining tartar sauce. Makes about 36 fritters.

PHOTO ON PAGE 43

Corn and Cheese Quesadillas
(*Flour Tortillas with Monterey Jack,*
Corn, and Chilies)

eight 7- to 8-inch or four 10-inch flour
   tortillas (page 103 or store-bought)
3 tablespoons unsalted butter, melted
2 cups grated Monterey Jack (about ½ pound)
1 cup cooked corn
2 fresh or pickled *jalapeño* chilies, or to taste,
   seeded and minced (wear rubber gloves)
guacamole (page 130) and tomato *salsa*
   (page 130) as accompaniments

Arrange half the tortillas in one layer on a large baking sheet and brush them lightly with some of the butter. Turn the tortillas over, divide the Monterey Jack, the corn, and the chilies evenly among them, and top the mixture with the remaining tortillas. Brush the tops lightly with some of the remaining butter and broil the *quesadillas* under a preheated broiler about 2 inches from the heat for 1 minute, or until the tops are golden and crisp. Turn the *quesadillas* carefully with a spatula, brush the tops lightly with the remaining butter, and broil the *quesadillas* for 1 minute more, or until the tops are golden and crisp. Serve the *quesadillas*, cut into wedges, with the *guacamole* and the *salsa*. Serves 4 as a first course or 6 as an hors d'oeuvre.

Cucumber Cups Filled with Herbed Yogurt and
Smoked Salmon

1 cup plain yogurt
a 14- to 16-inch seedless cucumber
3 scallions, minced
⅓ cup minced fresh dill plus dill sprigs
   for garnish
¼ pound thinly sliced smoked salmon

Drain the yogurt in a fine sieve set over a bowl, its surface covered with plastic wrap, chilled, overnight. Cut the cucumber crosswise into sixteen ¾-inch pieces and with a melon-ball cutter scoop out the centers, forming ¼-inch-thick cups. Sprinkle the cucumber cups with salt and let them drain, inverted, on paper towels for 10 minutes. In a bowl combine well the yogurt, the scallions, the minced dill, and salt and pepper to taste. Pat the cucumber cups dry gently and divide the yogurt mixture among them. Cut the salmon into eight 6- by ½-inch strips, halve the strips diagonally, and roll them up, beginning with the pointed ends and turning the edges slightly to form rose shapes. Arrange the salmon roses and the dill sprigs decoratively on the yogurt mixture. *The filled cucumber cups may be made 1 hour in advance and kept covered and chilled.* Makes 16 hors d'oeuvres.

Fruit Kebabs with Vanilla Mint Yogurt Sauce

1 cup plain yogurt
2 teaspoons sugar
⅛ teaspoon vanilla
2 tablespoons thinly sliced fresh mint leaves
1 pineapple, peeled, cored, and cubed
3 kiwi fruits, peeled and sliced
2 pints strawberries, hulled
1 honeydew melon, cubed
twenty-four 6-inch wooden skewers

In a bowl whisk together the yogurt, the sugar, the vanilla, and the mint. *The sauce may be made 1 day in advance and kept covered and chilled.*

Thread the fruits, alternating the pineapple, the kiwis, the strawberries, and the honeydew, onto the skewers. *The fruit kebabs may be made 1 day in advance and kept covered and chilled.* Serve the fruit kebabs with the yogurt sauce. Makes 24 kebabs.

PHOTO ON PAGE 43

Gingered Cream Cheese Grapes

6 ounces cream cheese, softened
2 tablespoons finely chopped crystallized ginger (available at specialty foods shops and some supermarkets)
30 green seedless grapes
1 cup pecans, toasted lightly, cooled completely, and chopped fine

In a bowl cream together the cream cheese and the ginger. Put 1 teaspoon of the mixture in the palm of one hand and roll it around a grape, using both palms to coat the grape completely. Coat the remaining grapes in the same manner and on a waxpaper–lined tray chill them for 15 minutes. Roll the cheese-coated grapes in the pecans, coating them completely, and chill them until the coating is firm. Makes 30 grapes.

Tiny Rib Lamb Chops with Minted Vinegar Dipping Sauce

For the dipping sauce
⅓ cup white-wine vinegar
¼ cup sugar
¼ cup plus 1 teaspoon minced fresh mint leaves

12 single New Zealand baby rib lamb chops (available at some butcher shops*), wholly frenched to the eye (about 1 pound)
1 garlic clove, halved crosswise
½ teaspoon dried thyme, crumbled
white pepper to taste

*For distribution information regarding frozen New Zealand baby lamb contact New Zealand Lamb Co., Inc., at 3 West Main Street, Elmsford, New York 10523 or telephone (914) 347-5488 or (800) 438-5262.

Make the dipping sauce: In a small saucepan combine the vinegar and the sugar and cook the mixture over moderate heat, stirring, until the sugar is dissolved. Stir in the mint and let the sauce cool. Season the sauce with salt and pepper and transfer it to a small bowl.

Pat the chops dry, rub them with the cut sides of the garlic, and sprinkle both sides of the chops with the thyme and the white pepper. Grill the chops in a well-oiled ridged grill pan over moderately high heat for 1 minute to 1½ minutes, depending on the thickness of the chops, on each side for rare meat. (Alternatively, the chops may be broiled under a preheated broiler about 4 inches from the heat for about 2 minutes on each side for rare meat.) Serve the chops with the dipping sauce. Makes 12 chops.

Lettuce Scoops with Coriander Yogurt Cheese

a 1-pound container plain yogurt
½ cup finely chopped seeded cucumber
½ cup finely chopped radish
⅓ cup finely chopped fresh coriander
12 small inner leaves of Bibb lettuce or
 romaine, rinsed and spun dry

In a large sieve lined with a double thickness of rinsed and squeezed cheesecloth and set over a bowl let the yogurt drain, covered and chilled, for 8 hours. Transfer the yogurt cheese to a bowl, discarding the liquid, and stir in the cucumber, the radish, the coriander, and salt to taste. Spoon about 1 tablespoon of the cheese mixture onto each lettuce leaf. (Do not combine the cheese and the vegetables more than 1 hour in advance or the mixture will become watery.) Serves 6.

PHOTO ON PAGE 15

Oriental Stuffed Mushrooms

2 tablespoons fresh lemon juice
24 large mushrooms (about 2½ pounds), the
 stems removed and chopped fine and the
 caps left whole
3 slices of lean bacon
¼ cup minced onion
4 teaspoons minced garlic
2 tablespoons soy sauce
1 tablespoon sesame seeds, toasted lightly
½ cup fine fresh bread crumbs plus
 1 tablespoon for sprinkling the mushrooms
1 scallion, sliced thin, for garnish

In a large saucepan combine 6 cups water with the lemon juice, add the mushroom caps, and bring the liquid to a boil. Simmer the mushroom caps for 6 minutes, transfer them to paper towels, and let them drain. (Blanching the mushroom caps will prevent them from wrinkling while they are baking.)

In a skillet cook the bacon over moderate heat until it is crisp, transfer it to paper towels, and let it drain. Pour off all but 1½ tablespoons of the fat from the skillet, in the remaining fat cook the onion, the garlic, and the mushroom stems over moderately low heat, stirring, until the vegetables are softened, and add the soy sauce, the sesame seeds, ½ cup of the bread crumbs, the bacon, crumbled, and pepper to taste. Cook the mixture, stirring, for 1 minute, or until it is slightly dry, divide it

among the mushroom caps, mounding it, and transfer the stuffed mushrooms to a jelly-roll pan. *The mushrooms may be prepared up to this point 1 day in advance and kept covered tightly with plastic wrap and chilled.*

Sprinkle the remaining 1 tablespoon bread crumbs over the mushrooms and bake the mushrooms in the middle of a preheated 325° F. oven for 7 minutes, or until the filling is heated through. To make the filling crisper the cooked mushrooms may be put under a preheated broiler about 4 inches from the heat for 1 minute. Garnish the mushrooms with the scallion. Makes 24 stuffed mushrooms.

PHOTO ON PAGE 42

Parmesan Puffs

¼ cup milk
½ stick (¼ cup) unsalted butter
¼ teaspoon salt
½ cup all-purpose flour
2 large eggs
1 cup freshly grated Parmesan

In a small heavy saucepan combine the milk, ¼ cup water, the butter, and the salt and bring the mixture to a boil over high heat. Reduce the heat to moderate, add the flour all at once, and beat the mixture with a wooden spoon until it leaves the side of the pan and forms a ball. Transfer the mixture to a bowl, whisk in the eggs, 1 at a time, whisking well after each addition, and stir in the Parmesan and pepper to taste. On a buttered baking sheet drop the batter in 8 mounds and bake the puffs in the upper third of a preheated 400° F. oven for 20 minutes, or until they are crisp and golden. The puffs may be served as an hors d'oeuvre or as an accompaniment to soups, meats, and poultry and may be stored overnight in an airtight container. Makes 8 puffs.

*Peperoncini Stuffed with
Smoked Salmon and Dill Cream*

35 to 40 (three to four 9-ounce jars)
 peperoncini (pickled Tuscan peppers),
 drained
8 ounces cream cheese, softened
½ stick (¼ cup) unsalted butter, softened
¼ cup minced fresh dill
3 tablespoons minced shallot
1 tablespoon fresh lemon juice

6 ounces thinly sliced smoked salmon,
   chopped fine

Trim the stem ends of the *peperoncini* at an angle and, wearing rubber gloves, discard the seeds and ribs. Let the *peperoncini* drain on paper towels. In a bowl cream the cream cheese with the butter until the mixture is smooth, add the dill, the shallot, and the lemon juice, and combine the mixture well. Stir in the salmon and salt and pepper to taste, transfer the mixture to a pastry bag fitted with a ½-inch decorative or plain tip, and pipe the smoked salmon and dill cream into the *peperoncini*. *The* peperoncini *may be prepared 1 day in advance and kept covered and chilled.* Makes 35 to 40 stuffed *peperoncini hors d'oeuvres*.

PHOTO ON PAGE 82

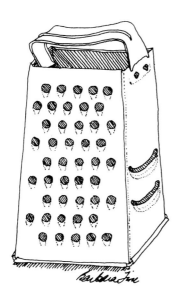

Potato Samosa Tartlets

For the filling

¾ cup minced onion

¼ cup minced canned green chilies (wear rubber gloves)

4 teaspoons minced peeled fresh gingerroot

1¾ teaspoons curry powder

1 teaspoon chili powder

½ teaspoon ground cumin

¼ teaspoon ground cloves

¼ teaspoon cinnamon

½ teaspoon salt

¼ cup vegetable oil

2 large boiling potatoes (1 pound), peeled and minced (about 2 cups), reserved in a bowl of cold water

1 small tomato, peeled, seeded, and chopped fine (⅓ cup)

2 tablespoons chopped fresh coriander

2 tablespoons plain yogurt

2 recipes *pâte brisée* (page 120)

½ cup finely chopped bottled mango chutney, or to taste

an egg wash made by beating 1 large egg with 2 teaspoons water

Make the filling: In a large skillet cook the onion, the chilies, the gingerroot, the curry powder, the chili powder, the cumin, the cloves, the cinnamon, and the salt in the oil over moderately low heat, stirring, until the onion is softened. While the onion is cooking, in a large saucepan of boiling salted water cook the potatoes for 3 to 5 minutes, or until they are tender, and drain them well. Add the potatoes to the skillet and cook the mixture, stirring, for 3 minutes. Stir in the tomato, the coriander, the yogurt, and black pepper to taste, cook the mixture, stirring, for 1 minute (do not let it boil), and let it cool. *The filling may be made 2 days in advance and kept covered and chilled.*

On a lightly floured surface roll out half the dough ⅛ inch thick and chill the remaining half, covered with wax paper. Cut out 54 rounds with a 2-inch round cutter and fit them into lightly oiled ⅛-cup gem tins. Spoon 1 level teaspoon of the filling into each tartlet shell and spoon a small dollop of the chutney on top of the filling. Roll out the remaining dough ⅛ inch thick, with the cutter cut out 54 more rounds, and fit the rounds on top of the filled shells. Press around the edge of each tartlet to seal the 2 pieces of dough, brush the tartlets with the egg wash, and prick each tartlet once with a fork. Bake the tartlets in the bottom third of a preheated 400° F. oven for 20 to 25 minutes, or until they are pale golden. Makes 54 tartlets.

PHOTO ON PAGE 42

CANAPÉS AND SPREADS

Roasted Red Bell Pepper Canapés

3 tablespoons white-wine vinegar
1 small garlic clove, minced
2 tablespoons golden raisins, soaked in
    boiling water for 5 minutes
½ teaspoon brown sugar
3 tablespoons olive oil
2 teaspoons shredded fresh basil leaves plus
    additional for garnish if desired
1 large red bell pepper, roasted (procedure on
    page 135) and cut into thin strips
six 1-inch-thick slices of French
    or Italian bread

In a small saucepan combine the vinegar, the garlic, the raisins, drained, and the brown sugar, bring the mixture to a boil, and boil it for 2 minutes, or until the garlic is softened. Let the mixture cool slightly and whisk in the oil and 2 teaspoons of the basil, whisking until the dressing is emulsified. Stir in the roasted bell pepper and season the mixture with salt and black pepper. On a baking sheet broil the bread slices under a preheated broiler about 3 inches from the heat until the tops are light golden and turn them over. Brush the untoasted sides with some of the liquid from the bell pepper mixture and broil the slices until the tops are golden. Top each slice with some of the roasted bell pepper mixture, drizzling the liquid over the top, and garnish the canapés with the additional basil. Serves 2 or 3 as a first course.

Yellow Bell Pepper Salsa with Cumin Tortilla Chips

1½ teaspoons ground cumin
1 teaspoon salt
vegetable oil for frying the tortillas
nine 6-inch corn tortillas, each cut into
    8 wedges
2 small yellow bell peppers, chopped fine
1 avocado (preferably California),
    chopped fine
1 onion, chopped fine
2 tomatoes (about 1 pound), seeded and
    chopped fine
1 small purple or red bell pepper,
    chopped fine

a 2-inch fresh *jalapeño* including the seeds,
    minced (wear rubber gloves)
½ cup lightly packed fresh coriander,
    chopped fine
3 tablespoons fresh lime juice
2 tablespoons fresh lemon juice

In a small bowl combine well the cumin and the salt. In a large deep heavy skillet heat ¾ inch of the oil to 375° F. on a deep-fat thermometer and in it fry the tortilla wedges in batches for 30 seconds to 1 minute, or until they are crisp and most of the bubbling subsides, transferring the chips with a slotted spoon as they are fried to paper towels to drain. Sprinkle the warm chips with the cumin mixture. *The cumin tortilla chips may be made 1 day in advance and kept in an airtight container.*

In a bowl combine well the yellow bell peppers, the avocado, the onion, the tomatoes, the purple bell pepper, the *jalapeño*, the coriander, the lime juice, and the lemon juice and chill the *salsa*, its surface covered with plastic wrap, for at least 1 hour and up to 6 hours. Transfer the *salsa* to serving bowls and serve it with the chips. Makes 4½ cups.

Miniature Roquefort Napoleons

a 17¼-ounce package (2 sheets) frozen puff
    pastry, thawed
¾ cup walnuts, chopped fine
6 ounces Roquefort at room temperature,
    mashed with a fork
4 ounces cream cheese, softened
¼ cup heavy cream
1 teaspoon fresh lemon juice
white pepper to taste

On a lightly floured surface, working with 1 pastry sheet at a time, roll out the pastry to form 16- by 12-inch rectangles and transfer each rectangle to a baking sheet. On 1 of the pastry sheets draw 2 shallow crosswise lines with a blunt knife dividing the sheet into thirds and sprinkle the walnuts over two thirds of that pastry sheet. Cover each pastry sheet directly with the buttered bottom surface of another baking sheet to weight it. Bake the pastry sheets in a preheated 400° F. oven for 5 minutes, remove the baking sheet weights, and with a fork prick the pastry sheets all over. Return the baking sheet weights to the pastry sheets, bake the pastry sheets for 10 minutes more, and remove the baking sheet weights.

Prick the pastry sheets again, switch the baking sheets in the oven so the pastry sheets bake evenly, and bake the pastry sheets for 7 to 10 minutes more, or until they are crisp and golden. While the pastry sheets are still warm, with a pastry wheel cut each sheet crosswise into sixteen 1-inch strips and cut the strips into sixths, making ninety-six 2- by 1-inch rectangles per sheet. *The pastry rectangles may be made 1 day in advance and kept, covered with plastic wrap, on the baking sheet.*

In a bowl with an electric mixer beat together the Roquefort, the cream cheese, the cream, the lemon juice, the white pepper, and salt to taste until the mixture is creamy and smooth. *The filling may be made 2 days in advance and kept covered and chilled. Let the filling return to room temperature before spreading it.*

Spread a thin layer of the filling on each of the rectangles without walnuts. To assemble each napoleon stack 2 Roquefort-topped layers and top them with a walnut-topped layer. Makes 64 napoleons.

PHOTO ON PAGE 42

Shrimp Toast with Pickled Ginger

4 shallots
4 garlic cloves
1 teaspoon minced peeled fresh gingerroot
2 teaspoons dry Sherry
½ teaspoon salt
1 teaspoon sugar
1 tablespoon cornstarch
1 tablespoon beaten egg white
1 tablespoon finely chopped fresh coriander
  plus small leaves for garnish
1 tablespoon light soy sauce
1 pound shrimp (about 24), shelled, deveined
  if desired
12 slices of homemade-type white bread,
  crusts discarded
1 cup fine fresh bread crumbs
vegetable oil for deep-frying
¼ cup pickled ginger (available at Asian
  markets and some specialty foods shops),
  drained and cut into julienne strips,
  for garnish

In a food processor blend the shallots, the garlic, the gingerroot, the Sherry, the salt, the sugar, the cornstarch, the egg white, the chopped coriander, and the soy sauce, add the shrimp, pulsing the motor, and purée the mixture until it is paste-like but not completely smooth.

Spread 1 heaping tablespoon of the shrimp mixture on each slice of bread, rounding off the top, dip the coated side of each slice in the bread crumbs, shaking off the excess, and cut each slice into 4 triangles. *The shrimp toasts may be prepared up to this point 1 day in advance and kept covered tightly with plastic wrap and chilled.*

In a large heavy skillet heat 1½ inches of the oil to 360° F. and in it fry the shrimp toasts, coated sides down first, in batches, for 1 minute on each side, or until they are golden. Let the shrimp toasts drain well on paper towels, garnish each shrimp toast with some of the pickled ginger and 1 of the coriander leaves, and serve the shrimp toasts immediately. Makes 48 shrimp toasts.

PHOTO ON PAGE 41

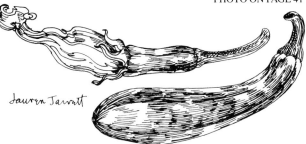

Lauren Jarrett

Herbed Zucchini Spirals

3 zucchini, scrubbed
2 cups parsley sprigs
1 to 2 garlic cloves, or to taste
⅔ cup walnuts
3 tablespoons freshly grated Parmesan

Using a mandoline or similar slicing device cut the zucchini lengthwise into ⅛-inch slices. Arrange the slices on a steamer rack set over simmering water and steam them, covered, for 3 to 5 minutes, or until they are just tender. (The zucchini slices should be barely flexible enough to roll. They will soften more as they cool.) In a food processor purée the parsley, the garlic, the walnuts, 2 tablespoons of the Parmesan, and salt to taste until the mixture is smooth. Arrange the zucchini slices on a work surface and dot each slice along its length with a heaping teaspoon of the purée. Roll up each slice jelly-roll fashion and fasten the spirals with wooden picks. Arrange the spirals in a shallow baking dish, sprinkle them with the remaining 1 tablespoon Parmesan, and bake them in the upper third of a preheated 425° F. oven for 5 minutes, or until the cheese is melted and the spirals are heated through. Serves 6.

PHOTO ON PAGE 15

*Cheddar and Green
Pepper Spread*

¼ pound extra-sharp yellow Cheddar,
    grated coarse
¼ pound extra-sharp white Cheddar,
    grated coarse
1 green bell pepper, cut into very thin
    1-inch-long strips
½ cup thinly sliced scallion
½ cup bottled mayonnaise
1½ teaspoons Dijon-style mustard
Saltine crackers as an accompaniment

In a bowl toss together the Cheddars, the bell pepper, and the scallion, add the mayonnaise, the mustard, and black pepper to taste, and combine the mixture well. *The spread keeps, covered and chilled, for 1 week.* Serve the spread with the crackers. Makes about 2 cups.

*Tapenade
(Provençal Olive Spread with Tuna)*

1½ cups firmly packed drained Niçoise olives
    (available at specialty foods shops and
    some supermarkets) or other brine-cured
    black olives, patted dry
4 flat anchovy fillets
¼ cup drained chunk light tuna (packed in oil)
3 tablespoons drained bottled capers
3 tablespoons extra-virgin olive oil

Crush the olives lightly with the flat side of a large knife on a cutting board, discard the pits, and in a food processor purée the olives well. Add the anchovies, the tuna, the capers, and the oil and purée the mixture well. Serve the *tapenade* as a spread for toasted French bread slices or thin slices of chilled *daikon* radish as an hors d'oeuvre. Makes about 1½ cups.

BREADS

YEAST BREADS

Soft Breadsticks with Fennel Seeds

a ¼-ounce package (2½ teaspoons) active
    dry yeast
a pinch of sugar
3 to 3½ cups all-purpose flour
2 teaspoons salt
2 teaspoons fennel seeds
¼ teaspoon pepper
an egg wash made by beating together 1 large
    egg yolk with 2 teaspoons water

In the bowl of an electric mixer proof the yeast with the sugar in ¼ cup lukewarm water for 5 minutes, or until it is foamy. With the paddle attachment beat in 1 cup warm water, 3 cups of the flour, the salt, the fennel seeds, and the pepper and beat the dough until it is smooth. With the dough hook of the electric mixer or by hand knead the dough, kneading in enough of the remaining ½ cup flour to form a smooth, elastic dough, for 10 minutes. Form the dough into a ball, put it in a well-buttered large bowl, turning it to coat it with the butter, and let it rise, covered with plastic wrap, in a warm place for 1 hour, or until it is double in bulk. Punch down the dough and, working with one small piece of dough at a time, form it into ¼-inch-thick ropes, each about 8 inches long. Arrange the ropes on buttered baking sheets, brush them lightly with the egg wash, and bake them in batches in the upper third of a preheated 450° F. oven for 15 minutes, or until they are golden. *The breadsticks may be made 1 day in advance and kept in an airtight container. Reheat the breadsticks, wrapped in foil, before serving.* Makes about 45 breadsticks.

PHOTO ON PAGE 21

Ham and Münster Buns with Honey Mustard

a ¼-ounce package (2½ teaspoons)
    active dry yeast
1 tablespoon sugar
2 tablespoons unsalted butter
½ cup milk
3½ to 3¾ cups all-purpose flour
2½ teaspoons salt
¼ cup Dijon-style mustard plus additional
    as an accompaniment
1 tablespoon honey
⅔ pound grated Münster
¾ pound very thinly sliced Black Forest ham
    or other smoked ham (not boiled)
mango chutney as an accompaniment

In a large bowl proof the yeast with the sugar in ¾ cup warm water for 5 minutes, or until the mixture is foamy. In a small saucepan melt the butter, add the milk, and heat the mixture to lukewarm. Add the milk mixture to the yeast mixture with 3½ cups of the flour and the salt. Stir the dough until it forms a ball, turn it out onto a floured surface, and knead it, incorporating as much of the remaining ¼ cup flour as necessary to prevent the dough from sticking, for 10 minutes, or until it is smooth and elastic. Form the dough into a ball, put it in a buttered large bowl, and turn it to coat it with the butter. Let the dough rise, covered, in a warm place for 1 hour, or until it is double in bulk.

Turn the dough out onto a floured surface and roll it into a 21- by 14-inch rectangle. In a small bowl combine well ¼ cup of the mustard and the honey, spread the mixture over the dough, and sprinkle the dough with the Münster. Cover the Münster with the ham and, starting with a long side, roll up the dough tightly, jelly-roll fashion. Trim the ends of the dough, cut the roll crosswise with a sharp knife into 16 equal pieces, and transfer the pieces, cut sides up, to 16 well-buttered ½-cup muffin tins, pressing them in slightly. Let the buns rise, covered, in a warm place for 45 minutes, or until they are almost double in bulk, and bake them in the middle of a preheated 375° F. oven for 30 minutes, or until they are golden. Run a knife around the buns, lifting them out of the tins, and let the buns cool upside down on a rack. *The buns may be made 1 day in advance and kept wrapped well and chilled.* Serve the buns warm or at room temperature with the chutney and the additional mustard. Makes 16 buns.

PHOTO ON PAGE 82

Potato Rosemary Focaccia

2½ teaspoons (a ¼-ounce package) active
   dry yeast
4½ cups all-purpose flour
2 cups mashed cooked russet (baking)
   potatoes (about 1¼ pounds)
1 tablespoon salt
2 garlic cloves, sliced thin
1 teaspoon dried rosemary, crumbled
⅓ cup olive oil
1½ pounds small red potatoes

In a small bowl sprinkle the yeast over 1 cup warm water and let it proof for 5 minutes, or until it is foamy. In a large bowl combine well 4 cups of the flour with the mashed potatoes and the salt until the mixture resembles coarse meal, add the yeast mixture, and stir the dough until it is combined well. Turn the dough out onto a floured surface and knead it, incorporating as much of the remaining ½ cup flour as necessary to prevent it from sticking, for 8 to 10 minutes, or until it is smooth and elastic. Form the dough into a ball, put it in an oiled bowl, and turn it to coat it with the oil. Let the dough rise, covered with plastic wrap, in a warm place for 1½ hours, or until it is double in bulk. While the dough is rising, in a small bowl stir together the garlic, the rosemary, and the oil and let the mixture stand, covered. Turn the dough out into a well-oiled 15½- by 10½-inch jelly-roll pan, press it evenly into the pan, and let it rise, covered loosely, in a warm place for 45 minutes, or until it is almost double in bulk. Using a *mandoline* or hand-held slicer cut the red potatoes into paper-thin slices, arrange the slices on the dough, overlapping them, and brush them with the oil mixture, discarding the garlic. Sprinkle the *focaccia* with salt and pepper to taste and bake it in the bottom third of a preheated 400° F. oven for 40 to 50 minutes, or until it is golden. Let the *focaccia* cool in the pan on a rack and serve it warm or at room temperature.

Parmesan Rolls

a ¼-ounce package (2½ teaspoons) active
   dry yeast
2 tablespoons olive oil
3½ to 4 cups all-purpose flour
2 teaspoons salt
1 cup freshly grated Parmesan

In a small bowl sprinkle the yeast over 1¼ cups warm water, let it proof for 5 minutes, or until it is foamy, and stir in the oil. In a large bowl whisk together 3½ cups of the flour, the salt, and the Parmesan, stir in the yeast mixture, and turn the dough out onto a floured surface. Knead the dough, incorporating as much of the remaining ½ cup flour as necessary to prevent the dough from sticking, for 8 to 10 minutes, or until it is smooth and elastic. Form the dough into a ball, put it into an oiled bowl, and turn it to coat it with the oil. Let the dough rise, covered with plastic wrap, in a warm place for 1½ to 2 hours, or until it is double in bulk. Turn the dough out onto a floured surface, divide it into 12 equal pieces, and form each piece into a ball. Transfer the rolls to a lightly oiled baking sheet and let them rise, covered loosely with a kitchen towel, in a warm place for 1 hour, or until they are almost double in bulk. Bake the rolls in the middle of a preheated 425° F. oven for 15 to 20 minutes, or until they are golden. Makes 12 rolls.

PHOTO ON PAGE 27

Dilled Walnut and Cottage Cheese Cloverleaf Rolls

a ¼-ounce package (2½ teaspoons) active
   dry yeast
2½ to 3¼ cups all-purpose flour
1 cup creamed cottage cheese
1 large egg, beaten lightly
2 tablespoons finely chopped fresh dill
1 tablespoon dill seeds
¼ cup finely chopped walnuts
1 tablespoon freshly grated lemon zest
1½ teaspoons salt
about 2 tablespoons unsalted butter, melted
   and cooled

In a large bowl proof the yeast in ½ cup lukewarm water for 5 minutes, or until it is foamy. Add 1 cup of the flour, the cottage cheese, the egg, the dill, the dill seeds, the walnuts, the zest, and the salt and beat the mixture with a wooden spoon until it is combined well. Stir in 1½ cups of the remaining flour, ½ cup at a time, and beat the mixture with the spoon until it is combined well. Turn the dough out onto a floured surface and knead it for 8 to 10 minutes, incorporating enough of the remaining ¾ cup flour, if necessary, to form a soft, slightly sticky dough. Transfer the dough to an oiled bowl, turning it to coat it with the oil, and let it rise, covered with plastic wrap, in a warm place for 1½ hours, or until it is double in bulk.

Stir down the dough, halve it, and on a lightly floured surface roll each half into a rope about 1 inch in diameter. Cut each rope into 24 pieces with a sharp knife and form the pieces into balls. Put 3 balls of dough into each of 16 buttered ⅓-cup muffin tins, brush them with the melted butter, and let the rolls rise, uncovered, in a warm place for 45 minutes to 1 hour, or until they are almost double in bulk. Bake the rolls in the middle of a preheated 400° F. oven for 18 to 20 minutes, or until they are golden. *The rolls may be made 1 week in advance and kept wrapped tightly and frozen. Reheat the rolls, wrapped in foil, in a preheated 400° F. oven for 25 to 30 minutes, or until they are heated through.* Makes 16 rolls.

QUICK BREADS

Cornmeal Biscuits

¾ cup all-purpose flour
¼ cup plus 1 teaspoon yellow cornmeal
1½ teaspoons double-acting baking powder
½ teaspoon sugar
¼ teaspoon salt
2½ tablespoons cold unsalted butter,
    cut into bits
6 tablespoons half-and-half

In a bowl stir together the flour, ¼ cup of the cornmeal, the baking powder, the sugar, and the salt, add the butter, and blend the mixture until it resembles coarse meal. Add the half-and-half and stir the mixture until it just forms a sticky dough. Gather the dough into a ball, knead the ball gently 6 times on a lightly floured surface, and roll or pat it out ½ inch thick. Cut out 6 rounds with a 2½-inch cutter dipped in flour and transfer them to an ungreased baking sheet. Sprinkle the remaining 1 teaspoon cornmeal over the tops of the rounds and bake the biscuits in the middle of a preheated 450° F. oven for 12 to 14 minutes, or until they are golden. Makes 6 biscuits.

Apple Cheese Quick Bread

1 stick (½ cup) unsalted butter, softened
⅓ cup sugar

⅓ cup honey
2 large eggs
1 cup whole-wheat flour
1 cup all-purpose flour
1 teaspoon double-acting baking powder
½ teaspoon baking soda
½ teaspoon salt
1½ cups grated Granny Smith apples (about 2)
½ cup grated Swiss cheese
½ cup chopped walnuts
cream cheese as an accompaniment

In a large bowl cream together the butter and the sugar and beat in the honey and the eggs. Into the butter mixture sift together the flours, the baking powder, the baking soda, and the salt, stir the mixture until it is combined well, and stir in the apples, the cheese, and the walnuts. Spoon the batter into a buttered loaf pan, 9 by 5 by 3 inches, and bake it in the middle of a preheated 350° F. oven for 50 to 60 minutes, or until a tester comes out clean. Turn the bread out onto a rack, and let it cool completely, and serve it sliced with the cream cheese.

Brown Oatmeal Soda Bread

2¼ to 2½ cups all-purpose flour
2 teaspoons baking soda
1 teaspoon double-acting baking powder
2 teaspoons salt
2 cups whole-wheat flour
1 cup old-fashioned rolled oats plus additional
    for sprinkling the bread
2 cups buttermilk
1 large egg, beaten lightly

Into a large bowl sift together 2¼ cups of the all-purpose flour, the baking soda, the baking powder, and the salt and stir in the whole-wheat flour and 1 cup of the oats. Add the buttermilk and the egg and stir the mixture until it forms a dough. Turn the dough out onto a floured surface and knead it, kneading in as much of the remaining ¼ cup all-purpose flour as necessary, until it forms a manageable but sticky dough. Halve the dough, form the halves into round loaves, and put them on a greased baking sheet. Sprinkle the loaves lightly with the additional oats, dust them with flour, and bake them in the middle of a preheated 350° F. oven for 30 to 35 minutes, or until they are browned lightly. Let the loaves cool on a rack. Makes two 7-inch loaves.

Olive Mint Quick Bread

1½ cups firmly packed drained Kalamata or
    other brine-cured black olives
2½ cups all-purpose flour
2 tablespoons double-acting baking powder
2 tablespoons sugar
1 teaspoon salt
½ cup fresh mint leaves, chopped
2 large eggs
⅓ cup olive oil
½ cup grated onion
⅔ cup milk

Crush the olives lightly with the flat side of a large knife on a cutting board and discard the pits. Drain the olives on paper towels and chop them. In a large bowl stir together the flour, the baking powder, the sugar, the salt, and the mint, add the olives, and toss the mixture well. In a small bowl whisk together the eggs, the oil, the onion, and the milk and add the egg mixture to the flour mixture, stirring until the batter is just combined. Transfer the batter to a greased loaf pan, 8 by 4 by 2½ inches, and bake the bread in the middle of a preheated 350° F. oven for 1 hour and 15 minutes, or until a tester comes out clean. Turn the bread out onto a rack and let it cool. Makes 1 loaf.

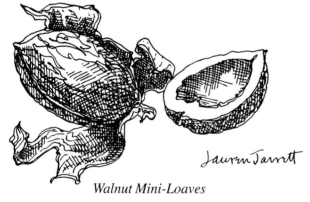

Walnut Mini-Loaves

1 cup all-purpose flour
1¼ teaspoons double-acting baking powder
½ teaspoon salt
¾ cup coarsely chopped toasted walnuts
1½ tablespoons vegetable shortening
⅓ cup firmly packed light brown sugar
1 large egg, beaten lightly
½ cup milk
¼ teaspoon vanilla

In a bowl stir together the flour, the baking powder, the salt, and ½ cup of the walnuts. In another bowl cream together the shortening and the brown sugar, beat in the egg, the milk, and the vanilla, and stir in the flour mixture until the batter is just combined. Divide the batter between 2 greased and floured 5- by 2-inch mini-loaf pans, sprinkle it with the remaining ¼ cup walnuts, and bake the loaves in the middle of a preheated 375° F. oven for 30 to 35 minutes, or until a tester inserted in the center comes out clean. Serve the loaves warm. Makes 2 mini-loaves.

Spiced Potato Doughnuts

3½ cups all-purpose flour
4 teaspoons double-acting baking powder
1 teaspoon salt
2 teaspoons ground cinnamon
1 teaspoon freshly grated nutmeg
2 large eggs
3 tablespoons unsalted butter, melted
¾ cup sugar
1½ cups mashed cooked russet (baking)
    potatoes (about 1 pound)
½ cup milk
2 teaspoons freshly grated orange zest
    if desired
1 teaspoon vanilla
vegetable oil for deep-frying
For the coating
½ cup sugar
½ teaspoon ground cinnamon,
    or to taste

Into a bowl sift together the flour, the baking powder, the salt, the cinnamon, and the nutmeg. In a small bowl whisk together the eggs, the butter, the sugar, the potatoes, the milk, the zest, and the vanilla until the mixture is combined well, add the potato mixture to the flour mixture, and stir the dough until it is just combined. Chill the dough, covered, for 1 hour, or until it is cold and can be handled easily. Roll out half the dough ½ inch thick on a well-floured surface and with a 3- to 3½-inch doughnut cutter cut out doughnuts, reserving the center pieces. With the other half of the dough either cut out round doughnuts in the same manner or shape the dough into crullers. For the crullers, roll the dough into a ½-inch-thick rectangle about 14- by 5-inches and cut it into 5- by ½-inch strips. To form each cruller twist 2 strips of dough together and pinch the ends to secure them. Fry the round doughnuts, the reserved doughnut centers, and the crullers in batches in 2 inches of 375° F. oil, turning them once, for 2 to 3 minutes, or until they are golden, transferring them as they are fried to paper towels to drain.

Make the coating: In a shallow bowl stir together the sugar and the cinnamon.

While the doughnuts are still warm roll them, 1 at a time, in the sugar mixture, coating them well. The doughnuts keep, wrapped in plastic, for 1 day. Makes about 20 doughnuts.

Apple Raisin Muffins

1½ cups all-purpose flour
1 teaspoon cinnamon
1 teaspoon baking soda
1 large egg
1 cup firmly packed dark brown sugar
1 cup sour cream
1 teaspoon vanilla
1 cup (about 6 ounces) dried apples,
　　chopped coarse
½ cup raisins
⅔ cup coarsely chopped walnuts, toasted
　　lightly and cooled

Into a bowl sift together the flour, the cinnamon, the baking soda, and a pinch of salt. In a large bowl with an electric mixer beat together the egg and the brown sugar until the mixture is thick and pale, add the sour cream and the vanilla, and beat the mixture until it is combined well. Beat in the flour mixture, a little at a time, and beat the batter until it is just combined. Stir in the dried apples, the raisins, and the walnuts and divide the batter among 16 paper-lined ½-cup muffin tins. Bake the muffins in the middle of a 350° F. oven for 20 to 25 minutes, or until a tester comes out clean, turn them out onto a rack, and let them cool. The muffins keep in an airtight container for 3 days. Makes 16 muffins.

Blueberry Corn Muffins

1 cup all-purpose flour
1 cup yellow cornmeal
1 tablespoon double-acting baking powder
1 teaspoon salt
1 stick (½ cup) unsalted butter, melted
　　and cooled
1 large egg

⅓ cup honey
⅓ cup sugar
¾ cup milk
2 cups picked over blueberries

In a bowl whisk together the flour, the cornmeal, the baking powder, and the salt. In a small bowl whisk together the butter, the egg, the honey, the sugar, and the milk, stir the butter mixture into the flour mixture, stirring until the batter is just combined, and fold in the blueberries. Divide the batter among 12 buttered ½-cup muffin tins, bake the muffins in the middle of a preheated 425° F. oven for 15 to 20 minutes, or until they are golden and a tester comes out clean, and turn them out onto a rack. Makes 12 muffins.

Corn Cakes

1 cup cornmeal
¾ teaspoon baking soda
¾ teaspoon salt
1 large egg, beaten lightly
1 cup buttermilk plus additional to thin the
　　batter if necessary
2 tablespoons unsalted butter, melted, plus
　　additional for brushing the griddle
1 cup fresh or frozen corn, cooked, drained,
　　and patted dry

In a bowl whisk together the cornmeal, the baking soda, and the salt, add the egg, 1 cup of the buttermilk, and 2 tablespoons of the butter, and whisk the batter until it is smooth. Stir in the corn and let the batter stand for 10 minutes. The batter should be the consistency of thick pancake batter; if it is too thick, thin it with the additional buttermilk. Heat a griddle over moderate heat until it is hot, brush it lightly with some of the additional butter, and drop the batter by tablespoons onto the griddle. Cook the cakes for 1 minute, or until the undersides are golden, turn them, and cook them for 1 minute more, or until the undersides are golden. Transfer the cakes to a heated platter and make more cakes with the remaining batter in the same manner, brushing the griddle lightly with some of the additional butter before cooking each batch. *The cakes may be made 1 day in advance and kept covered and chilled. Reheat them in a baking dish, covered tightly with foil, in a preheated 350° F. oven for 15 minutes.* Makes about 25 corn cakes.

PHOTO ON PAGE 38

Radish Sandwiches on Zucchini Basil Muffins

1¼ cups all-purpose flour
¾ teaspoon salt
½ teaspoon baking soda
1 teaspoon double-acting baking powder
½ teaspoon pepper
2 tablespoons vegetable shortening, softened
1 tablespoon sugar
1 large egg
¼ cup buttermilk
1 cup coarsely grated well-scrubbed zucchini
½ cup finely chopped fresh basil leaves
3 tablespoons unsalted butter, softened
8 radishes, sliced thin

In a small bowl whisk together the flour, the salt, the baking soda, the baking powder, and the pepper. In a bowl cream together the shortening and the sugar, beat in the egg and the buttermilk, beating until the mixture is combined well, and stir in the zucchini and the basil. Add the flour mixture to the zucchini mixture, stir the batter until it is just combined, and divide it among 24 well-buttered gem tins (each ⅛ cup). Bake the muffins in the middle of a preheated 400° F. oven for 15 to 18 minutes, or until a tester comes out clean, turn the muffins out onto a rack, and let them cool. Halve the muffins horizontally, spread the cut sides with the butter, and sandwich the radish slices between the muffin halves. Makes 24 sandwiches.

PHOTO ON PAGE 82

Dried Cherry Buttermilk Scones

½ cup buttermilk plus ¼ cup for brushing
   the scones
1 large egg
3 tablespoons light brown sugar
1 teaspoon vanilla
2¼ cups cake flour (not self-rising)
1 tablespoon double-acting baking powder
½ teaspoon baking soda
½ teaspoon salt
¾ stick (6 tablespoons) cold unsalted butter,
   cut into bits
½ cup dried sour cherries (available at
   specialty foods shops)
granulated sugar for sprinkling

In a bowl whisk together ½ cup of the buttermilk, the egg, the brown sugar, and the vanilla until the mixture is combined well. In another bowl stir together the flour, the baking powder, the baking soda, and the salt and blend in the butter until the mixture resembles coarse meal. Stir in the cherries and the buttermilk mixture with a fork until the mixture just forms a sticky but manageable dough. Knead the dough gently for 30 seconds on a lightly floured surface, pat it into a ¾-inch-thick round, and cut it into 8 wedges. On an ungreased baking sheet brush the wedges with the remaining ¼ cup buttermilk and sprinkle them with the granulated sugar. Bake the scones in the middle of a preheated 400° F. oven for 15 to 18 minutes, or until they are golden. Makes 8 scones.

Miniature Cream Scones with Currants

½ cup heavy cream plus additional for
   brushing the scones
1 large egg
1 teaspoon vanilla
3 tablespoons sugar plus additional for
   sprinkling the scones
2¼ cups cake flour (not self-rising)
½ teaspoon salt
1 tablespoon double-acting baking powder
½ teaspoon baking soda
¾ stick (6 tablespoons) cold unsalted butter,
   cut into bits
½ cup dried currants

In a bowl whisk together ½ cup of the cream, the egg, the vanilla, and 3 tablespoons of the sugar until the mixture is combined well. In another bowl stir together the flour, the salt, the baking powder, and the baking soda and blend in the butter until the mixture resembles coarse meal. Stir in the currants and the cream mixture with a fork until the mixture just forms a sticky but manageable dough. Knead the dough gently on a lightly floured surface for 30 seconds, pat it into a ½-inch-thick round, and with a 1½-inch fluted cutter cut it into rounds. Gather the scraps, repat the dough, and cut out more rounds. On an ungreased baking sheet brush the scones with the additional cream and sprinkle them with the additional sugar. Bake the scones in the middle of a preheated 400° F. oven for 15 to 18 minutes, or until they are golden. Makes about 16 miniature scones.

Oatmeal Date Drop Scones

¾ cup milk
1 large egg
3 tablespoons light brown sugar
1 teaspoon vanilla
2¼ cups cake flour (not self-rising)
1 cup old-fashioned rolled oats
1 tablespoon double-acting baking powder
½ teaspoon baking soda
½ teaspoon salt
¾ stick (6 tablespoons) cold unsalted butter,
    cut into bits
½ cup chopped pitted dates

In a bowl whisk together the milk, the egg, the brown sugar, and the vanilla until the mixture is combined well. In another bowl stir together the flour, the oats, the baking powder, the baking soda, and the salt and blend in the butter until the mixture resembles coarse meal. Stir in the dates and the milk mixture until the mixture just forms a sticky dough. Drop the dough by ⅓-cup measures onto an ungreased baking sheet and bake the scones in the middle of a preheated 400° F. for 15 to 18 minutes, or until they are golden. (Alternatively the scones may be dropped onto a hot greased griddle and cooked over moderate heat, turning them, for 15 to 18 minutes, or until they are golden on both sides and cooked through.) Makes about 12 scones.

Pine Nut and Cardamom Scones

½ cup milk
1 large egg
3 tablespoons light brown sugar
1 teaspoon vanilla
2¼ cups cake flour (not self-rising)
½ teaspoon salt
1 tablespoon double-acting baking powder
½ teaspoon baking soda
2 teaspoons ground cardamom
¼ teaspoon cinnamon
¼ teaspoon freshly grated nutmeg
2 teaspoons freshly grated lemon zest
¾ stick (6 tablespoons) cold unsalted butter,
    cut into bits
⅓ cup pine nuts, toasted lightly
an egg wash made by beating 1 large egg with
    2 tablespoons milk
granulated sugar for sprinkling the scones

In a bowl whisk together the milk, the egg, the brown sugar, and the vanilla until the mixture is combined well. In another bowl stir together the flour, the salt, the baking powder, the baking soda, the cardamom, the cinnamon, the nutmeg, and the zest and blend in the butter until the mixture resembles coarse meal. Stir in the milk mixture and three fourths of the pine nuts with a fork until the mixture just forms a sticky but manageable dough. Knead the dough gently on a lightly floured surface for 30 seconds, pat it into a ¾-inch-thick round, and with a 2½-inch fluted cutter cut it into rounds. On an ungreased baking sheet press the remaining pine nuts lightly into the scones, brush the scones with the egg wash, and sprinkle them with the granulated sugar. Bake the scones in the middle of a preheated 400° F. oven for 15 to 18 minutes, or until they are golden. Makes about 12 scones.

TOASTS

Goat Cheese Toasts

twelve ⅓-inch-thick diagonally cut slices
    of Italian or French bread
olive oil for brushing the toasts
¼ pound soft mild goat cheese

On a baking sheet broil the bread slices under a preheated broiler about 3 inches from the heat for 1 to 2 minutes on each side, or until they are golden, and brush one side of each toast lightly with the oil. Spread the oiled sides evenly with the goat cheese, covering them completely, and sprinkle the cheese with pepper to taste. Return the goat cheese toasts to the broiler and broil them for 1 minute, or until the cheese is melted slightly and glistening. Serve the toasts warm or at room temperature. Makes 12 toasts.

PHOTO ON PAGE 44

Herbed Melba Toasts

1 tablespoon unsalted butter, melted
⅛ teaspoon dried dill, crumbled
⅛ teaspoon dried thyme, crumbled
4 slices of homemade-style white bread

In a small bowl stir together the butter, the dill, the thyme, and salt and pepper to taste. Roll each slice of bread as thin as possible with a rolling pin and trim and discard the crusts. Brush both sides of the bread with the butter mixture, cut each slice diagonally into 2 triangles, and bake the triangles on a baking sheet in the middle of a preheated 350° F. oven, turning them once, for 15 minutes, or until they are browned lightly and crisp. Let the toasts cool on a rack. Serves 2.

Ripe Olive and Goat Cheese Toasts

1 cup firmly packed pitted ripe olives,
   drained well
6 ounces soft mild goat cheese
1 small garlic clove, if desired, minced and
   mashed to a paste with ¼ teaspoon salt
3 tablespoons minced scallion
Tabasco to taste
20 thin diagonal slices of French or Italian
   bread, toasted

In a food processor chop the olives, add the goat cheese, the garlic paste, the scallion, and the Tabasco, and blend the mixture until the olives are chopped fine. Spread the mixture evenly on the toasts, arrange the toasts on a baking sheet, and broil them under a preheated broiler about 2 inches from the heat for 1 minute, or until the cheese is just melted. Makes 20 toasts.

Whole Baked Garlic with Toasts

1 large head of garlic
3 tablespoons olive oil
ten ⅓-inch-thick diagonal slices of Italian
   or French bread

Cut off the top quarter of the garlic with a sharp knife to expose the cloves, set the garlic in the middle of a large piece of foil, and drizzle it with 2 teaspoons of the oil. Crimp the foil around the garlic to enclose it completely and bake the garlic in the middle of a preheated 425° F. oven for 40 minutes. While the garlic is baking,

brush the bread slices with the remaining oil and bake them on a baking sheet in the lower third of the oven (below the garlic), turning them once, for 10 to 12 minutes, or until they are golden and crisp. Unwrap the garlic and put it on a serving plate surrounded by the toasts.

To serve the garlic: Remove the softened cloves with a knife or fork or turn the head of garlic upside down and squeeze out the cloves. Spread the garlic on the toasts. Serves 2 as a first course.

OTHER BREADS

Vegetable Pita Pizzas

two 6-inch whole-wheat *pita* loaves
3 tablespoons olive oil plus additional for
   brushing the *pita* rounds
1⅓ cups grated mozzarella
1 small red onion, sliced thin
2 garlic cloves, minced
1 small red bell pepper, sliced thin
1 small green bell pepper, sliced thin
¾ cup thinly sliced zucchini
4 mushrooms, sliced
1 teaspoon dried orégano, crumbled
⅔ cup chopped seeded fresh tomato
3 tablespoons shredded fresh basil leaves
3 tablespoons freshly grated Parmesan

Halve the *pita* loaves horizontally to form 4 rounds, arrange the rounds, rough sides up, on a baking sheet, and brush the tops lightly with the additional oil. Sprinkle the rounds with salt to taste and toast them in the middle of a preheated 350° F. oven for 5 minutes, or until they are pale golden and crisp. Sprinkle half the mozzarella onto the rounds and bake the rounds for 1 minute, or until the mozzarella is melted. While the rounds are toasting, in a large skillet cook the onion and the garlic in the remaining 3 tablespoons oil over moderately low heat, stirring, until the onion is softened, add the bell peppers, and cook the mixture, stirring, for 4 minutes, or until the peppers are softened. Add the zucchini, the mushrooms, the orégano, and salt and black pepper to taste and cook the mixture, stirring, for 2 minutes, or until the zucchini is softened. Stir in half the remaining mozzarella and divide the mixture among the rounds, mounding it slightly. Top the rounds with the remaining mozzarella, the tomato, the basil, and the Parmesan and broil them under a preheated broiler about 4 inches from the heat for 3 minutes, or until the cheeses are melted and bubbly. Makes 4 pizzas, serving 2.

Flour Tortillas

2 cups all-purpose flour
¼ cup cold vegetable shortening, cut
   into pieces
1 teaspoon salt

In a bowl blend the flour and the shortening until the mixture resembles fine meal. In a small bowl stir together the salt and ⅔ cup warm water, add the salted water to the flour mixture, and toss the mixture until the liquid is incorporated. Form the dough into a ball and knead it on a lightly floured surface for 2 to 3 minutes, or until it is smooth. Divide the dough into 12 equal pieces (or 4 equal pieces for 10-inch tortillas), form each piece into a ball, and let the dough stand, covered with plastic wrap, for at least 30 minutes and up to 1 hour. Heat a griddle over moderately high heat until it is hot, on a lightly floured surface roll 1 of the balls of dough into a 7- or 10-inch round, and on the griddle cook the tortilla, turning it once, for 1 to 1½ minutes, or until it is puffy and golden on both sides. Wrap the tortilla in a kitchen towel and make tortillas with the remaining dough in the same manner, stacking and enclosing them in the towel as they are done. *The tortillas may be made 1 day in advance and kept chilled in a plastic bag.* Makes twelve 7-inch or four 10-inch tortillas.

To Warm Tortillas

In the oven: Stack 6 tortillas at a time, wrap each stack in foil, and heat the tortillas in the middle of a preheated 325° F. oven for 5 minutes for corn tortillas and 15 minutes for flour tortillas. If the tortillas are very dry to begin with, pat each tortilla between dampened hands before stacking them.

In the microwave: Stack 6 tortillas at a time, wrap each stack in a microwave-safe plastic bag, and heat the tortillas in a microwave oven at high power (100%) for 30 seconds to 1 minute, or until they are heated through and pliable.

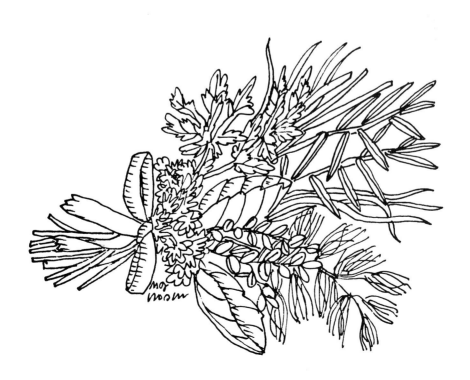

SOUPS

Apricot, Orange, and Carrot Soup

¾ pound carrots, peeled and cut into
  ½-inch-thick pieces
1½ cups fresh orange juice
1 cup apricot nectar
¼ cup fresh lemon juice
plain yogurt for garnish

In a steamer rack set over boiling water steam the carrots, covered, for 15 minutes, or until they are very tender. In a blender purée the carrots with the orange juice, the apricot nectar, the lemon juice, and a pinch of salt until the soup is smooth. Serve the soup at room temperature or chilled and drizzle each serving with some of the yogurt. Makes about 4 cups, serving 4 to 6.

Beet and Cabbage Borscht

1 onion, chopped
1 tablespoon vegetable oil
1 garlic clove, minced
½ teaspoon cuminseed
2 cups chopped cabbage (about ½ pound)
a 6-ounce boiling potato, peeled and
  grated coarse
2 cups beef broth
a 16-ounce jar whole beets, drained, reserving
  the liquid, and shredded
1 to 2 tablespoons red-wine vinegar,
  or to taste
sour cream or plain yogurt for garnish
  if desired
minced fresh dill for garnish if desired

In a large saucepan cook the onion in the oil over moderately low heat, stirring, until it is softened, add the garlic, the cuminseed, the cabbage, and the potato, and cook the mixture, stirring, for 1 minute. Add the broth, ½ cup water, the beets, the reserved beet liquid, the vinegar, and salt and pepper to taste, bring the liquid to a boil, and simmer the soup, covered partially, for

25 minutes. Divide the soup between 2 bowls and garnish it with the sour cream and the dill. Makes about 5 cups, serving 2.

Red Cabbage and Orzo Soup

¾ cup chopped red cabbage
1 tablespoon olive oil
1½ cups chicken broth
3 tablespoons *orzo* (rice-shaped pasta)
1 teaspoon soy sauce
4 thin lemon slices
1 tablespoon thinly sliced scallion greens

In a saucepan cook the cabbage in the oil over moderate heat, stirring, until it is tender, stir in the broth and ½ cup water, and bring the mixture to a boil. Add the *orzo*, simmer the mixture, stirring occasionally, for 6 to 8 minutes, or until the *orzo* is tender, and add the soy sauce and pepper to taste. Divide the soup between 2 heated bowls and top each serving with half the lemon slices and half the scallion greens. Makes about 3 cups, serving 2.

Cantaloupe Peach Soup

1 ripe cantaloupe, peeled, seeded, and
  cut into pieces
½ cup fresh orange juice
2 peaches
¼ cup light rum
plain yogurt for garnish

In a blender purée the cantaloupe with the orange juice and transfer the purée to a bowl. In the blender purée the peaches, peeled and pitted, with the rum, add the peach purée to the bowl, and combine the soup well. Serve the soup at room temperature or chilled and garnish each serving with a dollop of the yogurt. Makes about 8 cups, serving 8.

Chilled Curried Carrot Soup

1 onion, sliced thin
4 carrots, sliced thin (about 2 cups)
1 tablespoon vegetable oil
1 teaspoon curry powder
1 cup chicken broth
chopped fresh chives for garnish

In a large heavy saucepan cook the onion and the carrots in the oil, covered, over moderately low heat, stirring occasionally, until the onion is softened, add the curry, and cook the mixture, stirring, for 1 minute. Add the broth and 3 cups water, bring the liquid to a boil, and simmer the mixture for 15 to 20 minutes, or until the carrots are very tender. In a blender or food processor purée the soup in batches, let it cool completely, and chill it, covered, until it is cold. *The soup may be made 1 day in advance and kept covered and chilled.* Divide the soup among 4 bowls and sprinkle it with the chives. Makes about 3½ cups, serving 4.

PHOTO ON PAGE 17

Cauliflower Caraway Potato Soup

½ pound boiling potatoes
½ cup chopped cauliflower leaves
¼ cup chopped white part of scallion
¼ teaspoon caraway seeds
2 cups 1-inch cauliflower flowerets
⅓ cup thinly sliced scallion greens
freshly grated Parmesan to taste

In a saucepan combine the potatoes, peeled and cut into ½-inch pieces, the cauliflower leaves, the white part of scallion, the caraway seeds, and 3½ cups water, simmer the mixture for 15 minutes, or until the potatoes are very tender, and in a blender or food processor purée the mixture coarse. In the pan combine the purée and the flowerets, simmer the soup for 5 minutes, or until the flowerets are tender, and stir in the scallion greens and salt and pepper to taste. Serve the soup sprinkled with the Parmesan. Makes about 3½ cups, serving 2.

Cheddar and Roasted Red Bell Pepper Soup

a ½-pound russet (baking) potato
1 cup chopped onion
2 tablespoons vegetable oil
2 cups milk
2 large red bell peppers, roasted (procedure on
    page 135) and diced
1 teaspoon Worcestershire sauce
¼ teaspoon Tabasco, or to taste
14 ounces extra-sharp Cheddar, grated coarse
finely chopped fresh coriander for garnish
croutons for garnish if desired

In a kettle cook the potato, peeled and diced, and the onion in the oil over moderately low heat until the onion is softened, add 1 cup water, and simmer the mixture, covered, for 5 to 10 minutes, or until the potato is tender. In a blender purée the mixture with the milk and in the kettle combine the mixture with the roasted peppers, the Worcestershire sauce, and the Tabasco. Heat the mixture over moderately low heat, stirring in handfuls of the Cheddar, until the Cheddar is melted and the soup is hot (but do not let it boil), and garnish the soup with the coriander and the croutons. Makes about 6 cups, serving 6.

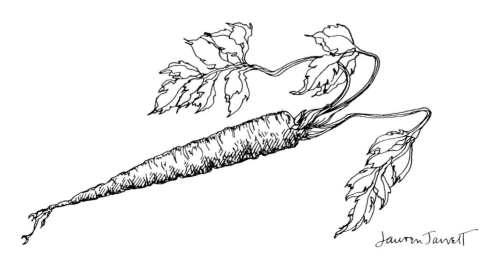

Lauren Jarrett

Chestnut and Celery Soup

1 cup finely chopped onion
2 garlic cloves, minced
1 bay leaf
½ teaspoon dried thyme, crumbled
2 tablespoons unsalted butter
2 cups thinly sliced celery (about 4 large ribs)
2 carrots, sliced thin
1 pound (about 2½ cups) canned
  or vacuum-packed whole chestnuts, rinsed,
  drained well, and patted dry if using canned
1 large boiling potato (about ½ pound)
3 cups chicken broth
sour cream as an accompaniment

In a kettle cook the onion, the garlic, the bay leaf, and the thyme in the butter over moderately low heat, stirring, until the onion is softened, add the celery and the carrots, and cook the mixture over moderate heat, stirring, for 5 minutes. Add the chestnuts, the potato, peeled and cut into 1-inch pieces, the broth, 2½ cups water, and salt and pepper to taste, simmer the mixture, covered, for 20 to 25 minutes, or until the chestnuts and the potato are very tender, and discard the bay leaf. In a blender purée the mixture in batches until it is smooth and return it to the kettle. *The soup may be prepared 1 day in advance, cooled uncovered, and kept covered and chilled.* Heat the soup, stirring, until it is hot and serve it with the sour cream. Makes about 9 cups, serving 6 to 8.

Chilled Cucumber Avocado Soup

1 cup buttermilk
2 cucumbers, peeled, seeded,
  and chopped
1 avocado (preferably California)
¼ cup chicken broth
2 tablespoons fresh lemon juice
¼ teaspoon ground cumin, or to taste

In a large measuring cup combine the buttermilk and enough ice cubes to measure 1½ cups total. In a blender blend the buttermilk mixture with half the cucumber, the avocado, peeled and pitted, the broth, the lemon juice, and the cumin until the mixture is smooth. Divide the soup between chilled bowls and stir half the remaining cucumber into each serving. Makes about 3½ cups, serving 2.

Chilled Cucumber and Bell Pepper Soup

1 garlic clove, minced and mashed to a paste
  with ¼ teaspoon salt
enough homemade-type white bread, crusts
  discarded and the rest torn into small
  pieces, to measure ½ cup
1 tablespoon white-wine vinegar
1 tablespoon olive oil
8 ounces plain yogurt
1 cup packed watercress sprigs, rinsed
  and spun dry
1 cucumber, peeled, seeded, and chopped fine
1 green bell pepper, chopped fine
3 tablespoons minced scallion
Tabasco to taste
croutons as an accompaniment

In a blender blend the garlic paste with the bread, the vinegar, the oil, the yogurt, the watercress, and salt and black pepper to taste until the mixture is smooth. Stir in the cucumber, the bell pepper, the scallion, and the Tabasco, chill the soup for 20 minutes, and serve it with the croutons. Serves 2.

Finnan Haddie and Watercress Soup

a ½-pound boiling potato
2 cups chopped onion
¾ stick (6 tablespoons) unsalted butter
a ¾-pound piece center-cut finnan haddie
  (smoked haddock, available at some fish
  markets and specialty foods shops)
1 cup milk
3 bunches of watercress, rinsed and coarse
  stems discarded (about 6 cups sprigs)
2 teaspoons fresh lemon juice

In a kettle cook the potato, peeled and diced, and the onion in 4 tablespoons of the butter over moderately low heat, stirring occasionally, until the onion is softened. While the vegetables are cooking, put the finnan haddie in a deep skillet just large enough to hold it, add the milk, the remaining 2 tablespoons butter, and 2 cups water, and bring the liquid to a simmer over moderate heat. Turn the finnan haddie and cook it, covered, at a bare simmer for 3 minutes. Transfer the finnan haddie with a slotted spoon to a plate. To the kettle add the fish poaching liquid and 2 cups water and simmer the mixture, covered, until the potatoes are soft. Stir in the watercress and simmer the soup, uncovered, for 3 minutes. In a blender purée the soup in batches until it is smooth, return it to the kettle, and stir in the lemon juice and salt and pepper to taste. *The soup and the finnan haddie may be prepared 1 day in advance and kept covered separately and chilled.* Heat the soup, stirring, until it is hot, ladle it into heated bowls, and garnish each serving with some of the finnan haddie, flaked. Makes about 9 cups, serving 8.

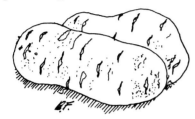

Portuguese Kale and Potato Soup

2 garlic cloves, minced
1½ cups finely chopped onion
¾ cup sliced carrot
¼ cup olive oil
1 pound (about 2 large) russet (baking) potatoes, peeled and cut into 1-inch pieces
4 cups chicken broth
¾ pound Spanish *chorizo* (cured spicy pork sausage, available at Hispanic markets and some specialty foods shops), cut into ¼-inch pieces
¾ pound kale, stems discarded and the leaves washed well, spun dry, and shredded thin (about 8 cups packed)
1 pound red potatoes

In a kettle cook the garlic, the onion, and the carrot in the oil over moderately low heat, stirring, until the vegetables are softened. Add the russet potatoes, the broth, and 4 cups water, bring the mixture to a boil, and simmer it, covered, for 10 to 15 minutes, or until the potatoes are tender. While the potatoes are cooking, in a skillet cook the *chorizo* over moderate heat, stirring, until it is browned lightly and transfer it with a slotted spoon to paper towels to drain. With the slotted spoon transfer the cooked potatoes to a blender with about 1½ cups of the cooking liquid and purée the mixture until it is smooth. Stir the purée into the broth mixture, add the *chorizo*, the kale, the red potatoes, cut into 1-inch pieces, and salt and pepper to taste, and simmer the soup, covered, for 10 minutes, or until the potatoes are tender. Makes about 10 cups, serving 6 to 8.

Parsnip Soup

½ cup finely chopped onion
1 garlic clove, minced
1 teaspoon minced peeled fresh gingerroot
½ cup thinly sliced carrot
½ cup thinly sliced celery
⅛ teaspoon dried thyme, crumbled
2 tablespoons unsalted butter
¾ pound parsnips (about 3), peeled and cut into ⅛-inch slices (about 2 cups)
2 cups chicken broth
freshly grated nutmeg to taste

In a heavy saucepan cook the onion, the garlic, the gingerroot, the carrot, the celery, and the thyme in the butter over moderately low heat, stirring, until the onion is softened. Add the parsnips and the broth, bring the liquid to a boil, and simmer the mixture, covered, for 15 minutes, or until the vegetables are very tender. Purée the soup in a blender and return it to the pan. Stir in the nutmeg, enough water to thin the soup to the desired consistency if necessary, and salt and pepper to taste. Makes about 3 cups, serving 2.

Pear, Pea, and Watercress Soup

1 onion, chopped
1 large pear, peeled, cored, and chopped
½ stick (¼ cup) unsalted butter
a 10-ounce package frozen peas, thawed
4 cups chicken broth
¼ cup medium-dry Sherry
¼ teaspoon dried thyme, crumbled
1 bunch of watercress, rinsed and coarse stems discarded

In a kettle cook the onion and the pear in the butter over moderately low heat, stirring occasionally, until the onion is softened, add the peas, the broth, the Sherry, and the thyme, and simmer the mixture for 8 minutes. Add the watercress and simmer the soup for 3 minutes. In a blender purée the soup in batches, season it with salt and pepper, and serve it warm or chilled. Makes about 8 cups, serving 8.

Curried Pear and Apple Soup

2 cups chicken broth
4 pears
1 Granny Smith apple
1 small potato (¼ pound)
½ cup coarsely chopped celery
    plus ¼ cup coarsely chopped celery leaves
½ small onion, chopped
1 teaspoon curry powder
2 tablespoons fresh lemon juice
2 cups half-and-half
⅛ teaspoon freshly grated nutmeg,
    or to taste

In a kettle combine the broth with 3 of the pears, peeled, cored, and chopped, the apple, peeled, cored, and chopped, the potato, peeled and chopped, the celery, the celery leaves, the onion, the curry powder, and the lemon juice and simmer the mixture, stirring occasionally, for 15 minutes, or until the potato is very tender. In a blender purée the mixture in batches with the half-and-half, season the purée with the nutmeg and salt and pepper, and stir in the remaining pear, peeled, cored, and diced. Serve the soup at room temperature or chilled. Makes about 7 cups, serving 6 to 8.

Mashed-Potato Soup

½ cup minced onion
1 small rib of celery including the leaves,
    chopped fine
1 carrot, grated coarse
2 tablespoons unsalted butter
2 cups chicken broth
a scant ¼ teaspoon dried rosemary,
    crumbled
2½ cups mashed potatoes
1 teaspoon white-wine vinegar
⅓ cup minced fresh parsley leaves

In a large saucepan cook the onion, the celery, and the carrot in the butter over moderately low heat, stirring, until the vegetables are tender, stir in the broth and the rosemary, and bring the mixture to a boil. Whisk in the potatoes, a little at a time, bring the soup to a boil, whisking, and stir in the vinegar, the parsley, and salt and pepper to taste. Makes about 4½ cups, serving 4 to 6.

Butternut Squash Soup with Green Chili Coriander Chutney

For the chutney
¼ cup sliced blanched almonds
¼ cup sweetened flaked coconut
2 *jalapeño* chilies, seeded and chopped coarse
    (wear rubber gloves)
2 cups loosely packed coriander
For the soup
2 cups chopped onion
2 tablespoons unsalted butter
2 tablespoons vegetable oil
a 3- to 3½-pound butternut squash, peeled,
    halved, the seeds and strings discarded, and
    the flesh cut into ½-inch pieces
6 cups chicken broth
two 4-inch strips of orange zest
1½ cups fresh orange juice

8 coriander sprigs for garnish

Make the chutney: In a blender or food processor blend the almonds, the coconut, the *jalapeños*, a pinch of salt, and ⅓ cup water until the mixture is ground fine. Add the coriander and blend the mixture until it is ground fine. (This recipe makes what is known as a dry chutney, which has a slightly grainy texture.) *The chutney may be made 8 hours in advance and kept covered and chilled.* Makes about 1 cup.

Make the soup: In a kettle cook the onion in the butter and the oil over moderately low heat, stirring, until it is softened, add the squash and ½ cup water, and cook the mixture, covered, over moderately low heat for 20 to 30 minutes, or until the squash is tender. Add the broth, the zest, and the juice and simmer the mixture, uncovered, for 15 minutes. In a blender or food processor purée the mixture in batches and strain it through a sieve into a large bowl. *The soup may be made 1 day in advance and kept covered and chilled.*

Ladle the soup into 8 bowls and garnish each serving with about a tablespoon of the chutney, to be stirred into the soup, and a coriander sprig. Makes about 10 cups, serving 8.

PHOTO ON PAGE 71

Tortilla Soup

1 whole chicken breast (about 1¼ pounds)
4 cups chicken broth

1 onion, sliced
3 garlic cloves
2 tablespoons vegetable oil plus additional
    for frying the tortillas
a 14- to 16-ounce can tomatoes, drained
⅓ cup fresh lime juice
2 fresh or pickled *jalapeño* chilies, or to taste,
    seeded and minced (wear rubber gloves)
six 7-inch corn tortillas, halved and cut
    crosswise into ¼-inch-wide strips
chopped fresh coriander for garnish if desired

In a large saucepan combine the chicken breast, the broth, and 3 cups water, bring the liquid to a boil, and simmer the chicken, covered, for 20 minutes, or until it is cooked through. Let the chicken cool in the broth. Transfer the chicken to a bowl, reserving the broth, discard the skin and bones, and shred the meat. In a heavy skillet cook the onion and the garlic in 2 tablespoons of the oil over moderate heat, stirring, until the onion is golden and in a blender or food processor purée the mixture with the tomatoes. Stir the purée into the reserved broth with the lime juice and the chilies and simmer the soup for 5 minutes.

While the soup is simmering, in the skillet, cleaned, heat ¼ inch of the additional oil over moderately high heat until it is hot but not smoking. Fry the tortilla strips in the oil in batches for 30 to 45 seconds, or until they are crisp, and transfer them as they are fried with a slotted spoon to paper towels to drain. Add the shredded chicken and the tortilla strips to the soup and simmer the soup for 1 to 2 minutes, or until it is heated through. Ladle the soup into heated bowls and garnish it with the coriander. Makes about 8 cups, serving 6.

Turkey Noodle Soup with Tomatoes

the carcass of 1 turkey, broken into
    large pieces
2 ribs of celery,
    chopped coarse
3 carrots, chopped coarse
3 garlic cloves
2 small onions, quartered
1 teaspoon black peppercorns
a 28-ounce can plum tomatoes, chopped
    coarse and drained well in a colander
6 ounces wide egg noodles
¼ cup finely chopped fresh
    parsley leaves

In a large kettle or stockpot combine the carcass, the celery, the carrots, the garlic, the onions, the peppercorns, and enough water to cover the mixture by 2 inches (about 6 quarts) and simmer the mixture, uncovered, for 3 hours. Strain the stock through a large sieve into a large bowl, leaving the solids in the sieve, return the stock to the kettle, and boil it until it is reduced to about 10 cups.

When the solids in the sieve are cool enough to handle, remove any turkey meat from the carcass and add it to the stock with the carrots, crushed lightly, discarding the remaining solids. Add the tomatoes and bring the soup to a boil. Stir in the noodles, boil the soup, stirring occasionally, for 8 to 10 minutes, or until the noodles are tender, and stir in the parsley and salt and pepper to taste. *The soup may be made in advance, cooled completely, uncovered, and kept covered and chilled for 2 days or covered and frozen for 2 months.* Makes about 12 cups, serving 8.

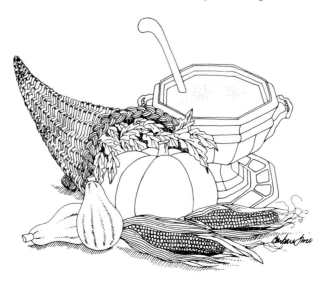

Scandinavian Vegetable Soup with Shrimp

1 carrot, sliced thin
⅓ cup shelled fresh peas or frozen peas,
    thawed
1 cup ½-inch cauliflower flowerets
1 small boiling potato, peeled, cut into ¼-inch
    dice, and reserved in a bowl of water
¼ pound green beans, trimmed and cut into
    ½-inch pieces
2 ounces fresh spinach, coarse stems
    discarded and the leaves washed well, spun
    dry, and chopped fine (about 1 cup)
½ cup half-and-half
1 large egg yolk
¼ pound small shrimp, shelled, deveined
    if desired
1 teaspoon salt
1 tablespoon finely chopped fresh dill plus
    2 dill sprigs for garnish
1 teaspoon dry Sherry if desired

In a large saucepan combine the carrot, the peas, the cauliflower, the potato, drained, and the green beans with 2 cups salted cold water and boil the mixture for 7 minutes, or until the vegetables are tender. Add the spinach and cook the mixture, stirring, for 1 minute. In a small bowl whisk together the half-and-half and the yolk, stir in 1 cup of the vegetable mixture, a little at a time, and stir the yolk mixture gradually back into the pan. Cook the mixture, stirring, for 1 minute, or until a thermometer registers 160° F. (but do not let it boil). Add the shrimp and simmer the mixture for 1 minute, or until the shrimp are pink and just firm. Add the salt, the chopped dill, pepper to taste, and the Sherry, divide the soup between 2 large soup bowls, and garnish each serving with a dill sprig. Serves 2.

Zucchini Coriander Soup

½ cup chopped onion
2 tablespoons olive oil
¾ pound zucchini, scrubbed and cut into
    ½-inch pieces
1½ cups chicken broth
1½ cups chopped fresh coriander
2 teaspoons fresh lemon juice, or to taste

In a large saucepan cook the onion in the oil over moderately low heat, stirring, until it is softened, add the zucchini and salt and pepper to taste, and cook the mixture, covered, stirring occasionally, for 4 minutes. Add the broth and 1¼ cups water and simmer the mixture, covered, for 10 minutes, or until the zucchini is tender. Remove the pan from the heat, stir in the coriander, and let the mixture cool. In a blender or food processor purée the mixture in batches, transferring the soup as it is puréed to a bowl. Stir in the lemon juice, season the soup with salt and pepper, and serve it at room temperature or chilled. Makes about 4 cups, serving 4.

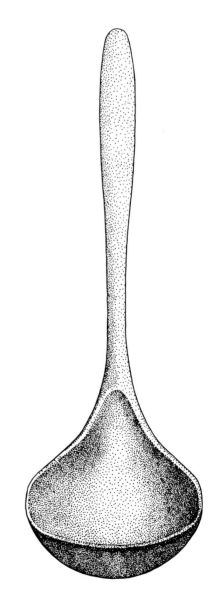

STOCKS

Turkey Giblet Stock

the giblets from 1 turkey (excluding the liver),
   chopped
3 cups chicken broth
1 onion stuck with 1 clove
1 carrot, halved
1 rib of celery, chopped
3 long parsley sprigs
¼ teaspoon dried thyme
½ bay leaf

In a saucepan combine the giblets, the stock, 3 cups water, the onion, the carrot, and the celery, bring the liquid to a boil, and skim the froth as it rises to the surface. Add the parsley, the thyme, and the bay leaf and cook the mixture over moderately low heat for 1 hour. Strain the stock through a fine sieve into a bowl, pressing hard on the solids, and let it cool. Chill the stock and remove the fat. The stock may be frozen. Makes about 3 cups.

White Veal Stock

2 pounds meaty veal knuckles, sawed into
   2-inch pieces
1 large onion stuck with 2 cloves
2 leeks, halved lengthwise and washed well
1 carrot
1 rib of celery, halved
1 teaspoon salt
a cheesecloth bag containing 4 parsley sprigs,
   ½ teaspoon dried thyme, and 1 bay leaf
1 pound chicken giblets (excluding the livers),
   chopped, or the chopped carcass of a raw or
   cooked chicken

In a kettle cover the veal knuckles with 12 cups cold water, bring the water to a boil, and skim the froth. Add ½ cup cold water, bring the stock to a simmer, and skim any froth. Add the onion, the leeks, the carrot, the celery, the salt, and the cheesecloth bag and simmer the stock, skimming the froth, for 4 hours. Add the giblets and simmer the stock, skimming the froth and adding boiling water if necessary to keep the ingredients barely covered, for 2 hours more. Strain the stock through a fine sieve set over a bowl, pressing hard on the solids, and let it cool. Chill the stock and remove the fat. The stock may be frozen. Makes about 6 cups.

FISH AND SHELLFISH

FISH

Fish Fillets with Tomatoes and Olives in Parchment

four 20- by 15-inch pieces of parchment paper
vegetable oil for brushing the parchment
four 6- to 8-ounce skinless flounder
   or orange roughy fillets
twelve ¼-inch-thick tomato slices
8 Kalamata or other brine-cured black olives,
   pitted and sliced thin
½ teaspoon dried hot red pepper flakes
1½ tablespoons unsalted butter, cut into bits
the zest from ½ orange removed with a
   vegetable peeler and cut into
   thin julienne strips
4 fresh herb sprigs, such as sage, thyme,
   or parsley

On a work surface brush 1 of the pieces of parchment with the oil, turn it over, and brush the other side with the oil. Arrange a second piece of parchment on top of the first, brush it with the oil, and layer the remaining 2 pieces on top in the same manner. Season the fish with salt and pepper, arrange 1 of the fillets on one half of the top piece of parchment, and top it with 3 tomato slices, one fourth of the olives, ⅛ teaspoon of the red pepper flakes, one fourth of the butter, one fourth of the zest, and 1 herb sprig. Fold the other half of the parchment over the fillet, beginning with a folded corner twist and fold the edges together forming a half-heart-shaped packet, and seal the end tightly by twisting it. Make 3 more packets with the remaining parchment and ingredients in the same manner. (Alternatively, the fish mixture can be wrapped in sheets of foil, oiling only the inside.) Bake the packets on a baking sheet in the middle of a preheated 450° F. oven for 10 minutes and cut them open before serving. Serves 4.

Herbed Fish Rolls in White Wine with Grapes

⅔ cup seedless green grapes
¾ cup dry white wine
four 6- to 8-ounce skinless flounder
   or orange roughy fillets
⅓ cup minced fresh parsley leaves
1 tablespoon minced fresh thyme leaves or
   ¾ teaspoon dried, crumbled
¼ cup minced onion
2 tablespoons unsalted butter
1 tablespoon all-purpose flour
¼ cup heavy cream
1 teaspoon fresh lemon juice

Reserve 8 of the grapes, halve the remaining grapes, and in a small saucepan let the grape halves macerate in the wine for 1 hour. Halve the fillets lengthwise, season them with salt and pepper, and sprinkle the skinned sides with the parsley and the thyme. Roll up each fillet half with 1 of the reserved grapes in the middle and secure it with a wooden pick. Stand the fish rolls up in a saucepan just large enough to hold them in one layer without crowding them. Transfer the macerated grapes with a slotted spoon to a small bowl, bring the wine to a boil, and pour it over the fish rolls. Cook the fish rolls, covered, at a bare simmer for 10 to 15 minutes, or until they just flake. Transfer the fish rolls with a slotted spoon to a plate, reserving the cooking liquid, and keep them warm, covered.

In a small saucepan cook the onion in the butter over moderate heat, stirring, for 5 minutes, stir in the flour, and cook the *roux* over moderately low heat, stirring, for 3 minutes. Remove the pan from the heat and strain the reserved cooking liquid through a fine sieve into the pan. Add the cream, the macerated grapes, the lemon juice, and salt and pepper to taste and boil the sauce, stirring, for 3 minutes. Pour off any liquid that has accumulated on the plate, divide the fish rolls among 4 heated plates, and spoon the sauce over them. Serves 4.

Crisp-Fried Fish Fillets Oriental

⅓ cup soy sauce
2 tablespoons white-wine vinegar
1½ tablespoons minced peeled fresh
 gingerroot
1 teaspoon sugar
four 6- to 8-ounce skinless flounder
 or orange roughy fillets
cornstarch for dredging the fish
2 large eggs
½ teaspoon salt
1⅓ cups fresh bread crumbs
¼ cup sesame seeds
vegetable oil for frying the fish

In a small saucepan combine the soy sauce, the vinegar, the gingerroot, the sugar, and pepper to taste and heat the mixture over low heat while preparing the fish. Pat the fish dry and season it with salt and pepper. Have ready in separate shallow dishes the cornstarch, the eggs beaten with the salt, and the bread crumbs combined with the sesame seeds. Dredge each fillet in the cornstarch, coating it thoroughly and shaking off the excess, dip it in the egg mixture, letting the excess drip off, and dredge it in the bread crumb mixture, pressing the mixture to help it adhere.

In a skillet large enough to hold 2 of the fillets comfortably heat ¼ inch of the oil over moderately high heat until it just begins to smoke, in it fry the fillets, 2 at a time, reheating the oil between batches, for 45 seconds to 1 minute on each side, or until they are golden brown, and transfer them to paper towels to drain. Transfer the fillets to 4 heated plates, bring the soy sauce mixture to a boil, and spoon it over the fish. Serves 4.

Marinated Fried Fish Strips and Potatoes with Onions and Green Peppers

vegetable oil for frying the potatoes
 and the fish
2 russet (baking) potatoes
1 pound skinless flounder or orange roughy
 fillets, cut into 2- by ½-inch strips
⅓ cup milk
all-purpose flour seasoned with salt and
 pepper for dredging the fish
4 garlic cloves, halved
¼ cup olive oil
2½ cups thinly sliced red onion

1 green bell pepper, cut into thin rings
½ teaspoon dried orégano
¾ cup dry white wine
½ cup white-wine vinegar
1 teaspoon sugar

In a large deep skillet heat 1 inch of the vegetable oil to 375° F. and in it fry the potatoes, peeled, halved lengthwise, and cut crosswise ¼ inch thick, in 2 batches for 8 minutes, or until they are golden brown. Transfer the potatoes with a slotted spoon to paper towels to drain and sprinkle them with salt to taste. In a small bowl combine the fish with the milk. Put the seasoned flour in a bowl, remove the fish strips from the milk, letting the excess drip off, and dredge them, a few at a time, in the flour, shaking off the excess. Reheat the vegetable oil to 375° F., in it fry the fish in 2 batches for 3 to 5 minutes, or until it is golden brown, and transfer it with a slotted spoon to paper towels to drain. In a large baking dish combine the fish and the potatoes.

In a large skillet cook the garlic in the olive oil over moderate heat, stirring, until it is golden, add the onion, the bell pepper, and the orégano, and cook the mixture over moderately low heat, stirring, for 5 minutes. Add the wine, the vinegar, the sugar, and salt and black pepper to taste, boil the liquid for 2 minutes, and pour the mixture over the fish and potatoes. Chill the dish, covered, for at least 8 hours or overnight. Let it stand at room temperature for 30 minutes before serving. Serves 6 to 8 as a first course or luncheon entrée.

Peanut-Crusted Fish Fillets with Fried Bananas

2 unripe bananas
2 tablespoons unsalted butter
1 tablespoon vegetable oil
two 6- to 8-ounce skinless flounder
    or orange roughy fillets
½ teaspoon ground cumin
1 large egg
¼ teaspoon salt
⅔ cup finely chopped unsalted peanuts
4 teaspoons fresh lime juice plus lime wedges
    as an accompaniment

Peel the bananas and cut them lengthwise into ¼-inch-thick slices. In a large ovenproof skillet heat 1 tablespoon of the butter and the oil over moderately high heat until the foam subsides, in the fat sauté the banana slices for 1 minute on each side, or until they are golden, and transfer them with a spatula to a plate. Pat the fish dry and sprinkle it with the cumin and salt and pepper to taste. Have ready in separate shallow dishes the egg beaten with the salt and the peanuts. Dip each fillet in the egg mixture, letting the excess drip off, and dredge it in the peanuts. To the skillet add the remaining 1 tablespoon butter, heat it over moderately high heat until the foam subsides, and in it sauté the fillets for 3 minutes. Turn the fillets, top them with the banana slices, and sauté them for 2 minutes more. Drizzle the fish with the lime juice and transfer the skillet to the middle of a preheated 450° F. oven. Bake the fish for 5 minutes. Transfer the fillets with a spatula to 2 heated plates and serve them with the lime wedges. Serves 2.

Grilled Fish Fillets with Lentil Salsa

¾ cup lentils, picked over
1 green bell pepper, chopped fine
½ cup finely chopped onion
2 tomatoes, chopped
¼ cup chopped fresh coriander
3 tablespoons olive oil

3 tablespoons red-wine vinegar
four 6- to 8-ounce skinless flounder
    or orange roughy fillets
all-purpose flour for dredging the fish

In a large saucepan of boiling water boil the lentils for 15 to 20 minutes, or until they are just tender, drain them in a sieve, and rinse them briefly under cold water. Drain the lentils well and in a bowl toss them with the bell pepper, the onion, the tomatoes, the coriander, the oil, the vinegar, and salt and black pepper to taste.

Pat the fillets dry, season them with salt and pepper, and dredge them in the flour, shaking off the excess. Grill the fillets on an oiled rack set about 6 inches over glowing coals or in an oiled ridged grill pan over moderately high heat for 4 to 5 minutes on each side, or until they just flake. Divide the *salsa* among 4 plates and top each serving with a fillet. Serves 4.

Fish Tacos

For the filling
1½ pounds scrod fillets or other firm-fleshed
    white fish fillets, cooked, drained well,
    and flaked
½ cup Kalamata or other brine-cured black
    olives, pitted and chopped
1 cup seeded and chopped tomatoes
    (about ½ pound)
3 scallions, sliced thin
2 fresh or pickled *jalapeño* chilies, or to taste,
    seeded and minced (wear rubber gloves)
2 tablespoons fresh lime juice, or to taste
2 tablespoons white-wine vinegar, or to taste
3 tablespoons olive oil
3 tablespoons chopped fresh coriander
    if desired

vegetable oil for frying the tortillas
twelve 7-inch corn tortillas
3 cups shredded romaine or iceberg lettuce
1½ cups coarsely grated radishes

Make the filling: In a bowl toss together the scrod, the olives, the tomatoes, the scallions, the chilies, the lime juice, the vinegar, the oil, the coriander, and salt and black pepper to taste and chill the filling, covered, for at least 1 hour or overnight.

In a skillet heat ½ inch of the oil over moderately high

heat until it is hot but not smoking, in it fry the tortillas, 1 at a time, folding them almost in half with tongs to form taco shells, for 1 minute, or until they are crisp and golden, and transfer them as they are fried with the tongs to paper towels to drain. Divide the filling among the tacos and top it with the lettuce and the radishes. Makes 12 tacos, serving 6.

Creamy Monkfish, Tomato, and Shellfish Potpie with Puff Pastry Crust

1 onion, minced
1 rib of celery, sliced thin
2 teaspoons minced garlic
2 tablespoons olive oil
½ teaspoon fennel seeds
1 cup bottled clam juice
a 14-ounce can tomatoes including the juice
a dash of Tabasco
¼ pound mushrooms, cut into eighths
1 pound boiling potatoes
½ teaspoon dried thyme, crumbled
½ teaspoon dried basil, crumbled
½ cup heavy cream
3 tablespoons cornstarch
1½ pounds monkfish fillets, cut into
    1-inch pieces
½ pound sea scallops, halved crosswise
½ pound shrimp, shelled
2 tablespoons finely chopped fresh
    parsley leaves
1 sheet of frozen puff pastry, thawed

In a kettle cook the onion, the celery, and the garlic in the oil over moderately low heat, stirring, until the onion is softened, add the fennel seeds, the clam juice, the tomatoes with the juice, the Tabasco, the mushrooms, the potatoes, peeled and cut into ¾-inch pieces, the thyme, and the basil, and simmer the mixture for 15 minutes, or until the potatoes are barely tender. In a small bowl whisk together the cream and the cornstarch, whisk the mixture into the potato mixture, and boil the mixture, whisking, for 1 minute. Stir in the monkfish, the scallops, the shrimp, the parsley, and salt and pepper to taste and transfer the mixture to a 3-quart oval baking dish.

On a floured surface roll out the puff pastry into an oval to fit the dish and brush the edge of the dish with water. Arrange the pastry over the dish and roll the roll-ing pin over the edge of the dish to cut the pastry. Bake the potpie in the middle of a preheated 425° F. oven for 17 to 20 minutes, or until the crust is puffed and golden brown. To serve the potpie, cut the crust into 8 pieces, arrange 1 piece on each of 8 heated dinner plates, and divide the filling among the plates. Serves 8.

Grilled Red Snapper with Thyme

2 tablespoons vegetable oil
4 sprigs of fresh thyme or 1 teaspoon
    dried, crumbled
four 6-ounce red snapper fillets
coriander sprigs for garnish
papaya coriander *salsa* as an accompaniment
    (recipe follows)

In a small saucepan combine the oil and the thyme, heat the oil over moderate heat until it begins to sizzle, and let the mixture cool to room temperature. In a shallow baking dish large enough to hold the snapper fillets in one layer arrange the snapper, skin side down, brush it with the oil mixture, and let it stand, covered and chilled, overnight. Grill the snapper, seasoned with salt and pepper, skin side down, on an oiled rack set 5 to 6 inches over glowing coals for 3 minutes, turn it with a spatula, and grill it for 1 to 2 minutes more, or until it just flakes. (Alternatively the snapper may be grilled in a ridged grill pan.) Garnish the snapper with the coriander and serve it with the *salsa*.

PHOTO ON PAGE 18

Papaya Coriander Salsa

1 cup papaya (about 1 papaya), halved,
    seeded, and chopped coarse
3 tablespoons minced shallot
a 2½-inch fresh *jalapeño* chili, chopped fine
    (wear rubber gloves)
2 tablespoons minced fresh coriander
½ teaspoon salt
3 tablespoons fresh lime juice

In a bowl combine well the papaya, the shallot, the *jalapeño*, the coriander, the salt, and 2 tablespoons of the lime juice, let the *salsa* stand, covered and chilled, for at least 1 hour and up to 3 hours, and stir in the remaining 1 tablespoon lime juice. Makes about 1 cup.

PHOTO ON PAGE 18

Salmon, Scallop, and Pea Terrine

¾ pound sea scallops, rinsed, drained, and
　patted dry
1 cup shelled fresh or frozen peas, cooked
　until tender, drained, and cooled
1 tablespoon lightly beaten egg white
2 tablespoons heavy cream
1 teaspoon salt
½ teaspoon dried tarragon, crumbled
1 pound skinless salmon fillet, cut into
　½-inch cubes
chive butter sauce (recipe follows) or *tsatsiki*
　(page 205)

In a food processor purée the scallops and the peas
until the mixture is almost smooth, add the egg white,
the cream, the salt, and the tarragon, and purée the mixture until it is smooth. Transfer the mixture to a bowl,
fold in the salmon, and transfer the mixture to a buttered
1-quart rectangular terrine, smoothing the top and rap-
ping the terrine on a hard surface to expel air bubbles.

Cover the terrine with buttered wax paper and the
lid or a double thickness of foil, put it in a baking pan,
and add enough hot water to the pan to come halfway
up the sides of the terrine. Bake the terrine in a preheated
375° F. oven for 45 minutes. Remove the terrine from
the baking pan and remove the lid and the wax paper.
Let the terrine stand for 10 minutes, carefully pour off
the excess liquid, and invert the terrine onto a platter.
*The terrine may be made 1 day in advance and kept cov-
ered and chilled. Let the terrine return to room temperature before serving.* Cut the terrine into ½-inch
slices and serve it warm with the chive butter sauce or at
room temperature with the *tsatsiki*. Serves 4.

PHOTO ON PAGE 51

Chive Butter Sauce

¼ cup minced shallot
¼ cup dry vermouth or dry white wine
2 tablespoons white-wine vinegar
½ stick (¼ cup) cold unsalted butter, cut
　into 4 pieces
2 teaspoons minced fresh chives

In a small heavy saucepan combine the shallot, the
vermouth, and the vinegar, bring the liquid to a boil,
and simmer it until the liquid is reduced to about 1 tablespoon. Reduce the heat to moderately low and whisk in

the butter, 1 piece at a time, lifting the pan from the heat
occasionally to cool the mixture and adding each new
piece before the previous one has melted completely.
(The sauce must not get hot enough to liquefy. It should
be the consistency of hollandaise.) Stir in the chives and
salt to taste. Makes about ½ cup.

PHOTO ON PAGE 51

Spicy Grilled Salmon Steaks with Black Butter

1½ teaspoons freshly ground black pepper
½ teaspoon paprika
¼ teaspoon cayenne
1 teaspoon minced garlic
1 tablespoon minced onion
½ teaspoon dried thyme, crumbled
¼ teaspoon salt
1 tablespoon olive oil
2 salmon steaks (1 pound), each about
　1 inch thick
1 tablespoon unsalted butter

In a bowl stir together the black pepper, the paprika,
the cayenne, the garlic, the onion, the thyme, the salt,
and the oil until the mixture forms a stiff paste. Pat the
paste onto both sides of each salmon steak. Heat an
oiled ridged grill pan over moderately high heat until it
is smoking and in it sauté the salmon, for 3 to 4 minutes
on each side, or until it is cooked through. While the
salmon is cooking, in a small skillet cook it over moderate heat, swirling the skillet, until it is dark brown, being careful not to let it burn. Transfer the salmon to
heated plates and pour the butter over it. Serves 2.

Norwegian-Style Poached Salmon
with Anchovy Butter

1½ tablespoons unsalted butter, softened
1½ tablespoons minced fresh parsley leaves
¾ teaspoon anchovy paste or mashed
　anchovy fillet
1 onion, sliced
⅓ cup distilled white vinegar
¼ cup sugar
½ teaspoon black peppercorns
1 teaspoon coriander seeds
½ teaspoon mustard seeds
1 teaspoon salt
two 1-inch-thick salmon steaks

In a small bowl combine well the butter, the parsley, the anchovy paste, and freshly ground black pepper to taste and reserve the anchovy butter, covered. In a saucepan combine the onion, the vinegar, the sugar, the peppercorns, the coriander seeds, the mustard seeds, the salt, and 4 cups water, bring the mixture to a boil, and simmer it for 15 minutes. Strain the mixture through a fine sieve into a deep heavy skillet just large enough to hold the salmon in one layer. Add the salmon, bring the liquid to a simmer, and poach the salmon, covered, for 8 to 10 minutes, or until it just flakes. Transfer the salmon steaks with a slotted spatula to plates, letting the poaching liquid drain off, and divide the reserved anchovy butter between them. Serves 2.

Smoked Salmon and Avocado with Lemon Caper Butter on Pumpernickel Bread

5 tablespoons unsalted butter, softened
1 tablespoon fresh lemon juice
1 tablespoon drained bottled capers
8 slices of pumpernickel bread
½ pound thinly sliced smoked salmon
1 small red onion, sliced thin
1 avocado (preferably California), pitted, peeled, cut into 12 wedges, and sprinkled with the juice of ½ lemon
1 cup alfalfa sprouts

In a small bowl cream together the butter, the lemon juice, the capers, and salt and pepper to taste and spread the lemon caper butter on one side of each slice of bread. Layer half the bread slices with the salmon, the onion, the avocado, and the sprouts and top the sandwiches with the remaining bread slices, pressing them firmly. Makes 4 sandwiches.

Smoked Salmon and Herbed Yogurt Roulade

1 egg sponge (page 164)
2 cups plain yogurt, drained in a fine sieve, covered, overnight
1 cup loosely packed flat-leafed parsley leaves, chopped fine
½ cup finely chopped scallion greens
1 tablespoon drained bottled capers, chopped fine
3 ounces sliced smoked salmon, cut into ½-inch-wide strips

Make the egg sponge and let it cool to room temperature, covered with a sheet of wax paper. In a bowl combine well the yogurt, the parsley, the scallion greens, and the capers. Spread the egg sponge evenly with the yogurt mixture, leaving a ½-inch border on all 4 sides, arrange the salmon strips in 6 lengthwise rows about 2 inches apart on the yogurt mixture, and starting with a long side roll up the egg sponge jelly-roll fashion. Trim the ends of the egg sponge diagonally and slice the *roulade*. Serves 8 to 10 as a first course.

Sardine Roulade with Jalapeño, Monterey Jack, and Tomato Sauce

1 egg sponge (page 164)
For the sauce
1 garlic clove, minced
2 teaspoons olive oil
a 14-ounce can plum tomatoes including
  the juice

a 3¾-ounce can brisling sardines packed in
  oil, drained and chopped coarse
2 teaspoons minced pickled *jalapeño* chili
  (wear rubber gloves)
1¼ cups grated Monterey Jack
unsalted butter, softened, for brushing
  the *roulade*

Prepare the egg sponge and while it is baking make the sauce.

Make the sauce: In a saucepan cook the garlic in the oil over moderately low heat, stirring occasionally, until it is golden, add the tomatoes with the juice, and simmer the mixture, breaking up the tomatoes, for 15 minutes, or until the sauce is thickened. Season the sauce with salt and pepper.

Assemble the *roulade*: Spread the sauce on the warm egg sponge, leaving a 1-inch border on the long sides, sprinkle it with the sardines, the *jalapeño*, and 1 cup of the Monterey Jack, and starting with a long side roll up the egg sponge jelly-roll fashion. With the aid of the towel and the wax paper transfer the *roulade*, seam side down, to a shallow baking pan, brush the top lightly with the butter, and sprinkle it with the remaining ¼ cup Monterey Jack. Bake the *roulade* in the upper third of a preheated 375° F. oven for 8 to 10 minutes, or until the Monterey Jack is melted, and slice it. Serves 4 to 6.

Scallops with Pink Grapefruit Beurre Blanc

¾ pound sea scallops, patted dry and
  cut into ½-inch-thick slices
1 tablespoon flour
2 tablespoons olive oil
¼ cup dry white wine
2 tablespoons bottled clam juice
1 tablespoon minced shallot
⅓ cup fresh pink grapefruit juice
½ teaspoon grated pink grapefruit zest
½ teaspoon sugar

3 tablespoons cold unsalted butter,
  cut into bits
1 tablespoon thinly sliced scallion
fresh pink grapefruit sections for garnish

In a bowl toss together the scallops, the flour, and salt and pepper to taste. In a skillet large enough to hold the scallops in one layer heat the oil over moderately high heat until it is hot but not smoking and in it sauté the scallops, stirring, for 2½ to 3 minutes, or until they are just firm and lightly golden. Transfer the scallops to a plate. Add the wine to the skillet, deglaze the skillet, scraping up the brown bits, and stir in the clam juice, the shallot, the grapefruit juice, the zest, and the sugar. Boil the liquid until it is reduced to about ⅓ cup and strain the mixture through a fine sieve set over a saucepan. Set the pan over low heat and whisk in the butter, 1 bit at a time, lifting the pan from the heat occasionally to cool the mixture and adding each new bit of butter before the previous one has melted completely. (The sauce should not get hot enough to liquefy. It should be the consistency of thin hollandaise.) Add the scallion and the scallops with any juices that have accumulated on the plate and heat the mixture until the scallops are heated through. Divide the mixture between 2 plates and garnish each plate with some of the grapefruit sections. Serves 2.

PHOTO ON PAGE 11

Grilled Scallops with Curried Tomato Coulis

2 large shallots, sliced thin
2 tablespoons olive oil
1 teaspoon mustard seeds
1½ teaspoons curry powder
½ teaspoon sugar
6 plum tomatoes, seeded and chopped
2 teaspoons balsamic vinegar
vegetable oil for brushing the grill pan
¾ pound sea scallops

In a skillet cook the shallots in the olive oil over moderate heat, stirring, until they are softened, stir in the mustard seeds and the curry powder, and cook the mixture, stirring, for 1 minute. Stir in the sugar, the tomatoes, and salt and pepper to taste and cook the mixture, stirring, for 2 minutes, or until the tomatoes begin to release their juices. Stir in the balsamic vinegar and keep the *coulis* warm. Heat a well-seasoned ridged grill pan over moderately high heat until it is hot and brush it with the vegetable oil. Add the scallops, patted dry, and grill them for 2½ minutes on each side, or until they are just firm. Divide the *coulis* between 2 plates and top each serving with half the scallops. Serves 2.

Sea Bass with Lemon Caper Fettuccine

2 tablespoons olive oil (preferably extra-virgin)
2 teaspoons fresh lemon juice
1 tablespoon drained bottled capers
⅛ teaspoon cayenne
1 tablespoon minced fresh parsley leaves
¼ pound fettuccine
two 6-ounce sea bass or salmon fillets
1 teaspoon vegetable oil

In a large bowl combine the olive oil, the lemon juice, the capers, the cayenne, and the parsley and transfer 1 tablespoon of the mixture to a small bowl. In a large saucepan of boiling salted water cook the fettuccine until it is *al dente*, drain it well, and in the large bowl toss it with the lemon mixture and salt to taste until the mixture is combined well.

Pat the fillets dry and season them with salt and pepper. In a non-stick skillet heat the vegetable oil over moderately high heat until it is hot but not smoking and in it sauté the fillets, skin sides up, for 4 minutes. Turn the fillets and sauté them for 4 minutes more, or until they are crisp and just flake. Divide the fettuccine between 2 heated plates, top it with the fillets, and drizzle the fillets with the remaining 1 tablespoon lemon mixture. Serves 2.

Fillet of Sole with Leek Sauce

2 tablespoons unsalted butter
the white and pale green parts of 2 leeks, split lengthwise, washed well, and sliced thin crosswise (about 2 cups)
⅓ cup dry white wine
2 sole fillets (about ¾ pound total)
⅓ cup heavy cream
fresh lemon juice to taste
minced fresh parsley leaves for garnish

In a microwave-safe glass casserole microwave the butter at high power (100%) for 1 minute, or until it is

melted. Stir in the leek and salt to taste and microwave the mixture, covered with the lid, at high power (100%) for 10 minutes, or until the leek is tender. Transfer the leek mixture to a saucepan and add the wine. Season the sole with salt and pepper and fold the fillets, skinned sides in, into thirds. Arrange the fillets in the casserole and microwave them, covered with the lid, at high power (100%) for 3 minutes, or until they just flake. While the fish is cooking, boil the leek mixture until almost all the liquid is evaporated. Transfer the fish with a slotted spatula to heated plates and keep it warm, covered with foil. Add the fish liquid remaining in the casserole to the leek mixture and boil the mixture until the liquid is reduced by half. Add the cream and boil the mixture, stirring, until the sauce is thickened slightly. Season the sauce with the lemon juice and salt and pepper, spoon it around the fish, and garnish each serving with the parsley. Serves 2.

Sautéed Swordfish with Niçoise Vinaigrette

5 tablespoons olive oil
two 1-inch-thick swordfish steaks
¼ cup finely chopped pitted Kalamata or other brine-cured black olives
¼ cup finely chopped drained bottled roasted red pepper
3 tablespoons finely chopped fresh parsley leaves, preferably flat-leafed
1 tablespoon drained bottled capers, chopped fine
1 flat anchovy fillet, minced
1 small garlic clove, minced and mashed to a paste with ¼ teaspoon salt
2 tablespoons minced scallion
1½ tablespoons balsamic or red-wine vinegar
lemon wedges as an accompaniment

In a skillet, preferably non-stick, heat 1½ tablespoons of the oil over moderately high heat until it is hot but not smoking and in it sauté the swordfish steaks, patted dry, for 4 to 5 minutes on each side, or until they are just cooked through. While the fish is cooking, in a small bowl stir together the olives, the roasted red pepper, the parsley, the capers, the anchovy, the garlic paste, the scallion, the vinegar, the remaining 3½ tablespoons oil, and salt and pepper to taste. Transfer the swordfish to plates, spoon the sauce over it, and serve it with the lemon wedges. Serves 2.

Grilled Swiss Cheese, Tuna, and Red Pepper Sandwiches

¼ cup minced drained bottled roasted
    red peppers
2 tablespoons mayonnaise
1 teaspoon fresh lemon juice
a pinch of ground cumin
a 6½-ounce can tuna packed in oil,
    drained well
1 hard-boiled large egg, minced
1 hot cherry pepper, seeded and minced
two 5-inch-long soft Italian rolls
½ small red onion, sliced thin
4 slices of Swiss cheese
2 tablespoons olive oil

In a bowl whisk together the roasted peppers, the mayonnaise, the lemon juice, and the cumin, add the tuna, flaked, the egg, the cherry pepper, and salt and black pepper to taste, and combine the mixture well. Split the rolls, divide the mixture between the bottoms, and top each portion with half the onion, 2 slices of the Swiss cheese, and the tops of the rolls. In a large skillet heat the oil over moderate heat until it is hot but not smoking and in it cook the sandwiches, pressing them with a spatula and turning them, for 8 minutes, or until the bread is golden brown and the cheese is melted. Serves 2.

SHELLFISH

Clam, Potato, and Bacon Potpie

6 slices of lean bacon
2 tablespoons unsalted butter
1 onion, chopped fine
3 tablespoons all-purpose flour
1 cup heavy cream
1 cup milk
1 pint shucked hard-shelled clams, chopped
    coarse, reserving ¼ cup of the liquor
¼ teaspoon Worcestershire sauce
3 boiling potatoes, cooked, peeled, and cut
    into ½-inch cubes
¼ teaspoon dried thyme, crumbled
2 tablespoons finely chopped fresh
    parsley leaves
1 teaspoon fresh lemon juice

2 recipes *pâte brisée* (recipe follows)
an egg wash made by beating 1 large egg with
    2 teaspoons water

In a kettle cook the bacon over moderately low heat until it is crisp. Transfer it with tongs to paper towels to drain. Pour off all but 2 tablespoons of the fat, add the butter, and in the fat cook the onion, stirring occasionally, until it is softened and lightly golden. Add the flour and cook the *roux*, stirring, for 3 minutes. Add the cream, the milk, the reserved clam liquor, and the Worcestershire sauce and cook the mixture, stirring, for 5 minutes, or until it is thickened. Add the potatoes, the clams, the thyme, the parsley, the lemon juice, the bacon, crumbled, and salt and pepper to taste and combine the mixture well.

Divide the dough in half. Roll out one piece of the dough ⅛ inch thick on a lightly floured surface, fit it into a 10-inch (1½-quart capacity) pie plate, and trim the dough, leaving a 1-inch overhang. Pour the filling into the shell. Roll out the remaining dough ⅛ inch thick, arrange it over the filling, and crimp the edge decoratively. Brush the top crust with the egg wash and bake the potpie in the lower third of a preheated 400° F. oven for 35 minutes, or until the crust is golden. Serves 6 to 8.

Pâte Brisée

1¼ cups all-purpose flour
¾ stick (6 tablespoons) cold unsalted butter,
    cut into bits
2 tablespoons cold vegetable shortening
¼ teaspoon salt

In a large bowl blend the flour, the butter, the vegetable shortening, and the salt until the mixture resembles meal. Add 3 tablespoons ice water, toss the mixture until the water is incorporated, and form the dough into a ball. Knead the dough lightly with the heel of the hand against a smooth surface for a few seconds to distribute the fat evenly and re-form it into a ball. Dust the dough with flour and chill it, wrapped in wax paper, for 1 hour.

Clams Casino

4 slices of lean bacon, chopped fine
½ cup chopped onion
1 large garlic clove, minced
1 tablespoon olive oil

½ cup finely diced red bell pepper
½ cup finely diced green bell pepper
¼ teaspoon dried orégano, crumbled
1 teaspoon wine vinegar
1 tablespoon freshly grated Parmesan
12 medium (2½-inch) hard-shelled clams,
    shucked (procedure follows) and the
    bottom shells reserved
coarse salt for filling the pan and platter

In a heavy skillet cook the bacon over moderate heat, stirring, until it begins to brown but is not crisp, transfer it with a slotted spoon to paper towels to drain, and discard the fat from the skillet. In the skillet, wiped clean, cook the onion and the garlic in the oil over moderately low heat until they are softened, add the bell peppers and the orégano, and cook the mixture, stirring, until the bell peppers are crisp-tender. Transfer the mixture to a small bowl and stir in the bacon, the vinegar, the Parmesan, and salt and black pepper to taste. *The bell pepper mixture may be made 1 day in advance and kept covered and chilled.*

Arrange the clams in the reserved shells in a jelly-roll pan filled with some of the rock salt (to balance the shells), divide the bell pepper mixture among them, and bake the clams in a preheated 400° F. oven for 12 to 15 minutes, or until they are just cooked through. Arrange the clams on a platter filled with more of the rock salt. Makes 12 baked clams.

PHOTO ON PAGE 81

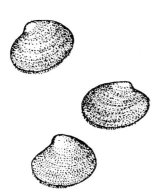

To Shuck Hard-Shelled Clams

Scrub the clams thoroughly with a stiff brush under cold water, discarding any clams that have cracked shells or that are not shut tightly. Hold each clam in a kitchen towel on a work surface with the hinged end away from you. Insert a clam knife between the shells, cut around the inside edges to sever the connecting muscles, and twist the knife slightly to open the shells. If the clams are not to be served raw they may be opened in the oven: Arrange the clams in one layer in a baking pan and put the pan in a preheated 450° F. oven for 3 to 5 minutes, or until the shells have opened. Reserve the liquor and discard any unopened clams.

Crisp-Fried Clams with Spinach Tartar Sauce in Pita Pockets

2½ cups shredded well-washed spinach leaves
½ cup mayonnaise
2 tablespoons finely chopped sweet pickle
2 tablespoons drained bottled capers
2 teaspoons Dijon-style mustard
2 teaspoons fresh lemon juice, or to taste
24 soft-shelled steamer clams, scrubbed
all-purpose flour for dredging the clams
2 large eggs
½ teaspoon salt
¼ teaspoon cayenne
cornmeal for dredging the clams
vegetable oil for deep-frying
four 6-inch *pita* loaves

In a small bowl combine well the spinach leaves, the mayonnaise, the pickle, the capers, the mustard, the lemon juice, and salt and black pepper to taste and chill the tartar sauce, covered.

In a large saucepan of boiling water blanch the clams for 2 minutes, drain them in a colander, and rinse them under cold water. Remove the clams from their shells, peeling off and discarding the dark membranes, rinse them briefly under cold water, and drain them well. In three separate shallow dishes have ready the flour, the eggs beaten with the salt and the cayenne, and the cornmeal. Dredge the clams, 1 at a time, in the flour, shaking off the excess, dip them in the egg mixture, letting the excess drip off, and dredge them in the cornmeal, transferring them as they are coated to a sheet of wax paper. In a kettle heat 1 inch of the oil to 375° F. on a deep-fat thermometer, in it fry the clams in 2 batches for 1 minute, or until they are crisp, and transfer them with a slotted spoon to paper towels to drain. Cut ¼ inch off one end of each *pita*, open the *pita* to form a pocket, and divide the fried clams among the *pita* pockets. Spoon some of the tartar sauce into each pocket, spreading it over the clams. Makes 4 sandwiches.

Spicy Steamed Clams with Fennel

1 large garlic clove, minced
¼ teaspoon dried hot red pepper flakes,
   or to taste
¾ teaspoon dried orégano, crumbled
2 tablespoons olive oil
½ cup finely chopped onion
1¼ cups thinly sliced fennel bulb, or celery
   combined with ½ teaspoon fennel seeds
a 14-ounce can plum tomatoes, drained,
   reserving the juice, and chopped
½ cup dry white wine
24 small hard-shelled clams, scrubbed well
2 tablespoons minced fresh parsley leaves
   plus parsley sprigs for garnish
crusty bread as an accompaniment

In a heavy saucepan cook the garlic, the pepper flakes, and the orégano in the oil over moderately low heat, stirring, for 1 minute, add the onion and the fennel, and cook the mixture over moderate heat, stirring, until the fennel is softened. Add the tomatoes with the reserved juice, the wine, and salt and pepper to taste and simmer the mixture, uncovered, stirring occasionally, for 5 minutes. Add the clams, steam them, covered, for 5 to 7 minutes, or until they have opened, and discard any unopened ones. Transfer the clams to a serving dish, stir the minced parsley into the fennel mixture, and spoon the mixture over the clams. Garnish the clams with the parsley sprigs and serve them with the bread. Serves 2.

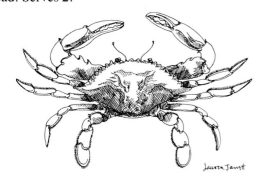

Crab Cakes with Red Bell Pepper

½ pound lump crab meat, picked over
¼ teaspoon salt
½ red bell pepper, minced
½ stick (¼ cup) unsalted butter
1½ teaspoons fresh lemon juice
2 tablespoons lightly beaten egg
1½ teaspoons Worcestershire sauce
1 hard-boiled large egg, one half chopped fine
   and, for garnish, the other half quartered
⅓ cup fresh white bread crumbs
1 tablespoon vegetable oil
lemon wedges for garnish if desired
bottled tartar sauce as an accompaniment
   if desired

In a bowl combine the crab meat, the salt, and black pepper to taste. In a small saucepan cook the bell pepper in 3 tablespoons of the butter over moderately low heat, stirring, until it is softened. Remove the pan from the heat, stir in the lemon juice, the beaten egg, and the Worcestershire sauce, and stir the mixture into the crab meat. Add the chopped hard-boiled egg and the bread crumbs, combine the mixture gently but thoroughly, and form it into 4 patties, each about ½ inch thick.

In a large heavy skillet heat the oil with the remaining 1 tablespoon butter over moderately high heat until the foam subsides and in the fat sauté the crab cakes, turning them carefully, for 4 to 5 minutes on each side, or until they are golden brown and crisp. Serve the crab cakes with the lemon wedges, the remaining hard-boiled egg, and the tartar sauce. Serves 2.

Broiled Open-Faced Crab-Meat Sandwiches

¼ cup finely chopped red bell pepper
¼ cup finely chopped green bell pepper
¼ cup finely chopped onion
1 garlic clove, minced
2 tablespoons unsalted butter
½ pound lump crab meat, picked over
2 tablespoons fresh lemon juice
1 hard-boiled large egg, chopped
1 teaspoon Worcestershire sauce, or to taste
2 tablespoons mayonnaise
1 teaspoon Dijon-style mustard
⅛ teaspoon cayenne, or to taste
2 English muffins, halved, buttered lightly,
   and toasted
2 tablespoons freshly grated Parmesan

In a large skillet cook the bell peppers, the onion, and the garlic in the butter over moderately low heat, stirring, until the vegetables are softened. Stir in the crab meat, the lemon juice, the egg, the Worcestershire sauce, the mayonnaise, the mustard, and the cayenne and divide the crab-meat mixture among the muffin halves, mounding it slightly. Sprinkle the sandwiches with the Parmesan and broil them under a preheated broiler about 4 inches from the heat for 3 to 4 minutes, or until the tops are just golden. Serves 4.

Curried Crab Meat and Mushroom Salad

¾ cup mayonnaise
4 teaspoons curry powder, or to taste
2 teaspoons minced fresh tarragon, or to taste, plus tarragon sprigs for garnish
1½ pounds king crab meat, picked over
½ pound small white mushrooms, sliced thin
4 tablespoons fresh lemon juice, or to taste
6 ribs of celery, cut into matchsticks and soaked in a bowl of ice and cold water for about 20 minutes

In a bowl whisk together the mayonnaise, the curry powder, the minced tarragon, and 1 to 2 tablespoons water, or enough to thin the sauce to the desired consistency. Stir in the crab meat, the mushrooms, and the lemon juice and on salad plates mound the mixture on the celery, drained. Garnish the salads with the tarragon sprigs. Serves 8.

Baked Oysters with Spinach Fennel Purée and Crisp-Fried Shallots

3 tablespoons vegetable oil
½ cup thinly sliced shallots
1 pound fresh spinach, coarse stems discarded and the leaves washed well
1 teaspoon fennel seeds
3 tablespoons unsalted butter
1 cup finely chopped fennel bulb plus fennel sprigs for garnish
12 oysters, shucked (procedure on page 124) and the bottom shells reserved
coarse salt for filling the pan and platter

In a small skillet heat the oil over moderately high heat until it is hot but not smoking and in it fry the shallots, stirring, until they are browned and crisp. Transfer the shallots with a slotted spoon to paper towels to drain, discarding the oil from the skillet, and sprinkle them with salt to taste. *The fried shallots may be made 2 days in advance and kept wrapped in the paper towels at room temperature.*

In a kettle cook the spinach in the water clinging to the leaves with the fennel seeds, covered, over moderate heat, stirring occasionally, for 3 minutes, or until it is wilted. In a colander drain the spinach mixture and press out the excess liquid. In a food processor purée the spinach mixture with 2 tablespoons of the butter and salt and pepper to taste and transfer the purée to a small bowl. In the small skillet cook the fennel bulb in the remaining 1 tablespoon butter over moderately low heat, stirring, until it is just tender and stir it into the spinach purée. *The spinach fennel purée may be made 1 day in advance and kept, its surface covered with plastic wrap, chilled.*

Arrange the oysters in the reserved shells in a jelly-roll pan filled with some of the rock salt (to balance the shells), divide the spinach fennel purée among them, and bake the oysters in a preheated 400° F. oven for 12 to 15 minutes, or until they are just cooked through. Top the oysters with the fried shallots, garnish them with the fennel sprigs, and arrange them on a platter filled with more of the rock salt. Makes 12 baked oysters.

PHOTO ON PAGE 81

Fried Oysters with Radicchio and Balsamic Vinegar

2 large eggs
2 tablespoons heavy cream
1½ cups cracker crumbs
24 oysters, shucked (procedure on page 124)
vegetable oil for frying
24 *radicchio* leaves
balsamic vinegar (available at specialty foods shops and many supermarkets) to taste for sprinkling the oysters

In a small bowl whisk together the eggs and the cream and have the crumbs ready in another small bowl. Working in batches, dip the oysters in the egg mixture, letting the excess drip off, dredge them in the crumbs, shaking off the excess, and put them in one layer on a platter. Chill the oysters for 30 minutes. In a skillet fry the oysters in batches in ½ inch of 375° F. oil for 30 to 45 seconds on each side, or until they are golden, transferring them as they are fried with a slotted spoon to paper towels. On the platter put a fried oyster in each *radicchio* leaf and sprinkle the oysters with the vinegar. Makes 24 hors d'oeuvres or serves 6 as a first course.

To Shuck Oysters

Scrub the oysters thoroughly with a stiff brush under running cold water. Hold each oyster flat side up on a work surface with the hinged end away from you, insert an oyster knife between the shells at the hinged end, twisting the knife to pop open the shell, and slide the blade against the flat upper shell to cut the large muscle and free the upper shell. If the shell crumbles and cannot be opened at the hinge, insert the knife between the shells at the curved end of the oyster, pry the shells open, and sever the large muscle. Break off and discard the upper shell and slide the knife under the oyster to release it from the bottom shell.

Shrimp, Chicken, and Pineapple Kebabs with Sweet Jalapeño Basting Sauce

¾ cup *jalapeño* chili jelly (available at specialty foods shops and many supermarkets)
2 tablespoons fresh lemon juice
36 jumbo shrimp, shelled, leaving the tail and the first joint of the shell intact, and deveined
1½ pounds skinless boneless chicken breasts, cut into ¾-inch pieces
1 pineapple, peeled, cored, and cut into ¾-inch pieces
vegetable oil for brushing the kebabs

In a shallow dish let twelve 12-inch wooden skewers soak in water to cover for 30 minutes. In a small saucepan combine the *jalapeño* jelly and the lemon juice and heat the mixture over moderately low heat, stirring, until the jelly is melted. Thread the shrimp, the chicken, and the pineapple, alternating them, onto the skewers, drained, and in a large deep skillet of boiling salted water cook the kebabs in batches for 6 minutes. Transfer the kebabs as they are cooked to paper towels and let them drain.

Brush the kebabs with the *jalapeño* jelly mixture, season them with salt and black pepper, and on an oiled rack set 5 to 6 inches over glowing coals grill them, turning them, for 1 to 2 minutes, or until the chicken is golden. Serves 6.

PHOTO ON PAGE 56

Shrimp with Orange Beurre Blanc

12 large shrimp, shelled, reserving the shells, and deveined
½ cup dry vermouth
¼ cup fresh orange juice
1 teaspoon freshly grated orange zest
3 tablespoons cold unsalted butter, cut into 6 pieces
1 teaspoon minced fresh chives for garnish
lemon juice to taste

In a small saucepan combine the reserved shrimp shells, the vermouth, the orange juice, and the zest and simmer the mixture, covered, for 5 minutes. Strain the mixture through a fine sieve into another small saucepan, discarding the shells. In a non-stick skillet melt 1 piece of the butter over moderately high heat, in it sauté the shrimp, stirring, for 2 minutes, or until they are cooked through, and keep them warm, covered.

Bring the orange mixture to a boil, reduce the heat to moderately low, and whisk in the remaining 5 pieces of butter, 1 piece at a time, lifting the skillet from the heat occasionally to cool the mixture and adding each new piece of butter before the previous one has melted completely. (The sauce should not get hot enough to liquefy. It should be the consistency of hollandaise.) Stir in the chives, the lemon juice, and salt and pepper to taste, divide the shrimp between 2 plates, and spoon some of the sauce over each serving. Serves 2.

Curried Chili Shrimp

2 shallots, minced
1 tablespoon minced peeled fresh gingerroot
1 garlic clove, minced
1 teaspoon minced bottled pickled *jalapeño* chili (wear rubber gloves)
1 teaspoon salt
1 tablespoon vegetable oil
⅛ teaspoon turmeric
1 teaspoon curry powder
1 small onion, sliced thin crosswise
½ cup thick coconut milk (recipe follows)
¾ pound (about 12) large shrimp, shelled, leaving the tail and the first joint of the shell intact, and deveined
scallion rice (page 179) as an accompaniment if desired

On a work surface with the flat side of a knife mash together the shallots, the gingerroot, the garlic, and the *jalapeño* chili with the salt until the mixture forms a coarse paste. In a heavy skillet heat the oil over moderate heat until it is hot but not smoking and in it cook the paste, stirring, for 1 minute. Add the turmeric, the curry powder, and the onion and cook the mixture over moderately low heat, stirring, for 2 minutes. Stir in the coconut milk and ½ cup water and simmer the mixture for 4 to 6 minutes, or until the liquid is reduced to about ½ cup. Add the shrimp in one layer and cook them, turning them once, for 3 to 4 minutes, or until they are just firm. Serve the shrimp mixture over the rice, tossing the rice with the sauce. Serves 2.

Thick Coconut Milk

1 coconut without any cracks and containing
    liquid

With an ice pick or a skewer test the 3 eyes of the coconut to find the weakest one and pierce it to make a hole. Drain the liquid and reserve it for another use. Bake the coconut in a preheated 400° F. oven for 15 minutes, break it with a hammer, and with the point of a strong knife lever the flesh carefully out of the shell.

Chop into small pieces enough of the coconut meat to measure 1 cup, reserving the remainder for another use, and in a blender or food processor blend it with ½ cup boiling water for 30 seconds. In a cheesecloth-lined sieve set over a bowl let the mixture drain for 5 minutes and squeeze it in the cheesecloth to extract more coconut milk. Makes about ½ cup.

Dill and Garlic Shrimp Skewers

18 large garlic cloves, unpeeled
1 tablespoon dill seeds
2 tablespoons minced fresh dill
2 tablespoons fresh lemon juice
½ teaspoon dried hot red pepper flakes
⅔ cup vegetable oil
eighteen 8-inch wooden skewers, soaked in
    warm water for 1 hour
18 large shrimp, shelled

In a saucepan of boiling water boil the garlic for 15 to 20 minutes, or until it is tender but not soft, drain it, and discard the peel carefully, leaving the cloves whole. In a bowl whisk together the dill seeds, the fresh dill, the lemon juice, and the red pepper flakes, add the oil in a stream, whisking, and whisk the marinade until it is emulsified. Onto the end of each skewer thread 1 shrimp and 1 garlic clove. Arrange the skewers, shrimp end down, in a bowl just large enough to hold them, pour the marinade over the shrimp, and let the shrimp marinate, covered loosely and chilled, basting them occasionally, for 3 hours. Drain the shrimp, arrange them in a shallow baking pan, and bake them in the upper third of a preheated 425° F. oven for 1 to 2 minutes, or until they are just cooked through. Serves 6.

PHOTO ON PAGE 15

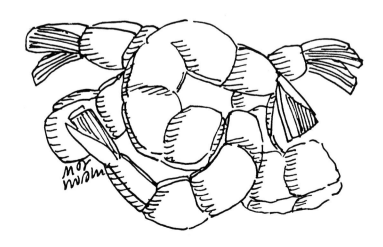

MEAT

BEEF

Carpaccio with Arugula and Artichoke Dressing

a ¾-pound trimmed piece of beef fillet
   (preferably cut from the thicker end of
   the fillet)
For the dressing
⅓ cup chopped drained marinated
   artichoke hearts
1 tablespoon Sherry vinegar or
   red-wine vinegar
2 tablespoons fresh lemon juice
¼ cup olive oil (preferably extra-virgin)

1 cup thinly sliced *arugula*, washed well
   and spun dry
20 Parmesan curls made by shaving a wedge
   of Parmesan with a vegetable peeler,
   or to taste
freshly ground black pepper to taste

Freeze the beef, wrapped in plastic wrap, for 1 hour, or until it is firm but not frozen solid, and with a very sharp knife cut it across the grain into ⅛-inch-thick slices. Arrange the slices about 3 inches apart on sheets of plastic wrap, cover them with additional sheets of plastic wrap, and with a rolling pin roll the slices thin, testing the first rolled slice to make sure it is not too thin to be lifted from the plastic without tearing. Roll up the sheets of plastic loosely and chill the beef for at least 1 hour, or up to 3 hours.

Make the dressing: In a blender purée the artichoke hearts with the vinegar, the lemon juice, and salt and pepper to taste, add the oil in a stream and 2 tablespoons warm water, and blend the mixture until it is emulsified.

Divide the beef slices among 4 chilled plates, lining the plates with a single layer of the slices, and mound the *arugula* and Parmesan curls in the center of each plate. Sprinkle each serving with the pepper to taste, drizzle some of the dressing over each serving, and serve the remaining dressing separately. Serves 4.

*Fillet of Beef on Garlic Croutons with Roasted Onion,
   Caper, and Tarragon Sauce*

2 tablespoons vegetable oil
a 3-pound fillet of beef, halved crosswise
2 loaves of Italian bread (each about 14 inches
   long), cut diagonally into ½-inch slices
about ¼ cup olive oil for brushing the bread
2 large garlic cloves
about 2 cups roasted onion, caper, and
   tarragon sauce (recipe follows)
tarragon sprigs for garnish

In a heavy flameproof roasting pan heat the vegetable oil over moderately high heat until it is hot but not smoking and in it brown the beef, patted dry and seasoned with salt and pepper, turning it every 2 minutes, for 10 minutes. Roast the beef in the middle of a preheated 475° F. oven for 12 to 15 minutes, or until a meat thermometer registers 130° F. for medium-rare meat, and let it cool to room temperature. *The beef may be roasted 2 days in advance and kept wrapped and chilled.* Slice the beef thin.

Brush both sides of each bread slice lightly with some of the olive oil and on baking sheets toast the slices on both sides under a preheated broiler about 3 inches from the heat until they are golden. Rub one side of each crouton with the garlic, spread it with about 1 teaspoon of the sauce, and top the croutons with the beef. Season the beef with salt and pepper, drizzle it with the remaining sauce, and arrange the croutons on a platter garnished with the tarragon sprigs. Serves 12.

PHOTO ON PAGE 81

Roasted Onion, Caper, and Tarragon Sauce

2 large onions (about ¾ pound each),
    unpeeled and untrimmed
2 tablespoons unsalted butter
2 tablespoons all-purpose flour
¾ cup heavy cream
¼ cup dry white wine
3 tablespoons drained bottled capers
1 teaspoon white-wine vinegar
1 tablespoon minced fresh tarragon leaves or
    ¾ teaspoon dried, crumbled
2 tablespoons minced fresh parsley leaves
1 tablespoon thinly sliced fresh chives or
    scallion greens

In a baking pan roast the onions in the middle of a pre-heated 475° F. oven for 2 hours. While the onions are roasting, in a small saucepan melt the butter over low heat, whisk in the flour, and cook the *roux*, whisking, for 3 minutes. Add the cream and the wine in a stream, whisking, bring the mixture to a boil, whisking, and simmer it, whisking, for 5 minutes. Remove the saucepan from the heat and stir in the capers, the vinegar, the tarragon, the parsley, and the chives.

Let the onions cool until they can be handled, discard the tough outer layers, the stems, the root ends, and the juices in the baking pan, and in a food processor purée the onions until they are smooth. Transfer the purée to a small saucepan, bring it to a boil, and boil it, stirring, until it is thickened and the excess liquid is evaporated. Stir the purée into the cream sauce and stir in salt and pepper to taste. *The sauce may be made 1 day in advance and kept covered and chilled.* Serve the sauce warm or at room temperature. Makes about 2 cups.

Roast Fillet of Beef with Chipotle Red Pepper Sauce and Mustard Chive Sauce

2 tablespoons vegetable oil
a 3½-pound fillet of beef at room temperature
chipotle red pepper sauce and mustard chive
    sauce (recipes follow) as accompaniments

In a heavy flameproof roasting pan heat the oil over moderately high heat until it is hot but not smoking, add the beef, patted dry and seasoned with salt and pepper, and brown it, turning it every 2 minutes, for 10 minutes. Roast the beef in a preheated 500° F. oven for 12 to 15 minutes, or until a meat thermometer registers 130° F.

The narrow end of the beef will be medium-rare; the wide end will be rare. Serve the beef with the sauces. Serves 8.

PHOTO ON PAGE 36

Chipotle Red Pepper Sauce

3 cups thinly sliced red bell pepper
    (about 3 large peppers)
2 tablespoons olive oil
1 canned *chipotle* chili in *adobo*
    (available at Mexican markets and some
    supermarkets), unseeded
2 teaspoons Worcestershire sauce

In a heavy skillet cook the bell peppers in the oil, covered, over moderately low heat, stirring occasionally, for 25 to 30 minutes, or until they are soft. In a blender purée the mixture with the *chipotle*, the Worcestershire sauce, and salt to taste. *The sauce may be made 2 days in advance and kept covered and chilled.* Transfer the sauce to a sauceboat and serve it warm or at room temperature. Makes about 1 cup.

PHOTO ON PAGE 36

Mustard Chive Sauce

½ cup dry mustard
3 tablespoons distilled white vinegar
1½ teaspoons sugar
1½ teaspoons salt
¾ stick (6 tablespoons) unsalted butter, cut
    into bits and softened
3 tablespoons minced fresh chives

In a small bowl stir together the mustard, the vinegar, the sugar, the salt, and 3 tablespoons water, making a smooth paste, and let the mixture stand, covered, for 10 minutes. Transfer the mixture to the top of a double boiler set over barely simmering water and whisk in the butter until it is just melted and thoroughly combined. Remove the pan from the heat and stir in the chives. Transfer the sauce to a sauceboat and serve it warm or at room temperature. Makes about 1 cup.

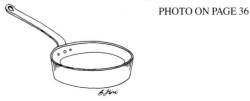

PHOTO ON PAGE 36

Roast Beef and Couscous Rolls

3 tablespoons olive oil
½ teaspoon salt
¾ cup couscous
2 tablespoons red-wine vinegar
½ cup finely chopped celery
⅓ cup freshly grated Parmesan
¼ cup thinly sliced scallion
3 tablespoons fresh orange juice
3 tablespoons minced fresh parsley leaves
1 pound thinly sliced rare roast beef
1 red bell pepper, cut lengthwise into
  ¼-inch-thick strips
Bibb lettuce leaves, rinsed and spun dry,
  for garnish

In a small saucepan bring 1 cup water to a boil with 1 tablespoon of the oil and the salt, stir in the couscous, and let the mixture stand off the heat, covered, for 5 minutes. Stir in the remaining 2 tablespoons oil, the vinegar, the celery, the Parmesan, the scallion, the orange juice, the parsley, and salt and black pepper to taste and let the mixture cool to room temperature. Press about 2 tablespoons of the couscous mixture in the palm of one hand, forming a log, and arrange it across a short end of 1 roast beef slice. Arrange 1 pepper strip along each side of the log and roll up the couscous and the bell pepper tightly in the roast beef. With a sharp knife cut the roll into 1-inch lengths, trimming the ends. Make rolls with the remaining roast beef, couscous mixture, and bell pepper in the same manner. *The rolls may be prepared 8 hours in advance and kept wrapped in plastic wrap and chilled.* Line a platter with the lettuce and arrange the rolls on top. Makes about 52 rolls.

PHOTO ON PAGE 49

Roast Beef, Saga Blue, and Watercress with Horseradish Mayonnaise on French Bread

four 5-inch lengths of French bread, split
  horizontally leaving the halves attached
⅓ pound Saga blue cheese, softened and the
  rind discarded
2 cups watercress sprigs
1 pound thinly sliced rare roast beef
¼ cup mayonnaise
1 tablespoon drained bottled horseradish,
  or to taste

Open the bread lengths, spread the cut sides with the blue cheese, and top the cheese with the watercress and the roast beef. In a small bowl combine well the mayonnaise and the horseradish and drizzle the horseradish mayonnaise over the roast beef. Season the sandwiches with salt and pepper and close them, pressing them firmly. Makes 4 sandwiches.

Beef Potpies with Yorkshire Pudding Crusts

5 cups ½-inch pieces cooked rare roast beef
  (about 2 pounds)
a 10-ounce package frozen peas, thawed
1 pound boiling potatoes (about 4), cooked
  and cut into ½-inch pieces
1 onion, sliced thin
1 tablespoon unsalted butter plus
  2 tablespoons unsalted butter, melted
  (or 2 tablespoons roast beef drippings, heated)
1 garlic clove, minced
1 tablespoon Worcestershire sauce
1½ teaspoons bottled horseradish
¼ cup heavy cream
For the Yorkshire pudding batter
2 large eggs
½ teaspoon salt
1 cup all-purpose flour
1 cup milk
1 large egg white at room temperature

In a large bowl combine the roast beef, the peas, and the potatoes. In a skillet cook the onion in the 1 tablespoon unmelted butter over moderately low heat, stirring occasionally, until it is softened, add the garlic, and cook the mixture for 3 minutes. Stir in the Worcestershire sauce, the horseradish, and the cream and cook the mixture, stirring, until it is thickened. Add the sauce to the roast beef mixture, season the mixture with salt and pepper, and combine it well. Divide the mixture among six 1½-cup gratin dishes.

Make the Yorkshire pudding batter: In a blender blend the eggs, the salt, the flour, and the milk for 30 seconds and chill the mixture, covered, for 30 minutes. In a small bowl beat the egg white until it forms soft peaks and fold it into the mixture.

Pour the melted butter around the edges of the gratin dishes and heat the potpies in the middle of a preheated 450° F. oven for 2 minutes. Pour ⅓ cup of the Yorkshire pudding batter around the edge of each gratin dish and bake the potpies for 15 minutes (do not open the oven door). Reduce the heat to 400° F. and bake the potpies for 10 to 15 minutes more, or until the pudding is puffed and browned. Serves 6.

Herbed Shell Steaks with Sautéed Onions

1 garlic clove, minced and mashed to a paste
   with 1 teaspoon salt
½ teaspoon pepper
½ teaspoon dried orégano
two 1-inch-thick boneless shell steaks
   (each about ½ pound)
¼ cup vegetable oil
2 onions, halved lengthwise and sliced
   thin crosswise

On a work surface mash together the garlic paste, the pepper, and the orégano. Rub the mixture onto the steaks. In a heavy skillet, preferably cast-iron, heat the oil over moderately high heat until it is hot but not smoking, in it sauté the onions, stirring occasionally, for 6 minutes, or until they are golden, and transfer them with a slotted spoon to paper towels to drain. Heat the oil remaining in the skillet over moderately high heat until it is hot but not smoking, in it sauté the steaks for 3½ minutes on each side for medium-rare meat, and transfer the steaks with tongs to plates. Pour off the fat from the skillet, add ¼ cup water, and boil it, scraping up the brown bits, for 15 seconds. Stir in the onions and spoon the onion mixture over the steaks. Serves 2.

Stir-Fried Beef and Broccoli

For the beef
2 teaspoons soy sauce
¼ teaspoon sugar
¼ teaspoon salt
¾ pound boneless sirloin, cut across
   the grain into ¼-inch-thick slices
For the sauce
1 tablespoon cornstarch
1 tablespoon soy sauce
1 tablespoon medium-dry Sherry or Scotch
¼ cup chicken or beef broth or water
1 teaspoon sugar
2 teaspoons Oriental sesame oil

3 tablespoons vegetable oil
1 tablespoon minced peeled fresh gingerroot
1 tablespoon minced garlic
a 4-inch fresh red chili, seeded and minced
   (wear rubber gloves) or ½ teaspoon dried hot
   red pepper flakes
1 pound broccoli, cut into flowerets
   and the stems peeled and cut into
   ½-inch-thick sticks
cooked rice as an accompaniment

Prepare the beef: In a small bowl stir together the soy sauce, the sugar, and the salt, add the beef, and let it marinate for 20 minutes.

Make the sauce while the beef is marinating: In a bowl dissolve the cornstarch in the soy sauce and stir in the Sherry, the broth, the sugar, and the sesame oil.

Heat a wok or large heavy skillet over high heat until it is hot, add 2 tablespoons of the vegetable oil, and heat it until it just begins to smoke. Stir-fry the beef in the oil in batches for 1 minute, or until it is no longer pink, and transfer it as it is cooked with a slotted spoon to a plate. Add the remaining 1 tablespoon vegetable oil to the wok, heat it until it is hot but not smoking, and in the oil stir-fry the gingerroot, the garlic, and the chili for 30 seconds, or until the mixture is fragrant. Add the broccoli and stir-fry the mixture for 1 minute. Add ⅓ cup water and steam the broccoli, covered, for 1½ to 2 minutes, or until it is crisp-tender. Stir the sauce, add it to the wok with the beef and any juices that have accumulated on the plate, and cook the mixture, stirring, for 2 minutes, or until the sauce is thickened and the beef is heated through. Transfer the mixture to a heated platter and serve it with the rice. Serves 2.

Beef Fajitas
(*Grilled Marinated Skirt Steak with Bell Peppers,
Onions, and Flour Tortillas*)
For the marinade
4 garlic cloves, minced and mashed to
 a paste with 1 teaspoon salt
¼ cup fresh lime juice
1½ teaspoons ground cumin
2 tablespoons olive oil

2 pounds skirt steak, trimmed and cut into
 large pieces to fit on a grill or broiler pan
 or in a ridged grill pan
2 tablespoons vegetable oil
3 assorted colored bell peppers, sliced thin
1 large red onion, sliced thin
2 garlic cloves, minced
twelve 7- to 8-inch flour tortillas (page 103),
 warmed (procedure on page 103)
guacamole and tomato *salsa* (recipes follow)
 as accompaniments

Make the marinade: In a large bowl whisk together
the garlic paste, the lime juice, the cumin, and the oil.
 Add the steak to the marinade, turning it to coat it
well, and let it marinate, covered and chilled, for at least
1 hour or overnight. Grill the steak, drained, on a well-
oiled rack set about 5 inches over glowing coals or in a
hot well-seasoned ridged grill pan over moderately high
heat for 3 to 4 minutes on each side, or until it is just
springy to the touch, for medium-rare meat. (Alternatively, the steak may be broiled on the rack of a broiler
pan under a preheated broiler about 4 inches from the
heat for 3 to 4 minutes on each side for medium-rare
meat.) Transfer the steak to a cutting board and let it
stand for 10 minutes. While the steak is standing, in a
large skillet heat the oil over moderately high heat until
it is hot but not smoking, add the bell peppers, the onion, and the garlic, and sauté the mixture, stirring, for
5 minutes, or until the bell peppers are softened. Slice
the steak thin across the grain on the diagonal and arrange the slices on a platter with the bell pepper mixture.
Drizzle any steak juices over the steak and the pepper
mixture and serve the steak and the pepper mixture with
the tortillas, the *guacamole*, and the *salsa*.
 Assemble a *fajita*: Spread some of the *guacamole* on
a tortilla, top it with a few slices of the steak, some of the
pepper mixture, and some of the *salsa*. Roll up the tortilla to enclose the filling. Makes 12 *fajitas*, serving 6.

Guacamole
2 ripe avocados (preferably California)
1 small onion, minced
1 garlic clove, minced and mashed to a paste
 with ½ teaspoon salt
4 teaspoons fresh lime juice, or to taste
½ teaspoon ground cumin
1 fresh or pickled *jalapeño* chili if desired,
 seeded and minced (wear rubber gloves)
3 tablespoons chopped fresh coriander
 if desired

Halve and pit the avocados and scoop the flesh into a
bowl. Mash the avocados coarse with a fork and stir in
the onion, the garlic, the lime juice, the cumin, the chili,
and the coriander. *The guacamole may be made 2 hours
in advance, its surface covered with plastic wrap, and
chilled.* Makes about 2 cups.

Tomato Salsa
1 pound tomatoes, peeled if desired, seeded,
 and chopped
1 small onion, minced
1 fresh or pickled *jalapeño* chili, or to taste,
 seeded and minced (wear rubber gloves)
1 tablespoon fresh lime juice
2 tablespoons chopped fresh coriander
 if desired

In bowl toss together the tomatoes, the onion, the
chili, the lime juice, the coriander, and salt to taste and
let the *salsa* stand for 30 minutes. *The salsa may be
made 4 hours in advance and kept covered and chilled.
Let the salsa come to room temperature before serving.*
Makes about 2 cups.

Shredded Beef Flautas
(*Crisp-Fried Beef-Stuffed Corn Tortillas*)
For the filling
2 pounds boneless beef chuck, cut into
 2-inch pieces
2 onions
3 garlic cloves
1 teaspoon salt
2 tablespoons olive oil
½ cup tomato sauce

1 fresh or pickled *jalapeño* chili, or to taste,
   seeded and chopped (wear rubber gloves)
¾ teaspoon ground cumin

twelve 7-inch corn tortillas, warmed
   (procedure on page 103)
vegetable oil for frying the *flautas*
3 cups shredded romaine or
   iceberg lettuce
guacamole (page 130) and sour cream as
   accompaniments

Make the filling: In a large saucepan combine the beef, 1 of the onions, sliced, 1 of the garlic cloves, the salt, and water to cover, bring the water to a boil, and simmer the mixture, covered partially, for 1½ to 2 hours, or until the beef is tender. Let the beef cool in the broth, drain it, reserving ⅓ cup of the broth, and with a fork shred it. In a large skillet cook the remaining onion, minced, and the remaining 2 garlic cloves, minced, in the oil over moderately low heat, stirring,

until the onion is softened, add the shredded beef, the tomato sauce, the chili, the cumin, the reserved broth, and salt and black pepper to taste, and simmer the mixture, stirring, for 3 to 5 minutes, or until it is thickened. Let the filling cool.

Working with 1 warmed tortilla at a time and keeping the others covered, spread about 2 rounded tablespoons of the filling down the center of each tortilla, roll up the tortillas, enclosing the filling, and secure the ends closed with wooden picks. Keep the rolled tortillas covered with plastic wrap. *The flautas may be prepared up to this point 2 hours in advance and kept covered tightly with plastic wrap and chilled.*

In a large skillet heat ½ inch of the oil over moderately high heat until it is hot but not smoking, in it fry the *flautas* in batches, turning them, for 1 to 2 minutes, or until they are crisp, and transfer them with tongs as they are fried to paper towels to drain. Spread the lettuce on a platter or divide it among 6 plates, arrange the *flautas* on it, and top them with the *guacamole* and the sour cream. Serves 6.

Lauren Jarrett

Chili con Carne with Chili Cheddar Shortcakes

For the shortcake biscuits

1½ cups all-purpose flour

2 teaspoons double-acting baking powder

½ teaspoon baking soda

½ teaspoon salt

2 tablespoons cold unsalted butter,
   cut into bits

¼ pound sharp Cheddar, grated coarse
   (about 1½ cups)

four 2-inch pickled *jalapeño* chilies, seeded
   and minced (wear rubber gloves)

1 cup sour cream

For the chili con carne

2 large onions, chopped (about 3 cups)

¼ cup vegetable oil

1 tablespoon minced garlic

2 carrots, sliced thin

3 pounds boneless beef chuck, ground coarse
   in batches in a food processor or
   by the butcher

¼ cup chili powder

1 tablespoon ground cumin

2 tablespoons paprika

1 tablespoon dried orégano, crumbled

1 tablespoon dried hot red pepper flakes,
   or to taste

two 8-ounce cans tomato sauce

1¼ cups beef broth

3 tablespoons cider vinegar

a 19-ounce can kidney beans, rinsed
   and drained

2 green bell peppers, chopped

Make the shortcake biscuits: Into a bowl sift together the flour, the baking powder, the baking soda, and the salt, add the butter, and blend the mixture until it resembles coarse meal. Stir in the Cheddar and the chilies, add the sour cream, and stir the mixture until it just forms a soft but not sticky dough. Knead the dough gently 6 times on a lightly floured surface, roll or pat it out ½ inch thick, and with a 3½-inch cookie cutter cut out 6 rounds. Bake the rounds on an ungreased baking sheet in the middle of a preheated 425° F. oven for 15 to 17 minutes, or until they are golden.

Make the chili con carne: In a kettle cook the onions in the oil over moderately low heat, stirring often, until they are softened, add the garlic and the carrots, and cook the mixture, stirring, for 1 minute. Add the chuck and cook it over moderate heat, stirring and breaking up any lumps, for 10 minutes, or until it is no longer pink. Add the chili powder, the cumin, the paprika, the orégano, and the red pepper flakes and cook the mixture, stirring, for 1 minute. Add the tomato sauce, the broth, and the vinegar, bring the mixture to a boil, and simmer it, covered, stirring occasionally, for 50 minutes to 1 hour, or until the meat is tender. Add the kidney beans, the bell peppers, and salt and black pepper to taste and simmer the mixture, uncovered, for 15 minutes, or until the bell peppers are tender.

Arrange a biscuit, heated and split, on each of 6 dinner plates, spoon the chili con carne over the bottom half, and cover it with the top half of the biscuit. Serves 6.

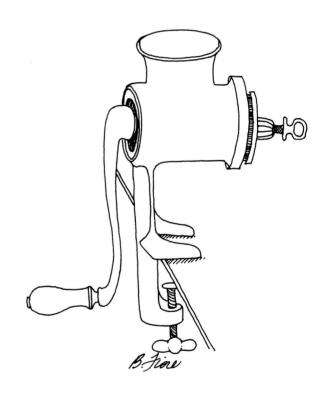

B. Fiore

Open-Faced Burgers with Horseradish-Cheese Sauce

1 garlic clove, minced and mashed to a paste
   with ½ teaspoon salt

1 tablespoon unsalted butter

1 kaiser roll, halved

⅓ cup sour cream
½ cup grated extra-sharp Cheddar
1 tablespoon drained bottled horseradish
1 tablespoon minced bottled sweet pickle
1 teaspoon minced bottled pickled *jalapeño*
   chili (wear rubber gloves)
1 tablespoon vegetable oil
¾ pound ground chuck, formed into two
   ½-inch-thick patties

In a small saucepan combine the garlic paste and the butter and heat the mixture over moderately low heat, stirring, until the butter is melted. Brush the cut sides of the roll with the butter mixture and toast the roll halves lightly. In a saucepan combine the sour cream and the Cheddar, heat the mixture over moderately low heat, stirring occasionally, until the cheese is melted, but do not let it boil, and stir in the horseradish, the pickle, and the *jalapeño* chili. In a heavy skillet (preferably cast-iron) heat the oil over moderately high heat until it is hot but not smoking and in it cook the patties, seasoned with salt and black pepper, turning them once, for 8 minutes for medium-rare meat. Transfer the burgers to the roll halves and spoon the horseradish-cheese sauce over them. Serves 2.

Guacamole Hamburgers with Monterey Jack and Chilies

1½ pounds ground chuck
a 2-ounce piece of Monterey Jack, cut into
   4 pieces
4 teaspoons finely chopped seeded pickled
   jalapeño chilies (wear rubber gloves)
For the guacamole
1 avocado (preferably California)
2½ teaspoons fresh lemon juice
⅓ cup finely diced seeded tomato
3 tablespoons minced scallion
¼ teaspoon ground cumin
2 tablespoons chopped fresh coriander,
   or to taste

4 sesame hamburger buns or English muffins,
   split and toasted

Handling the chuck as little as possible, divide it into fourths, shape each fourth into a ball, and with your thumb make a depression in the center of each ball. Fill each depression with a piece of the Monterey Jack and 1 teaspoon of the *jalapeño* chilies and form the meat around the cheese mixture into a 1-inch-thick patty. Season the hamburgers with salt and black pepper and grill them on an oiled rack set 5 to 6 inches over glowing coals for 5 minutes on each side for medium-rare meat.

Make the *guacamole* while the hamburgers are grilling: Halve, pit, and peel the avocado, in a bowl mash the flesh coarse with a fork, and stir in the lemon juice, the tomato, the scallion, the cumin, the coriander, and salt and pepper to taste.

Transfer the hamburgers to the buns and top them with the *guacamole*. Serves 4.

Roquefort Hamburgers on Grilled Garlic Toasts

¼ cup crumbled Roquefort or other
   blue cheese
2 tablespoons unsalted butter, softened
1½ pounds ground chuck
For the toasts
eight ⅓-inch-thick diagonal slices of French
   or Italian bread
olive oil for brushing the toasts
1 garlic clove, halved crosswise

In a food processor purée the Roquefort with the butter, transfer the Roquefort mixture to a sheet of wax paper, and using the wax paper shape it into a log. Freeze the log, wrapped in the wax paper, for 20 minutes, or until it is firm. *The Roquefort butter may be made 4 days in advance and kept wrapped in foil and frozen.*

Handling the chuck as little as possible, divide it into fourths, shape each fourth into a ball, and with your thumb make a depression in the center of each ball. Cut the Roquefort butter into 4 pieces, insert a piece of butter in each depression, and form the meat around each piece of butter into a 1-inch-thick patty. Season the hamburgers with salt and pepper and grill them on an oiled rack set 5 to 6 inches over glowing coals for 5 minutes on each side for medium-rare meat.

Make the toasts while the hamburgers are grilling: Arrange the bread slices on the rack around the hamburgers and grill them for 1 to 2 minutes on each side, or until they are golden. Transfer the toasts to a platter, brush one side of each toast with the oil, and rub it with the garlic, cut side down.

Transfer the hamburgers to 4 of the garlic toasts and top them with the remaining garlic toasts. Serves 4.

Tarragon Hamburgers with Pickled Red Onions
For the pickled onions
1 small red onion, cut into very thin rings
¼ cup tarragon vinegar
½ teaspoon salt

½ stick (¼ cup) unsalted butter, softened
3 tablespoons minced fresh tarragon leaves
1½ teaspoons tarragon vinegar
1½ pounds ground chuck
4 English muffins, split, toasted, and buttered

Make the pickled onions: In a small saucepan combine the onion rings, the vinegar, the salt, and ¾ cup water, bring the liquid to a boil, and simmer the mixture for 4 minutes. Transfer the mixture to a bowl and let it cool. *The onions may be made 4 days in advance and kept covered and chilled.*

In a food processor or in a bowl with an electric mixer cream the butter with the tarragon and blend in the vinegar and salt and pepper to taste. Transfer the butter mixture to a sheet of wax paper, using the wax paper shape it into a log, and freeze it, wrapped in the wax paper, for 20 minutes, or until it is firm. *The tarragon butter may be made 4 days in advance and kept wrapped in foil and frozen.*

Handling the chuck as little as possible, divide it into fourths, shape each fourth into a ball, and with your thumb make a depression in the center of each ball. Cut the tarragon butter into 4 pieces, insert a piece of butter in each depression, and form the meat around each piece of butter into a 1-inch-thick patty. Season the hamburgers with salt and pepper and grill them on an oiled rack set 5 to 6 inches over glowing coals for 5 minutes on each side for medium-rare meat. Transfer the hamburgers to the English muffins and top them with the pickled onions, drained. Serves 4.

Steak Sandwiches with Crispy Onions
1 cup thinly sliced onions
2 tablespoons unsalted butter
1 tablespoon olive oil
¾ cup thinly sliced mushrooms
1 garlic clove, minced
¾ cup beef broth
1½ tablespoons heavy cream
3 tablespoons ketchup

1½ tablespoons Worcestershire sauce, or to taste
1 teaspoon Dijon-style mustard
1 pound grilled steak, cut into ⅛-inch-thick slices
1 long loaf of Italian-style bread, halved horizontally and each half buttered lightly, cut into 4 pieces, and toasted

In a skillet cook the onions in the butter and the oil over moderate heat, stirring occasionally, until they are crisp and golden and transfer them with a slotted spoon to paper towels to drain. In the fat remaining in the skillet cook the mushrooms and the garlic over moderately low heat, stirring occasionally, until the mushrooms begin to turn brown and transfer the mixture to a plate. Add the broth to the skillet and deglaze the skillet, scraping up the brown bits. Add the cream, the ketchup, the Worcestershire sauce, and the mustard and stir in the mushroom mixture and the steak slices. Divide the steak mixture among the bottom bread pieces, sprinkle it with some of the onions, and top the onions with the remaining bread pieces. Serves 4.

Sliced Shell Steak on Parmesan Toasts with Shallot and Sour Cream Sauce
2 slices of thin homemade-type white bread, crusts discarded
2 tablespoons freshly grated Parmesan
2 tablespoons unsalted butter
2 shallots, minced
3 tablespoons sour cream
½ teaspoon Worcestershire sauce
5 drops of Tabasco
¾ pound shell (New York strip) steak (about 1½ inches thick)
vegetable oil for brushing the rack

Toast the bread slices on a rack in a preheated 350° F. oven until they are golden, sprinkle one side of each toast with the Parmesan, and broil the toasts under a preheated broiler about 4 inches from the heat for 1 minute, or until the cheese is bubbly.

In a skillet heat the butter over moderately low heat until the foam subsides and in it cook the shallots, stirring, until they are softened. Remove the skillet from the heat, whisk in the sour cream, the Worcestershire sauce, the Tabasco, and salt and pepper to taste, and keep the sauce warm, covered.

Broil the steak on the rack of a broiler pan, brushed with the oil, under the preheated broiler about 8 inches from the heat, turning it once, for 7 minutes on each side, or until it is medium-rare, transfer it to a carving board, and let it stand for 1 minute. Slice the steak, reserving any juices, and divide it between the toasts, arranging it in overlapping slices. Nap the steak with the reserved juices and serve it with the sauce. Serves 2.

VEAL

Veal Chops with Eggplant and Pepper Stuffing and Roasted Red Pepper Sauce

For the stuffing
1 small onion, minced
2 tablespoons olive oil
1½ tablespoons minced shallot
2 garlic cloves, minced
1 yellow bell pepper, cut into ¼-inch pieces (about ½ cup)
¼ pound eggplant, peeled and cut into ¼-inch pieces (about 1 cup)
1 plum tomato, seeded and chopped fine
1 teaspoon *herbes de Provence* (available at specialty foods shops) or equal parts crumbled dried thyme, rosemary, and savory
¼ teaspoon dried sage, crumbled
¼ teaspoon dried basil, crumbled
1 teaspoon finely chopped fresh parsley leaves
½ teaspoon salt

two 1-inch-thick rib veal chops, trimmed and the bones frenched (about ¾ pound)
1 tablespoon vegetable oil
For the sauce
1 large red bell pepper, roasted (procedure follows) and chopped
2 tablespoons extra-virgin olive oil
¾ teaspoon fresh lemon juice, or to taste
¾ teaspoon balsamic vinegar, or to taste
cayenne to taste

finely chopped fresh parsley leaves for garnish

Make the stuffing: In a large skillet cook the onion in the oil over moderately low heat until it is softened. Add the shallot, the garlic, the bell pepper, and the eggplant and cook the mixture, stirring, for 6 to 8 minutes, or until the eggplant is softened. Stir in the tomato, the *herbes de Provence*, the sage, the basil, the parsley, the salt, and black pepper to taste, cook the stuffing, stirring, for 1 minute, and let it cool.

With a sharp paring knife make a 1-inch-long incision along the fat side of each chop and cut a pocket in each chop by moving the knife back and forth carefully through the incision. Stuff each chop with half of the stuffing and secure the pockets with wooden picks. Brush the chops with some of the oil and in a roasting pan brushed with the remaining oil roast them in a preheated 475° F. oven, basting them with any pan juices, for 7 minutes on each side, or until they are cooked through but the flesh is still slightly pink near the bone.

Make the sauce while the chops are roasting: In a blender blend together the bell pepper, the oil, the lemon juice, the vinegar, the cayenne, 1 tablespoon water, and salt and black pepper to taste.

Transfer the chops to a cutting board, let them stand for 3 minutes, and discard the wooden picks. Arrange the chops on heated plates, pour the sauce, heated, on the plates, and sprinkle each serving with some of the parsley. Serves 2.

PHOTO ON PAGE 12

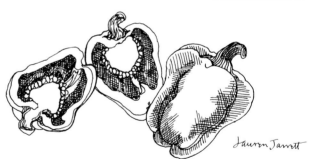

To Roast Peppers

Using a long-handled fork char the peppers over an open flame, turning them, for 2 to 3 minutes, or until the skins are blackened. (Or broil the peppers on the rack of a broiler pan under a preheated broiler about 2 inches from the heat, turning them every 5 minutes, for 15 to 25 minutes, or until the skins are blistered and charred.) Transfer the peppers to a bowl and let them steam, covered, until they are cool enough to handle. Keeping the peppers whole, peel them starting at the blossom end, cut off the tops, and discard the seeds and ribs. (Wear rubber gloves when handling hot peppers.)

Loin of Veal with Shiitake Stuffing

For the stuffing

1½ ounces dried *shiitake* mushrooms, soaked
    in 1½ cups hot water for 20 minutes and
    drained, reserving the liquid
½ cup minced shallots
2 tablespoons olive oil
¼ cup minced celery
¾ cup minced carrot
2 garlic cloves, minced
½ teaspoon finely chopped fresh rosemary or
    ⅛ teaspoon dried, crumbled
½ teaspoon finely chopped fresh sage or
    ⅛ teaspoon dried, crumbled
½ teaspoon finely chopped fresh marjoram or
    ⅛ teaspoon dried, crumbled
½ teaspoon finely chopped fresh thyme or
    ⅛ teaspoon dried, crumbled
1½ tablespoons finely chopped fresh
    parsley leaves
1 tablespoon Cognac
2 teaspoons fresh lemon juice
¼ cup chicken broth
¼ pound small white mushrooms, chopped
    fine (about 1¼ cups)
⅓ cup heavy cream
½ cup fresh bread crumbs

a 2½- to 3-pound boned veal loin (preferably
    naturally raised*) trimmed, a 1½-inch-wide
    slit cut lengthwise through the center of the
    loin, and the loin tied at 1-inch intervals
    with kitchen string
1½ cups white veal stock (page 111) or
    chicken broth
thin slices of fatback for covering the veal
white pepper to taste
16 dried *shiitake* mushrooms (about 1 ounce),
    soaked in 1 cup hot water for 20 minutes,
    drained, and patted dry, for garnish
    if desired
1 tablespoon olive oil if desired
thyme sprigs for garnish

Make the stuffing: Cut the stems from the *shiitake*, discarding them, and chop the *shiitake* fine. (There should be about 1 cup packed finely chopped *shiitake*.) Strain the reserved liquid through a fine sieve to remove any grit and reserve it for the sauce. In a large skillet cook the shallots in the oil over moderately low heat, stirring, until they are softened, stir in the celery, the carrot, and the garlic, and cook the mixture, stirring, until the vegetables are softened. Stir in the rosemary, the sage, the marjoram, the thyme, the parsley, and the Cognac and cook the mixture, stirring, for 1 minute. Add the lemon juice, the broth, the white mushrooms, and the chopped *shiitake* and cook the mixture, its surface covered with a round of buttered wax paper, stirring occasionally, until the mushrooms are tender. Boil the mixture, uncovered, stirring occasionally, until the liquid is evaporated. Stir in the cream and the bread crumbs, season the mixture with salt and pepper, and cook it over moderate heat, stirring, until it is thickened. Let the stuffing cool. *The stuffing may be made 1 day in advance, kept covered and chilled, and brought to room temperature before the veal is stuffed.*

Using the handle of a wooden spoon, pack the stuffing into the veal a little at a time. Transfer the veal to a roasting pan just large enough to hold it and add 1 cup of the stock. Cover the veal with the fatback and roast it in the middle of a preheated 325° F. oven, basting it every 20 minutes with the pan juices, for 1 hour. Remove the fatback and roast the veal for 45 minutes to 1 hour more, or until it registers 150° F. on a meat thermometer. Transfer the veal to a cutting board and let it stand for 15 minutes.

While the veal is standing, skim the fat from the pan juices, add the remaining ½ cup stock, and deglaze the pan over high heat, scraping up the brown bits, until the mixture is reduced by half. Strain the mixture through a fine sieve set over a saucepan, bring it to a boil, whisking, with the reserved *shiitake* liquid, and simmer the mixture for 5 minutes, or until it is thickened slightly. Season the sauce with salt and the white pepper. In a skillet sauté the *shiitake* in the oil over moderately high heat, stirring occasionally, until they are heated through. Cut the veal into 16 slices, arrange 2 slices on each plate, and garnish each serving with 2 of the sautéed *shiitake* and some of the thyme sprigs. Serve the sauce separately. Serves 8.

PHOTO ON PAGE 78

*naturally raised prepared veal loin is
    available by mail order from Summerfield
    Farm, HCR 4, Box 195A, Brightwood, VA
    22715. Tel. (703)948-3100

Braised Veal Shanks with White Bean Tomato Sauce

    5 tablespoons olive oil
    2 tablespoons unsalted butter
    6 large 2-inch-thick veal shanks (about
        4½ pounds), each patted dry and tied
        securely with kitchen string to keep the
        meat and bone attached
    1½ cups chopped onion
    1 cup chopped carrot
    1 cup chopped celery
    2 garlic cloves
    2 bay leaves
    2 fresh thyme sprigs or 1 teaspoon
        dried thyme, crumbled
    5 large parsley sprigs plus additional parsley
        sprigs for garnish
    two 2-inch strips of lemon zest removed with
        a vegetable peeler
    a 15- to 19-ounce can white beans, rinsed
        and drained
    a 28-ounce can plum tomatoes, drained
        and chopped
    1 cup dry white wine
    2 cups chicken broth
For the gremolata
    ¼ cup finely chopped parsley leaves
    1 tablespoon freshly grated lemon zest
    1½ teaspoons minced garlic,
        or to taste

In a kettle heat 2 tablespoons of the oil and the butter over moderately high heat until the foam subsides, in the fat brown the veal shanks, and transfer them to a plate. Pour off the fat from the kettle, add the remaining 3 tablespoons oil, and in it cook the onion, the carrot, the celery, the garlic, the bay leaves, and salt and pepper to taste over moderate heat, stirring, until the vegetables are softened. Return the shanks to the kettle, add the thyme, 5 of the parsley sprigs, the zest, the beans, the tomatoes, the wine, and the broth, and bring the liquid to a boil. Braise the mixture, covered, in the middle of a preheated 350° F. oven, basting the shanks every 30 minutes, for 2 hours, transfer the shanks with a slotted spoon to a plate, and keep them warm, covered. Discard the thyme sprigs and the bay leaves and in a blender or food processor purée the vegetable mixture in batches. (For a chunky sauce, purée half the vegetable mixture and stir the purée into the remaining vegetable mixture.)

Make the *gremolata*: In a small bowl stir together the parsley, the zest, and the garlic.

Serve the veal shanks topped with the sauce and sprinkled with the *gremolata*. Garnish each serving with a parsley sprig. Serves 6.

PHOTO ON PAGE 27

*Wild Mushroom and Veal Terrine with Roasted
Yellow Pepper Coulis*

For the terrine

3 slices of white bread, crusts discarded and
   the bread torn into pieces
½ cup heavy cream
1 large egg white
2 garlic cloves, minced
½ cup finely chopped onion
½ stick (¼ cup) unsalted butter
1¼ pounds white mushrooms, chopped fine
   (preferably in a food processor)
4 tablespoons Cognac or other brandy
¾ pound ground lean veal
½ cup minced shallots
¾ pound wild mushrooms such as
   chanterelles, *shiitake*, or *porcini*, or an
   assortment (available at specialty produce
   markets and some supermarkets), chopped
⅓ cup chicken broth
⅓ cup dry white wine

For the coulis

4 large yellow bell peppers, roasted
   (procedure on page 135)
4 tablespoons olive oil
2 tablespoons red-wine vinegar
1 tablespoon balsamic vinegar

diced orange bell peppers for garnish
minced fresh chives for garnish

Make the terrine: In a small bowl combine the bread, ¼ cup of the cream, and the egg white. In a large skillet cook the garlic and the onion in 2 tablespoons of the butter over moderately low heat, stirring, until the onion is softened, add the white mushrooms, and cook the mixture over moderate heat, stirring, for 5 minutes, or until the mushrooms are softened and begin to give off their liquid. Add 2 tablespoons of the Cognac and cook the mixture, stirring, until all the liquid has evaporated. Let the mixture cool, transfer it to a food processor, and purée it with the bread mixture. Add the veal, the remaining ¼ cup cream, and salt and pepper to taste and blend the mixture, scraping down the sides, until it is smooth. Transfer the veal mixture to a bowl and keep it covered and chilled while cooking the wild mushrooms. In the skillet, cleaned, cook the shallots with salt and pepper to taste in the remaining 2 tablespoons butter over moderately low heat, stirring, until they are soft-

ened, add the wild mushrooms, and cook the mixture over moderate heat, stirring, for 2 minutes. Add the broth, the wine, and the remaining 2 tablespoons Cognac and boil the mixture, uncovered, stirring occasionally, until all the liquid has evaporated. Let the mixture cool, stir it into the veal mixture, and spoon the mixture into a well-buttered 1-quart terrine, smoothing the top. Cover the terrine with a buttered sheet of foil and the lid, put the terrine in a baking pan, and add enough hot water to the pan to reach halfway up the sides of the terrine. Bake the terrine in the middle of a preheated 350° F. oven for 1 hour to 1 hour and 15 minutes, or until a meat thermometer registers 165° F. Let the terrine cool and pour off any excess liquid. Invert the terrine onto a plate and chill it, covered, overnight.

Make the *coulis*: In a blender or food processor blend together the roasted peppers, the oil, the vinegars, and salt and black pepper to taste until the mixture is smooth.

Cut the terrine into ½-inch-thick slices and pour about ¼ cup of the *coulis* onto each of 8 serving plates. Put a slice of terrine over the *coulis* and sprinkle each serving with some of the diced bell peppers and the chives. Serves 8.

PORK

Ham Biscuits

2 cups all-purpose flour
1 tablespoon double-acting baking powder
½ teaspoon salt
1¼ cups heavy cream plus additional for
   brushing the rounds
unsalted butter, softened, for spreading
   on the biscuits
¼ cup firmly packed brown sugar, or to taste
about ½ pound thinly sliced cooked country
   ham, such as Smithfield

In a bowl whisk together the flour, the baking powder, and the salt, add 1¼ cups of the cream, and stir the mixture until it just forms a dough. Gather the dough into a ball, knead it gently 6 times on a lightly floured surface, and roll or pat it out ½ inch thick. Cut out as many biscuits as possible with a 2-inch round cutter dipped in flour and transfer them to an ungreased baking sheet. Gather the scraps, reroll the dough, and cut out more biscuits in the same manner. Brush the tops of the biscuits with the additional cream, prick them lightly with a fork, and bake the biscuits in the middle of a pre-heated 425° F. oven for 15 minutes, or until they are pale golden. Transfer the biscuits to a rack and let them cool. *The biscuits may be made 1 day in advance and kept in an airtight container.*

Halve the biscuits horizontally with a fork, spread each half with some of the butter, and sprinkle it with about ¼ teaspoon of the brown sugar, or to taste. On a baking sheet broil the halves under a preheated broiler about 2 inches from the heat for 45 seconds to 1½ minutes, or until the sugar is melted and bubbly. Sandwich the ham between the biscuit halves. Makes about 22 ham biscuits.

PHOTO ON PAGE 39

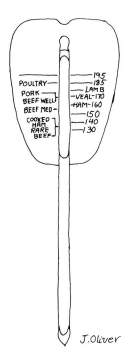

J.Oliver

Fresh Ham with Cracklings and Pan Gravy

an 8- to 10-pound fresh ham (shank end
   leg of pork)
vegetable oil for rubbing the ham
1 tablespoon coarse salt
½ teaspoon dried thyme, crumbled
½ teaspoon dried sage, crumbled
½ teaspoon pepper
1 teaspoon dry English-style mustard
12 ounces beer (not dark)

For the gravy
2 tablespoons all-purpose flour
1 cup beef broth
½ teaspoon dry English-style mustard
¼ teaspoon dried sage, crumbled
⅛ teaspoon dried thyme, crumbled
¼ teaspoon sugar
2 teaspoons cider vinegar

watercress sprigs for garnish

With a small sharp knife prick the ham skin all over, make 4 parallel ¼-inch-deep incisions through the skin the entire length of the ham, and rub the ham lightly with the oil. In a small bowl rub together the coarse salt, the thyme, the sage, the pepper, and the mustard and rub the mixture over the entire surface of the ham. Put the ham on a roasting rack set in a roasting pan and put the pan in a preheated 500° F. oven. Reduce the tempera-ture immediately to 325° F. and roast the ham for 1 hour. Pour half the beer over the ham, roast the ham for 30 minutes more, and pour the remaining beer over the ham. Roast the ham for 2½ hours more, or until a meat thermometer registers 170° F., and let it cool on the rack in the pan for 15 minutes. Pull off the brown crisp skin, leaving the layer of fat on the ham, with scis-sors cut the skin into small pieces, and arrange the cracklings in one layer in a baking pan. Sprinkle the cracklings with salt and bake them in the middle of a preheated 350° F. oven, stirring occasionally, for 15 minutes, or until they are crisp and browned. Transfer the cracklings to paper towels and let them drain. Cut the remaining fat from the ham, slice the meat thinly across the grain, and arrange it on a platter. Keep the ham warm, covered.

Make the gravy: Skim off the fat from the juices in the roasting pan, add 1 cup water, and deglaze the pan over moderate heat, scraping up the brown bits. Transfer the liquid to a saucepan. In a small bowl whisk together the flour and ¼ cup of the broth until the flour is dissolved and whisk the mixture into the deglazing liquid with the remaining ¾ cup broth, the mustard, the sage, the thyme, and the sugar. Bring the mixture to a boil, whisking, add the vinegar and pepper to taste, and sim-mer the gravy, whisking, for 5 minutes.

Garnish the ham with the cracklings and the water-cress sprigs and serve it with the gravy. Serves 8 with leftovers.

PHOTO ON PAGE 24

Baked Ham with Cucumber, Tarragon, and Mushroom Sauce

1 tablespoon unsalted butter
4 large mushrooms, sliced thin
1 cucumber, peeled, seeded, and sliced thin
    crosswise (about 1½ cups)
2 teaspoons finely chopped fresh tarragon
    leaves plus tarragon sprigs for garnish
    if desired
2 tablespoons heavy cream
¼ teaspoon Dijon-style mustard
a ¾-pound ham steak, trimmed

In a skillet melt the butter over moderate heat until the foam subsides and in it cook the mushrooms, stirring, until they begin to give off their liquid. Add the cucumber and cook the mixture, stirring, for 3 to 5 minutes, or until the cucumber is softened slightly. Stir in the chopped tarragon, the cream, and the mustard and cook the mixture until it is thickened slightly. Put the ham in a baking dish and spread it with the cucumber mixture. Bake the ham in the middle of a preheated 350° F. oven for 10 minutes, or until it is heated through, and garnish the top with the tarragon sprigs. Serves 2.

Barbecue Pork Burgers with Coleslaw

For the barbecue sauce
½ cup minced onion
2 garlic cloves, minced
2 tablespoons unsalted butter
1 cup ketchup
3 tablespoons Worcestershire sauce
2 teaspoons dry mustard
¼ cup cider vinegar
¼ cup firmly packed brown sugar
2½ teaspoons chili powder
½ teaspoon Tabasco

1½ pounds ground pork
3 tablespoons fresh bread crumbs
For the coleslaw
2 cups thinly shredded cabbage
¼ cup coarsely grated carrot
¼ cup thinly sliced red onion
2 teaspoons fresh lemon juice
3 tablespoons mayonnaise, or to taste

4 sesame hamburger buns, split and toasted

Make the barbecue sauce: In a heavy saucepan cook the onion and the garlic in the butter over moderately low heat, stirring, until the onion is softened, add the ketchup, the Worcestershire sauce, the mustard, the vinegar, the brown sugar, the chili powder, and the Tabasco, and simmer the mixture. Stir it occasionally for 15 minutes. Transfer the sauce to a bowl and let it cool. *The barbecue sauce may be made 4 days in advance and kept covered and chilled.*

In a bowl combine well the pork, the bread crumbs, and 1/3 cup of the barbecue sauce and form the mixture into four 1-inch-thick patties. Season the burgers with salt and pepper and grill them on an oiled rack set 5 to 6 inches over glowing coals, basting them often and turning them several times, for 8 to 9 minutes on each side, or until they are just cooked through.

Make the coleslaw while the burgers are grilling: In a bowl stir together well the cabbage, the carrot, the onion, the lemon juice, the mayonnaise, and salt and pepper to taste.

Put the burgers in the buns and top them with the coleslaw. Serve the remaining barbecue sauce separately. Serves 4.

Chinese-Style Pork Burgers

1 tablespoon cornstarch
3 tablespoons soy sauce
1½ tablespoons sugar
1½ tablespoons Scotch
¾ cup chicken broth
1 tablespoon vegetable oil
1½ tablespoons minced peeled fresh
    gingerroot
2 teaspoons minced garlic
¾ teaspoon dried hot red pepper flakes
1½ teaspoons Oriental sesame oil
1½ pounds ground pork
12 canned water chestnuts, blanched in
    boiling water for 1 minute, drained, and
    chopped fine
3 tablespoons fresh bread crumbs
4 sesame hamburger buns, split and toasted
shredded iceberg lettuce as an accompaniment

In a small bowl dissolve the cornstarch in the soy sauce and stir in the sugar, the Scotch, and the broth. In a small saucepan heat the vegetable oil over moderately high heat until it is hot but not smoking, add the gingerroot, the garlic, and the red pepper flakes, and stir-fry the mixture for 30 seconds. Stir the soy sauce mixture, add it to the pan, and bring the mixture to a boil, stirring. Simmer the sauce for 1 minute, transfer it to a bowl, and stir in the sesame oil. Let the sauce cool.

In a bowl combine well the pork, the water chestnuts, ¼ cup of the sauce, and the bread crumbs and form the mixture into four 1-inch-thick patties. Grill the burgers on an oiled rack set 5 to 6 inches over glowing coals. Baste them often with the remaining sauce and turn them several times, for 8 to 9 minutes on each side, or until they are just cooked through. Transfer the burgers to the buns and top them with the iceberg lettuce. Serves 4.

Picadillo Tostadas
(Corn Tortillas with Sweet-and-Savory Ground Pork)

For the picadillo
1 large onion, chopped fine
3 garlic cloves, minced
2 tablespoons vegetable oil
2 pounds ground pork
⅓ cup raisins
1½ cups tomato sauce
½ cup sliced pimiento-stuffed green olives
¾ teaspoon cinnamon
¼ teaspoon ground cloves

vegetable oil for frying the tortillas
twelve 7-inch corn tortillas
3 cups shredded romaine or iceberg lettuce
1½ cups thinly sliced red onion or coarsely
  grated radishes

Make the *picadillo*: In a large heavy skillet cook the onion and the garlic in the oil over moderately low heat, stirring, until the onion is softened, add the pork, and cook the mixture over moderate heat, stirring and breaking up any lumps, until the pork is no longer pink. Pour off any excess fat, add the raisins, the tomato sauce, the olives, the cinnamon, the cloves, and salt and pepper to taste, and simmer the mixture, stirring occasionally, for 10 to 15 minutes, or until it is thickened. *The picadillo may be made 1 day in advance, kept covered and chilled, and reheated before proceeding.*

In a skillet heat ¼ inch of the oil over moderately high heat until it is hot but not smoking, in it fry the tortillas, 1 at a time, for 30 seconds to 1 minute, or until they are crisp and golden, and transfer them with tongs as they

are fried to paper towels to drain. Arrange the *tostada* shells in one layer on platters, divide the *picadillo* among them, and top it with the lettuce and the onion. Makes 12 *tostadas*, serving 6 to 8.

Pork Chops with Sautéed Apples
and Applejack Cream

3½ tablespoons unsalted butter
six 1-inch-thick loin pork chops
  (about 2 pounds)
3 Granny Smith or Golden Delicious apples
2 tablespoons firmly packed light brown sugar
2 tablespoons applejack or Calvados
¼ cup dry white wine
½ cup heavy cream
¼ teaspoon celery salt
⅛ teaspoon dried sage, crumbled

In a large skillet heat 2 tablespoons of the butter over moderately high heat until the foam subsides, in it brown the chops, patted dry and seasoned with salt and pepper, in batches for 2 minutes on each side, and transfer them to a plate. Pour off the fat from the skillet, add the remaining 1½ tablespoons butter, and in it sauté the apples, peeled, cored, and cut into eighths, with 1 tablespoon of the brown sugar over moderately high heat, turning them, for 3 minutes, or until they are golden. Add the applejack, the wine, the remaining tablespoon brown sugar, the cream, the celery salt, and the sage, bring the mixture to a boil, and add the chops with any juices that have accumulated on the plate. Simmer the mixture, covered, for 20 minutes, or until the chops and the apples are tender, and transfer the chops and the apples to a heated platter. Cook the sauce for 1 minute, or until it is thickened, and pour it over the chops and apples. Serves 6.

Pork Chops with Fruitcake Stuffing

⅓ cup minced onion
⅓ cup minced green bell pepper
3 tablespoons unsalted butter
1 cup finely chopped fruitcake
four 1-inch-thick rib pork chops
   (about ½ pound each)
1 tablespoon vegetable oil

In a heavy skillet cook the onion and the bell pepper in 2 tablespoons of the butter over moderately low heat, stirring, until the vegetables are softened, stir in the fruitcake and salt and black pepper to taste, and let the stuffing cool. With a sharp paring knife make a 1-inch-long horizontal incision along the side of each chop and cut a deep, wide pocket in the chop. Fill the chops with the stuffing and close the openings with wooden picks. Pat the chops dry with paper towels and season them with salt and black pepper.

In a heavy ovenproof skillet (preferably cast-iron) heat the remaining 1 tablespoons butter and the oil over moderately high heat until the foam subsides and in the fat brown the pork chops. Add ¼ cup water, bake the chops, covered, in the middle of a preheated 350° F. oven, turning them once, for 30 minutes, and transfer them to plates. On top of the stove boil the pan juices until they are reduced to about ⅓ cup, strain them through a sieve into a bowl, and spoon them over the chops. Serves 4.

Braised Pork Chops with Apricots

1 tablespoon vegetable oil
two 1-inch-thick loin pork chops
1½ tablespoons unsalted butter
½ cup finely chopped shallot
½ teaspoon ground cumin
½ teaspoon ground coriander
½ teaspoon freshly grated orange zest
1 teaspoon grated peeled fresh gingerroot
⅓ cup dry white wine
1 cup chicken broth
½ cup thinly sliced dried apricots
1½ teaspoons all-purpose flour
1½ tablespoons minced fresh coriander

In a heavy skillet heat the oil over moderately high heat until it is hot but not smoking, in it brown the pork chops, patted dry and seasoned with salt and pepper, and transfer them to a plate. Add 1 tablespoon of the butter to the skillet and in it cook the shallot, the cumin, the ground coriander, the zest, and the gingerroot over moderately low heat, stirring, until the shallot is softened. Add the wine, the broth, and the apricots, bring the liquid to a simmer, and in it braise the pork chops, covered, over moderately low heat for 20 minutes, or until they are tender. Transfer the chops to a serving plate with a slotted spatula and keep them warm. In a small bowl stir together well the remaining ½ tablespoon butter, softened, and the flour until the mixture is combined well, add the *beurre manié* to the braising liquid, and bring the sauce to a boil, stirring. Simmer the sauce for 1 to 2 minutes, or until it is thickened, stir in the fresh coriander and salt and pepper to taste, and pour the sauce over the pork chops. Serves 2.

Braised Pork Chops with Peppers

1 teaspoon unsalted butter
two ¾-inch-thick rib pork chops
⅓ cup chicken broth
2 tablespoons plus 1 teaspoon balsamic
   vinegar
1 cup coarsely chopped red bell pepper
1 cup coarsely chopped green bell pepper
1 teaspoon cornstarch dissolved in
   2 teaspoons water

In a non-stick skillet heat the butter over moderately high heat until the foam subsides and in it brown the pork chops, patted dry and seasoned with salt and black pepper. Add the broth and the vinegar, bring the liquid to a boil, and transfer the mixture to a microwave-safe baking dish just large enough to hold the chops in one layer. Sprinkle the chops with the bell peppers and microwave the mixture, covered with microwave-safe plastic wrap, at medium power (50%) for 6 minutes. Stir the cornstarch mixture into the cooking juices and microwave the mixture, covered, at high power (100%) for 1 minute. Serves 2.

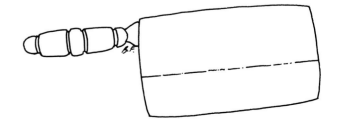

Barbecued Spareribs

2 racks of pork spareribs (about 6 pounds)
Southern-style tomato barbecue sauce (recipe
   follows)

In a large kettle combine the sparerib racks with
enough water to cover them, bring the water to a boil,
and simmer the spareribs, skimming the froth as necessary, for 45 minutes. Drain the spareribs well. *The
spareribs may be prepared up to this point 1 day in
advance and kept wrapped in foil and chilled.* Pat the
spareribs dry, brush them all over with some of the
sauce, and grill them on an oiled rack set 5 to 6 inches
over glowing coals for 6 minutes on each side, brushing
them with more of the sauce as they are turned. Serve
the remaining barbecue sauce separately with the spareribs. Serves 6.

PHOTO ON PAGE 54

Southern-Style Tomato Barbecue Sauce

2 small onions, quartered
2¼ cups distilled white vinegar
1½ cups bottled chili sauce
¾ cup coarsely grated peeled
   Granny Smith apple
3 tablespoons dark molasses
⅓ cup vegetable oil
1 large garlic clove, chopped
1 bottled sweet pickled gherkin, chopped,
   plus 3 tablespoons juice
3 tablespoons Dijon-style mustard
1 teaspoon celery salt
2 tablespoons Worcestershire sauce
1 tablespoon Tabasco
cayenne to taste
¾ teaspoon turmeric

In a blender or food processor purée the onions in
batches with the vinegar, the chili sauce, the apple, the
molasses, the oil, the garlic, the gherkin with the juice,
the mustard, the celery salt, the Worcestershire sauce,
the Tabasco, the cayenne, and the turmeric. In a saucepan simmer the mixture, stirring occasionally, for 40 to
45 minutes, or until it is reduced to about 4 cups, and
let the sauce cool. *The sauce may be made 1 week in
advance and kept covered and chilled.* Makes about
4 cups.

PHOTO ON PAGE 54

Pork Tamale Potpie with Corn-Bread Crust

For the pork mixture
1 cup chopped onion
1 cup chopped green bell pepper
2 tablespoons vegetable oil
1½ pounds lean ground pork
a 12-ounce can tomato sauce
2 tablespoons tomato paste
a 10-ounce package frozen corn, thawed
1 tablespoon ground cumin
½ teaspoon ground allspice
2 teaspoons chili powder
1 tablespoon Worcestershire sauce
1 teaspoon Tabasco plus additional to taste
1 tablespoon yellow cornmeal
For the topping
1 cup all-purpose flour
1 cup yellow cornmeal
3 tablespoons sugar
2 teaspoons double-acting baking powder
3 tablespoons unsalted butter, melted and cooled
¾ cup milk
1 large egg, beaten lightly
½ cup grated Monterey Jack
a 4-ounce can green chili peppers, drained
   and chopped

Make the pork mixture: In a large skillet cook the onion and the bell pepper in the oil over moderately low
heat, stirring, until the onion is softened, add the pork,
and cook the mixture over moderate heat, stirring and
breaking up any lumps, until the pork is no longer pink.
Stir in the tomato sauce, the tomato paste, the corn, the
cumin, the allspice, the chili powder, the Worcestershire sauce, 1 teaspoon of the Tabasco, the cornmeal,
and salt and black pepper to taste, simmer the mixture, stirring occasionally, for 30 minutes, and add the
additional Tabasco. Spoon the mixture into a shallow
2½-quart casserole. *The mixture may be made 1 day
in advance and kept, covered and chilled.*

Make the topping: Into a bowl sift together the flour,
the cornmeal, the sugar, and the baking powder, add the
butter, the milk, and the egg, and stir the batter until it is
just combined. Stir in the Monterey Jack and the chili
peppers and drop the batter by large spoonfuls around
the edge of the casserole.

Bake the potpie in the middle of a preheated 400° F.
oven for 10 minutes, reduce the heat to 350° F., and
bake the potpie for 30 minutes more. Serves 6.

LAMB

Curried Lamb Burgers with Chutney Mustard
vegetable oil for frying the onion
1 onion, sliced very thin
1½ pounds lean ground lamb
1½ teaspoons curry powder
½ teaspoon ground cumin
¼ cup Dijon-style mustard
3 tablespoons Major Grey chutney, or to taste
4 onion rolls, split and toasted

In a deep skillet heat ½ inch of the oil over moderately high heat until it is hot but not smoking and in it fry the onion in 2 batches, stirring, for 30 seconds to 1 minute, or until it is golden brown, being careful not to let it burn. Transfer the onion as it is fried with a slotted spoon to paper towels to drain and let it cool.

Handling the lamb as gently as possible, in a bowl combine it with the fried onion, crumbled, the curry powder, and the cumin and form the mixture into four 1-inch-thick patties. Season the burgers with salt and pepper and grill them on an oiled rack set 5 to 6 inches over glowing coals for 8 to 9 minutes on each side, or until the lamb is cooked but still pink within.

While the burgers are grilling, in a small bowl stir together the mustard and the chutney. Transfer the burgers to the rolls and serve them with the chutney mustard. Serves 4.

Greek-Style Lamb Burgers with Minted Yogurt Sauce
For the sauce
an 8-ounce container of plain yogurt
1 garlic clove, minced and mashed to a paste
    with ¼ teaspoon salt
2 tablespoons shredded fresh mint leaves,
    or to taste
For the burgers
1½ pounds ground lamb
⅓ cup crumbled Feta
⅓ cup (about 8) Kalamata or other brine-cured
    black olives, pitted and chopped fine

4 small *pita* loaves, each split halfway around
    the edge to form a pocket
1 tomato, sliced
1 green bell pepper, cut into rings
1 small red onion, sliced thin

Make the sauce: Put the yogurt in a sieve lined with a dampened paper towel set over a bowl and let it drain for 30 minutes. Transfer the yogurt to a small bowl and stir in the garlic paste and the mint.

Make the burgers: Handling the lamb as gently as possible, in a bowl combine it with the Feta and the olives and form the mixture into four 1-inch-thick patties. Season the burgers lightly with salt and pepper and grill them on an oiled rack set 5 to 6 inches over glowing coals for 8 to 9 minutes on each side, or until the lamb is cooked but still pink within.

Transfer the burgers to the *pita* pockets, top them with the tomato slices, the bell pepper rings, and the onion slices, and serve them with the yogurt sauce. Serves 4.

Lamb Chops on Spiced Tomatoes and Onions
¼ teaspoon ground cumin
¼ teaspoon ground cardamom
½ teaspoon salt
½ teaspoon freshly ground pepper
2 tablespoons olive oil
four ½-inch slices of tomato
four ¼-inch slices of onion
four ¾-inch-thick rib lamb chops
    (about 1 pound total)

In a bowl combine well the cumin, the cardamom, the salt, and the pepper. In a large non-stick skillet heat 1 tablespoon of the oil over moderately high heat until it is hot but not smoking and in it cook the tomato and the onion in one layer for 3 minutes. Turn the vegetables, sprinkle them with the spice mixture, and cook them for 3 minutes more, or until they are just tender. Divide the vegetables between 2 heated plates, arranging them in one layer. Add the remaining 1 tablespoon oil to the skillet, in it sauté the chops, patted dry, over moderately high heat for 5 minutes on each side for medium-rare meat, and arrange them on top of the vegetables. Serves 2.

Balsamic-Marinated Lamb Chops
½ cup balsamic vinegar (available at specialty
    foods shops and many supermarkets)

3 large garlic cloves, chopped coarse
3 large shallots, chopped coarse
¾ teaspoon dried thyme, crumbled
¾ teaspoon salt
½ teaspoon freshly ground pepper
six 1½-inch-thick loin lamb chops
vegetable oil for brushing the chops
pimiento butter (recipe follows) as an
    accompaniment

In a bowl whisk together the vinegar, the garlic, the shallots, the thyme, the salt, and the pepper. In a sturdy sealable large plastic bag combine the chops and the marinade, seal the bag, forcing out as much air as possible, and let the chops marinate, chilled, turning them several times, for at least 8 hours or overnight. Drain the chops, pat them dry with paper towels, and let them come to room temperature. Brush the chops well with the oil and grill them on a well-oiled rack set 5 to 6 inches over glowing coals for 8 minutes on each side for medium-rare meat, or until they are just springy to the touch. Transfer the chops to a platter and let them stand for 5 minutes. Top each chop with a dollop of the butter, either by piping it from a pastry bag fitted with a fluted tip or using a spoon. Serves 6.

Pimiento Butter

¾ stick (6 tablespoons) unsalted butter,
    softened
¼ cup drained bottled pimiento or roasted red
    pepper, patted dry and chopped
½ teaspoon fresh lemon juice

In a food processor blend together the butter, the pimiento, and the lemon juice until the pimiento is minced and the butter is orange-colored and season the butter with salt and pepper. Makes about ½ cup.

Broiled Lamb Chops with Lemon Caper Sauce

two 1½-inch-thick loin lamb chops
1 tablespoon unsalted butter
1 teaspoon freshly grated lemon zest
1 teaspoon drained bottled capers
1 tablespoon fresh lemon juice

Pat the lamb chops dry, sprinkle them with salt and pepper to taste, and broil them on the rack of a broiler pan under a preheated broiler about 4 inches from the heat for 6 minutes. Turn the chops, broil them for 4 minutes more for medium-rare meat, and let them stand for 5 minutes. While the chops are standing, in a small saucepan melt the butter and stir in the zest, the capers, the lemon juice, and salt and pepper to taste. Transfer the chops to 2 plates and pour the sauce over them. Serves 2.

Herbed Lamb Kebabs with Yogurt Sauce

a ¾-pound piece of boneless lamb shoulder,
    trimmed
2 tablespoons fresh lemon juice
¼ teaspoon dried thyme, crumbled
¼ teaspoon dried rosemary, crumbled
¼ teaspoon dried orégano, crumbled
¼ teaspoon pepper
¼ teaspoon salt
¼ cup olive oil
eight 8-inch wooden skewers, soaked in water
    for 15 minutes
2 tablespoons plain yogurt

Cut the lamb shoulder across the grain into thin slices with a sharp knife, flatten the slices between sheets of plastic wrap until they are ⅛ inch thick, and cut them into 1-inch-wide strips.

In a saucepan whisk together the lemon juice, the thyme, the rosemary, the orégano, the pepper, and the salt, add the oil in a stream, whisking, and whisk the marinade until it is emulsified. Add the lamb strips, stir the mixture to coat the strips well with the marinade, and thread them onto the skewers, reserving the remaining marinade. Arrange the kebabs on the rack of a broiling pan, broil them under a preheated broiler about 3 inches from the heat, turning them once, for 6 minutes, and transfer them to a plate. Transfer 2 tablespoons of the juices from the broiler pan to the reserved marinade and bring the mixture to a boil. Remove the pan from the heat, whisk in the yogurt and salt and pepper to taste. Spoon the sauce over the kebabs. Serves 2.

Herbed Roast Leg of Lamb with Roasted Onions and Potatoes

⅓ cup Dijon-style mustard
1 large garlic clove, minced and mashed to a
    paste with ¼ teaspoon salt
1 tablespoon finely chopped fresh rosemary
    leaves or 1 teaspoon dried, crumbled, plus
    fresh rosemary sprigs for garnish if desired
1 tablespoon finely chopped fresh thyme
    leaves or 1 teaspoon dried, crumbled, plus
    fresh thyme sprigs for garnish if desired
1½ tablespoons soy sauce
¼ cup dry white wine
4 tablespoons olive oil
an 8-pound leg of lamb, the pelvic bone
    removed and the lamb tied
2 pounds (about 40) small white onions,
    blanched in boiling water for 2 minutes,
    drained, and peeled
2 large carrots, cut into ½-inch pieces
2½ pounds (about 40) small red or white
    potatoes, cooked in boiling salted water
    for 10 minutes, drained, and halved
For the gravy
1 cup dry red wine
2 cups beef broth
2 tablespoons unsalted butter, softened
3 tablespoons all-purpose flour

In a small bowl whisk together the mustard, the garlic paste, the chopped rosemary, the chopped thyme, the soy sauce, the wine, and salt and pepper to taste, add 2 tablespoons of the oil in a stream, whisking, and whisk the mixture until it is combined well. Brush the lamb generously on all sides with the mustard mixture, reserving the remaining mustard mixture, and let it marinate in a lightly oiled roasting pan, covered and chilled, for at least 6 hours or overnight.

Let the lamb come to room temperature and brush it with the reserved mustard mixture. In a bowl toss the onions with 1 tablespoon of the remaining oil, add the onions and the carrots to the pan, and roast them with the lamb in the middle of a preheated 450° F. oven for 15 minutes. In the bowl toss the potatoes with the remaining 1 tablespoon oil and add them to the pan. Reduce the heat to 350° F. and roast the lamb and vegetables, stirring the vegetables occasionally, for 1 hour and 15 minutes, or until a meat thermometer registers 140° F. for medium-rare meat. Transfer the lamb to a large platter

and let it stand for 20 minutes. Transfer the onions and the potatoes with a slotted spoon to a serving dish, leaving the carrots in the pan, and keep them warm, covered.

Make the gravy: Pour off the fat from the pan, add the wine, and deglaze the pan over moderately high heat, scraping up the brown bits. Boil the mixture until it is reduced by half and strain it through a sieve into a saucepan, pressing hard on the carrots. Add the broth and bring the mixture to a boil. In a small bowl knead together the butter and the flour until the mixture is combined well and add the mixture to the gravy a little at a time, whisking. Add any juices that have accumulated on the platter and salt and pepper to taste and simmer the gravy, whisking occasionally, for 3 minutes, or until it is thickened.

Remove the string from the lamb, spoon some of the potatoes and onions around the lamb, and garnish the lamb with the thyme and rosemary sprigs. Serve the lamb, carved, with the gravy. Serves 8.

PHOTO ON PAGE 30

Lamb and Eggplant Potpie with Feta Potato Crust

For the lamb mixture
two 1-pound eggplants, cut into ½-inch cubes
    (about 8 cups)
5 tablespoons vegetable oil
1 large onion, chopped
1 tablespoon minced garlic
2 pounds lean ground lamb
1¼ teaspoons cinnamon
2 teaspoons dried mint, crumbled
1¼ teaspoons dried orégano, crumbled
½ teaspoon ground allspice
a 35-ounce can Italian plum tomatoes,
    drained, reserving 1 cup of the juice,
    and chopped
2 tablespoons tomato paste
¼ cup freshly grated Parmesan
For the topping
3 pounds russet (baking) potatoes (about 6)
2 tablespoons unsalted butter
⅓ cup freshly grated Parmesan
⅓ pound grated Feta

1 tablespoon unsalted butter

Make the lamb mixture: In a colander sprinkle the

eggplant with salt and let it drain for 30 minutes. In a large skillet heat 4 tablespoons of the oil over moderate heat, in it cook the eggplant, patted dry, in batches, stirring, for 15 minutes, or until it is tender but still holds its shape, and transfer it with a slotted spoon to a bowl. In the skillet heat the remaining 1 tablespoon oil over moderate heat and in it cook the onion, stirring, until it is softened. Add the garlic and cook the mixture, stirring, for 1 minute. Add the lamb and cook the mixture, stirring and breaking up any lumps, until the lamb is no longer pink. Pour off any excess fat from the skillet, add the cinnamon, the mint, the orégano, and the allspice, and cook the mixture, stirring, for 1 minute. Add the tomatoes with the reserved juice, the tomato paste, and salt and pepper to taste and cook the mixture, stirring, for 15 minutes, or until it is thickened. Transfer the mixture to a large bowl and stir in the Parmesan. *The lamb mixture improves in flavor if made up to this point and kept, covered and chilled, overnight.* Add the eggplant to the lamb mixture, combine the mixture well, and spread it in a buttered shallow 3-quart gratin dish.

Make the topping: In a large saucepan combine the potatoes, peeled and cut into 1-inch pieces, with enough cold water to cover them by 1 inch, bring the water to a boil, and simmer the potatoes for 10 to 15 minutes, or until they are tender. Drain the potatoes, return them to the pan, and cook them over moderate heat, shaking the pan, for 30 seconds to evaporate any excess liquid. Force the potatoes through a ricer or the medium disk of a food mill into a bowl, add the butter, the Parmesan, the Feta, and salt and pepper to taste, and stir the mixture until it is combined well and the butter is melted.

Spoon the topping over the lamb mixture, spreading it to cover the lamb mixture completely, and dot the surface with the butter, cut into bits. Bake the potpie in the middle of a preheated 400° F. oven for 35 to 40 minutes, or until it is browned lightly. Serves 8.

OTHER MEATS

Calf's Liver with Apples and Onions

4 slices of lean bacon
½ stick (¼ cup) unsalted butter
2 large onions, sliced thin
3 Granny Smith apples
2 tablespoons white-wine vinegar
1 teaspoon sugar
¼ cup dry white wine
1½ pounds calf's liver, sliced ⅓ inch thick
    and cut into 2- by 1-inch strips
finely chopped fresh parsley leaves plus
    additional sprigs for garnish
lemon wedges for garnish

In a large skillet cook the bacon over moderate heat until it is crisp, transfer it to paper towels to drain, and pour off all but 2 tablespoons of the fat. To the fat remaining in the skillet add 2 tablespoons of the butter and cook the onions in the fat over moderate heat, stirring occasionally, until they are softened and light golden. Add the apples, cored and cut into eighths, and cook the mixture until the apples are light golden. Add the vinegar, the sugar, and the wine, bring the mixture to a boil, and boil it for 3 minutes, or until it is thickened. Transfer the mixture to a heated platter.

In the skillet, cleaned, heat the remaining 2 tablespoons butter over high heat until the foam subsides and in it sauté the liver, patted dry, turning it, for 3 to 4 minutes, or until it is browned and slightly pink within. Arrange the liver over the apple mixture, sprinkle the bacon, crumbled, and the chopped parsley over it, and garnish the platter with the parsley sprigs and the lemon wedges. Serves 6.

Spiced Venison Steaks with Red-Cabbage Confit and Red-Wine Sauce

a 3½- to 4-pound boneless loin of venison,*
    trimmed and cut crosswise into eight 4- to
    6-ounce steaks, reserving any remaining for
    another use
2 tablespoons black peppercorns
2 tablespoons Szechwan peppercorns
    (available at Oriental markets, specialty
    foods shops, and some supermarkets)
2 tablespoons dried allspice berries
1 stick (½ cup) plus 3 tablespoons unsalted
    butter, softened
3 tablespoons vegetable oil
½ cup minced white part of scallion
    plus ⅓ cup thinly sliced scallion green
1 cup dry red wine
red-cabbage *confit* (recipe follows) as an
    accompaniment

*Venison is available at many butcher shops, specialty foods shops, and some supermarkets. It can be ordered directly from D'Artagnan by calling (800) DARTAGNAN or in New Jersey (201) 792-0748. Alternatively, eight 6-ounce filets mignons of beef may be substituted for the venison.

Flatten each steak to a ¾-inch thickness between 2 pieces of plastic wrap. In a heavy-duty sealable plastic bag or between 2 sheets of wax paper crush the peppercorns and the allspice berries coarse with the bottom of a heavy skillet. Press the peppercorn mixture into both sides of the steaks and chill the steaks, covered with plastic wrap, for at least 2 hours or overnight.

In each of 2 heavy skillets heat ½ tablespoon of the butter and 1½ tablespoons of the oil over moderately high heat until the foam subsides and in the fat sauté the steaks, seasoned with salt, for 3 to 4 minutes on each side, or until they are just springy to the touch for rare meat. Transfer the steaks with a slotted spatula to a platter and keep them warm, covered loosely. Pour off the fat remaining in the skillets, to each skillet add 1 tablespoon of the remaining butter and half the minced white scallion, and cook the scallion over moderate heat, stirring, until it is softened. Deglaze each skillet with ½ cup of the wine, scraping up any brown bits clinging to the skillet, and pour the wine mixture from one skillet into the other. Boil the wine mixture until it is reduced to a glaze, remove the skillet from the heat, and whisk in the remaining 8 tablespoons butter, 1 tablespoon at a time, adding each new piece just before the previous one has melted completely. Whisk in the scallion green and salt and black pepper to taste. Divide the red-cabbage *confit* among 8 dinner plates, arrange a venison steak over each serving, and spoon some of the sauce over each steak. Serves 8.

PHOTO ON PAGE 66

Red-Cabbage Confit

8 cups thinly sliced red cabbage
    (about 2 pounds)
1 large onion, sliced thin (about 3 cups)
1 bay leaf
¼ teaspoon dried thyme, crumbled
4 dried allspice berries
2 garlic cloves, crushed
2 tablespoons olive oil
1 Granny Smith apple, peeled and
    grated coarse
1 cup dry red wine
¼ cup red-wine vinegar plus
    additional to taste
2 tablespoons sugar
⅓ cup dried currants

In a kettle of boiling salted water blanch the cabbage for 2 minutes and drain it. In the kettle, cleaned, cook the onion, the bay leaf, the thyme, the allspice berries, the garlic, and salt and pepper to taste in the oil over moderately low heat, stirring, until the onion is softened, add the cabbage, the apple, the wine, ¼ cup of the vinegar, the sugar, and ¾ cup water, and bring the liquid to a boil. Simmer the mixture, covered, stirring occasionally, for 30 to 35 minutes, or until the cabbage is tender, discard the allspice berries, and add the currants. Simmer the mixture, uncovered, stirring occasionally, for 10 to 15 minutes more, or until most of the liquid has evaporated, discard the bay leaf and the garlic, and season the *confit* with salt and pepper and the additional vinegar. *The confit may be made 2 days in advance, kept covered and chilled, and reheated just before serving.* Makes about 6 cups.

PHOTO ON PAGE 66

POULTRY

CHICKEN

Chicken Cacciatora with Fusilli

¼ cup vegetable oil
a 3½-pound chicken, cut into serving pieces
1 onion, chopped fine
½ pound mushrooms, sliced thin
1 garlic clove, minced
a 28-ounce can plum tomatoes including
 the juice
½ cup dry red wine
2 flat anchovy fillets, rinsed, patted dry,
 and mashed to a paste
1 teaspoon dried orégano, crumbled
1 pound *fusilli* (corkscrew-shaped pasta)
½ cup minced fresh parsley leaves if desired

In a kettle heat the oil over moderately high heat until it is hot but not smoking and in it brown the chicken, patted dry, in batches, transferring it as it is browned to a bowl. Pour off and discard all but about 3 tablespoons of the oil and in the remaining oil cook the onion and the mushrooms over moderate heat, stirring occasionally, until the onion is golden. Add the garlic and cook the mixture, stirring, for 1 minute. Add the tomatoes with the juice, the wine, the chicken with any juices that have accumulated in the bowl, the anchovy paste, and the orégano and simmer the mixture, covered, stirring occasionally and breaking up the tomatoes, for 30 to 35 minutes, or until the chicken is tender. *The chicken mixture may be made 2 days in advance, cooled to room temperature, and kept covered and chilled. Reheat the chicken mixture before serving.*

In a kettle of boiling salted water cook the *fusilli* for 10 to 12 minutes, or until it is *al dente*, drain it well, and in a large bowl toss it with the chicken mixture. Sprinkle the chicken *cacciatora* with the parsley. Serves 4.

PHOTO ON PAGE 33

Chicken Club on Brioche Toast

4 slices of lean bacon
1 whole skinless boneless chicken breast
 (about ½ pound)
12 slices of brioche bread cut from large
 round or rectangular loaves, toasted lightly
½ cup mayonnaise
8 lettuce leaves, rinsed and spun dry
8 thin slices of tomato
8 thin slices of red onion

In a small heavy skillet cook the bacon over moderate heat, turning it, until it is crisp, transfer it to paper towels to drain, and pour off all but 1 tablespoon of fat from the skillet. In the fat in the skillet sauté the chicken, patted dry and seasoned with pepper, for 6 to 8 minutes on each side, or until it is just springy to the touch, and transfer it to a work surface. Let the chicken stand for 10 minutes and cut it into thin slices. Spread one side of each brioche toast with some of the mayonnaise, sprinkle it with pepper to taste, and layer 4 of the toasts with a lettuce leaf, a tomato slice, an onion slice, and a bacon slice. Top each sandwich with a brioche toast, a lettuce leaf, an onion slice, a tomato slice, and one fourth of the chicken and cover each sandwich with a brioche toast, pressing it firmly. Makes 4 sandwiches.

Chicken and Apple Curry

2 tablespoons vegetable oil
3 tablespoons unsalted butter
a 3½-pound chicken, cut into serving pieces
2 ribs of celery, chopped fine
1 large onion, chopped fine
2 garlic cloves, minced
2 Granny Smith apples
1 red bell pepper, chopped
1 tablespoon curry powder
½ teaspoon cinnamon
½ teaspoon ground cumin
2 tablespoons all-purpose flour
2 cups chicken broth
finely chopped fresh parsley leaves for garnish
steamed rice (recipe follows) as an
    accompaniment
apple ginger chutney (page 216) as an
    accompaniment

In a flameproof casserole heat the oil and 1 table-spoon of the butter over moderately high heat until the foam subsides, in it brown the chicken, patted dry and seasoned with salt, and transfer the chicken with a slotted spoon to a plate. Pour off the fat from the casserole, add the remaining 2 tablespoons butter, and in it cook the celery, the onion, and the garlic over moderately low heat, stirring occasionally, until the vegetables are softened. Add the apples, cored and chopped, and cook the mixture, stirring occasionally, for 5 minutes. Add the bell pepper, the curry powder, the cinnamon, and the cumin and cook the mixture, stirring, for 1 minute. Stir in the flour and cook the mixture over moderate heat, stirring, for 3 minutes. Add the broth and the chicken with any juices that have accumulated on the plate, bring the liquid to a boil, and cook the chicken mixture, covered, at a bare simmer for 15 to 20 minutes, or until the chicken is cooked through and tender. Transfer the chicken with a slotted spoon to a serving plate, boil the vegetable mixture, stirring, for 3 to 5 minutes, or until it is thickened slightly, and season the sauce with salt and black pepper. Pour the sauce over the chicken and top it with the parsley. Serve the curry with the rice and the chutney. Serves 4 to 6.

Steamed Rice

1 tablespoon salt
2 cups unconverted long-grain rice

In a large saucepan bring 5 quarts water to a boil with the salt. Sprinkle in the rice, stirring until the water returns to a boil, and boil it for 10 minutes. Drain the rice in a large colander and rinse it. Set the colander over a large saucepan of boiling water and steam the rice, covered with a kitchen towel and the lid, for 15 minutes, or until it is fluffy and dry. Makes about 6 cups.

Chicken and Dill Fricassee with Sour Cream Shortcakes

For the shortcake biscuits
1¾ cups all-purpose flour
2 teaspoons double-acting baking powder
½ teaspoon baking soda
½ teaspoon salt
½ teaspoon sugar
2 tablespoons finely chopped fresh dill
4 tablespoons cold vegetable shortening
⅔ cup sour cream
¼ cup milk
For the fricassee
¼ pound mushrooms, sliced
½ stick (¼ cup) unsalted butter
3 tablespoons minced shallot
¼ cup all-purpose flour
3 cups chicken broth
¾ cup heavy cream
a 10-ounce package frozen peas, thawed
1 tablespoon fresh lemon juice
1 teaspoon salt
2½ tablespoons finely chopped fresh dill
4 cups bite-size pieces cooked chicken
¼ pound cooked ham, cut into cubes
    (about ¾ cup)

Make the shortcake biscuits: Into a bowl sift together the flour, the baking powder, the baking soda, the salt, and the sugar, add the dill and the shortening, and blend the mixture until it resembles meal. Stir in the sour cream and the milk and stir the mixture until it just forms a soft but sticky dough. On a floured surface roll or pat out the dough ½ inch thick and with a 3½-inch cookie cutter cut out 6 rounds. Bake the rounds on an ungreased baking sheet in the middle of a preheated 425° F. oven for 15 to 17 minutes, or until they are golden.

Make the fricassee: In a skillet cook the mushrooms in 1 tablespoon of the butter over moderate heat, stirring occasionally, until they give off their liquid and reserve the mixture. In a large saucepan melt the remaining 3 tablespoons butter over moderate heat and in it cook the shallot until it is softened. Add the flour and cook the *roux*, stirring, for 3 minutes. Add the broth in a stream, stirring, and cook the mixture, stirring, for 5 minutes. Add the cream and boil the mixture, stirring occasionally, for 10 minutes. Add the peas, the lemon juice, the salt, the dill, the chicken, the ham, the reserved mushroom mixture, and pepper to taste and simmer the mixture for 10 minutes, or until the chicken is heated through.

Arrange a biscuit, heated and split, on each of 6 dinner plates, spoon some of the fricassee over the bottom half, and cover it with the top half of the biscuit. Serves 6.

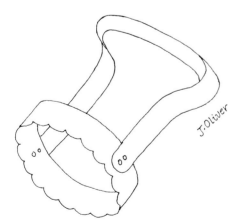

Chicken and Swiss Chard Enchilada Casserole

1 pound Swiss chard, rinsed well
   and drained
2 garlic cloves, minced
1 tablespoon olive oil
1 large whole chicken breast
   (about 1½ pounds), cooked, boned,
   and shredded (about 1¼ cups meat)
vegetable oil for frying the tortillas
twelve 7-inch corn tortillas, dried at room
   temperature for 30 minutes, or until they
   are leathery and curled but not crisp
2½ cups Mexican-style tomato sauce
   (page 165)
½ cup chicken broth
1½ cups grated Monterey Jack
   (about 6 ounces)
½ cup freshly grated Parmesan

Cut the stems from the Swiss chard leaves and chop them and the leaves separately. In a large skillet cook the garlic in the oil over moderate heat, stirring, until it is fragrant, stir in the Swiss chard stems and ¼ cup water, and cook the mixture, covered, for 5 minutes. Add the leaves and cook the mixture, covered, stirring occasionally, for 3 to 5 minutes, or until the leaves are tender. Drain the Swiss chard mixture and in a bowl toss it with the shredded chicken and salt and pepper to taste.

In a skillet heat ¼ inch of the oil over moderately high heat until it is hot but not smoking, in it fry the tortillas, 1 at a time, turning them, for 3 to 4 seconds, or until they are softened, and transfer them with tongs as they are fried to paper towels to drain. In a bowl thin the tomato sauce with the broth, spoon about ⅓ cup of it into the bottom of a greased 13- by 9-inch baking dish, and arrange 4 of the tortillas in one layer over it. Spread the tortillas with half the chicken mixture and half the Monterey Jack, spoon about ½ cup of the remaining sauce over the mixture, and cover it with 4 of the remaining tortillas in one layer. Spread the tortillas with the remaining chicken mixture and the remaining Monterey Jack, top the mixture with ½ cup of the remaining sauce, and cover it with the remaining 4 tortillas. Pour the remaining sauce evenly over the tortillas and sprinkle it with the Parmesan. Bake the enchiladas, covered with foil, in the middle of a preheated 350° F. oven for 15 minutes, remove the foil, and bake the enchiladas, uncovered, for 5 to 10 minutes more or until the cheese is bubbling. Serves 6.

Arroz con Pollo
(Rice with Chicken)

a rounded ¼ teaspoon saffron threads
¼ cup olive oil
a 3½-pound chicken, cut into
    serving pieces
2 onions, chopped
2 small green bell peppers,
    chopped
¾ pound plum tomatoes (about 6), peeled,
    seeded, and chopped
2 garlic cloves, minced
4 teaspoons paprika
3 cups Arborio rice (Italian short-grain rice,
    available at Italian markets and some
    specialty foods shops)
6 cups chicken broth
1 large red bell pepper, roasted (procedure on
    page 135) and cut into strips
1 cup thawed frozen peas
¼ cup minced fresh parsley leaves
    if desired

Set a rack over a saucepan of boiling water, put the saffron in a saucer on the rack, and let it steam for 3 to 4 minutes, or until it is brittle. Remove the saucer and the rack and crumble the saffron in the saucer. In a large heavy skillet heat the oil over moderately high heat until it is hot but not smoking and reduce the heat to moderately low. Cook the chicken, patted dry, in batches in the oil, turning it, for 15 to 18 minutes, or until it is cooked through, transferring it as it is cooked to a bowl. Pour off all but 3 tablespoons of the fat from the skillet and in the skillet cook the onions and the green bell peppers over moderately low heat, stirring occasionally, until the vegetables are softened. Add the tomatoes, the garlic, the paprika, and the saffron and cook the mixture, stirring, for 1 minute. Add the rice and cook the mixture, stirring, for 3 minutes. Add the broth, heated, and simmer the mixture, stirring occasionally, for 7 minutes. Transfer the rice mixture to a shallow 5-quart baking dish and arrange the chicken over it. Bake the *arroz con pollo* in the middle of a preheated 325° F. oven for 15 minutes, sprinkle the red bell pepper and the peas over it, and bake the *arroz con pollo* for 5 to 10 minutes more, or until the liquid is absorbed and the rice is *al dente*. Sprinkle the *arroz con pollo* with the parsley. Serves 6.

PHOTO ON PAGE 69

Chicken with Riesling and Grapes

2 tablespoons unsalted butter
1 tablespoon olive oil
1 whole chicken breast, halved
1 shallot, minced
1 garlic clove, minced
2 teaspoons all-purpose flour
⅓ cup Riesling
½ cup chicken broth
2 teaspoons fresh lemon juice
⅛ teaspoon dried thyme, crumbled
¼ pound green seedless grapes, halved
    crosswise (about ¾ cup)

In a large skillet heat the butter and the oil over moderately high heat until the foam subsides, in the fat brown the chicken on all sides for 8 minutes, or until it is golden, and transfer it with tongs to a plate. Reduce the heat to moderately low and in the fat remaining in the skillet cook the shallot and the garlic for 3 minutes. Stir in the flour and cook the *roux*, stirring, for 2 minutes. Add the Riesling and cook the mixture, stirring, for 1 minute. Add the broth, the lemon juice, the thyme, and salt and pepper to taste and bring the mixture to a boil, stirring. Return the chicken to the skillet with any juices that have accumulated on the plate and simmer the mixture, covered, for 15 minutes. Add the grapes and simmer the mixture, uncovered, stirring occasionally, for 3 to 5 minutes, or until the chicken is cooked through. Serves 2.

Coq au Vin

2 slices of lean bacon
10 pearl onions
1 onion, chopped
1 garlic clove, minced
2 tablespoons unsalted butter
3 mushrooms, cut into ¼-inch slices
½ cup chicken broth
¼ cup dry red wine
1 tablespoon Worcestershire sauce
a pinch of dried thyme
1 whole skinless boneless chicken breast
    (about ¾ pound), halved
cooked rice as an accompaniment

Arrange the bacon on a double thickness of microwave-safe paper towels, top it with a double thickness of microwave-safe paper towels, and microwave it at high power (100%) for 2 minutes. Let the bacon cool and crumble it coarse. In a microwave-safe baking dish combine the pearl onions with 1 tablespoon water and microwave them, covered with a microwave-safe lid, at high power (100%) for 1 minute. Transfer the pearl onions to a bowl, let them cool, and peel them. In the dish microwave the chopped onion and the garlic in the butter, covered with the lid, at high power (100%), stirring after 2 minutes, for 5 minutes. Add the mushrooms, the broth, the wine, the Worcestershire sauce, the thyme, and salt and pepper to taste and microwave the mixture, covered with the lid, at high power (100%) for 10 minutes. Add the chicken, the bacon, and the pearl onions, baste them with the cooking liquid, and microwave the mixture, covered with the lid, for 10 minutes, or until the chicken is cooked through. Serve the mixture with the rice. Serves 2.

Austrian-Style Fried Chicken

two 3-pound chickens
all-purpose flour seasoned with salt and
  pepper for dredging the chicken
3 large eggs, beaten lightly
2 cups stale fine bread crumbs
vegetable oil for deep-frying
fresh thyme branches for garnish
tomato chutney (page 217) as an
  accompaniment

Quarter each chicken, discarding the first 2 joints of the wings. Remove the breastbones and ribs and remove the skin and any fat. Have ready in 3 wide shallow bowls the flour, the eggs, and the bread crumbs. Dredge the chicken in the flour, shaking off the excess, dip it in the egg, letting the excess drip off, and coat it well with the bread crumbs, shaking off the excess. Arrange the chicken on a baking sheet lined with wax paper and chill it, uncovered, for 30 minutes. *The chicken may be prepared up to this point 1 day in advance and kept uncovered and chilled.*

In a large deep skillet heat 1 inch of the oil to 360° F. and in it fry the chicken in batches without crowding, turning it, for 5 minutes, or until it is golden brown, transferring it as it is fried to paper towels to drain. Arrange the chicken on a rack in a shallow pan and bake it in the middle of a preheated 350° F. oven for 15 minutes for the breast pieces and 20 minutes for the leg

pieces. Arrange the chicken on heated platters, garnish it with the thyme, and serve it with the chutney. Serves 8.

PHOTO ON PAGE 61

Balsamic Vinegar Chicken with Wild Mushrooms

1 ounce (about 1 cup) dried *porcini*
  (available at specialty foods shops)
6 chicken thighs (about 1½ pounds), rinsed
  and patted dry
all-purpose flour for dredging
two ¼-inch-thick slices of slab bacon (about
  ¼ pound), cut crosswise into ⅓-inch pieces
1 tablespoon olive oil
3 garlic cloves, minced
½ cup fruity red wine, such as Beaujolais
½ cup beef broth
¼ cup balsamic vinegar (available at specialty
  foods shops and many supermarkets)
1 teaspoon arrowroot dissolved in 2 teaspoons
  cold water
¾ cup drained and chopped canned tomatoes
minced fresh flat-leafed parsley leaves
  for garnish

In a small bowl let the *porcini* soak in 1 cup boiling water for 10 minutes, or until they are soft, and drain them well, reserving the liquid. Season the chicken with pepper and dredge it in the flour, shaking off the excess. In a large heavy skillet cook the bacon over moderate heat, stirring, until it is golden and crisp, transfer it with a slotted spoon to paper towels, and let it drain. Add to the skillet the chicken, skin side down, and cook it, turning it occasionally, for 20 minutes, or until it is golden and crisp. Transfer the chicken with a slotted spoon to a plate, season it with salt, and discard the fat in the skillet. Add the oil to the skillet and in it cook the garlic over low heat, stirring, for 1 minute. Add the reserved *porcini* liquid, the wine, the broth, and 3 tablespoons of the vinegar and boil the mixture for 4 minutes. Add the arrowroot mixture in a stream, stirring, stir in the tomatoes, and add the chicken, turning it to coat it with the sauce. Simmer the mixture, covered, for 10 minutes, stir in the *porcini* and the bacon, and simmer the mixture, covered, for 10 minutes. Stir in the remaining 1 tablespoon vinegar with salt and pepper to taste and sprinkle the mixture with the parsley. Serves 6.

Crisp Coconut Chicken with Roasted Red Bell Pepper Sauce

1 red bell pepper, roasted (page 135)
  and chopped
½ teaspoon fresh lemon juice
¼ teaspoon sugar
cayenne to taste
1 tablespoon olive oil
1 garlic clove, minced and mashed to a paste
  with ¼ teaspoon salt
⅛ teaspoon ground ginger
1 tablespoon Dijon-style mustard
1 whole skinless boneless large chicken breast
  (about 10 ounces), halved
all-purpose flour seasoned with salt and black
  pepper for dredging the chicken
an egg wash made by beating 1 large egg with
  1 teaspoon water
1 cup sweetened flaked coconut
2 tablespoons unsalted butter
2 tablespoons dry Sherry

In a blender purée the bell pepper with the lemon juice, the sugar, the cayenne, the oil, and salt and black pepper to taste until the sauce is smooth. In a small bowl whisk together the garlic paste, the ginger, and the mustard and spread the mixture onto both sides of the chicken. In separate bowls have ready the seasoned flour, the egg wash, and the coconut. Dredge the chicken in the flour, shaking off the excess, dip it in the egg wash, letting the excess drip off, and coat it thoroughly with the coconut, pressing the coconut to make it adhere.

In a large ovenproof skillet heat the butter over moderately high heat until the foam subsides and in it sauté the chicken for 2 minutes on each side, or until the coconut is golden. Add the Sherry, transfer the skillet to a preheated 375° F. oven, and bake the chicken for 10 to 12 minutes, or until it is just cooked through. Divide the sauce between 2 large plates and arrange the chicken on it. Serves 2.

Grilled Chicken with Corn and Sun-Dried Tomato Salsa

½ cup cooked corn kernels (from about 1 ear)
2 tablespoons minced drained sun-dried
  tomatoes packed in oil
2 tablespoons thinly sliced scallion
2 tablespoons finely chopped red onion
1 garlic clove, minced and mashed to a paste
  with ¼ teaspoon salt
1 teaspoon minced seeded fresh *jalapeño*, or
  to taste (wear rubber gloves)
1 tablespoon fresh lime juice
1½ teaspoons white-wine vinegar
2 tablespoons olive oil plus additional for
  brushing the chicken
2 to 3 tablespoons finely chopped fresh
  coriander, or to taste
1 boneless whole chicken breast
  (about 1 pound), halved

In a bowl stir together the corn, the tomatoes, the scallion, the red onion, the garlic paste, the *jalapeño*, the lime juice, the vinegar, 2 tablespoons of the oil, the coriander, and salt and pepper to taste. Brush the chicken with the additional oil, season it with salt and black pepper, and grill it on a rack set 5 to 6 inches over glowing coals or in a hot well-seasoned ridged grill pan, covered, over moderately high heat, for 4 to 5 minutes on each side, or until it is cooked through. Divide the chicken and the *salsa* between 2 plates. Serves 2.

Pennsylvania Dutch–Style Chicken Potpie

a 3½-pound chicken
2 cups all-purpose flour
1 tablespoon cold vegetable shortening
1 teaspoon salt
1 large egg, beaten lightly
2 carrots, sliced thin
1 rib of celery, sliced thin
1 onion, minced
1 pound boiling potatoes (about 4)
⅓ cup finely chopped fresh parsley leaves

Season the cavity of the chicken with salt and pepper, put the chicken in a kettle just large enough to hold it, and add 14 cups water. Bring the water to a boil, simmer the chicken, covered, skimming the froth, for 45 minutes, or until it is tender, and transfer it to a large bowl. When the chicken is cool enough to handle, discard the skin and bones, cut the meat into bite-size pieces, and chill it, covered. Measure the stock remaining in the kettle and boil it until it is reduced to about 10 cups. Strain the stock through a sieve into a bowl, let it cool, uncovered, and chill it, covered, overnight.

In a bowl blend together the flour, the shortening,

and the salt. In a small bowl whisk together the egg and ⅔ cup cold water, add the mixture to the flour mixture, and stir the mixture until it forms a soft but not sticky dough. Halve the dough, keeping half of it under an inverted bowl, roll out the other half on a heavily floured surface into a 12- by 10-inch rectangle, and cut it with a pastry wheel into 2-inch squares. Transfer the squares to a lightly floured baking sheet and roll and cut out the remaining dough in the same manner.

Discard the fat from the stock, return the stock to the kettle, and bring it to a boil with the chicken, the carrots, the celery, the onion, the potatoes, peeled and sliced thin, and salt and pepper to taste. Add the noodle squares, a few at a time, stirring gently, simmer the mixture, covered, for 20 to 30 minutes, or until the vegetables and noodles are tender, and stir in the parsley. Serves 6 to 8.

Sesame Chicken and Stir-Fried Vegetables

1 whole boneless chicken breast, halved
2 teaspoons sesame seeds
1 tablespoon vegetable oil plus additional for
　brushing the grill pan
¼ pound fresh *shiitake* or white mushrooms,
　stems discarded and the caps sliced thin
½ pound cabbage, sliced thin (about 2 cups)
1 small red bell pepper, cut into julienne strips
2 teaspoons white-wine vinegar
2 teaspoons soy sauce
1 teaspoon Oriental sesame oil
½ teaspoon minced peeled fresh gingerroot
¼ teaspoon sugar

Coat the chicken with the sesame seeds and season it with salt and black pepper. Heat a ridged grill pan or heavy skillet over moderately high heat until it is hot, brush it with the additional vegetable oil, and in it sauté the chicken for 7 to 9 minutes on each side, or until it is just springy to the touch.

While the chicken is cooking, in a large skillet heat the remaining 1 tablespoon vegetable oil over moderately high heat until it is hot but not smoking and in it stir-fry the mushrooms for 3 minutes. Add the cabbage and the bell pepper and stir-fry the vegetables for 5 minutes, or until they are crisp-tender. In a small bowl combine well the vinegar, the soy sauce, the sesame oil, the gingerroot, and the sugar, add the mixture to the vegetables with salt and black pepper to taste, and stir-fry the

mixture over moderately high heat for 1 minute. Divide the vegetable mixture between 2 heated plates, cut the chicken against the grain into ¼-inch-thick slices, and arrange it on top of the vegetables. Serves 2.

Teriyaki-Style Chicken

2½ tablespoons soy sauce
½ teaspoon minced peeled fresh gingerroot
5 teaspoons honey
1 tablespoon medium-dry Sherry
1 tablespoon white-wine vinegar
1 garlic clove, minced and mashed to a paste
　with ½ teaspoon salt
1 boneless whole chicken breast (about
　1 pound) with the skin on, halved

In a bowl whisk together the soy sauce, the gingerroot, the honey, the Sherry, the vinegar, and the garlic paste. Flatten the chicken breast halves between sheets of plastic wrap until they are about ½ inch thick and let them marinate in the soy mixture, turning them once, for 20 minutes. Transfer the chicken, reserving the marinade in a small saucepan, skin sides down, to the oiled rack of a broiler pan and broil it under a preheated broiler about 6 inches from the heat for 5 minutes. While the chicken is cooking boil the reserved marinade until it is reduced by half. Brush the chicken with some of the marinade, turn it, and brush it with the remaining marinade. Broil the chicken for 6 to 8 minutes more, or until it is just cooked through, transfer it to a cutting board, and cut it on the diagonal into ½-inch-thick slices. Serves 2.

Port-Glazed Chicken Livers and Onions

2 onions, sliced
2 tablespoons unsalted butter
¾ pound chicken livers, halved and trimmed
2 tablespoons all-purpose flour
1 tablespoon olive oil
¼ cup Tawny Port
¼ cup minced fresh parsley leaves
2 tablespoons hazelnuts, toasted and skinned
   (procedure follows) and chopped

In a heavy skillet sauté the onions in the butter over moderately high heat, stirring, until they are golden brown and transfer them to a plate. In a bowl toss the chicken livers, patted dry, with the flour and salt and pepper to taste, heat the oil in the skillet over moderately high heat until it is hot but not smoking, and in it sauté the chicken livers, turning them, for 3 minutes, or until they are just cooked through but still pink within. Add the onions, the Port, and 3 tablespoons water and cook the mixture over moderate heat, stirring, for 2 minutes, or until the liquid is thickened. Stir in 2 tablespoons of the parsley and salt and pepper to taste, divide the mixture between 2 heated plates, and top each serving with half the remaining parsley and half the hazelnuts. Serves 2.

To Toast and Skin Hazelnuts

Toast the hazelnuts in one layer in a baking pan in a preheated 350° F. oven for 10 to 15 minutes, or until they are colored lightly and the skins blister. Wrap the nuts in a kitchen towel and let them steam for 1 minute. Rub the nuts in the towel to remove the skins and let them cool.

Braised Chicken Thighs with Lemons and Olives

1 tablespoon olive oil
4 chicken thighs (about 1½ pounds),
   rinsed
1 onion, chopped
2 garlic cloves, minced
¾ teaspoon ground cumin
¼ teaspoon cinnamon
¼ cup fresh lemon juice
½ cup chicken broth
8 large pimiento-stuffed
   green olives
4 lemon slices
2 teaspoons cornstarch dissolved in
   1 tablespoon cold water

In a heavy flameproof casserole heat the oil over moderately high heat until it is hot but not smoking and in it brown the chicken, patted dry and seasoned with salt and pepper, transferring it as it is browned with a slotted spoon to a plate. Add the onion to the casserole and cook it over moderately low heat, stirring, until it is softened. Add the garlic, the cumin, and the cinnamon and cook the mixture, stirring, for 1 minute. Return the chicken to the casserole and add the lemon juice, the broth, the olives, and the lemon slices. Bring the liquid to a boil and braise the chicken, covered, in a preheated 350° F. oven for 20 minutes, or until it is tender. Remove the lid and bring the chicken mixture to a boil on top of the stove. Stir the cornstarch mixture, add it to the chicken mixture, stirring, and simmer the mixture for 1 minute. Serves 2.

Parmesan Mustard Chicken Wings

1 stick (½ cup) unsalted butter,
   melted
2 tablespoons Dijon-style mustard
⅛ teaspoon cayenne
1 cup dry bread crumbs
½ cup freshly grated Parmesan
1 teaspoon ground cumin
20 chicken wings, wing tips cut off and
   discarded and the wings halved at the joint

In a shallow dish whisk together the butter, the mustard, and the cayenne. In another shallow dish combine well the bread crumbs, the Parmesan, the cumin, and salt and black pepper to taste. Dip the chicken wings, a few at a time, in the butter mixture, letting the excess drip off, coat them with the crumb mixture, and arrange them without touching in a greased shallow baking pan. Bake the chicken wings in the lower third of a preheated 425° F. oven for 30 minutes. (If extra-crisp chicken wings are desired, turn the wings after 20 minutes.) Serves 6.

PHOTO ON PAGE 15

ASSORTED FOWL

Roasted Cornish Hen with Mustard Seed Topping

a 1½-pound Cornish hen
1½ tablespoons olive oil
1 tablespoon Dijon-style mustard
2 tablespoons mustard seeds
½ teaspoon dried rosemary, crumbled
1 garlic clove, minced
¼ cup dry white wine
¼ cup chicken broth

Remove the backbone from the hen with poultry shears or a sharp knife, put the hen, skin side up, on a work surface, and press down the breastbone to flatten the hen. In an ovenproof skillet roast the hen, skin side up, in a preheated 450° F. oven for 10 minutes. While the hen is roasting, in a small bowl whisk together the oil, the mustard, the mustard seeds, the rosemary, the garlic, and salt and pepper to taste. Remove the hen from the oven, spread the mustard mixture over the skin, and roast the hen for 15 minutes. Transfer the hen to a preheated broiler and broil it about 4 inches from the heat for 4 to 5 minutes, or until the skin is crisp. (Do not let the mustard seeds burn.) Transfer the hen to a platter and keep it warm. To the skillet add the wine and boil the mixture over high heat until it is reduced by half. Add the broth, boil the mixture for 1 minute, scraping up any brown bits, and add any juices that have accumulated on the platter. Strain the sauce through a fine sieve onto 2 plates, cut the hen in half with a sharp knife, and arrange each half on top of the sauce. Serves 2.

Sweet-and-Spicy Cornish Hens

½ cup apple jelly
1½ tablespoons fresh lemon juice
1½ tablespoons fresh lime juice
1 tablespoon Worcestershire sauce
1 teaspoon minced pickled *jalapeño* chili
  (wear rubber gloves)
two 1¼- to 1½-pound Cornish hens, halved
  and backbones discarded

In a saucepan combine the jelly, the lemon and lime juices, the Worcestershire sauce, and the *jalapeño* and heat the mixture over moderate heat, stirring, until the jelly is just melted. Pat the Cornish hens dry, sprinkle them with salt and black pepper, and arrange the halves, skin sides down, on a rack in a foil-lined roasting pan. Brush the halves with some of the sauce and roast them in the lower third of a preheated 500° F. oven for 15 minutes. Baste the halves with the sauce, turn them, and roast them, basting them after 7 minutes, for 15 minutes, or until the juices run clear when a thigh is pricked with a skewer. Serves 2.

Lauren Jarrett

Roast Quail with Cranberry Madeira Sauce

a 12-ounce bag fresh or thawed frozen
    cranberries (about 3¼ cups)
⅔ cup firmly packed dark brown sugar
½ cup apple juice
½ cup cranberry juice
⅓ cup Sercial Madeira
¼ teaspoon freshly grated nutmeg
¼ teaspoon ground ginger
¼ teaspoon dry mustard
1 cup chicken broth
½ stick (¼ cup) unsalted butter
the zest of 1 orange, removed with a
    vegetable peeler
twelve 5- to 6-ounce quail,* rinsed, patted dry,
    and the legs tied together with kitchen string
12 slices of homemade-type white bread, each
    slice toasted and cut into a decorative shape

*available by mail from
    Wylie Hill Farm,
    P.O. Box 35,
    Craftsbury Common, VT 05827
    tel. (802) 586-2887,
    or at specialty butcher shops

In a saucepan combine the cranberries, the brown sugar, the apple juice, the cranberry juice, the Madeira, the nutmeg, the ginger, the mustard, ½ cup of the broth, 2 tablespoons of the butter, the zest, and salt and pepper to taste. Bring the liquid to a boil and simmer the mixture, stirring occasionally, for 25 minutes, or until it is thickened and the berries have burst. Strain the glaze through a sieve into a bowl, pressing hard on the solids and discarding them. *The glaze may be made 1 day in advance, kept covered and chilled, and reheated.*

Transfer ½ cup of the glaze to a small bowl and reserve it. In a large ovenproof skillet heat the remaining 2 tablespoons butter over moderately high heat until the foam subsides, in it brown the quail, turning them, for 4 minutes, and arrange the quail breast sides up. Baste the quail generously with some of the remaining glaze and roast them in the top third of a preheated 450° F. oven for 10 minutes. Reduce the heat to 400° F. and roast the quail, basting them with some of the remaining glaze every 10 minutes, for 40 minutes more, or until the leg meat is no longer pink. Transfer the quail to a plate, discard the string, and pour off the fat in the skillet.

Deglaze the skillet with the remaining ½ cup broth over moderately high heat, scraping up the brown bits, stir in the reserved ½ cup glaze, and boil the mixture, whisking, until it is thickened. Strain the sauce through a fine sieve into a heated sauceboat and season it with salt and pepper. Arrange 2 of the toasts on each of 6 dinner plates, top each toast with 1 of the quail, and serve the sauce with the quail. Serves 6.

PHOTO ON PAGE 75

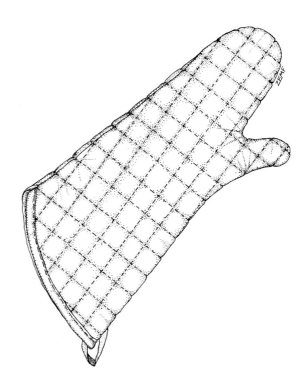

*Roast Turkey with Corn Bread and Kale Stuffing
and Paprika Pan Gravy*

For the stuffing
2 large onions, chopped (about 4 cups)
4 ribs of celery, chopped
1 stick (½ cup) unsalted butter
1 large bunch of kale, stems discarded and
    the leaves rinsed well and chopped
    (about 10 cups)

about 4 cups corn bread for stuffing (recipe
    follows) or packaged corn bread stuffing
1 tablespoon dried sage, crumbled

a 12- to 14-pound turkey, the neck and giblets
    (excluding the liver) reserved for making
    turkey giblet stock
1½ sticks (¾ cup) unsalted butter,
    softened
⅔ cup turkey giblet stock (page 111)
    or chicken broth
For the gravy
⅓ cup all-purpose flour
1 teaspoon paprika, or to taste
4 cups turkey giblet stock (page 111) or
    chicken broth

fresh kale leaves for garnish
paprika peppers (available at specialty
    produce markets) or drained bottled cherry
    peppers for garnish

Make the stuffing: In a large skillet cook the onions
and the celery with salt and pepper to taste in the butter
over moderately low heat, stirring, until the vegetables
are softened. Add the kale in batches, stirring until each
batch is wilted, and cook the mixture until the kale is
bright green. In a bowl combine the mixture with the
corn bread, stir in the sage and salt and pepper to taste,
and toss the stuffing gently until it is combined well. Let
the stuffing cool. *The stuffing may be made 1 day in
advance and kept covered and chilled. (To prevent bac-
terial growth, do not stuff the turkey in advance.)*

Rinse the turkey inside and out, pat it dry, and season
it with salt and pepper. Pack the neck cavity loosely
with some of the stuffing, fold the neck skin under the
body, and fasten it with a skewer. Pack the body cavity
loosely with some of the remaining stuffing and tie the
drumsticks together with kitchen string. Transfer the remaining stuffing to a buttered baking dish and reserve
it, covered and chilled. Spread the turkey with ½ stick of
the butter and season it with salt and pepper.

Roast the turkey on a rack in a flameproof roasting
pan in a preheated 425° F. oven for 30 minutes. In a
saucepan melt the remaining 1 stick butter and let it
cool. Reduce the oven temperature to 325° F., baste the
turkey with the pan juices, and drape it with a piece of
cheesecloth, soaked in the melted butter. Roast the turkey, lifting the cheesecloth and basting the turkey every

20 minutes, for 2½ to 3 hours more, or until a meat thermometer inserted in the fleshy part of a thigh registers
180° F. and the juices run clear when the thigh is pierced
with a skewer. During the last hour of roasting bake the
reserved stuffing, drizzled with the stock and ½ cup of
the pan juices and covered loosely.

Discard the cheesecloth and the trussing string and
transfer the turkey to a heated platter, reserving the
juices in the roasting pan. Let it stand, covered loosely
with foil, for 25 minutes.

Make the gravy: Skim all but ⅓ cup of the fat from the
roasting pan, add the flour to the pan, and cook the *roux*
over moderate heat, whisking, for 3 minutes. Add the
paprika and cook the mixture for 30 seconds. Add the
stock in a stream, whisking, bring the mixture to a boil,
whisking, and add salt and pepper to taste. Simmer the
gravy, stirring occasionally, for 10 minutes and transfer
it to a heated sauceboat.

Garnish the turkey with the kale leaves and the paprika peppers. Serves 8 with leftovers.

PHOTO ON PAGE 72

Corn Bread for Stuffing

1 cup all-purpose flour
1½ cups yellow cornmeal
1 tablespoon double-acting baking powder
1 teaspoon salt
1 cup milk
1 large egg
3 tablespoons unsalted butter, melted and
    cooled

In a bowl stir together the flour, the cornmeal, the
baking powder, and the salt. In a small bowl whisk together the milk, the egg, and the butter, and stir the mixture into the cornmeal mixture, stirring until the batter is
just combined. Pour the batter into a greased 8-inch-
square baking pan and bake the corn bread in the middle
of a preheated 425° F. oven for 20 to 25 minutes, or until
the top is pale golden and a tester comes out clean. Let
the corn bread cool in the pan for 5 minutes, invert it
onto a rack, and let it cool completely. Crumble the corn
bread coarse into 2 shallow baking pans and toast it in
the middle of a preheated 325° F. oven, stirring occasionally, for 30 to 35 minutes, or until it is dried and
deep golden. Makes about 4 cups.

Thai-Style Turkey Burgers with Pickled Cucumbers

For the pickled cucumbers
⅓ cup distilled white vinegar
1½ tablespoons firmly packed light
  brown sugar
¾ teaspoon salt
½ teaspoon dried hot red pepper flakes
1 small seedless cucumber, sliced very thin

For the burgers
1 large garlic clove
1 teaspoon finely chopped peeled
  fresh gingerroot
⅓ cup chopped fresh coriander
⅓ cup chopped fresh mint leaves
¼ cup chopped fresh basil leaves
2 tablespoons fresh lime juice
2 teaspoons sugar
1 flat anchovy fillet
1½ pounds ground turkey
3 tablespoons fresh bread crumbs
¼ teaspoon cayenne, or to taste

4 sesame hamburger buns or onion rolls, split
  and toasted

Make the pickled cucumbers: In a small bowl stir together the vinegar, the brown sugar, the salt, and the red pepper flakes until the sugar and the salt are dissolved, add the cucumber, stirring to coat it well with the marinade, and let the mixture stand for 30 minutes.

Make the burgers: Into a food processor with the motor on, drop the garlic and the gingerroot, add the coriander, the mint, the basil, the lime juice, the sugar, and the anchovy, and blend the mixture well. In a bowl combine well the turkey, the herb mixture, the bread crumbs, and the cayenne and form the mixture into four 1-inch-thick patties. Season the burgers with salt and black pepper and grill them on an oiled rack set 5 to 6 inches over glowing coals for 8 to 9 minutes on each side, or until they are just cooked through.

Transfer the burgers to the buns and top them with the pickled cucumbers, drained. Serves 4.

Turkey and Sweet Potato Croquettes
with Cranberry Apple Salsa

For the croquettes
⅓ cup chopped onion
2 tablespoons unsalted butter
¼ cup all-purpose flour plus ½ cup additional
  for dredging the croquettes
¼ cup milk
¼ cup chicken broth
2 cups finely chopped cooked turkey
½ cup mashed sweet potatoes
⅛ teaspoon cayenne
an egg wash made by beating lightly 2 large
  eggs with 1 tablespoon water
1½ cups fine fresh bread crumbs

For the salsa
½ cup finely chopped picked-over
  fresh cranberries
¾ cup finely chopped Granny Smith apple
  tossed with 1 tablespoon lemon juice
1 tablespoon honey
2 scallions, chopped fine
3 tablespoons golden raisins, chopped fine
2 fresh *jalapeño* or *serrano* chilies, or to taste,
  seeded and minced (wear rubber gloves)

vegetable oil for deep-frying the croquettes

Make the croquettes: In a small saucepan cook the onion in the butter over moderately low heat, stirring, for 5 minutes, stir in ¼ cup of the flour, and cook the *roux* mixture over low heat, stirring, for 3 minutes. Stir in the milk and the broth, cook the mixture, stirring, until it forms a paste, and cook the paste, stirring, for 3 minutes. Remove the pan from the heat, stir in the turkey, the sweet potatoes, the cayenne, and salt and black pepper to taste, and combine the mixture well. Chill the turkey mixture, covered, for 2 hours, or until it is firm, and roll level tablespoons of it into balls. Dredge the balls in the additional ½ cup flour, shaking off the excess, coat them thoroughly with the egg wash, letting the excess drip off, and dredge them in the bread crumbs. Transfer them to wax paper as they are coated. *The croquettes may be made up to this point 1 month in advance and kept wrapped well and frozen. Thaw the croquettes for 1 hour.* If serving the croquettes immediately, let them dry at room temperature for 1 hour.

Make the *salsa* while the croquettes are thawing or drying: In a small bowl combine well the cranberries, the apple, the honey, the scallions, the raisins, the chilies, and salt to taste and chill the *salsa*, covered, for 1 hour.

In a large saucepan heat 2 inches of the oil until a deep-fat thermometer registers 365° F., in it fry the croquettes in batches for 1 to 1½ minutes, or until they are golden brown, and transfer them with a slotted spoon to paper towels to drain. Serve the croquettes with the *salsa*. Makes about 24 croquettes.

Turkey Chili

2 cups chopped onion
4 garlic cloves, chopped fine
¼ cup olive oil
two 35-ounce cans plum tomatoes including
 the juice
a 15-ounce can tomato purée
¼ cup chili powder
1½ tablespoons ground cumin
1 tablespoon dried hot red pepper flakes
1 teaspoon dried orégano
½ teaspoon cinnamon
1 tablespoon salt
½ teaspoon black pepper
the drumsticks, legs, and wings from a
 cooked turkey
2 green bell peppers, chopped coarse
two 19-ounce cans kidney beans, rinsed and
 drained well
sour cream as an accompaniment if desired
coarsely grated Cheddar as an accompaniment
 if desired

In a large kettle cook the onion and the garlic in the oil over moderate heat, stirring, until they are golden, add the tomatoes with the juice, the tomato purée, 2 cups water, the chili powder, the cumin, the red pepper flakes, the orégano, the cinnamon, the salt, and the black pepper, and combine the mixture well. Add the turkey parts and simmer the chili, uncovered, stirring occasionally, for 2 hours. Transfer the turkey parts with a slotted spoon to a plate and let them cool until they can be handled. Stir the bell peppers and the beans into the chili, add the turkey meat, discarding the skin and bones, and simmer the chili, stirring occasionally, for 40 minutes more, or until the bell peppers are tender. *The chili may be made in advance, cooled completely, uncovered, and kept covered and chilled for 2 days or covered and frozen for 2 months.* Serve the chili topped with a dollop of the sour cream and sprinkled with the Cheddar. Makes about 12 cups, serving 8.

Sautéed Turkey Cutlets with Cranberry Orange Glaze

1 large egg white
½ teaspoon salt
1 cup fine dry bread crumbs seasoned
 with pepper
four ¼-inch-thick turkey cutlets (about
 ¾ pound), pounded to ⅛-inch thickness
 between sheets of plastic wrap
1 cup cranberry juice
2 tablespoons lightly packed brown sugar
2 tablespoons cider vinegar
¼ teaspoon freshly grated orange zest
vegetable oil for frying

In a bowl whisk the egg white and the salt until the mixture is frothy and have the bread crumbs ready in a shallow dish. Dip the cutlets in the egg white, letting the excess drip off, coat them with the bread crumbs, patting the crumbs to make them adhere, and transfer the cutlets to a rack set on a baking sheet. Chill the cutlets, uncovered, for 15 minutes.

While the cutlets are chilling, in a small saucepan boil the cranberry juice until it is reduced to about ½ cup, add the brown sugar and the vinegar, and boil the mixture until it is syrupy and reduced to about 3 tablespoons. Stir in the zest and keep the glaze warm.

In a large heavy skillet heat ¼ inch of the oil over moderately high heat until it is hot but not smoking and in it fry the cutlets in 2 batches, turning them once, for 1½ minutes. Transfer the cutlets to paper towels, let them drain, and divide them between plates. Drizzle the cutlets with the glaze. Serves 2.

Turkey Hash

1 onion, chopped fine
1 red bell pepper, chopped fine
1 green bell pepper, chopped fine
¾ stick (6 tablespoons) unsalted butter
½ cup all-purpose flour
3 cups chicken broth
¾ cup medium-dry Sherry
½ cup half-and-half
5 cups diced cooked turkey
1½ cups diced cooked potato
1 tablespoon Worcestershire sauce
1 tablespoon fresh lemon juice, or to taste
Tabasco to taste
½ cup minced fresh parsley leaves

In a large heavy skillet cook the onion and the bell peppers in the butter over moderately low heat, stirring, until they are softened, add the flour, and cook the *roux* mixture, stirring, for 3 minutes. Add the broth, the Sherry, and the half-and-half, whisking, bring the mixture to a boil, whisking, and stir in the turkey, the potato, the Worcestershire sauce, the lemon juice, the Tabasco, and salt and black pepper to taste. Simmer the mixture, stirring occasionally, for 10 minutes, thinning the mixture with water if necessary. *The hash may be prepared up to this point 2 days in advance and kept covered and chilled. Reheat the hash, thinning the mixture with water if necessary.* Stir in the parsley and transfer the hash to a chafing dish. Serves 8.

PHOTO ON PAGE 39

Creamy Rosemary Turkey and Vegetable Potpie with Herbed Dumplings

For the stew turkey mixture
2 tablespoons unsalted butter
1 onion, minced
4 carrots, cut into 2-inch julienne strips
    (about 2 cups)
2 ribs of celery, cut into 2-inch julienne strips
    (about 1 cup)
⅓ cup dry white wine
2 tablespoons all-purpose flour
3 cups chicken broth
¾ cup heavy cream
2 large egg yolks
4 cups bite-size pieces cooked turkey

¾ teaspoon finely chopped fresh rosemary
    or ½ teaspoon dried, crumbled
For the dumpling batter
1 cup all-purpose flour
1½ teaspoons double-acting baking powder
½ teaspoon salt
½ teaspoon dried rosemary, crumbled
1 tablespoon minced fresh parsley leaves
½ cup milk

Make the turkey mixture: In a kettle melt the butter over moderately low heat and in it cook the onion, the carrots, and the celery, stirring occasionally, until the vegetables are softened. Add the wine and cook the mixture for 3 minutes. Add the flour and cook the *roux*, stirring, for 3 minutes. Add the broth in a stream and bring the sauce to a boil, whisking. In a bowl whisk together the cream and the yolks, whisk about ½ cup of the sauce into the bowl to temper the cream mixture, and add the cream mixture, in a stream, to the sauce. Cook the mixture over moderately low heat, whisking, until it is thickened (do not let it boil) and stir in the turkey, the rosemary, and salt and pepper to taste.

Make the dumpling batter: In a bowl whisk together the flour, the baking powder, the salt, the rosemary, the parsley, and pepper to taste, add the milk, and stir the batter until it is just combined.

Drop the batter by spoonfuls into 6 or 8 mounds onto the simmering turkey mixture (do not let the liquid boil), simmer the dumplings, uncovered, for 10 minutes, and simmer them, covered, for 10 minutes more. Serves 6 to 8.

Hot Browns
(Open-Faced Turkey Sandwiches with Mornay Sauce)

1½ teaspoons finely chopped onion
1½ tablespoons unsalted butter
2 tablespoons all-purpose flour
1½ cups milk
a pinch of cayenne
1 tablespoon dry Sherry
¾ cup grated extra-sharp Cheddar
4 slices of homemade-type white bread,
    toasted lightly
½ pound cooked turkey breast, sliced thin
4 thin slices of tomato
8 slices of cooked bacon
1 tablespoon freshly grated Parmesan

In a small saucepan cook the onion in the butter over moderately low heat, stirring, until it is softened, stir in the flour, and cook the *roux*, stirring, for 3 minutes. Remove the pan from the heat and add the milk, scalded, in a stream, whisking vigorously until the mixture is thick and smooth. Add the cayenne and salt and pepper to taste and simmer the sauce, stirring occasionally, for 10 to 15 minutes, or until it is thickened to the desired consistency. Strain the sauce through a fine sieve into a bowl and add the Sherry and the Cheddar, stirring until the mixture is smooth.

Arrange the toasts in a baking pan and divide the turkey among them. Top each sandwich with a tomato slice and 2 slices of the bacon and spoon the sauce evenly over the sandwiches. Sprinkle the sandwiches with the Parmesan and broil them under a preheated broiler about 4 inches from the heat for 5 to 7 minutes, or until the tops are brown and bubbly. Serves 4.

Turkey Tetrazzini

10 ounces mushrooms, sliced thin
  (about 4 cups)
5 tablespoons unsalted butter
¼ cup all-purpose flour
1¾ cups milk
2 cups chicken broth
¼ cup dry white wine

10 ounces spaghetti
3 cups coarsely chopped cooked turkey,
  including cooked giblets if desired
1 cup cooked peas
⅔ cup freshly grated Parmesan
⅓ cup fine fresh bread crumbs

In a large heavy saucepan cook the mushrooms in ¼ cup of the butter over moderate heat, stirring, until most of the liquid they give off has evaporated, stir in the flour, and cook the mixture over low heat, stirring, for 3 minutes. Add in a stream the milk, the broth, and the wine, stirring, bring the mixture to a boil, stirring, and simmer the sauce for 5 minutes. In a kettle of boiling salted water cook the spaghetti until it is *al dente* and drain it well.

In a large bowl combine well the spaghetti, the mushroom sauce, the turkey, the peas, and salt and pepper to taste, stir in ⅓ cup of the Parmesan, and transfer the mixture to a buttered shallow 3-quart casserole. In a small bowl combine well the remaining ⅓ cup Parmesan, the bread crumbs, and salt and pepper to taste, sprinkle the mixture evenly over the Tetrazzini, and dot the top with the remaining 1 tablespoon butter, cut into bits. *The Tetrazzini may be prepared up to this point 1 month in advance and kept frozen, covered.* Bake the Tetrazzini in the middle of a preheated 375° F. oven for 30 to 40 minutes, or until it is bubbling and the top is golden. Serves 4 to 6.

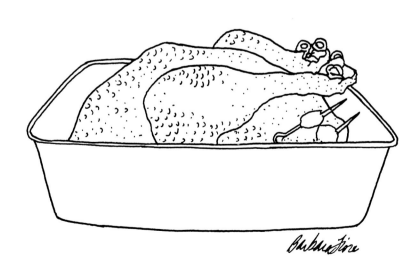

CHEESE, EGGS, AND BREAKFAST ITEMS

CHEESE

Cheddar and Black Bean Fritters

½ cup yellow cornmeal
¼ cup all-purpose flour
¼ teaspoon double-acting baking powder
¼ teaspoon cayenne
¼ teaspoon salt
½ teaspoon ground cumin
⅓ cup milk
1 large egg yolk
1 cup ¼-inch-diced extra-sharp Cheddar
    (about ¼ pound)
1 cup canned black beans, rinsed well in a
    sieve and patted dry between layers of
    paper towels
2 large egg whites
vegetable oil for frying the fritters
sour cream and tomato *salsa* (page 130) as
    accompaniments if desired

In a bowl whisk together well the cornmeal, the flour, the baking powder, the cayenne, the salt, and the cumin, whisk in the milk and the yolk, and stir in the Cheddar and the beans. In another bowl beat the whites until they hold soft peaks and fold them into the Cheddar mixture thoroughly. Heat ⅛ inch of the oil in a well-seasoned cast-iron or non-stick skillet over moderately high heat until it is hot but not smoking. Working in batches, drop heaping tablespoons of the batter into the skillet, spreading them slightly, fry the fritters for 1 minute on each side, or until they are golden brown, and let them drain on paper towels. Serve the fritters with the sour cream and the tomato *salsa*. Makes about 18 fritters.

Cheddar Grits and Bacon Roulade

1 egg sponge (recipe follows)
½ cup quick-cooking grits (not instant)
1 cup grated extra-sharp Cheddar
    (about ¼ pound)
10 slices (about ½ pound) of lean bacon,
    cooked until crisp, drained, and crumbled
¼ cup finely chopped white part of scallion
3 tablespoons unsalted butter, melted

Prepare the egg sponge and while it is baking, in a saucepan bring 2 cups water to a boil and add the grits, a little at a time. Bring the mixture to a boil and simmer the grits, stirring occasionally, for 5 minutes. Add ¾ cup of the Cheddar and salt and pepper to taste, cook the mixture over moderate heat, stirring, until the Cheddar is melted, and let it stand, covered, for 2 minutes.

Spread the warm grits mixture on the warm egg sponge, leaving a 1-inch border on the long sides, sprinkle the bacon and the scallion over the grits, and starting with a long side roll up the egg sponge jelly-roll fashion. With the aid of the kitchen towel and the wax paper transfer the *roulade*, seam side down, to a shallow baking dish, brush the top lightly with some of the butter, and sprinkle it with the remaining ¼ cup Cheddar. Bake the *roulade* in the upper third of a preheated 375° F. oven for 8 to 10 minutes, or until the Cheddar is melted, slice it, and drizzle the slices with the remaining butter. Serves 4 to 6.

Egg Sponge

3 tablespoons unsalted butter
6 tablespoons all-purpose flour
1¼ cups milk
4 large eggs, separated, the whites
    at room temperature

Line a buttered jelly-roll pan, 15½ by 10½ by 1 inches, with wax paper, butter the paper, and dust it with flour, knocking out the excess. In a saucepan melt the butter, add the flour, and cook the *roux* over moderately low heat, stirring, for 3 minutes. Add the milk in a stream, whisking, and simmer the mixture, whisking occasionally, for 5 minutes. Transfer the mixture to a large bowl and whisk in the yolks, 1 at a time, whisking well after each addition. In a bowl with an electric mixer beat the whites until they just hold stiff peaks, stir one third of them into the yolk mixture, and fold in the remaining whites gently but thoroughly. Spread the batter evenly in the prepared pan and bake it in the middle of a preheated 350° F. oven for 25 minutes, or until it is golden and firm to the touch. Cover the egg sponge with a sheet of buttered wax paper, buttered side down, and a kitchen towel, invert a baking sheet over the towel, and invert the egg sponge onto the baking sheet, removing the wax paper from the top carefully. Trim ¼ inch from the short sides of the egg sponge.

Chilaquiles
(Layered Corn Tortillas, Tomato Sauce, and Cheese)

vegetable oil for frying the tortillas
twelve 7-inch corn tortillas, cut into eighths
   and dried at room temperature for
   30 minutes, or until they are leathery
   and curled but not crisp
2½ cups Mexican-style tomato sauce
   (recipe follows)
½ cup chicken broth
2 fresh or pickled *jalapeño* chilies, or to taste,
   seeded and minced (wear rubber gloves)
2 cups grated Monterey Jack (about ½ pound)
⅓ cup sour cream

In a skillet heat ½ inch of the oil over moderately high heat until it is hot but not smoking, in it fry the tortillas in batches for 10 to 20 seconds, or until they are pale golden and almost crisp, and transfer them as they are fried with a slotted spatula to paper towels to drain. In a bowl stir together the tomato sauce, the broth, and the chilies. In a greased 1½-quart shallow baking dish layer the tortillas, the Monterey Jack, and the tomato sauce, beginning with a layer of the tortillas and ending with a layer of the Monterey Jack, and bake the *chilaquiles*, covered with foil, in the middle of a preheated 350° F. oven for 20 minutes. Thin the sour cream with 1 tablespoon water and drizzle the mixture decoratively over the *chilaquiles*. Serves 6.

Mexican-Style Tomato Sauce

a 35-ounce can plum tomatoes, drained
1 onion, chopped coarse
2 garlic cloves, chopped coarse
2 fresh or pickled *jalapeño* chilies, or to taste,
   seeded and minced (wear rubber gloves)
3 tablespoons vegetable oil

In a blender purée the tomatoes with the onion, the garlic, and the chilies. In a large skillet heat the oil over moderately high heat until it is hot but not smoking, add the tomato purée, and cook the mixture, stirring occasionally, for 5 minutes. Season the sauce with salt and black pepper. Makes about 2½ cups.

Croques-Monsieur
(Grilled Ham-and-Cheese Sandwiches)

1 cup finely grated Gruyère plus 2 tablespoons
   for sprinkling the sandwiches
2 tablespoons sour cream
¾ teaspoon Dijon-style mustard
¾ teaspoon kirsch
8 slices of homemade-type white bread
4 thin slices of cooked ham
½ stick (¼ cup) unsalted butter, softened

In a bowl stir together 1 cup of the Gruyère, the sour cream, the mustard, and the kirsch and spread 1 tablespoon of the mixture evenly over each bread slice. Arrange the ham on 4 of the bread slices and top it with the remaining bread slices, spread side down. Remove the crusts with a sharp knife and spread the tops of the sandwiches lightly with 2 tablespoons of the butter. Invert the sandwiches into a large skillet, spread the tops with the remaining 2 tablespoons butter, and grill the sandwiches over moderately high heat, turning them once, for 6 to 8 minutes, or until they are golden brown on both sides. Transfer the sandwiches with a metal spatula to a baking sheet, sprinkle them with the remaining 2 tablespoons Gruyère, and broil them under a preheated broiler about 4 inches from the heat for 2 to 3 minutes, or until the Gruyère is just melted. Serves 4.

Goat Cheese, Salami, and Tomato on Mini-Bagels

10 mini-bagels, halved horizontally and
   toasted lightly
6 ounces soft mild goat cheese
10 slices of hard salami, each quartered
   into triangles
60 slices of cherry tomato (about 20 tomatoes)
20 small basil sprigs

Spread the bagel halves with the goat cheese, top each half with 2 salami triangles, 3 slices of tomato, and a basil sprig, and sprinkle the toppings lightly with pepper. Makes 20 open-faced sandwiches.

PHOTO ON PAGE 82

Mozzarella in Carrozza
(Sautéed Breaded Mozzarella)

1 large egg
2 tablespoons milk
½ cup toasted fresh bread crumbs
eight ¼-inch-thick slices of Italian bread
1¾ teaspoons anchovy paste, or to taste
¼ pound whole-milk mozzarella cut into four
   ¼-inch-thick slices
2 tablespoons olive oil
1 tablespoon unsalted butter
1 tablespoon fresh lemon juice
1 plum tomato, seeded and minced
¼ teaspoon drained bottled green peppercorns
   (available at specialty foods shops and
   many supermarkets)
finely chopped fresh parsley leaves
   for garnish

In a bowl whisk together the egg and the milk and transfer the mixture to a shallow bowl. Put the bread crumbs in another shallow bowl. Spread the bread slices with 1½ teaspoons of the anchovy paste, put 1 slice of the mozzarella on each of 4 bread slices, and top the mozzarella with the remaining bread slices, forming sandwiches. Working with 1 sandwich at a time, dip the sandwiches into the egg mixture, letting the excess drip off, and coat them with the bread crumbs. In a large heavy skillet heat the oil and the butter over moderately high heat until the fat is hot but not smoking and in the fat sauté the sandwiches, turning them and gently flattening them with a spatula, for 6 minutes, or until the mozzarella is melted and the bread is golden. Divide the

sandwiches between 2 heated plates and keep them warm. To the skillet add the lemon juice, the tomato, the green peppercorns, the remaining ¼ teaspoon anchovy paste, and salt and black pepper to taste and cook the mixture over high heat, whisking, until it is heated through. Spoon the sauce over the sandwiches and sprinkle the sandwiches with the parsley. Serves 2 as a first course.

Smoked Mozzarella and Roasted Pepper with
Olive Dressing on Italian Bread

4 Kalamata or other brine-cured black olives,
   pitted
1 tablespoon fresh lemon juice
¼ cup olive oil
½ garlic clove, or to taste
⅛ teaspoon cayenne, or to taste
four 4-inch-lengths of Italian bread,
   halved horizontally
1 large yellow or red bell pepper, roasted
   (procedure on page 135) and quartered
½ pound smoked mozzarella, sliced thin
1 cup loosely packed fresh basil leaves

In a blender blend the olives, the lemon juice, the oil, the garlic, and the cayenne until the mixture is smooth and brush the cut sides of the bread with the olive dressing. Divide the roasted pepper, the mozzarella, and the basil among the bottom halves of the bread and cover the sandwiches with the top halves of the bread, pressing them firmly. Makes 4 sandwiches.

Three-Cheese Fondue with Tomato Onion Chutney

½ pound Gruyère, grated coarse
   (about 2½ cups)
½ pound Emmenthal, grated coarse
   (about 2½ cups)
½ pound Doux de Montagne, Havarti, or
   Vacherin Fribourgeois, grated coarse
   (about 2½ cups)
2 tablespoons cornstarch
1 garlic clove, halved
1 cup dry white wine
2 teaspoons fresh lemon juice
2 tablespoons Calvados
⅓ cup tomato onion chutney (recipe follows)

Accompaniments
soft breadsticks with fennel seeds (page 95)
roasted potatoes with garlic (page 192)
assorted cooked vegetables such as broccoli,
    cauliflower, carrots, and pearl onions
cooked *tortellini* or *tortelloni*

In a large bowl toss together well the cheeses and the cornstarch. Rub the inside of a heavy saucepan with the garlic, leaving it in the pan, add the wine, ¾ cup water, and the lemon juice, and boil the mixture for 1 minute. Stir in the cheese mixture gradually and bring the mixture to a simmer over moderate heat, stirring. Stir in the Calvados and simmer the mixture, stirring, for 2 minutes. Transfer the fondue to a fondue pot, swirl in the chutney, and set the fondue pot on its stand over a low flame. Serve the breadsticks, the potatoes, the vegetables, and the *tortellini* for dipping into the fondue. Stir the fondue often to keep it combined. Serves 6.

PHOTO ON PAGE 21

Tomato Onion Chutney

2½ cups chopped onion
1 teaspoon mustard seeds
3½ tablespoons unsalted butter
a 14-ounce can tomatoes, drained well
    in a colander
1 tablespoon red-wine vinegar
1 tablespoon sugar
⅛ teaspoon ground allspice
2 tablespoons minced fresh parsley leaves

In a heavy skillet cook the onion and the mustard seeds in the butter over moderate heat until the onion be-gins to turn golden. Add the tomatoes, the vinegar, the sugar, and the allspice, cook the mixture, stirring and breaking up the tomatoes with a wooden spoon, until the chutney is very thick, and add the parsley and salt and pepper to taste. *The chutney may be made 3 days in advance and kept covered and chilled.* Makes about 2 cups.

Welsh Rabbit with Tomato

2 tablespoons unsalted butter
3 tablespoons all-purpose flour
⅔ cup beer (not dark)
a 13½- to 14½-ounce can tomatoes, drained in
    a sieve, chopped, and drained again well
10 ounces extra-sharp Cheddar, grated coarse
½ teaspoon English-style dry mustard
1 teaspoon Worcestershire sauce
¼ teaspoon Tabasco, or to taste
eighteen 1-inch slices of Italian bread
    or 12 English muffin halves, toasted
flat-leafed parsley sprigs for garnish
bacon as an accompaniment if desired

In a saucepan combine the butter and the flour and cook the *roux* over low heat, stirring, for 3 minutes. Whisk in the beer and the tomatoes and boil the mixture, whisking, for 3 minutes. Reduce the heat to moderately low, stir in the Cheddar, the mustard, the Worcestershire sauce, and the Tabasco, and cook the mixture, stirring, until it is hot (but do not let it boil). Arrange 3 of the toasts or 2 of the muffin halves on each of 6 plates and spoon the Cheddar mixture on top. Garnish the Welsh rabbit with the parsley and serve it with the bacon. Serves 6.

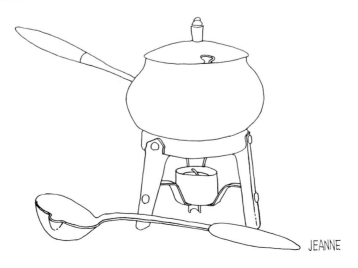

JEANNE

EGGS

Baked Mashed Potato and Vegetable Omelet

1 red bell pepper, chopped fine
1 green bell pepper, chopped fine
1 cup finely chopped onion
1½ cups sliced mushrooms
4 tablespoons olive oil
8 large eggs
3 cups mashed cooked russet (baking)
   potatoes (about 2 pounds)
½ cup freshly grated Parmesan
¼ cup finely chopped fresh parsley leaves

In a 12-inch non-stick skillet cook the bell peppers, the onion, and the mushrooms with salt and black pepper to taste in 2 tablespoons of the oil over moderately low heat, stirring, for 5 to 10 minutes, or until the vegetables are tender and all the liquid the mushrooms give off is evaporated. In a large bowl whisk together the eggs, the potatoes, the Parmesan, the parsley, and salt and black pepper to taste until the mixture is combined well and stir in the vegetable mixture. In the skillet heat the remaining 2 tablespoons oil over moderate heat until it is hot but not smoking, pour in the egg mixture, and bake the omelet in the middle of a preheated 325° F. oven for 20 to 30 minutes, or until it is set. (If the skillet handle is plastic, wrap it heavily in foil.) Cut the omelet into wedges and serve it warm. Serves 6 to 8.

Creamy Scrambled Eggs with Crispy Potatoes

⅔ cup vegetable oil
1 russet (baking) potato, cut into thin julienne
   strips and reserved in a bowl of cold water
4 large eggs
2 tablespoons heavy cream
2 tablespoons unsalted butter
lightly buttered toast as an accompaniment

In a large skillet heat the oil over high heat until it is hot but not smoking and in it fry the potato, rinsed, drained, and patted dry, stirring, for 6 minutes, or until it is crisp and golden. Transfer the potato with a slotted spoon to paper towels to drain and sprinkle it with salt to taste.

In a bowl whisk together the eggs and the cream. In a skillet melt the butter over moderately low heat and in it cook the eggs, stirring, until they are barely set. Stir in the potatoes, cook the mixture, stirring, until the eggs are set, and add salt and pepper to taste. Divide the egg mixture between 2 heated plates and serve it with the toast. Serves 2.

Lobster-Salad-Stuffed Eggs

¼ pound cooked lobster meat or the meat of
   1 cooked King crab leg, chopped fine
   (about ½ cup)
2 radishes, chopped fine
2 tablespoons finely chopped scallion
2 tablespoons finely chopped celery
1 tablespoon minced fresh parsley leaves
2 tablespoons mayonnaise
2 teaspoons fresh lemon juice
⅛ teaspoon Tabasco
3 hard-boiled large eggs
½ cup finely shredded romaine for garnish
½ cup finely shredded cabbage for garnish

In a bowl combine well the lobster, the radishes, the scallion, the celery, the parsley, the mayonnaise, the lemon juice, the Tabasco, and salt and pepper to taste. Halve the eggs crosswise and remove the yolks. Chop 1 of the yolks, reserving the other 2 for another use, and stir it into the lobster salad. Divide the romaine and the cabbage between 2 salad plates, forming nests, fill the whites with the lobster salad, and arrange the eggs in the nests. Serves 2 as a first course.

Goat Cheese and Walnut Soufflés
with Watercress and
Frisée Salad

For the soufflés
¾ cup walnuts, toasted lightly, cooled, and
    chopped fine
3 tablespoons unsalted butter
4 tablespoons all-purpose flour
1 cup milk
4 large eggs, separated, the whites
    at room temperature
1½ cups (about 6 ounces) crumbled mild
    goat cheese such as Montrachet
1 teaspoon fresh thyme leaves
    or ¼ teaspoon dried, crumbled
a pinch of cream of tartar
For the salad
3 tablespoons Sherry vinegar*
¾ teaspoon Dijon-style mustard.
4 tablespoons walnut oil*
2 tablespoons olive oil
2 large bunches of watercress, rinsed, spun
    dry, and coarse stems discarded
    (about 5 cups)
5 cups torn *frisée* (French or Italian curly
    chicory, available at specialty produce
    markets), rinsed and spun dry

*available at specialty foods shops

Make the soufflés: Coat the bottom and sides of each of 8 buttered ½-cup ramekins with about 1 tablespoon of the walnuts and arrange the ramekins in a jelly-roll pan. In a small saucepan melt the butter over moderately low heat, whisk in the flour, and cook the *roux*, whisking, for 3 minutes. Add the milk in a stream, whisking, and boil the mixture over moderate heat, whisking, for 2 minutes, or until it is thick and smooth. Transfer the mixture to a bowl and let it cool slightly. Whisk in the yolks, 1 at a time, the goat cheese, the thyme, and salt and pepper to taste and whisk the mixture until it is combined well. In another bowl beat the whites with a pinch of salt until they are frothy, add the cream of tartar, and beat the whites until they just hold stiff peaks. Whisk one third of the whites into the cheese mixture and fold in the remaining whites gently but thoroughly. Divide the soufflé mixture among the ramekins, sprinkle each soufflé with about 1½ teaspoons of the remaining walnuts, and bake the soufflés in the upper third of a pre-heated 400° F. oven for 20 minutes, or until they are puffed and golden.

Make the salad while the soufflés are baking: In a bowl whisk together the vinegar, the mustard, and salt and pepper to taste, add the oils in a stream, whisking, and whisk the dressing until it is emulsified. In a bowl toss the watercress and the *frisée* with the dressing and divide the salad among 8 plates.

Transfer a ramekin to each plate and serve the soufflés immediately. Serves 8.

Sausage and Red Bell Pepper Quiche

½ cup plus 2 tablespoons all-purpose flour
3 tablespoons cold unsalted butter,
    cut into bits
1 tablespoon cold vegetable shortening
½ teaspoon salt
¾ pound hot or sweet Italian sausages, casings
    discarded and the meat chopped
2 red bell peppers, minced (about 1¼ cups)
¼ cup grated Cheddar
2 tablespoons freshly grated Parmesan
2 large eggs
½ cup heavy cream
3 tablespoons milk

In a bowl blend together the flour, the butter, the shortening, and a pinch of the salt until the mixture resembles meal, add 1½ tablespoons ice water, and toss the mixture until the water is incorporated, adding more water if necessary to form the dough into a ball. Pat the dough into a 7½-inch tart pan with a removable rim and bake the shell in the bottom third of a preheated 425° F. oven for 7 minutes, or until it is just golden.

While the shell is baking, in a large skillet cook the sausage with the bell peppers, covered, over moderately high heat, stirring and breaking up any lumps, for 7 minutes, or until the sausage is no longer pink and the bell peppers are soft, and drain the mixture, discarding the excess fat. Transfer the mixture to a bowl, stir in the remaining salt, the Cheddar, and the Parmesan, and spread the mixture in the bottom of the shell. In a bowl whisk together the eggs, the cream, and the milk, pour the egg mixture over the sausage mixture, and bake the quiche on a baking sheet in the middle of a preheated 425° F. oven for 15 minutes. Reduce the temperature to 350° F. and bake the quiche for 10 minutes more. Serves 2 as an entrée.

BREAKFAST ITEMS

*Cheddar Biscuits with Fried Eggs, Ham,
and Brown Butter*

For the biscuits
¼ cup all-purpose flour
½ teaspoon double-acting baking powder
1 tablespoon cold unsalted butter, cut into bits
⅔ cup grated sharp Cheddar
2 tablespoons milk

1 tablespoon unsalted butter
2 large eggs
2 slices of imported ham
sliced scallion for garnish

Make the biscuits: Into a bowl sift together the flour, the baking powder, and a pinch of salt, add the butter, and blend the mixture until it resembles coarse meal. Stir in the Cheddar and add the milk, stirring, to form a soft sticky dough. On a floured surface pat the dough out into a 6-inch square and cut out 4 rounds with a 2¾-inch round cutter dipped in flour. Put 2 of the rounds on top of the remaining 2 rounds, press them together gently, and bake the biscuits on a buttered baking sheet in the middle of a preheated 425° F. oven for 15 minutes, or until they are pale golden. (Makes 2 large biscuits.)

While the biscuits are baking, in a large skillet heat the butter over moderate heat, swirling the skillet, until it just begins to turn golden brown, slide the eggs carefully into the skillet, and cook them, basting them with the butter, until the yolks are just set and the whites are slightly crisp around the edges. Halve the biscuits horizontally, arrange a ham slice, folding it, on each lower half, and top it with an egg. Drizzle the butter over the eggs, sprinkle the eggs with the scallion, and top them with the upper biscuit halves. Serve the sandwiches hot. Serves 2.

Melon, Nectarine, Grape, and Plum Compote
a 4½-pound piece of watermelon, scooped
   into ¾-inch balls (about 4 cups)
a 2-pound cantaloupe, scooped into
   ¾-inch balls

half a 5-pound honeydew melon, scooped into
   ¾-inch balls (about 3 cups)
2 plums, each cut into 6 wedges
2 nectarines, each cut into 8 wedges
2 cups green seedless grapes
1 tablespoon sugar
¼ teaspoon salt
3 tablespoons fresh lime juice

In a large bowl combine the watermelon, the cantaloupe, the honeydew, the plums, the nectarines, and the grapes. In a small bowl stir together the sugar, the salt, and the lime juice until the sugar and salt are dissolved, drizzle the syrup over the fruit, and toss the mixture gently until it is combined well. Chill the compote, covered, stirring gently once or twice, overnight. Serves 4 generously.

PHOTO ON PAGE 63

Apple and Cinnamon Oatmeal Pancakes
1¼ cups buttermilk
⅔ cup quick-cooking rolled oats (not instant)
1 large egg, beaten lightly
2 tablespoons firmly packed light brown sugar
⅔ cup firmly packed grated peeled Granny
   Smith apple, excess juice squeezed out
6 tablespoons all-purpose flour
6 tablespoons whole-wheat flour
1 teaspoon baking soda
½ teaspoon salt
1 teaspoon cinnamon
2 tablespoons vegetable oil plus additional
   for brushing the griddle
maple syrup as an accompaniment

In a bowl whisk together 1 cup of the buttermilk and the oats and let the mixture stand for 15 minutes. In a large bowl whisk together the egg, the brown sugar, and the apple. Stir in the flours, the baking soda, the salt, the cinnamon, 2 tablespoons of the oil, the oats mixture, and the remaining ¼ cup buttermilk and combine the batter well. Heat a griddle over moderate heat until it is hot enough to make drops of water scatter over its surface, brush it with the additional oil, and drop the batter by half-filled ¼-cup measures onto it. Cook the pancakes, for 1 to 2 minutes on each side, or until they are golden and cooked through. Serve the pancakes with the syrup. Makes twelve 4-inch pancakes, serving 2.

Blueberry Whole-Wheat Pancakes

2 cups buttermilk
3 large eggs
¾ stick (6 tablespoons) unsalted butter,
    melted and cooled, plus additional melted
    butter for brushing the griddle
¾ cup all-purpose flour
½ cup whole-wheat flour
¼ cup wheat germ
1 teaspoon salt
2 teaspoons double-acting baking powder
1½ teaspoons baking soda
3 tablespoons sugar
2 cups picked over blueberries
blueberry syrup (recipe follows) or maple
    syrup as an accompaniment

In a bowl whisk together the buttermilk, the eggs, and 6 tablespoons of the butter. In a large bowl whisk together the flours, the wheat germ, the salt, the baking powder, the baking soda, and the sugar, add the buttermilk mixture, and whisk the batter until it is just combined. Heat a griddle over moderately high heat until it is hot enough to make drops of water scatter over its surface and brush it with some of the additional melted butter. Working in batches, pour the batter onto the griddle by ⅓-cup measures, sprinkle each pancake with about 2 tablespoons of the blueberries, and cook the pancakes for 2 minutes on each side, or until they are golden. Transfer the pancakes as they are cooked to a heatproof platter and keep them warm in a preheated 200° F. oven. Serve the pancakes with the syrup. Makes about sixteen 5-inch pancakes.

Blueberry Syrup

6 cups picked over blueberries
3 cups sugar
the zest of 1 lemon, removed in strips
    with a vegetable peeler
¼ cup fresh lemon juice, or to taste

In a large saucepan combine the blueberries and 1½ cups water, bring the mixture to a boil, and simmer it, covered, for 10 minutes. Purée the mixture in batches in a blender or food processor and force it through a fine sieve into a bowl, discarding the solids. In the pan, cleaned, combine the sugar, the zest, and 3 cups water, bring the mixture to a boil, stirring until the sugar is dis-

solved, and boil it, uncovered, until a candy thermometer registers 220° F. Discard the zest, add the blueberry mixture, and boil the syrup, stirring, for 1 minute. Let the syrup cool, skim off any froth, and stir in the lemon juice. Pour the syrup into glass jars with tight-fitting lids. The syrup keeps, covered and chilled, for 3 months. Serve the syrup warm over pancakes or ice cream. Makes about 6 cups.

Mashed-Potato Pancakes

2 cups mashed potatoes
1 large egg, beaten lightly
6 tablespoons all-purpose flour
1½ tablespoons grated onion
½ teaspoon dried marjoram, crumbled
⅓ cup chopped cooked turkey liver if desired
vegetable oil for frying the pancakes

In a bowl combine well the potatoes and the egg, stir in the flour thoroughly, and stir in the onion, the marjoram, the liver, and salt and pepper to taste. In a large heavy skillet heat ⅛ inch of the oil over moderately high heat until it is hot but not smoking and in it fry heaping tablespoons of the potato mixture, flattening them slightly with the back of the spoon, for 1 minute on each side, or until they are golden brown. Transfer the pancakes as they are cooked to paper towels to drain and if desired keep them warm on a rack set on a baking sheet in a preheated 250° F. oven. Serve the pancakes as an accompaniment to meat, poultry, or eggs. Serves 6 to 8.

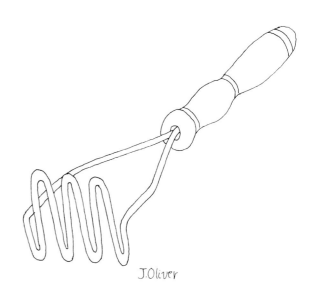

J.Oliver

Walnut and Wheat Germ Silver-Dollar Pancakes

1 cup all-purpose flour
1 teaspoon baking soda
½ teaspoon salt
1 teaspoon sugar
¼ cup wheat germ
1 large egg
1 cup buttermilk
¼ cup walnuts
vegetable oil for brushing the griddle
blackberry syrup (recipe follows) as an
   accompaniment
melted butter as an accompaniment
fresh blackberries for garnish if desired

In a blender blend the flour, the baking soda, the salt, the sugar, the wheat germ, the egg, and the buttermilk for 15 seconds and scrape down the sides. Add the walnuts and blend the batter until the walnuts are just chopped fine. *The batter may be made 1 day in advance and kept covered and chilled.*

Heat a griddle over moderate heat until it is hot enough to make drops of water scatter over its surface and brush it with some of the oil. Working in batches, pour the batter onto the griddle in 2-inch mounds, cook the pancakes for 1½ minutes on each side, or until they are golden, and transfer them as they are cooked to a heatproof platter, keeping them warm in a preheated 200° F. oven. Serve the pancakes with the blackberry syrup and the butter. Garnish them with the blackberries. Makes about 4 dozen 2-inch pancakes.

PHOTO ON PAGE 62

Blackberry Syrup

4 cups blackberries, picked over
¾ cup sugar
the zest of 1 lemon, removed in strips with a
   vegetable peeler

In a saucepan combine the blackberries and 1 cup water, bring the water to a boil, and simmer the berries, covered, for 10 minutes. Purée the mixture in a blender in batches and force it through a fine sieve into a bowl, discarding the solids. In the pan, cleaned, combine the sugar, the zest, and 2 cups water, bring the mixture to a boil, stirring until the sugar is dissolved, and boil it, uncovered, until it registers 220° F. on a candy thermometer. Remove the zest with a slotted spoon, discarding it, add the blackberry purée, and boil the syrup until it registers 210° F. Let the syrup cool, skimming off any froth, and serve it warm or at room temperature. The syrup keeps, covered and chilled, for 6 weeks. Makes about 2 cups.

PHOTO ON PAGE 62

PASTA AND GRAINS

PASTA

Whole-Wheat Fettuccine with Potatoes, Prosciutto, and Peas

1½ pounds small red potatoes
1 pound whole-wheat fettuccine or
    other whole-wheat pasta
2 garlic cloves, minced
1½ cups finely chopped onion
¼ teaspoon dried hot red pepper flakes,
    or to taste
1 teaspoon dried rosemary, crumbled
½ cup olive oil
½ cup chicken broth
½ cup dry white wine
a 10-ounce package frozen peas
¼ pound thinly sliced prosciutto,
    cut into thin strips
½ cup finely chopped fresh parsley leaves,
    preferably flat-leafed
freshly grated Parmesan to taste

In a large kettle of boiling salted water cook the red potatoes, cut crosswise into ¼-inch-thick slices or into ¼-inch dice, for 5 to 7 minutes, or until they are tender, and transfer them with a slotted spoon to a bowl, reserving the water for cooking the fettuccine. In a large heavy skillet cook the garlic, the onion, the red pepper flakes, and the rosemary in the oil over moderately low heat, stirring, until the onion is soft and add the broth, the wine, and the peas. Simmer the mixture for 3 minutes, or until the peas are tender, and stir in the prosciutto, the potatoes, the parsley, and salt and pepper to taste. Bring the reserved water in the kettle to a boil and in it cook the fettuccine until it is *al dente*. Drain the pasta and in a large bowl toss it with the potato mixture and the Parmesan. Serves 6.

Noodle Pancakes with Caraway

¼ pound very fine egg noodles
1 large egg, beaten lightly
¾ teaspoon caraway seeds
1 tablespoon vegetable oil
1½ teaspoons unsalted butter

In a saucepan of boiling salted water boil the noodles until they are *al dente* and drain them well. In a bowl toss the noodles with the egg and the caraway seeds until they are coated well. In a small non-stick skillet heat the oil and the butter until the foam subsides, add ½ cup of the noodle mixture, and form it into a pancake 4 inches in diameter, tidying the edges with a spatula. Cook the pancake over moderately high heat for 2 minutes, or until the underside is golden, turn it, and cook it for 2 minutes more. Slide the pancake onto a plate and keep it warm. Make pancakes with the remaining noodle mixture in the same manner. Serves 2.

Baked Olive and Mozzarella Orzo

1 pound *orzo* (rice-shaped pasta)
1½ cups chopped onion
2 tablespoons olive oil
2 tablespoons unsalted butter
2 cups chopped celery
2 tablespoons all-purpose flour
1 cup chicken broth
a 35-ounce can plum tomatoes, drained well
1 teaspoon dried basil, crumbled
¼ teaspoon cayenne, or to taste
½ pound Kalamata or other brine-cured black
    olives, pitted and sliced thin
¾ pound mozzarella

In a kettle of boiling salted water boil the *orzo* until it is *al dente*, drain it well, and transfer it to a large bowl. In a large heavy skillet cook the onion in the oil and the butter over moderately low heat, stirring, until it is softened, add the celery, and cook the mixture, stirring, for 5 minutes. Stir in the flour, cook the mixture, stirring, for 3 minutes, and stir in the broth, the tomatoes, chopping them with a spoon, the basil, and the cayenne. Simmer the mixture, stirring, for 5 minutes, stir it into the *orzo* with the olives, ½ pound of the mozzarella, cut into ¼-inch dice, and salt to taste, and transfer the mixture to a shallow 2-quart baking dish. Cut the remaining mozzarella into thin strips and arrange it decoratively on top of the *orzo*. Bake the *orzo* in the middle of a preheated 400° F. oven for 30 minutes, or until it is heated through and slightly crisp on top. Serves 12.

PHOTO ON PAGE 81

Saffron Orzo

1½ cups chicken broth
1 cup *orzo* (rice-shaped pasta)
¼ teaspoon crumbled saffron threads
2 tablespoons unsalted butter
¼ cup freshly grated Parmesan

In a saucepan bring the broth and 1½ cups water to a boil, add the *orzo*, and boil it for 5 to 7 minutes, or until it is *al dente*. In a small bowl dissolve the saffron in 1 tablespoon of the hot cooking liquid. Drain the *orzo* well, return it to the pan, and stir in the saffron mixture, the butter, the Parmesan, and salt and pepper to taste. Serves 6.

PHOTO ON PAGE 27

Pasta with Bell Peppers, Goat Cheese, and Basil

2 garlic cloves, minced
2 tablespoons olive oil
½ cup finely chopped onion
1 large red bell pepper, cut into julienne strips
    (about 1 cup)
1 large yellow bell pepper, cut into julienne
    strips (about 1 cup)
⅓ cup dry white wine
⅓ cup sliced pitted Kalamata or other brine-
    cured black olives
½ cup finely shredded fresh basil leaves
½ pound *rotelle* or *fusilli*
3 ounces (about 1 cup) mild goat cheese such
    as Montrachet, crumbled

In a skillet cook the garlic in the oil over moderately low heat, stirring, for 1 minute, add the onion, and cook the mixture, stirring, until the onion is softened. Add the bell peppers, cook the mixture over moderate heat, stirring, for 5 minutes, or until the peppers are just tender, and add the wine and the olives. Boil the wine until it is reduced by half, season the mixture with salt and black pepper, and stir in the basil. In a kettle of boiling salted water cook the pasta until it is *al dente* and drain it well, reserving ⅓ cup of the cooking water. In a serving bowl whisk two thirds of the goat cheese with the reserved cooking water until the cheese is melted and the mixture is smooth, add the pasta and the bell pepper mixture, and toss the mixture well. Sprinkle the pasta with the remaining goat cheese. Serves 2.

Pasta with Lentils

1½ cups finely chopped onion
¼ teaspoon dried thyme, crumbled
3 tablespoons olive oil
⅓ cup lentils
1 carrot, chopped fine
¼ pound *rotelle* or other small pasta
¼ cup minced fresh parsley leaves
freshly grated Parmesan as an accompaniment

In a large heavy skillet cook the onion with the thyme in the oil over moderate heat, stirring, until the onion is golden. While the onion is cooking, combine the lentils with 1⅓ cups water, bring the water to a boil, and simmer the lentils, covered, for 12 minutes. Add the carrot and simmer the mixture, covered, for 3 minutes, or until the lentils and carrot are just tender. Transfer the lentil mixture with the liquid to the skillet, season it with salt and pepper, and keep it at a bare simmer while cooking the pasta.

In a large saucepan of salted boiling water boil the pasta until it is *al dente*. Ladle out and reserve about ½ cup of the pasta liquid, drain the pasta, and add it to the lentil mixture. Simmer the pasta mixture, tossing it to combine it and adding some of the reserved pasta liquid to moisten the mixture if necessary, for 1 minute. Stir in the parsley and transfer the mixture to a heated serving bowl. Serve the pasta with the Parmesan. Serves 2.

Pasta with Summer Vegetables

1½ pounds fava beans, shelled (about 1 cup)
2 zucchini (about 1 pound), scrubbed, the skin and ¼ inch of the flesh removed with a knife in wide strips and cut into 2-inch julienne strips, reserving the core for another use
2 pints cherry tomatoes, quartered lengthwise
½ cup finely chopped red onion, soaked in cold water for 10 minutes if strong
2 garlic cloves, minced and mashed to a paste with ½ teaspoon salt
1 yellow bell pepper, cut into 2-inch julienne strips
¾ cup fresh flat-leafed parsley leaves
5 tablespoons extra-virgin olive oil
¾ pound *gemellini* (small pasta twists, available at some specialty foods shops) or other small tubular pasta
freshly grated Parmesan as an accompaniment if desired

In a saucepan of boiling water boil the fava beans for 4 to 5 minutes, or until they are tender. Drain the beans, let them cool until they can be handled, and peel off and discard the tough outer skins. In a steamer set over boiling water steam the zucchini, covered, for 1½ to 2 minutes, or until it is just tender. In a large bowl combine the beans, the zucchini, the tomatoes, the onion, drained well if soaked, the garlic, the bell pepper, the parsley, the oil, and salt and black pepper to taste and toss the mixture until it is combined well. In a kettle of boiling salted water boil the *gemellini* until it is *al dente*,

drain it, and while it is still hot add it to the vegetable mixture, tossing the mixture until it is combined well. Serve the pasta warm or at room temperature with the Parmesan. Serves 4.

PHOTO ON PAGE 44

Penne, Bell Peppers, and Smoked Salmon in Creamy Garlic Sauce

For the sauce
½ cup heavy cream
4 garlic cloves, crushed lightly
¼ cup fresh lemon juice
¾ cup olive oil
2 tablespoons minced fresh dill
2 tablespoons minced fresh parsley leaves

1 pound *penne* (quill-shaped macaroni) or other tubular pasta
1 large red bell pepper, cut into fine julienne strips about 2 inches long
1 large green bell pepper, cut into fine julienne strips about 2 inches long
1 small red onion, sliced thin
6 ounces thinly sliced smoked salmon, cut into 2- by ⅓-inch strips
a 4-ounce jar red salmon caviar or flying fish roe (available at specialty foods shops) for garnish if desired
8 dill sprigs for garnish

Make the sauce: In a saucepan bring the cream to a boil over moderate heat, add the garlic, and simmer the mixture for 15 minutes, or until the garlic is softened and the cream is reduced to about ¼ cup. In a blender or food processor purée the mixture until it is very smooth, add the lemon juice, and blend the mixture well. With the motor running add the oil in a slow stream, blending the mixture until it is emulsified. Blend in the dill, the parsley, and salt and pepper to taste.

In a large kettle of boiling salted water cook the *penne* until it is tender, drain it well, and transfer it to a large bowl. Toss together gently the *penne*, the bell peppers, the onion, and the smoked salmon, reserving 16 strips for garnish, add the sauce, and toss the mixture gently. Divide the mixture among 8 salad plates and garnish each serving with 2 of the reserved salmon strips, some of the caviar, and a dill sprig. Serve the *penne* warm or at room temperature. Serves 8 as a first course.

Crab-Meat Ravioli with Fennel Purée and Roasted Red Pepper Sauce

For the filling

¼ cup finely chopped shallot
2 tablespoons unsalted butter
¼ pound sole fillet, cut into strips
½ pound lump crab meat, picked over
1 tablespoon fresh lemon juice
2 tablespoons finely chopped fresh tarragon
   leaves
2 tablespoons fine dry bread crumbs
2 large egg yolks

For the fennel purée

¼ cup finely chopped onion
2 garlic cloves, minced
2 tablespoons olive oil
1 fennel bulb, chopped coarse (about 3 cups)
¼ cup chicken broth
1 tablespoon unsalted butter
2 teaspoons Pernod

For the sauce

1 large red bell pepper, roasted (procedure on
   page 135) and chopped
2 garlic cloves, crushed
2 tablespoons olive oil
1 tablespoon fresh orange juice
a 14-ounce can plum tomatoes, drained and
   chopped coarse
1 tablespoon unsalted butter
¼ teaspoon freshly grated orange zest

60 won ton wrappers (available at Oriental
   markets and many supermarkets), thawed if
   frozen

Make the filling: In a small heavy skillet cook the shallot in the butter over moderately low heat, stirring, until it is softened, add the sole, and cook the mixture, stirring, until the fish is cooked through. Transfer the mixture to a bowl, mash the fish with a fork, and let the mixture cool. Stir in the crab meat, the lemon juice, the tarragon, the bread crumbs, the yolks, and salt and pepper to taste and chill the filling, covered, for 1 hour, or until it is cold.

Make the fennel purée: In a heavy saucepan cook the onion and the garlic in the oil over moderately low heat, stirring, until the onion is softened, stir in the fennel, and cook the mixture, stirring, for 3 minutes. Add the broth and simmer the mixture gently, covered, for 15 to 20 minutes, or until the fennel is very tender. In a food processor purée the mixture and transfer the purée to the pan. Stir in the butter, the Pernod, and salt and pepper to taste and keep the purée warm, covered.

Make the sauce: In a small heavy saucepan cook the bell pepper and the garlic in the oil over moderately low heat, stirring, until the vegetables are very soft, stir in the orange juice and the tomatoes, and simmer the mixture, stirring occasionally, for 10 minutes. In a blender purée the mixture and transfer the purée to the pan. Stir in the butter, the zest, and salt and black pepper to taste and keep the sauce warm, covered, while preparing the ravioli.

Prepare the won ton ravioli (procedure follows). Spoon some of the fennel purée onto each of 6 heated plates, arrange 5 ravioli on each plate, and top each serving with some of the sauce. Serves 6.

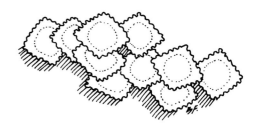

To Prepare Won Ton Ravioli

Put 1 won ton wrapper on a lightly floured surface, mound 1 tablespoon of the filling in the center of the wrapper, and brush the edges with water. Put a second wrapper over the first, pressing down around the filling to force out the air, seal the edges well, and trim the excess dough around the filling with a decorative cutter or sharp knife. Make won ton ravioli with the remaining wrappers and filling in the same manner, transferring them as they are formed to a dry kitchen towel, and turn them occasionally to let them dry slightly.

Bring a kettle of boiling salted water to a gentle boil and in it cook the ravioli in batches for 2 minutes, or until they rise to the surface and are tender. (Do not let the water boil vigorously once the ravioli have been added.) Transfer the ravioli as they are cooked with a slotted spoon to a dry kitchen towel or paper towels to drain and keep them warm.

Goat Cheese Ravioli with Garlic Tomato Sauce

For the filling

¾ pound mild creamy goat cheese, such as
   Montrachet, at room temperature
3 tablespoons ricotta
⅓ cup finely chopped prosciutto
   (about 2 ounces)
¼ cup finely chopped fresh basil leaves
½ teaspoon freshly grated lemon zest
1 large egg, beaten lightly

For the sauce

3 large garlic cloves, sliced thin
¼ cup olive oil
a 28-ounce can plum tomatoes, drained
   and chopped fine
1½ teaspoons fresh thyme

60 won ton wrappers (available at Oriental
   markets and many supermarkets), thawed
   if frozen

6 fresh basil sprigs for garnish if desired

Make the filling: In a bowl stir together well the goat cheese, the ricotta, the prosciutto, the basil, the zest, the egg, and salt and pepper to taste and chill the filling, covered, for 1 hour, or until it is cold.

Make the sauce: In a heavy skillet cook the garlic in the oil over moderately low heat, stirring, until it just begins to turn pale golden and discard it with a slotted spoon. Add the tomatoes, bring the mixture to a boil, and boil it over moderately high heat, stirring, for 10 minutes, or until it is thick. Stir in the thyme and salt and pepper to taste and keep the sauce warm, covered, while preparing the ravioli.

Prepare the won ton ravioli (procedure on page 176) and arrange 5 of them on each of 6 heated plates. Spoon the sauce over the ravioli and garnish each serving with a basil sprig. Serves 6.

Rigatoni with Hot Sausage and Fennel

½ pound hot Italian sausage, casings
   discarded
1 tablespoon olive oil
½ cup finely chopped onion
1 large garlic clove, minced
1 large red bell pepper, chopped (about 1 cup)
1 fennel bulb, sliced thin (about 2 cups)

⅓ cup dry white wine
½ cup chicken broth
¼ cup heavy cream
½ pound rigatoni or other tubular pasta
¼ cup minced fresh parsley leaves
freshly grated Parmesan to taste

In a heavy skillet cook the sausage over moderate heat, stirring and breaking up any lumps, until it is cooked through and transfer it with a slotted spoon to paper towels to drain. Add the oil to the skillet and in it cook the onion and the garlic over moderately low heat, stirring, until the onion is softened. Add the bell pepper and the fennel and cook the mixture over moderate heat, stirring occasionally, for 5 minutes, or until the bell pepper and fennel are softened. Add the wine and the broth, bring the liquid to a boil, and simmer the mixture, covered, for 5 minutes. Add the cream and boil the mixture until it is thickened slightly and reduced by about one third. In a kettle of boiling salted water cook the rigatoni until it is *al dente* and drain it well. Stir into the fennel mixture the parsley, the sausage, and salt and pepper to taste and in a bowl toss the sauce with the rigatoni and the Parmesan. Serves 2.

*Oriental Spaghetti with Cucumber
and Spicy Peanut Sauce*

¼ cup smooth peanut butter
1 tablespoon soy sauce
1 tablespoon fresh lemon juice
1 small garlic clove, minced
¼ teaspoon dried hot red pepper flakes,
   or to taste
¼ teaspoon sugar
6 ounces spaghetti
1 cucumber, peeled, seeded, and cut
   diagonally into ⅛-inch slices
⅓ cup thinly sliced scallion

In a blender blend the peanut butter, the soy sauce, the lemon juice, the garlic, the red pepper flakes, the sugar, and ¼ cup hot water until the sauce is smooth. In a kettle of boiling salted water boil the spaghetti until it is just tender, drain it in a colander, and rinse it briefly under cold water. Drain the spaghetti well, transfer it to a bowl, and toss it with the sauce, the cucumber, the scallion, and salt and pepper to taste. Serve the pasta at room temperature. Serves 2.

GRAINS

Couscous with Cuminseed and Scallion

1 tablespoon olive oil
¼ teaspoon cuminseed
¼ teaspoon salt
½ cup couscous
⅓ cup thinly sliced scallion
3 tablespoons minced fresh parsley leaves

In a small saucepan combine ¾ cup water, the oil, the cuminseed, and the salt and bring the mixture to a boil. Stir in the couscous and let the mixture stand, covered, off the heat for 5 minutes. Fluff the mixture with a fork and stir in the scallion, the parsley, and salt and pepper to taste. Serves 2.

Couscous with Sage

¾ cup chicken broth
a scant ½ teaspoon dried sage, crumbled
½ cup couscous
2 teaspoons unsalted butter, cut into bits

In a small saucepan bring the broth to a boil with the sage, stir in the couscous, and remove the pan from the heat. Let the couscous stand, covered, for 5 minutes, add the butter and salt and pepper to taste, and fluff the mixture with a fork until the butter is melted. Serves 2.

Kasha with Zucchini and Red Bell Pepper

1 cup chicken broth
3 tablespoons olive oil
1 cup whole kasha
1 large egg, beaten lightly
1 onion, chopped
1 garlic clove, minced
1 red bell pepper, chopped
1 zucchini, scrubbed, halved lengthwise,
    and cut into ¼-inch slices
plain yogurt for garnish

In a saucepan combine the broth, 1 cup water, and 1 tablespoon of the oil and bring the liquid to a boil. In a bowl combine the kasha and the egg, stirring to coat the kasha well with the egg, transfer the mixture to a deep skillet with a lid, and cook the kasha over moderately high heat, stirring and breaking up the lumps, for 2 to 4 minutes, or until the grains are separated. Remove the skillet from the heat, add the broth mixture slowly (the mixture will spatter), and cover the skillet tightly. Cook the kasha, covered, over low heat for 10 to 15 minutes, or until the liquid is absorbed.

While the kasha is cooking, in a skillet cook the onion, the garlic, and the bell pepper in the remaining 2 tablespoons oil over moderately low heat, stirring, until the vegetables are softened. Add the zucchini and salt and black pepper to taste, increase the heat to moderately high, and cook the mixture, stirring, for 3 minutes, or until the zucchini is just tender. Stir the vegetables into the kasha and serve the kasha with a dollop of the yogurt. Serves 2.

Browned Onion and Corn Pilaf

½ cup chopped onion
½ cup corn kernels, thawed if frozen
1 tablespoon unsalted butter
½ cup unconverted long-grain rice
1 teaspoon salt

In a heavy saucepan cook the onion and the corn in the butter over moderately high heat, stirring, until the vegetables are browned. Add the rice, stir the mixture until the rice is coated with the butter, and stir in 1 cup water and the salt. Bring the liquid to a boil, stirring, and cook the pilaf, covered, over low heat for 25 to 30 minutes, or until the liquid is absorbed. Serves 2.

Rice Pilaf with Pistachios and Golden Raisins

¼ cup finely chopped onion
¼ teaspoon turmeric
⅛ teaspoon ground cardamom
1½ tablespoons unsalted butter
⅓ cup long-grain rice
⅔ cup chicken broth
2 tablespoons pistachio nuts, toasted lightly,
    cooled, and chopped
2 tablespoons golden raisins, soaked in
    boiling water to cover for 1 minute
    and drained
2 tablespoons thinly sliced scallion greens

In a small heavy saucepan cook the onion with the turmeric and the cardamom in 1 tablespoon of the butter over moderately low heat, stirring, until the onion is softened. Add the rice and cook it, stirring, until it is coated with the butter. Add the broth, bring the liquid to a boil, covered, and simmer the mixture for 17 minutes, or until the liquid is absorbed and the rice is tender. Stir in the pistachios, the raisins, the scallion greens, the remaining ½ tablespoon butter, and salt and pepper to taste. Serves 2.

Rice and Tomatoes

1 teaspoon salt
1 cup unconverted long-grain rice
1 onion, chopped fine
1 tablespoon vegetable oil
a 13-ounce can plum tomatoes, drained,
    reserving ¼ cup juice, and chopped

In a large saucepan bring 4 quarts water to a boil with the salt. Sprinkle in the rice, stirring until the water returns to a boil, and boil it for 10 minutes. Drain the rice in a colander and rinse it. Set the colander over a large saucepan of boiling water and steam the rice, covered with a kitchen towel and the lid, for 15 minutes, or until it is fluffy and dry. *The rice may be made 1 day in advance and kept covered and chilled. Reheat the rice in a steamer over boiling water.*

In a saucepan cook the onion in the oil over moderately low heat, stirring occasionally, until it is softened, add the tomatoes with the reserved juice, and cook the mixture, stirring occasionally, for 3 minutes. In a bowl combine well the rice, the tomato mixture, and salt and pepper to taste. Serves 4.

PHOTO ON PAGE 18

Rice with Kale and Tomatoes

½ cup long-grain unconverted rice
1 small garlic clove, minced
1 tablespoon olive oil
a 14-ounce can plum tomatoes, drained,
    seeded, and chopped
2 cups finely chopped rinsed kale leaves

In a small heavy saucepan bring 1 cup water to a boil, add the rice and salt to taste, and cook the rice, covered, over low heat for 20 minutes, or until the liquid is absorbed and the rice is tender. In a heavy skillet cook the garlic in the oil over moderately low heat, stirring, until it is golden, add the tomatoes and the kale, and cook the mixture, stirring occasionally, for 3 to 5 minutes, or until the kale is tender. Fluff the rice with a fork and in a bowl combine well the rice, the kale mixture, and salt and pepper to taste. Serves 2.

Scallion Rice

2 teaspoons salt
⅔ cup unconverted long-grain rice
⅓ cup finely chopped white part of scallion
1 tablespoon unsalted butter
¼ cup thinly sliced scallion greens

In a large saucepan bring 4 quarts water to a boil with the salt. Sprinkle in the rice, stirring until the water returns to a boil, and boil it for 10 minutes. Drain the rice in a large colander and rinse it. Set the colander over a large saucepan of boiling water and steam the rice, covered with a kitchen towel and the lid, for 15 minutes, or until it is fluffy and dry. In a small skillet cook the white part of scallion in the butter over moderately low heat, stirring occasionally, until it is softened and in a bowl toss the rice with the scallion mixture, the scallion greens, and salt and pepper to taste. Serves 2.

VEGETABLES

Artichokes with Garlic Saffron Sauce

2 artichokes
½ lemon
10 unpeeled garlic cloves
1½ tablespoons white-wine vinegar
¼ teaspoon dried orégano
⅛ teaspoon saffron threads, crumbled
¼ teaspoon sugar
2 tablespoons olive oil
1 tablespoon minced fresh parsley leaves

Cut off the stems of the artichokes with a stainless-steel knife, break off the tough outer leaves, and cut off the top fourth of each artichoke. Snip off the tips of the remaining artichoke leaves with scissors and rub the cut edges with the lemon half. Arrange the artichokes upright in a microwave-safe dish, add 1 inch water and the garlic, and cover the dish tightly with microwave-safe plastic wrap. Microwave the artichokes at high power (100%) for 15 to 20 minutes, or until the bases of the artichokes are tender.

While the artichokes are cooking, in a blender blend together 3 tablespoons warm water, the vinegar, the orégano, the saffron, the sugar, and the oil. Transfer the cooked artichokes to 2 plates. Peel the garlic, in the blender purée it with the vinegar mixture until the mixture is smooth, and stir in the parsley and salt and pepper to taste. Transfer the sauce to a bowl and serve it with the artichokes. Serves 2.

Sautéed Baby Artichokes

1¼ pounds baby artichokes
1 tablespoon all-purpose flour
¼ cup olive oil
1 teaspoon minced garlic
¼ teaspoon dried rosemary, crumbled
¼ teaspoon dried orégano, crumbled

¼ teaspoon dried basil, crumbled
2 teaspoons fresh lemon juice, or to taste
1 cup dry white wine
⅛ teaspoon dried hot red pepper flakes,
  or to taste
1 teaspoon finely chopped fresh parsley leaves

Bend the outer leaves of the artichokes back until they snap off close to the base and remove several more layers of leaves in the same manner until the white inner leaves are reached. Trim the tips and quarter the artichokes. In a small bowl toss the artichokes with the flour and salt and black pepper to taste. In a skillet heat the oil with the garlic over moderate heat until it is hot but not smoking and cook the garlic until it is softened. Add the artichokes and sauté them over moderately high heat, stirring, for 6 minutes. Stir in the rosemary, the orégano, the basil, and the lemon juice and cook the mixture, stirring, for 1 minute. Add the wine, the red pepper flakes, and salt and black pepper to taste and simmer the mixture, covered, for 25 to 30 minutes, or until the artichokes are very tender. Add the parsley and boil the mixture, uncovered, over high heat for 1 minute, or until it is thickened slightly. Serves 2.

PHOTO ON PAGE 12

Bean Burrito Casserole

1 onion, chopped fine
4 garlic cloves, minced
3 tablespoons olive oil
two 1-pound cans black, pinto, or pink beans,
  rinsed and drained
1 cup tomato sauce
2 teaspoons ground cumin
4 fresh or pickled *jalapeño* chilies if desired,
  seeded and chopped (wear rubber gloves)
¼ cup chopped fresh coriander if desired

twelve 7- to 8-inch flour tortillas
  (page 103 or store-bought), warmed
  (procedure on page 103)
1½ cups grated Monterey Jack
  (about 6 ounces)
guacamole (page 130) and tomato *salsa*
  (page 130) as accompaniments

Make the filling: In a large heavy skillet cook the onion and the garlic in the oil over moderately low heat, stirring, until the onion is softened, add the beans, and mash about half of them coarse with the back of a wooden spoon. Add the tomato sauce, the cumin, the chilies, and salt and black pepper to taste, simmer the mixture, stirring, for 3 to 5 minutes, or until it is thickened slightly, and stir in the coriander.

Working with 1 warmed tortilla at a time and keeping the others covered, spread about 3 tablespoons of the filling down the center of each tortilla and roll the tortillas, enclosing the filling but keeping the ends open. Arrange the *burritos*, seam sides down, in one layer in a baking dish, sprinkle them with the Monterey Jack, and bake them, covered with foil, in the middle of a preheated 350° F. oven for 10 minutes. Serve the *burritos* with the *guacamole* and the *salsa*. Makes 12 *burritos*, serving 6.

Green Beans with Olives

½ pound green beans, trimmed
½ teaspoon dried orégano
4 Kalamata or other brine-cured black olives,
  pitted and chopped
1 tablespoon softened unsalted butter
lemon juice to taste

In a saucepan of boiling salted water boil the green beans with the orégano for 5 minutes, or until they are crisp-tender. Drain the beans, transfer them to a bowl, and toss them with the olives, the butter, and the lemon juice. Serves 2.

Buttered Haricots Verts
(Buttered Thin French Green Beans)

1 pound *haricots verts* (thin French green
  beans, available at specialty produce
  markets and some supermarkets)
2 tablespoons unsalted butter

In a kettle of boiling salted water boil the *haricots verts* for 4 to 6 minutes, or until they are crisp-tender, drain them, and plunge them into a bowl of ice and cold water to stop the cooking. Drain the beans again and pat them dry. *The beans may be prepared up to this point 1 day in advance and kept wrapped in dampened paper towels in a plastic bag and chilled.* Just before serving, in a large skillet melt the butter over moderately high heat and in it toss the *haricots verts* until they are heated through. Season the *haricots verts* with salt and pepper. Serves 8.

PHOTO ON PAGE 78

Beets with Stout and Sautéed Beet Greens

9 pounds beets including the greens
  (4½ pounds without the greens), trimmed,
  leaving 2 inches of the stem ends intact and
  reserving 1 pound of the beet greens
3 tablespoons Guinness stout
1 tablespoon red-wine vinegar
½ stick (¼ cup) unsalted butter
the reserved beet greens or 1 pound kale,
  coarse stems discarded and the leaves
  washed well, spun dry, and chopped
  very coarse

In a kettle cover the beets with 2 inches cold water, bring the water to a boil, and simmer the beets, covered, for 20 to 35 minutes (depending on their size), or until they are tender. Drain the beets and under cold running water slip off and discard their skins and stems. In a skillet bring to a boil the stout and the vinegar and whisk in 2 tablespoons of the butter. Stir in the beets, quartered, add salt and pepper to taste, and keep the beets warm, covered. In a large skillet heat the remaining 2 tablespoons butter over moderately high heat until the foam subsides, in it sauté the reserved beet greens, stirring, for 5 minutes, or until they are tender, and stir in salt and pepper to taste. Arrange the greens around the edge of a platter and mound the beets in the center. Serves 8.

PHOTO ON PAGE 24

Lemony Creamed Brussels Sprouts and Celery

4 ribs of celery, cut diagonally into
  ⅓-inch slices
2 tablespoons unsalted butter
¼ teaspoon celery seeds
3 tablespoons all-purpose flour
1 cup milk
1 teaspoon freshly grated lemon zest
2 teaspoons fresh lemon juice
1½ pounds Brussels sprouts, trimmed,
  blanched for 12 minutes in boiling salted
  water, or until they are tender, and drained,
  or two 10-ounce packages frozen, thawed

In a heavy saucepan cook the celery in the butter over
moderately low heat, stirring, for 3 minutes, or until it
begins to soften. Stir in the celery seeds and the flour
and cook the mixture, stirring, for 3 minutes. Add the
milk in a stream, whisking, and salt and pepper to taste
and simmer the sauce, stirring, until it is smooth and
thickened. Stir in the zest, the lemon juice, and the
Brussels sprouts and simmer the mixture, stirring occasionally, until the Brussels sprouts are heated through.
Transfer the creamed Brussels sprouts to a heated serving dish. Serves 8.

PHOTO ON PAGE 73

Cauliflower and Spinach Vinaigrette

2 tablespoons red-wine vinegar
2 tablespoons finely chopped pimiento-stuffed
  green olives
2 tablespoons finely chopped bottled roasted
  red peppers
1 tablespoon finely chopped fresh parsley
  leaves (preferably flat-leafed)
3 tablespoons olive oil
1 small head of cauliflower, separated into
  flowerets (about 6 cups)
6 ounces spinach, washed well and coarse
  stems discarded

In a small bowl whisk together the vinegar, the
olives, the roasted peppers, the parsley, and salt to
taste, add the oil, whisking, and whisk the dressing until
it is emulsified. In a shallow microwave-safe dish
arrange the cauliflower in one layer, add 2 tablespoons water, and microwave the cauliflower, covered
with a microwave-safe lid, at high power (100%) for 8

minutes, or until it is tender. Transfer the cauliflower
with a slotted spoon to a bowl. Put the spinach in the
microwave-safe dish and microwave it with the water
clinging to its leaves, covered with the lid, at high
power (100%) for 2 minutes. Blot the spinach dry with
paper towels, pressing out the excess liquid. Transfer
the spinach to a platter, mound the cauliflower on it, and
spoon the dressing over the vegetables. Serve the vegetables at room temperature. Serves 2 as a first course.

Grilled Corn

12 ears of corn in their husks, the outer layer
  of husks discarded or torn into strips for
  tying the corn
sage butter (page 188) as an accompaniment

Peel back the corn husks carefully, without breaking
them off, and discard the silks. Fold the husks back into
place and tie the ends together with the strips of outer
husk or kitchen string. Combine the corn in large bowls
with cold water to cover and let it soak for 10 minutes.
Drain the corn and grill it on a rack set 5 to 6 inches over
glowing coals, turning it occasionally, for 15 minutes.
Serve the corn with the sage butter. Serves 6.

PHOTO ON PAGE 55

Corn and Zucchini Timbales

2½ cups fresh corn kernels (cut from about
  5 ears of corn)
5 large eggs
1 tablespoon all-purpose flour
1 teaspoon sugar
1 teaspoon salt
2 zucchini, rinsed
1½ teaspoons minced fresh thyme leaves or
  ½ teaspoon dried, crumbled

In a blender purée the corn with ⅔ cup water for
1 minute, add the eggs, the flour, the sugar, and the salt,
and purée the mixture for 1 minute. Strain the purée
through a fine sieve into a bowl, pressing hard on the
solids. With a vegetable peeler cut 16 thin lengthwise
slices from the zucchini, avoiding the cores, and grate
enough of the remaining zucchini to measure 1 cup.
Squeeze the grated zucchini dry in a kitchen towel and
stir it into the corn mixture with the thyme.
  Arrange 2 zucchini slices decoratively in each of 8

buttered ½-cup timbale molds. Press the slices firmly against the sides of the molds and trim the ends. Divide the corn mixture among the molds. Arrange the molds in a baking dish, add enough hot water to the dish to come halfway up their sides, and bake the timbales in the middle of a preheated 350° F. oven for 35 to 40 minutes, or until they are firm. Transfer the molds to a work surface and let them stand for 3 minutes. Run a thin knife around the edge of each mold and invert the timbales onto platters. *The timbales may be made 1 day in advance and kept covered and chilled. Reheat the timbales in a baking dish, covered tightly with foil, in a preheated 350° F. oven for 15 minutes.* Serves 8.

PHOTO ON PAGE 61

Cucumber, Sweet Onion, and Mint with Curried Mayonnaise on Peasant Bread

½ cup mayonnaise
1 teaspoon curry powder, or to taste
8 slices of peasant or country-style bread
1 cucumber, peeled if desired and sliced
   thin diagonally
1 sweet onion, such as Vidalia, sliced thin
½ cup fresh mint leaves

In a small bowl combine well the mayonnaise and the curry powder and spread the curried mayonnaise on one side of each slice of bread. Layer half the bread slices with the cucumber, the onion, and the mint, sprinkle the mixture with salt and pepper to taste, and top the sandwiches with the remaining bread slices, pressing them firmly. Makes 4 sandwiches.

Eggplant Gratin

1½ cups finely chopped onion
3 tablespoons olive oil
a 1-pound eggplant, cut into ½-inch pieces
⅓ cup plus 2 tablespoons minced fresh
   parsley leaves
½ cup freshly grated Parmesan
¼ cup dry bread crumbs

In a heavy skillet cook the onion in 2 tablespoons of the oil over moderately low heat, stirring occasionally, until it is golden. While the onion is cooking, in a steamer set over boiling water steam the eggplant, covered, for 10 minutes, or until it is tender, transfer it to a colander, and let it drain for 5 minutes. In a bowl toss together the eggplant, the onion mixture, ⅓ cup of the parsley, and salt and pepper to taste and spread the mixture in a greased 3-cup shallow baking dish. In a small bowl stir together the Parmesan, the bread crumbs, and the remaining 2 tablespoons parsley, sprinkle the mixture over the eggplant mixture, and drizzle the top with the remaining 1 tablespoon oil. Bake the gratin in the middle of a preheated 400° F. oven for 20 minutes, or until the topping is golden and the mixture is bubbling around the edges. Serves 2.

Eggplant Stuffed with Scamorza Cheese

6 Japanese or small Italian eggplants
 (about 1½ pounds total)
1 cup finely chopped onion
5 tablespoons olive oil
¾ pound tomatoes, peeled, seeded, and
 chopped fine
2 tablespoons minced fresh parsley leaves
5 ounces *scamorza* cheese (available at cheese
 shops and some specialty foods shops) or
 provolone, cut into 12 sticks, each about
 3- by 1- by ½-inch
3 hard-boiled large eggs, the ends trimmed
 and each egg cut crosswise into 4 slices
2 plum tomatoes, each cut crosswise into
 6 slices

Cut off the stem end of each eggplant and halve the eggplants lengthwise. Scoop out the pulp from each eggplant with a spoon without piercing the skin, leaving a ¼-inch-thick shell, and chop the pulp fine.

In a large skillet cook the onion in 3 tablespoons of the oil over moderately low heat, stirring, until it is very soft, add the eggplant pulp, the chopped tomatoes, and salt and pepper to taste, and simmer the mixture, stirring, for 20 to 25 minutes, or until the eggplant is very tender. While the mixture is cooking, arrange the eggplant shells in one layer, cut sides up, in a lightly oiled baking dish and brush them with 1 tablespoon of the remaining oil. Bake the shells in the middle of a preheated 350° F. oven for 15 minutes, or until they are tender.

Stir the parsley into the eggplant filling and spoon about 1 tablespoon of the filling into the bottom of each eggplant shell. Put 1 stick of the cheese in each shell, put an egg slice over each stick of cheese, and divide the remaining filling among the shells, spreading it to cover the cheese and egg. Top each stuffed eggplant with a plum tomato slice, drizzle the tomatoes with the remaining 1 tablespoon oil, and bake the eggplants in the middle of the preheated 350° F. oven for 10 minutes, or until the cheese is melted. Serves 6 as a first course or 3 as an entrée.

Crisp-Fried Eggplant

⅓ cup cornstarch
1 large egg
½ teaspoon coarse salt plus additional for
 sprinkling the eggplant
1 cup fresh bread crumbs
1 small eggplant (about ¼ pound), cut
 crosswise into ¼-inch-thick slices
vegetable oil for deep-frying
lemon wedges if desired

Put the cornstarch, the egg beaten with ½ teaspoon of the salt, and the bread crumbs in separate small dishes. Dredge each eggplant slice in the cornstarch, coating it thoroughly and shaking off the excess, coat it with the egg mixture, and dredge it in the bread crumbs, pressing on the crumbs to make them adhere. Transfer the eggplant as it is coated to paper towels and let it dry slightly. In a deep heavy skillet fry the eggplant slices in batches in ½ inch of 375° F. oil for 1 minute on each side, or until they are golden brown, and transfer them with tongs to paper towels to drain. Sprinkle the eggplant lightly with the additional salt and serve it with the lemon wedges. Serves 2 as a side dish or first course.

Sweet-and-Sour Eggplant with Red Onion, Raisins, and Pine Nuts

1 cup thinly sliced red onion
2 tablespoons olive oil
1 eggplant, cut into ¼-inch dice
 (about 3 cups)
3 tablespoons red-wine vinegar plus
 additional to taste
1 tablespoon sugar
2 tablespoons golden raisins
1½ tablespoons pine nuts, toasted
2 tablespoons minced fresh parsley leaves
 (preferably flat-leafed)

In a skillet cook the onion in the oil over moderately low heat, stirring, until it is softened, add the eggplant and salt and pepper to taste, and cook the mixture over moderate heat, stirring, for 5 minutes. Cook the mixture, covered, stirring occasionally, for 3 to 5 minutes more, or until the eggplant is tender, and transfer it to a bowl. To the skillet add 3 tablespoons of the vinegar, the sugar, and the raisins, cook the mixture over moderate heat, stirring, until the sugar is dissolved, and pour it over the eggplant mixture. Stir in the pine nuts, the parsley, the additional vinegar, and salt and pepper to taste. Serve the sweet-and-sour eggplant warm or at room temperature. Serves 2.

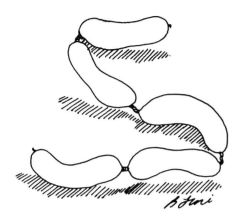

erate heat, stirring, and transfer it with a slotted spoon to paper towels to drain. Chop the reserved eggplant and in the fat remaining in the skillet cook it with the celery, the bell pepper, and the onions over moderate heat, stirring occasionally and scraping up the brown bits, until the mixture is golden. Add 1 cup water and cook the mixture, covered, stirring occasionally, for 10 minutes. Add 1 cup more water and cook the mixture, uncovered, stirring occasionally, for 2 minutes, or until the eggplant is very soft.

In a large bowl combine the eggplant mixture, the sausage, the rice, the scallion greens, the parsley, the cayenne, and salt and black pepper to taste. Divide the mixture among the eggplant shells, arrange the eggplants in 2 shallow 15½- by 10½- baking pans, and add 1 cup water to each pan. Bake the eggplants, covered with foil, in a preheated 350° F. oven for 30 minutes. Sprinkle the eggplants with the bread crumb mixture and broil them in batches under a preheated broiler about 4 inches from the heat for 2 to 3 minutes, or until the topping is golden. Serves 6 as an entrée.

Eggplants Filled with Sausage Jambalaya

⅓ cup fine dry bread crumbs
¼ cup freshly grated Parmesan
1½ cups short-grain rice (available at Oriental markets and some supermarkets)
3 eggplants (about 1½ pounds each)
1 pound smoked sausage, such as kielbasa, chopped coarse
3 ribs of celery, sliced thin crosswise
1 green bell pepper, chopped coarse
2 onions, chopped coarse
½ cup thinly sliced scallion greens
⅓ cup minced fresh parsley leaves
cayenne to taste

In a small bowl combine well the bread crumbs and the Parmesan. In a heavy saucepan combine the rice, 2 cups water, and salt to taste, bring the water to a boil, and cook the rice, covered, over low heat for 15 to 20 minutes, or until the water is absorbed and the rice is tender. Halve the eggplants lengthwise and with a melon-ball cutter scoop out the flesh, reserving 4 cups of it and leaving ¼-inch shells. In a kettle of boiling salted water blanch the eggplant shells in batches for 4 minutes and drain them, inverted, on paper towels.

In a large heavy skillet brown the sausage over mod-

Braised Belgian Endive Gratin

8 Belgian endives (about 2 pounds), trimmed and halved lengthwise, leaving the root ends intact
1½ tablespoons fresh lemon juice
3 tablespoons unsalted butter, cut into bits
½ teaspoon salt
2 teaspoons sugar
¾ cup chicken broth
⅔ cup finely grated Gruyère
1⅓ cups dry bread crumbs

In a heavy kettle combine the endives, cut sides down, in two layers, the lemon juice, the butter, the salt, the sugar, and the broth, cover the mixture with a buttered round of wax paper and the lid, and bring the liquid to a boil. Simmer the mixture, covered, for 20 to 30 minutes, or until the endives are very tender, and transfer them with a slotted spoon, cut sides down, to a buttered gratin dish just large enough to hold them in one layer. In a small bowl stir together the Gruyère and the bread crumbs, sprinkle the mixture evenly over the endives, and broil the gratin under a preheated broiler about 4 inches from the heat for 3 to 4 minutes, or until the topping is golden and the cheese is melted. Serves 8.

PHOTO ON PAGE 66

Grilled Leeks with Herbed Vinaigrette

12 medium leeks (about 4½ pounds), trimmed
    to about 7 inches, split lengthwise to within
    1½ inches of the root end, roots trimmed
    but root ends left intact, tough outer
    leaves discarded, and the leeks washed well
vegetable oil for grilling
For the vinaigrette
4 teaspoons Dijon-style mustard
3 tablespoons white-wine vinegar
½ cup extra-virgin olive oil
⅓ cup minced assorted fresh herbs, such as
    chives, parsley, mint, basil, and tarragon
¼ cup finely diced red bell pepper
¼ cup Kalamata or other brine-cured black
    olives, pitted and diced fine

Tie the leeks in 4 bundles with kitchen string, in a kettle of boiling salted water boil them for 6 minutes, or until they are just tender, and drain them in a colander. Refresh the leeks under cold water and discard the strings. Cut the leeks apart at the root ends and drain them on paper towels. *The leeks may be prepared up to this point 1 day in advance and kept covered and chilled.* Brush the leeks with the oil and grill them in batches in a heated oiled ridged grill pan over moderate heat or on an oiled rack set 4 to 5 inches over glowing coals for 3 to 4 minutes on each side, or until they are golden. Transfer the leeks as they are grilled to a platter and keep them warm, covered. *The leeks may be prepared up to this point 1 day in advance and kept covered and chilled. Reheat the leeks on a baking sheet in a preheated 350° F. oven for 10 minutes, or until they are heated through.*

Make the vinaigrette: In a bowl whisk together the mustard, the vinegar, and salt and black pepper to taste, add the oil in a stream, whisking, and whisk the dressing until it is emulsified. Whisk in the herbs, the bell pepper, and the olives.

Divide the leeks among 8 plates and spoon the vinaigrette over each serving. Serves 8 as a first course.

PHOTO ON PAGE 60

Horseradish Creamed Leeks

the white and pale green parts of 4 leeks
    (about 1 pound), trimmed, left whole, and
    each leek slit down one side to within
    1 inch of the base
2 tablespoons unsalted butter
⅓ cup chicken broth
⅓ cup heavy cream
1 tablespoon drained bottled horseradish,
    or to taste
3 tablespoons grated Gruyère

In a large bowl of cold water fan out the leaves of the leeks and rinse them well until there is no grit. In a large skillet heat the butter over moderate heat until the foam begins to subside, add the leeks, patted dry, and toss them to coat them with the butter. Add the broth and the cream, bring the liquid to a boil, and simmer the mixture, uncovered, stirring occasionally, for 25 to 35 minutes, or until the leeks are very tender. Transfer the leeks with a slotted spatula to a gratin dish. Stir the horseradish into the liquid remaining in the skillet and season the sauce with salt and pepper. Pour the sauce over the leeks, sprinkle it with the Gruyère, and broil the leeks under a preheated broiler about 4 inches from the heat for 2 minutes, or until the cheese is golden. Serves 2.

Mushroom and Onion Gratins

1 pound mushrooms, sliced thin
½ stick (¼ cup) unsalted butter
¼ cup all-purpose flour
2 large onions (about 1¾ pounds),
    sliced very thin
6 tablespoons heavy cream
1 cup grated Gruyère
¼ cup fresh fine bread crumbs

In a skillet cook the mushrooms in 2½ tablespoons of the butter over moderately low heat, stirring, until they are softened and most of the liquid they give off has evaporated. Stir in the flour and cook the mixture, stirring, for 3 minutes.

In each of six 1½-cup gratin dishes layer the onions, the remaining butter, cut into bits, the mushroom mixture, and salt and pepper to taste, beginning and ending with a layer of onions, and pour 1 tablespoon of the cream over the top of each gratin. In a small bowl combine well the Gruyère and the bread crumbs and sprinkle the mixture over the cream. (Alternatively, the gratin, layered in the same manner, may be prepared in one 2-quart gratin dish.) Bake the gratins in the middle of a preheated 325° F. oven for 50 minutes to 1 hour, or until the onions are tender and the tops are golden. *The gratins may be prepared 3 hours in advance, kept covered and chilled, and reheated in a preheated 400° F. oven for 5 minutes, or until they are heated through.* Serves 6 as a first course.

Mushroom Dill Roulade with Sour Cream Sauce

1 egg sponge (page 164)
For the sauce
½ cup sour cream
5 teaspoons fresh lemon juice
For the filling
1½ pounds mushrooms, chopped fine
1 onion, chopped fine
½ stick (¼ cup) unsalted butter
¼ cup fresh dill, chopped fine
½ cup minced fresh parsley leaves

Prepare the egg sponge and while it is baking make the sauce and the filling.

Make the sauce: In a small bowl whisk together the sour cream, the lemon juice, 2 teaspoons water, and salt and pepper to taste and chill the sauce, covered.

Make the filling: In a large skillet cook the mushrooms and the onion in the butter over moderate heat, stirring occasionally, until the liquid the mushrooms give off is evaporated and the mushrooms are browned. Stir in the dill and the parsley.

Assemble the *roulade*: Spread the filling on the warm egg sponge, leaving a 1-inch border on the long sides, and starting with a long side roll up the egg sponge jelly-roll fashion. Slice the *roulade* and serve the slices with the sauce. Serves 8 to 10 as a first course.

Sesame Mushrooms

¾ pound mushrooms, sliced thin
2 teaspoons Oriental sesame oil
1 teaspoon vegetable oil
2 tablespoons thinly sliced scallion greens

In a heavy skillet cook the mushrooms in the oils over moderate heat, stirring frequently, for 6 to 8 minutes, or until the liquid they give off is evaporated and they are golden. Stir in 1 tablespoon water, the scallion greens, and salt and pepper to taste and cook the mixture, stirring, for 1 minute. Serves 2.

Spicy Mushrooms and Leeks

3 small leeks, split lengthwise, washed well, drained, and the white and pale green parts sliced thin
2 tablespoons unsalted butter
¾ pound small mushrooms, quartered
2 tablespoons dry white wine
⅛ teaspoon dried hot red pepper flakes, or to taste
1½ teaspoons fresh lemon juice

In a microwave-safe dish combine the leeks and the butter and microwave the mixture, covered with microwave-safe plastic wrap, at high power (100%), stirring once, for 5 minutes. Remove the plastic wrap and microwave the mixture for 5 minutes more, or until the leeks are tender. Stir in the mushrooms, the wine, and the red pepper flakes and microwave the mixture, covered with the plastic wrap, at high power (100%) for 5 minutes. Stir the mixture and microwave it, uncovered, for 8 minutes more, or until the mushrooms are tender. Stir in the lemon juice and salt to taste. Serves 2.

Okra, Squash, and Onion Kebabs

24 pearl onions
twenty-four 1½-inch-diameter pattypan squash
24 small okra
olive oil for brushing the kebabs
sage butter (page 188) as an accompaniment

In a kettle of boiling salted water boil the onions for 2 minutes, add the squash, and boil the vegetables for 2 minutes. Add the okra and boil the vegetables for 1 minute. Drain the vegetables, plunge them into a bowl of ice and cold water to stop the cooking, and drain them again. Peel the onions. *The vegetables may be prepared up to this point 1 day in advance and kept covered and chilled.* Thread the onions, the squash, and the okra, alternating them, onto twelve 10-inch wooden skewers, brush the vegetables lightly with the oil, and season them with salt and pepper. Grill the kebabs on a rack set 5 to 6 inches over glowing coals, turning them, for 8 minutes, or until the squash is tender. Serve the kebabs with the sage butter. Serves 6.

PHOTO ON PAGE 55

Sage Butter

1 stick (½ cup) unsalted butter, softened
2 tablespoons finely chopped fresh sage plus
   whole sage leaves for garnish if desired

In a bowl combine well the butter, the chopped sage, and salt and pepper to taste and chill the sage butter, covered, for at least 1 hour or overnight. *The sage butter may be made 4 days in advance and kept covered and chilled.* Garnish the sage butter with the sage leaves. Makes about ½ cup.

PHOTO ON PAGES 54 AND 55

*Onions Filled with Hashed-Brown Potatoes
and Bacon*

six ¾-pound onions
6 slices of lean bacon
2 tablespoons unsalted butter
1 pound russet (baking) potatoes
1 small green bell pepper, chopped fine
⅓ cup minced fresh parsley leaves
1 teaspoon dried thyme, crumbled
1 cup grated sharp Cheddar

Cut ½ inch from the stem end of each onion, leaving the root end intact, and with a melon-ball cutter scoop out the centers, reserving 1½ cups of the centers and leaving ¼-inch shells. In a kettle of boiling salted water boil the onion shells gently for 5 minutes and let them drain, inverted, on paper towels. Chop fine the reserved onion. In a heavy skillet cook the bacon over moderate heat until it is crisp, transfer it with tongs to paper towels to drain, and crumble it. Pour all but 1 tablespoon of the fat from the skillet, add the butter, and heat the mixture over moderately high heat until the foam subsides. Add the potatoes, peeled and cut into ¼-inch dice, the chopped onion, and the bell pepper and sauté the vegetables, stirring frequently, for 4 to 6 minutes, or until the potatoes are golden brown and just tender. Remove the skillet from the heat and stir in the parsley, the thyme, ¾ cup of the Cheddar, and salt and pepper to taste.

Sprinkle the onion shells with salt and pepper, divide the potato mixture among them, and put the onions in a shallow 15½- by 10½-inch baking pan. Add 1 cup water to the pan and bake the onions in a preheated 350° F. oven for 30 minutes. Top the onions with the remaining ¼ cup Cheddar and bake them for 10 to 15 minutes more, or until the cheese is melted. Serves 6.

Thanksgiving Stuffed Onions

4 large onions (about ¾ pound each)
¼ cup chicken broth
¼ cup heavy cream
½ teaspoon sugar
2 cups chopped cooked turkey
1 cup cooked turkey stuffing
6 tablespoons cranberry sauce
½ cup turkey gravy or chicken broth
1⅓ cups mashed potatoes

Cut the top ½ inch from each onion, peel the onions, and with a melon-ball cutter scoop out the centers, reserving the onion pieces, leaving 2 layers of onion or ⅓-inch-thick shells, and leaving the bottoms slightly thicker. Transfer the reserved onion pieces to a 13- by 9-inch glass baking dish, drizzle the broth over them, and arrange the onion shells, inverted, on top. Cover the dish tightly with foil and bake the onions in the middle of a preheated 425° F. oven for 45 to 50 minutes, or until the shells are just tender. Remove and reserve the shells, into the onion pieces stir the cream, the sugar, and salt and pepper to taste, and bake the mixture, uncovered, in the 425° F. oven, stirring occasionally, for 25 minutes.

While the creamed onions are baking, in each reserved onion shell layer ¼ cup of the turkey, ¼ cup of the stuffing, 1½ tablespoons of the cranberry sauce, and another ¼ cup of the turkey and holding each shell in one hand pack the layers lightly. Arrange the stuffed onions on top of the baked creamed onions and pour 2 tablespoons of the gravy into each stuffed onion. Top each stuffed onion with ⅓ cup of the mashed potatoes, mounding them and scoring them with a fork, and bake the onions in the 425° F. oven, stirring the creamed onions occasionally, for 35 to 40 minutes, or until the potatoes are golden. Serves 4.

Petits Pois

two 10-ounce packages frozen *petits pois*
   (tiny peas)
2 tablespoons unsalted butter, softened
the zest of 1 lemon, removed with a vegetable
   peeler and cut into fine julienne strips

In a large saucepan bring 1 cup salted water to a boil, add the peas, and return the water to a boil, separating the peas with a fork. Simmer the peas, covered, for 3 to

4 minutes, or until they are heated through, and drain them well. Toss the peas with the butter and salt and pepper to taste, transfer them to a heated serving dish, and sprinkle them with the zest. Serves 6.

PHOTO ON PAGE 75

Minted Pea Purée

three 10-ounce packages frozen peas, thawed
⅓ cup fresh mint leaves plus fresh mint sprigs
    for garnish if desired
3 tablespoons half-and-half, or to taste
3 tablespoons unsalted butter, cut into bits

In a large saucepan combine the peas with ¾ cup water and the mint leaves and boil the mixture, covered, for 4 minutes, or until the peas are tender. Drain the mixture well and in a food processor purée it with the half-and-half, the butter, and salt and pepper to taste. *The purée may be made 1 day in advance, kept covered and chilled, and reheated.* Transfer the purée to a serving dish and garnish it with the mint sprigs. Serves 8.

PHOTO ON PAGE 30

Meatloaf-Filled Green Bell Peppers

6 green bell peppers (about ½ pound each)
½ cup fine dry bread crumbs
1 cup heavy cream
¾ cup finely chopped onion
3 tablespoons unsalted butter
1¼ pounds lean ground chuck
½ pound ground pork
¼ cup chopped scallion greens
¼ cup minced fresh parsley leaves
1½ teaspoons salt
⅛ teaspoon ground cloves

In a kettle of boiling salted water blanch the bell peppers, covered partially, for 3 minutes and transfer them to a bowl of ice and cold water to stop the cooking. Cut ¾ inch from the stem end of each bell pepper, reserving the bottoms, and chop fine the flesh from around the stems, discarding the stems. In a bowl let the bread crumbs soak in the cream for 8 minutes, or until the cream is absorbed. In a skillet cook the onion in the butter over moderately low heat, stirring occasionally, until it is softened and let it cool. Stir the onion mixture into the bread crumb mixture, stir in the chuck, the

pork, the scallion greens, the parsley, the salt, the cloves, and black pepper to taste, and divide the mixture among the bell peppers. Arrange the bell peppers in a shallow 15½- by 10½- baking pan, add 2 cups water to the pan, and bake the peppers in the middle of a preheated 375° F. oven for 1 hour, or until the meat is no longer pink. Serves 6 as an entrée.

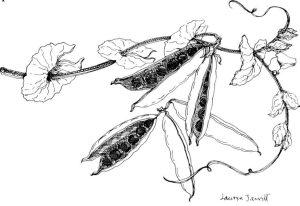

Lauren Jarrett

Red Bell Peppers Filled with Curried Rice

1 cup short-grain rice (available at Oriental
    markets and some supermarkets)
3 small red bell peppers, halved lengthwise
    and the seeds and ribs discarded
½ cup sliced almonds
3 tablespoons unsalted butter
1½ teaspoons curry powder
½ cup raisins, chopped coarse
4 scallions, chopped fine
cayenne to taste

In a heavy saucepan combine the rice, 1½ cups water, and salt to taste, bring the water to a boil, and cook the rice, covered, over low heat for 15 to 20 minutes, or until the water is absorbed and the rice is tender. In a kettle of boiling salted water blanch the bell pepper halves for 4 minutes, plunge them into a bowl of ice and cold water to stop the cooking, and let them drain well on paper towels.

In a skillet cook the almonds in the butter over moderate heat, stirring occasionally, until they begin to turn golden, add the curry powder, and cook the mixture, stirring, for 30 seconds. Add the raisins, the scallions, and ½ cup water and cook the mixture, stirring occasionally, until the liquid is reduced to about ⅓ cup. In a bowl combine well the rice, the almond mixture, the cayenne, and salt to taste, divide the mixture among the bell pepper halves, and serve the bell peppers at room temperature. Serves 6 as a side dish.

Potatoes Boulangère

1 tablespoon unsalted butter
2 tablespoons beef broth
1 unpeeled large (¾ pound) russet (baking)
    potato, scrubbed well and cut into
    ¼-inch-thick slices
1 onion, sliced thin
coarse salt to taste

In a 1-cup glass measure combine the butter and the broth and microwave the mixture at high power (100%) for 1 minute, or until the butter is melted. In a small microwave-safe bowl or casserole arrange one third of the potato slices, drained, in one layer, top them with one third of the onion slices, and layer the remaining vegetable slices in the same manner. Pour the butter mixture over the potato mixture and sprinkle the top with the salt and pepper to taste. Microwave the mixture, three fourths covered with microwave-safe plastic wrap, at high power (100%) for 10 to 12 minutes, or until the potatoes are tender. Serves 2.

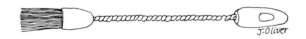

Baked Potato Skins

8 russet (baking) potatoes (about ½ pound
    each), scrubbed, patted dry, and rubbed
    with olive oil
olive oil for brushing the potato skins
sweet paprika for sprinkling the potato skins
fine sea salt or kosher salt for sprinkling the
    potato skins
sour cream as an accompaniment if desired

Prick the potatoes a few times with a fork and bake them in the middle of a preheated 425° F. oven for 1 hour. Let the potatoes cool, halve them lengthwise, and scoop them out, leaving a ¼-inch shell. Reserve the potato pulp for another use. Cut each shell lengthwise into 6 strips and arrange the strips on a baking sheet. Brush the strips with the oil, sprinkle them with the paprika, the salt, and pepper to taste, and bake them in the middle of the preheated 425° F. oven for 20 to 25 minutes, or until they are crisp and golden brown. Serve the potato skins with the sour cream. Serves 6.

PHOTO ON PAGE 15

Crusty Potato Galette

1 tablespoon unsalted butter,
    melted
1 tablespoon vegetable oil
¾ pound boiling or baking potatoes,
    scrubbed but not peeled
¼ teaspoon dried rosemary,
    crumbled

In a small bowl stir together the butter and the oil. In a food processor fitted with a 1-millimeter slicing blade or with a *mandoline* or similar hand-held slicing device, slice the potatoes thin. Working quickly to prevent the potatoes from discoloring, brush the bottom of a 9-inch cast-iron skillet with some of the butter mixture and cover it with a layer of the potato slices, overlapping them. Brush the potatoes with some of the remaining butter mixture, sprinkle them with some of the rosemary, and season them with salt and pepper. Layer the remaining potatoes with the remaining butter mixture and rosemary in the same manner. Heat the mixture over moderately high heat until it begins to sizzle, transfer the skillet to the middle of a preheated 450° F. oven, and bake the *galette* for 25 minutes, or until it is golden and the potatoes are tender. Cut the *galette* into wedges. Serves 2.

Baked Potatoes with Lebanese-Style Beef Filling

3 russet (baking) potatoes (about ½ pound
    each), scrubbed, patted dry, and rubbed
    with vegetable oil
2 teaspoons cornstarch
2¼ cups plain yogurt
1 large garlic clove, minced and mashed to a
    paste with 1½ teaspoons salt
⅓ cup coarsely chopped walnuts
3 tablespoons vegetable oil
1 onion, halved lengthwise and sliced
    thin crosswise
¾ pound ground chuck
¾ teaspoon cinnamon
½ cup minced fresh parsley leaves

Prick the potatoes a few times with a fork and bake them on a rack in the middle of a preheated 450° F. oven for 1½ hours.

While the potatoes are baking, in a small bowl dissolve the cornstarch in 2 tablespoons of the yogurt and in a saucepan simmer the cornstarch mixture and the remaining yogurt, whisking, for 5 minutes. Stir in the garlic paste, simmer the sauce, whisking, for 2 minutes, and keep it warm, covered. In a skillet cook the walnuts in the oil over moderate heat, stirring, for 1 to 2 minutes, or until they are golden, and transfer them with a slotted spoon to a large bowl. In the oil remaining in the skillet cook the onion, stirring occasionally, until it is golden, add the chuck, and brown the meat, breaking up the lumps.

While the baked potatoes are still warm, halve them lengthwise, scoop out the flesh, leaving crisp shells, and chop coarse the flesh. In the large bowl combine well the walnuts, the chuck mixture, the chopped potato, the cinnamon, the parsley, and salt and pepper to taste, divide the mixture among the potato shells, and top it with some of the sauce. Bake the potatoes on a baking sheet in the 450° F. oven for 10 to 15 minutes, or until the filling is hot. Serve them with the remaining sauce. Serves 6 as an entrée.

Dauphine Potatoes
(Deep-Fried Potato Croquettes)

1½ pounds russet (baking) potatoes (about 3)
3 tablespoons unsalted butter, cut into bits
1 teaspoon salt
a pinch of freshly grated nutmeg
½ cup all-purpose flour
2 large eggs
vegetable oil for deep-frying the potatoes
coarse salt for sprinkling the croquettes
    if desired

Bake the potatoes in a preheated 425° F. oven for 50 minutes to 1 hour, or until they are soft, halve them lengthwise, and scoop the potato out of the shells with a spoon, reserving the shells for another use. Force the scooped-out potato through a ricer or a food mill fitted with the medium disk into a large bowl. (There should be about 2 cups riced potato.)

In a saucepan combine ½ cup water, the butter, the salt, and the nutmeg, bring the mixture to a boil, and stir in the flour all at once. Reduce the heat to moderate and beat the mixture vigorously with a wooden spoon for 3 minutes, or until the paste pulls away from the side of the pan and forms a ball. Remove the pan from the heat, add the eggs, 1 at a time, beating after each addition,

and beat the mixture until it is smooth and shiny.

Add the potatoes and beat the mixture until it is combined well. *The potato mixture may be prepared up to this point 1 day in advance and kept covered and chilled.* In a deep fryer or large kettle heat 2 inches of the oil until it registers 340° F. on a deep-fat thermometer. Transfer the potato mixture to a large pastry bag fitted with a ½-inch star tip and pipe eight 2½-inch lengths, cutting them with kitchen shears or a small knife, directly into the oil. Fry the croquettes, turning them with a slotted spoon, for 3 minutes, or until they are crisp, golden, and cooked through, transfer them as they are fried to paper towels to drain, and sprinkle them with the salt. Make more croquettes in batches with the remaining potato mixture and transfer the drained croquettes to a rack set in a jelly-roll pan (to prevent them from becoming soggy). *The croquettes may be made 2 hours in advance, kept covered loosely with paper towels at room temperature, and reheated on the rack in a preheated 400° F. oven for 5 minutes, or until they are heated through and crisp.* If not making the croquettes in advance, keep them warm in a preheated 300° F. oven. Serves 6.

PHOTO ON PAGE 75

Dilled Potatoes Vinaigrette

1 pound small red boiling potatoes, scrubbed
¼ teaspoon Dijon-style mustard
1 tablespoon white-wine vinegar
1½ teaspoons dry vermouth or dry white wine
2 tablespoons olive oil
¼ cup minced fresh dill

Cut the potatoes lengthwise into fourths and in a steamer set over boiling water steam them, covered, for 7 to 10 minutes, or until they are just tender. In a bowl whisk together the mustard, the vinegar, the vermouth, and salt to taste, add the oil in a stream, whisking, and whisk the dressing until it is emulsified. Add the potatoes while they are still warm to the dressing and toss them gently with the dressing, the dill, and pepper to taste until they are coated well. Let the potato mixture stand, tossing it occasionally, for 30 minutes and serve it at room temperature. *The potato mixture may be made 1 day in advance and kept covered and chilled. Let the potato mixture return to room temperature before serving.* Serves 4.

PHOTO ON PAGE 51

Mashed-Potato Cakes with Olives and Capers

a ½-pound russet (baking) potato
1 teaspoon drained bottled capers,
    chopped fine
4 Kalamata or other brine-cured black olives,
    chopped fine
1 large egg, beaten lightly
⅓ cup dry bread crumbs
¼ cup vegetable oil
lemon wedges as an accompaniment

Peel the potato, cut it into ¾-inch pieces, and on a rack in a saucepan steam it over boiling water, covered, for 8 to 10 minutes, or until it is very tender. Let the potato cool for 5 minutes, in a bowl mash it, and stir in the capers, the olives, the egg, and salt and pepper to taste. Scoop the mixture by ¼-cup measures, form the scoops into ½-inch-thick cakes, and coat the cakes with the bread crumbs. In a large heavy skillet heat the oil over moderately high heat until it is hot but not smoking and in it sauté the cakes, turning them once, for 4 minutes, or until they are golden. Serve the cakes with the lemon. Makes about 4 cakes, serving 2.

Mashed Potatoes

3 pounds russet (baking) potatoes, scrubbed
⅓ cup milk
¾ stick (6 tablespoons) unsalted butter,
    melted

In a kettle combine the potatoes with enough cold water to cover them by 2 inches, bring the water to a boil, and add salt to taste. Simmer the potatoes for 1 hour, or until they are tender, drain them, and return them to the kettle. Steam the potatoes, covered, shaking the kettle, for 30 seconds, or until they are dry. Peel the potatoes while they are still warm, force them through a ricer or a food mill fitted with the coarse disk into a bowl, and beat in the milk, scalded, the butter, and salt and pepper to taste. Transfer the potatoes to a heated serving dish. Serves 8.

Mashed Potatoes with Scallion

3 pounds boiling potatoes, scrubbed
½ stick (¼ cup) unsalted butter, softened
¾ to 1 cup milk
½ cup thinly sliced scallion

In a large kettle cover the potatoes with 2 inches salted cold water, bring the water to a boil, and simmer the potatoes for 40 to 50 minutes, or until they are tender. Drain the potatoes and force them through a ricer or peel them and mash them with a potato masher. Stir in the butter and enough of the milk, heated, to reach the desired consistency. Stir in the scallion and salt and pepper to taste. Serves 8.

PHOTO ON PAGE 24

Roasted Potatoes with Garlic

2 pounds small red potatoes, quartered
2 large garlic cloves, sliced thin
1½ tablespoons olive oil

In a jelly-roll or large baking pan toss the potatoes with the garlic, the oil, and salt and pepper to taste and roast them in the middle of a preheated 500° F. oven, stirring once, for 30 minutes. Serves 6.

PHOTO ON PAGE 21

Roasted Rosemary Potato Slices

2½ tablespoons unsalted butter, melted
2 russet (baking) potatoes (about 1¼ pounds),
    scrubbed
1 teaspoon kosher salt plus additional
    if desired
½ teaspoon dried rosemary, crumbled

Into an 8-inch baking pan pour half the butter, making sure it covers the entire bottom, and in the pan layer the potatoes, cut into ¼-inch-thick slices, in separate rows, overlapping them slightly. Sprinkle the potatoes with the salt, the rosemary, and pepper to taste, pour the remaining butter over them, and bake the potatoes in the middle of a preheated 425° F. oven, turning each row once with a long thin spatula, for 45 minutes to 1 hour, or until they are crisp and golden. Sprinkle the potatoes with the additional salt. Serves 2.

PHOTO ON PAGE 11

Sautéed Potatoes Provençale

3 tablespoons red-wine vinegar
2 garlic cloves, minced
2 teaspoons freshly grated lemon zest
½ cup olive oil

3 pounds (about 6 large) boiling potatoes, peeled, sliced ¼ inch thick, and patted dry
⅓ cup minced fresh parsley leaves, preferably flat-leafed

In a small saucepan combine the vinegar, the garlic, the zest, and salt and pepper to taste, bring the mixture to a boil, and simmer it for 2 minutes. Remove the pan from the heat and whisk in ¼ cup of the oil. In each of 2 large skillets heat 2 tablespoons of the remaining oil over moderately high heat until it is hot but not smoking and in it cook the potatoes in one layer in batches over moderate heat, turning them, for 10 to 15 minutes, or until they are golden brown on the outside and tender within. Transfer the potatoes to a serving dish, pour the garlic mixture over them, and toss them with the parsley. Serves 6.

Old-Fashioned Scalloped Potatoes

2 cups thinly sliced onion
9 tablespoons unsalted butter
6 tablespoons all-purpose flour
3½ cups milk
2½ pounds boiling potatoes
1½ cups coarsely grated sharp Cheddar (about 6 ounces)
⅓ cup dry bread crumbs

In a skillet cook the onion in 2 tablespoons of the butter over moderately low heat, stirring, until it is very soft. In a heavy saucepan melt 6 tablespoons of the remaining butter over moderately low heat, whisk in the flour, and cook the *roux*, whisking, for 3 minutes. Add the milk, scalded, in a stream, whisking, and bring the sauce to a boil. Simmer the sauce, whisking, for 1 minute and add salt and pepper to taste. Peel the potatoes and slice them ⅛ inch thick. Spread about one third of the sauce in the bottom of a well-buttered 3-quart gratin dish at least 2½ inches deep, cover it with a layer of potato slices, overlapping the slices slightly, and cover the potatoes with one third of the onions. Sprinkle the onions with one third of the Cheddar and continue to layer the remaining sauce, potatoes, onions, and Cheddar in the same manner. Sprinkle the top with the bread crumbs, dot it with the remaining 1 tablespoon butter, cut into bits, and bake the potato mixture, covered with foil, in the middle of a preheated 400° F. oven for 20 minutes. Remove the foil and bake the potato mixture for 30 to 35 minutes more, or until the top is golden and the potatoes are tender. Serves 6 to 8.

Sherried Sweet Potatoes and Apples

3 large sweet potatoes
3 Granny Smith apples
½ stick (¼ cup) unsalted butter
¼ cup fresh lemon juice
¼ cup firmly packed light brown sugar
¼ teaspoon cinnamon
⅓ cup medium-dry Sherry

In a kettle combine the sweet potatoes with enough cold water to cover them by 1 inch and boil them for 35 minutes, or until they are just tender. Drain the sweet potatoes and let them cool until they can be handled. *The sweet potatoes may be prepared in advance up to this point and kept chilled overnight.* Peel the sweet potatoes, cut them lengthwise into sixths, and cut the lengths crosswise into ½-inch pieces. Peel, core, and cut the apples lengthwise into sixths and cut the wedges crosswise into ½-inch pieces. In a large heavy skillet cook the apples in the butter over moderate heat, stirring, for 3 minutes, or until they are softened. Stir in the lemon juice, the brown sugar, the cinnamon, and the Sherry, bring the liquid to a boil, and simmer the apples for 3 minutes. Add the sweet potatoes and cook the mixture, stirring gently and trying not to break up the sweet potatoes, for 2 minutes, or until it is combined well and heated through. Transfer the mixture to a heated serving dish. Serves 8.

PHOTO ON PAGE 73

Creamed Rutabaga and Sweet Potato

1½ tablespoons unsalted butter,
   cut into pieces
1½ tablespoons all-purpose flour
1 onion, chopped
¾ pound rutabaga, peeled and cut into
   ½-inch pieces
1 cup heavy cream
¾ pound sweet potato, peeled and cut into
   ½-inch pieces

In a microwave-safe 9-inch square baking dish microwave the butter at high power (100%) for 15 seconds, or until it is melted, stir in the flour, and microwave the *roux* at high power (100%), stirring it every minute, for 3 minutes. Stir in the onion and microwave the mixture at high power (100%) for 1 minute. Stir in the rutabaga, the cream, and 2 tablespoons water and microwave the mixture at high power (100%) for 5 minutes. Stir in the sweet potato and salt and pepper to taste, microwave the mixture at high power (100%) for 15 to 18 minutes, or until the vegetables are tender. Let the mixture stand, covered, for 5 minutes. Serves 2–3.

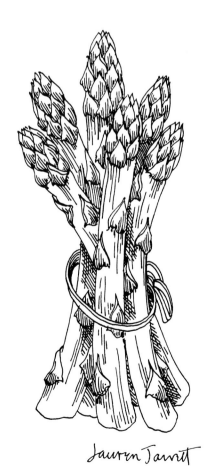

Lauren Jarrett

Roasted Shallot and Sesame Asparagus

2½ pounds asparagus, trimmed
1½ tablespoons olive oil
2 tablespoons minced shallot
2 tablespoons sesame seeds, toasted lightly
fresh lemon juice to taste

In a large shallow baking dish toss the asparagus with the oil, coating it well, and bake it in a preheated 500° F. oven, shaking the dish every 2 minutes, for 6 to 8 minutes, or until it is almost *al dente*. Sprinkle the asparagus with the shallot and the sesame seeds, bake it for 1 minute, or until it is *al dente*, and sprinkle it with the lemon juice and salt to taste. Serves 8.

PHOTO ON PAGE 36

Buttered Snow Peas

¼ pound snow peas, trimmed and the
   strings discarded
1 teaspoon unsalted butter

In a large saucepan of boiling salted water blanch the snow peas for 1 minute, or until they are crisp-tender. Drain the snow peas well and in a bowl toss them with the butter. Serves 2.

PHOTO ON PAGE 11

Spaghetti Squash with Mushrooms and Herbs

a 2- to 2½-pound spaghetti squash, halved
   lengthwise, reserving 1 half for another use
2 tablespoons unsalted butter
¼ cup finely chopped onion
1 cup thinly sliced mushrooms
2 tablespoons minced fresh parsley leaves
1 tablespoon minced fresh chives
¼ cup freshly grated Parmesan

Wrap the squash half in microwave-safe plastic wrap and microwave it, cut side up, at high power (100%) for 10 to 12 minutes, or until it feels soft when pressed. Let the squash stand for 5 minutes. In a small microwave-safe dish combine the butter, the onion, and the mushrooms and microwave the mixture at high power (100%), stirring once, for 5 minutes, or until the mushrooms are tender. Discard the seeds from the squash, scrape the flesh with a fork into a bowl, and toss it with the mushroom mixture, the parsley, the chives, the Parmesan, and salt and pepper to taste. Serves 2.

Tomatoes with Corn and Basil Filling

6 tomatoes (about 3 pounds)
3 ears of corn, shucked
2 tablespoons red-wine vinegar
⅓ cup olive oil
¼ cup chopped fresh basil leaves plus 6 basil
    sprigs for garnish
1 scallion, chopped fine
2 tablespoons unsalted butter
1 cup ¼-inch bread cubes

Cut ½ inch from the stem end of each tomato and with a melon-ball cutter scoop out and discard the seeds and pulp, leaving a ½-inch shell. Sprinkle the shells with salt and let them drain, inverted, on paper towels for 10 minutes. In a large saucepan combine the corn with enough salted cold water to cover it by 1 inch, bring the water to a boil, and boil the corn for 5 minutes. Drain the corn, let it cool until it can be handled, and, working over a bowl, cut the kernels from the cobs with a serrated knife.

In a small bowl whisk together the vinegar and salt and pepper to taste, add the oil in a stream, whisking, and whisk the dressing until it is emulsified. To the corn add the dressing, the chopped basil, the scallion, and salt and pepper to taste.

In a skillet melt the butter over moderately high heat and in it sauté the bread cubes, stirring occasionally, until they are golden. Toss the croutons with the corn mixture, spoon the mixture into the tomatoes, and arrange the basil sprigs decoratively on the tomatoes. Serves 6 as a side dish.

Grilled Vegetables on Onion Rolls

2 tablespoons white-wine vinegar
⅓ cup vegetable oil
2 red bell peppers, quartered
½ pound eggplant, cut crosswise into
    ¼-inch-thick slices
½ pound zucchini, scrubbed and cut
    diagonally into ¼-inch-thick slices
1 onion, cut crosswise into ¼-inch-thick slices
4 onion rolls, halved horizontally
¼ cup fresh coriander if desired

In a bowl whisk together the vinegar and salt and black pepper to taste, add the oil in a stream, whisking,

and whisk the dressing until it is emulsified. Brush the bell peppers with some of the dressing, grill them, skin sides down, on a rack set 4 to 6 inches over glowing coals for 10 to 15 minutes, or until the skin is charred, and transfer them to a bowl, discarding the charred skin. Brush the eggplant, the zucchini, and the onion with some of the remaining dressing, grill the vegetables on the rack, turning them, for 10 to 15 minutes, or until they are browned and tender, and transfer them to the bowl. Brush the cut sides of the rolls with the remaining dressing and grill the rolls, cut sides down, for 30 seconds, or until they are toasted lightly. (Alternatively, the vegetables and the rolls can be broiled on the rack of a broiler pan about 2 inches from the heat.) Divide the vegetables among the bottom halves of the rolls, top them with the coriander, and cover the sandwiches with the tops of the rolls, pressing them firmly. Makes 4 sandwiches.

Mixed Spring Vegetables

¾ pound (about 30) baby carrots,* trimmed
    and peeled
¾ pound (about 24) baby turnips,* trimmed,
    or 1 pound turnips, peeled and cut into
    1-inch pieces
¾ pound *haricots verts** (thin green beans),
    trimmed
¾ pound (about 30) baby pattypan squash,*
    trimmed
½ stick (¼ cup) unsalted butter
2 tablespoons minced fresh chives, or to taste

*available at specialty produce markets

In a steamer set over boiling water steam the carrots and the turnips, covered, for 5 to 7 minutes, or until they are just tender, and transfer them to a large bowl. In the steamer steam the *haricots verts*, covered, for 3 to 4 minutes, or until they are just tender, and transfer them to the bowl. In the steamer steam the squash, covered, for 3 minutes, or until they are just tender, and transfer them to the bowl. In a large skillet melt the butter over moderate heat, add the vegetables, the chives, and salt and pepper to taste, and cook the mixture, stirring, until the vegetables are combined well and heated through. Serves 8.

PHOTO ON PAGE 30

Roasted Autumn Vegetables

1½ pounds small red potatoes
1 pound shallots (about 24), peeled
    and trimmed
5 tablespoons olive oil
1 bay leaf
¼ teaspoon dried thyme, crumbled
4 garlic cloves, crushed
2 pounds butternut squash, peeled and cut
    into ¾-inch pieces (about 4 cups)
fresh thyme sprigs for garnish if desired

In a bowl toss together the potatoes, quartered, the shallots, 4 tablespoons of the oil, the bay leaf, the thyme, the garlic, and salt and pepper to taste. Spread the vegetables in a large oiled roasting pan and roast them in the middle of a preheated 375° F. oven, shaking the pan every 5 to 10 minutes, for 25 minutes. In a bowl toss the squash with the remaining 1 tablespoon oil and salt and pepper to taste and add it to the pan. Roast the vegetables, shaking the pan occasionally, for 10 to 20 minutes more, or until they are tender. Discard the bay leaf and garnish the vegetables with the thyme sprigs. Serves 8.

PHOTO ON PAGE 66

Zucchini in Mint Vinaigrette

½ teaspoon sugar
½ teaspoon salt
2 tablespoons fresh lemon juice
¼ cup vegetable oil
2 zucchini, each cut into ¼-inch slices
3 tablespoons chopped fresh mint leaves

In a small bowl whisk together the sugar, the salt, the lemon juice, and the oil. Transfer the vinaigrette to a skillet, bring it to a boil, and add the zucchini, stirring to coat it with the dressing. Simmer the zucchini for 3 minutes, or until it is crisp-tender, stir in the mint, and let the zucchini cool in the dressing. Serve the zucchini at room temperature. Serves 2.

Zucchini and Tomato Sauté with Herbs

½ cup finely chopped onion
2 tablespoons unsalted butter or olive oil
2 small zucchini, scrubbed and sliced thin
    (about 2 cups)
2 tomatoes, seeded and chopped fine
    (about ¾ cup)
2 tablespoons minced fresh mint, basil, or
    parsley leaves

In a skillet cook the onion in the butter over moderately low heat, stirring, until it is softened, add the zucchini, and sauté the mixture over moderate heat, stirring, for 3 to 5 minutes, or until the zucchini is just tender. Stir in the tomatoes, cook the mixture, covered, for 1 to 2 minutes, or until the tomatoes are just heated through, and stir in the mint and salt and pepper to taste. Serves 2.

Zucchini Boats with Tabbouleh Filling

½ cup *bulgur* (cracked wheat)
1 teaspoon salt
3 tablespoons fresh lemon juice
¼ cup olive oil
1 small garlic clove, minced
3 zucchini (about ½ pound each), scrubbed,
    trimmed, and halved lengthwise
½ cup minced fresh mint leaves plus mint
    sprigs for garnish
½ cup minced fresh parsley leaves
½ cup finely chopped, seeded, peeled
    cucumber
1 scallion, minced
1 tomato, seeded and chopped fine

In a bowl combine the *bulgur* with the salt, pour enough boiling water over the *bulgur* to cover it by 1 inch, and let the *bulgur* soak for 1 hour. Drain the *bulgur* and squeeze it dry in a kitchen towel. In a bowl stir together the *bulgur*, the lemon juice, the oil, and the garlic and let the *bulgur* marinate, covered and chilled, for at least 1 hour and up to 3 hours. With a melon-ball cutter scoop out the zucchini flesh, reserving it for another use and leaving ¼-inch shells. On a steamer rack set over boiling water steam the zucchini shells, cut sides up and covered partially, in batches for 3 to 5 minutes, or until they are just tender. Transfer the shells, cut sides down, to paper towels to drain and let them cool. Stir the minced mint, the parsley, the cucumber, the scallion, the tomato, and salt and pepper to taste into the *bulgur* mixture, divide the *tabbouleh* among the zucchini shells, and garnish the zucchini boats with the mint sprigs. Serves 6 as a side dish.

Grilled Marinated Zucchini

1 large garlic clove, minced and mashed to a
    paste with ½ teaspoon salt
2 tablespoons fresh lemon juice
1 teaspoon white-wine vinegar
¼ cup vegetable oil
2 zucchini (about 1½ inches in diameter), scrubbed

In a small bowl whisk together the garlic paste, the lemon juice, the vinegar, and pepper to taste and whisk in the oil. In a shallow baking dish large enough to hold the zucchini in one layer combine the zucchini, halved lengthwise, and the marinade and let the zucchini marinate, covered and chilled, turning them several times, overnight. Grill the zucchini on an oiled rack set 5 to 6 inches over glowing coals for 8 minutes and brush them with some of the marinade. Turn the zucchini, grill them for 6 to 8 minutes, or until they are tender, and transfer them to a work surface. (Alternatively, the zucchini may be grilled in a ridged grill pan.) Slice the zucchini diagonally. Serves 4.

PHOTO ON PAGE 18

SALADS AND SALAD TOPPINGS

ENTRÉE SALADS

Spicy Oriental Beef Salad

1 tablespoon vegetable oil
1 pound ground beef (preferably chuck)
1 tablespoon Worcestershire sauce
¼ cup fresh lime juice
¼ teaspoon cayenne
1 tablespoon sugar
1 tablespoon soy sauce
1 garlic clove, minced and mashed to a paste
   with ½ teaspoon salt
⅓ cup finely chopped scallion
½ cup chopped fresh coriander or fresh
   mint leaves
soft lettuce leaves for lining the plates
lime wedges for garnish

In a large skillet heat the oil over moderately high heat until it is hot but not smoking, in it stir-fry the beef for 1 minute, or just until it is no longer pink, and drain the beef in a sieve. In a bowl whisk together the Worcestershire sauce, the lime juice, the cayenne, the sugar, the soy sauce, and the garlic paste, add the beef, and stir it to combine it well with the dressing. Stir in the scallion and the coriander, divide the mixture between 2 plates, lined with the lettuce leaves, and garnish the salads with the lime wedges. Serves 2.

Grilled Chicken Salad with Corn, Peppers, and Tortilla Crisps

For the chicken
2 boneless whole chicken breasts with the skin
   (about 1½ pounds), halved
½ cup fresh lime juice
1 teaspoon dried orégano, crumbled
vegetable oil for brushing the chicken
For the tortilla crisps
4 corn tortillas, cut into long thin triangles
vegetable oil for frying the tortillas

2 cups cooked fresh corn kernels (cut from
   about 4 ears)
1 large red bell pepper, diced
3 scallions, sliced thin
2 tablespoons fresh lime juice, or to taste
1 tablespoon finely chopped fresh orégano or
   1 teaspoon dried, crumbled, or to taste
½ teaspoon ground cumin, or to taste
¼ cup olive oil
1 bunch of *arugula*, washed well and spun dry

Prepare the chicken: In a bowl let the chicken marinate in the lime juice with the orégano and salt and pepper to taste, covered and chilled, for at least 30 minutes, or up to 1 hour. Drain the chicken, pat it dry, and brush it with the oil. Grill the chicken, seasoned with salt and pepper, on a well-oiled rack set about 6 inches over glowing coals for 6 to 7 minutes on each side, or until it is just cooked through. (Alternatively, the chicken can be grilled on top of the stove in a ridged grill pan over moderately high heat for about the same length of time.) Transfer the chicken to a cutting board and let it stand for 10 minutes.

Make the tortilla crisps while the chicken is grilling: In a heavy skillet heat ½ inch oil to 375° F. on a deep-fat thermometer and in it fry the tortilla triangles in batches for 45 seconds to 1 minute, or until they are golden, transferring them with a slotted spatula as they are fried to paper towels to drain and sprinkling them with salt. *The tortilla crisps may be made 1 day in advance and kept in an airtight container.*

In a large bowl combine the corn, the bell pepper, and the scallions, add the lime juice, the orégano, the cumin, the oil, and salt and pepper to taste, and toss the mixture until it is combined well. Cut the chicken lengthwise into thin slices and add it to the corn mixture with any juices that have accumulated on the cutting board. Divide the *arugula* and the tortilla crisps decoratively among 4 plates and mound the chicken salad in the center of each plate. Serves 4.

PHOTO ON PAGE 45

Grilled Chicken and Ziti Salad

2 whole skinless boneless chicken breasts,
    halved (about 1½ pounds)
2 tablespoons fresh lemon juice
1 pound *ziti* or other tubular pasta
2 large red bell peppers, cut into ½-inch dice
2½ cups thinly sliced celery
1 red onion, chopped (about 1¼ cups)
1¼ cups Kalamata or other brine-cured black
    olives, pitted and sliced thin
¼ cup minced fresh dill
3 tablespoons white-wine vinegar
2 tablespoons mayonnaise
2 tablespoons Dijon-style mustard
⅔ cup olive oil

In an oiled ridged grill pan heated over moderately high heat or on a rack set 4 to 6 inches over glowing coals grill the chicken breasts for 8 to 10 minutes on each side, or until they are springy to the touch, and transfer them to a dish. Sprinkle the chicken with the lemon juice and let it cool. In a kettle of boiling salted water boil the *ziti* until it is tender. In a colander refresh the *ziti* under cold water and drain it well.

In a large bowl toss together the *ziti*, the bell peppers, the celery, the onion, the olives, and the dill. Remove the chicken from the dish, reserving the juices, slice it thin, and add it to the *ziti* salad. To the juices in the dish add the vinegar, the mayonnaise, the mustard, and salt and pepper to taste, whisk the mixture well, and add the oil in a stream, whisking until the dressing is emulsified. Add the dressing to the salad, toss the salad well, and season it with salt and pepper. Serves 8 to 10.

PHOTO ON PAGE 48

Chicken Pasta Salad in Creamy Curry Dressing

¼ pound *rotelle* or other spiral pasta
1 whole skinless boneless chicken breast
    (about ¾ pound), poached and cut into bite-
    size pieces (about 1½ cups)
5 cherry tomatoes, quartered
2 scallions, sliced thin
1 tablespoon finely chopped fresh
    basil leaves
For the dressing
½ teaspoon minced garlic
1 teaspoon minced peeled fresh gingerroot
1 tablespoon unsalted butter
¼ cup heavy cream
1 tablespoon white-wine vinegar
¾ teaspoon curry powder
dried hot red pepper flakes to taste
1 tablespoon finely chopped drained bottled
    mango chutney, or to taste

In a large kettle of boiling salted water cook the pasta for 10 minutes, or until it is tender, refresh it in a colander under cold water, and drain it well. In a large bowl combine the pasta, the chicken, the tomatoes, the scallions, and the basil.

Make the dressing: In a skillet cook the garlic and the gingerroot in the butter over moderately low heat, stirring, until the garlic is softened, add the cream, and cook the mixture, whisking, until it is thickened slightly. Whisk in the vinegar, the curry powder, the red pepper flakes, and the chutney.

Add the dressing to the pasta mixture, tossing the salad to combine it well, and season the salad with salt and pepper. Serves 2.

Red Leaf Lettuce and Vegetable Salad with Yogurt-Mustard Dressing

3 cups torn red leaf lettuce, rinsed well and
   spun dry
1 carrot, grated
½ small red onion, sliced thin
4 mushrooms, sliced thin
4 cherry tomatoes, quartered
¾ cup broccoli flowerets, cut into ½-inch
   pieces, blanched in boiling water
   for 1 minute, and drained well
½ red bell pepper, cut into strips
1 teaspoon fresh lemon juice
1 tablespoon olive oil
1½ teaspoons coarse-grained mustard
¼ teaspoon sugar
a pinch of cayenne
½ cup plain yogurt
1 teaspoon finely chopped fresh parsley leaves
1 hard-boiled large egg,
   quartered, for garnish if desired

In a large bowl toss together the lettuce, the carrot, the onion, the mushrooms, the tomatoes, the broccoli, and the bell pepper. In a bowl whisk together the lemon juice, the oil, the mustard, the sugar, the cayenne, the yogurt, the parsley, and salt and black pepper to taste and toss the salad with the dressing, combining it well. Divide the salad between 2 large salad plates and garnish it with the egg. Serves 2.

Shrimp, Arugula, and Beet Salad with Parmesan Vinaigrette

3 beets (about ½ pound), trimmed, leaving the
   roots and 1 inch of the stems attached, and
   scrubbed well
12 medium shrimp, shelled and deveined
¼ pound green beans, trimmed and cut
   into ½-inch pieces (about ⅔ cup)
1½ tablespoons minced shallot
1 teaspoon Dijon-style mustard
1½ tablespoons fresh lemon juice
1½ teaspoons balsamic vinegar
2 tablespoons freshly grated Parmesan
3 tablespoons olive oil
3 cups packed *arugula* leaves, rinsed
   and spun dry

In a microwave-safe bowl combine the beets with ¼ cup water and microwave them, covered tightly with microwave-safe plastic wrap, at high power (100%), turning them once, for 10 to 12 minutes, or until they are tender. Let the beets stand, covered, for 5 minutes, rinse them under cold water, discarding the skins, and cut them into ¼-inch pieces. In a microwave-safe dish just large enough to hold the shrimp in one layer combine the shrimp with ¼ cup water, microwave them, covered tightly with microwave-safe plastic wrap, at high power (100%) for 2 minutes, or until they are just cooked through, and let them cool. In a small microwave-safe bowl combine the beans with ¼ cup water and microwave them, covered tightly with microwave-safe plastic wrap, at high power (100%) for 2 minutes, or until they are just tender. Rinse the beans under cold water and drain them well.

In a blender or small food processor blend the shallot, the mustard, the lemon juice, the vinegar, the Parmesan, and salt and pepper to taste until the mixture is smooth and with the motor running add the oil in a stream, blending the dressing until it is emulsified. In a salad bowl toss the *arugula*, the shrimp, and the beans with the dressing, divide the mixture between 2 plates, and sprinkle each serving with half the beets. Serves 2.

Spanish-Style Shrimp and Scallop Salad

2 tablespoons olive oil
1 teaspoon minced garlic
¼ pound shrimp, shelled, and deveined
   if desired
¼ pound sea scallops, halved crosswise
¼ cup minced seeded tomato
8 pimiento-stuffed green olives, sliced thin
½ small red onion, sliced thin
1 tablespoon Sherry vinegar
a pinch of paprika
⅛ teaspoon sugar
1 small head of Bibb lettuce, rinsed, spun
   dry, and cut into julienne strips
8 romaine leaves, cut into julienne strips

In a skillet heat 1 tablespoon of the oil with the garlic over moderately high heat until it is hot but not smoking and in it sauté the shrimp and the scallops, stirring, for 2 minutes. Stir in the tomato, the olives, and the onion and transfer the mixture to a large bowl. In a bowl whisk together the remaining 1 tablespoon oil, 1 tablespoon water, the vinegar, the paprika, the sugar, and salt and pepper to taste. Add the lettuces and the dressing to the shrimp mixture and toss the salad to coat it well with the dressing. Serves 2.

Lauren Jarrett

Lebanese-Style Tuna Salad with Tahini Dressing

For the dressing
2 tablespoons *tahini* (sesame seed paste, available at natural foods stores and some supermarkets)
3 tablespoons fresh lemon juice
1 large garlic clove, minced and mashed to a paste with ½ teaspoon salt
⅛ teaspoon cayenne, or to taste
⅓ cup olive oil

four 6½-ounce cans tuna packed in oil, drained and flaked
2 pounds onions, sliced thin
⅓ cup vegetable oil
⅓ cup pine nuts
1 cup chopped fresh flat-leafed parsley leaves plus parsley sprigs for garnish
6 to 8 pita loaves, quartered and opened into pockets

Make the dressing: In a blender blend together the *tahini*, the lemon juice, the garlic paste, and the cayenne, with the motor running add the oil in a stream, blending until the dressing is emulsified, and season the dressing with salt.

In a bowl toss the tuna lightly with half the dressing and mound the mixture on a large platter. In a large heavy skillet cook the onions in the oil over moderate heat, stirring occasionally, for 50 minutes, or until they are golden brown, and season them with salt and pepper. With a fork scatter the onions over the tuna. In the skillet cook the pine nuts over moderately low heat, stirring, until they are golden and scatter them over the on-

ions. Drizzle the salad with the remaining dressing and sprinkle it with the chopped parsley. Garnish the salad with the parsley sprigs and serve it with the pita pockets. Serves 8 to 10.

PHOTO ON PAGE 48

SALADS WITH GREENS

Arugula Salad with Carrot and Yellow Pepper
4 teaspoons white-wine vinegar
½ cup olive oil
10 cups loosely packed bite-size pieces of leaf lettuce, rinsed and spun dry
3 cups *arugula*, coarse stems discarded and the leaves rinsed and spun dry
½ cup coarsely grated carrot
½ cup julienne strips of yellow bell pepper

In a small bowl whisk together the vinegar and salt and black pepper to taste, add the oil in a stream, whisking, and whisk the dressing until it is emulsified. In a large bowl combine the lettuce, the *arugula*, the carrot, and the bell pepper, drizzle the dressing over the salad, and toss the salad until it is combined well. Serves 4.

PHOTO ON PAGE 33

Bibb, Watercress, and Mint Salad
2½ tablespoons Sherry vinegar (available at specialty foods shops) or white-wine vinegar
2 teaspoons Dijon-style mustard
½ cup olive oil
5 heads of Bibb lettuce, leaves torn into bite-size pieces, rinsed, and spun dry (about 10 cups)
2 large bunches of watercress, coarse stems discarded, rinsed and spun dry (about 5 cups)
2 cups fresh mint leaves, rinsed and spun dry

In a bowl whisk together the vinegar, the mustard, and salt and pepper to taste, add the oil in a stream, whisking, and whisk the dressing until it is emulsified. In a large bowl toss the lettuce, the watercress, and the mint with the dressing. Serves 8.

PHOTO ON PAGE 39

Blue Cheese Caesar Salad

enough Italian bread, cut into ¾-inch cubes,
  to measure 1 cup
5 tablespoons olive oil
1 small garlic clove, minced and mashed to a
  paste with ¼ teaspoon salt
1 flat anchovy fillet, minced
½ cup crumbled blue cheese
2 tablespoons fresh lemon juice
½ teaspoon Worcestershire sauce
1 large egg
1 head of romaine, rinsed, spun dry, and torn
  into bite-size pieces (about 5 cups)
¼ cup freshly grated Parmesan

In a jelly-roll pan toss the bread cubes with 1 tablespoon of the oil and salt to taste, bake them in the middle
of a preheated 350° F. oven for 10 to 15 minutes, or until
they are golden, and let the croutons cool. In a small
bowl stir together well the garlic paste, the anchovy,
and half the blue cheese, whisk in the lemon juice and
the Worcestershire sauce, whisking until the mixture is
smooth, and whisk in the remaining oil and salt and pepper to taste, whisking until the dressing is combined
well. In a saucepan of boiling water boil the egg in the
shell for 30 seconds and drain it. In a salad bowl toss the
romaine with the dressing. Break the egg into the
greens, add the Parmesan, the remaining blue cheese,
and the croutons, and toss the salad until it is combined
well. Serves 2.

Escarole Salad with Tarragon

1½ tablespoons red-wine vinegar
⅓ cup olive oil
2 heads of escarole, rinsed and spun dry
1 tablespoon fresh tarragon leaves,
  chopped fine

In a small bowl whisk together the vinegar and salt
and pepper to taste, add the oil in a stream, whisking,
and whisk the dressing until it is emulsified. Cut off and
discard the tough stems from the escarole, chop the
leaves coarse, and in a large bowl toss them with the tarragon and the dressing until the salad is combined.
Serves 6.

PHOTO ON PAGE 69

Frisée, Radicchio, and Asian Pear Salad with Hazelnut Vinaigrette

8 cups torn *frisée* (French or Italian curly
  chicory, available at specialty produce
  markets), rinsed and spun dry
1 head of *radicchio* (about ¾ pound),
  separated into leaves, rinsed, spun dry, and
  shredded (about 6 cups)
2 Asian pears (available at specialty produce
  markets), cored and cut into ½-inch pieces
3 tablespoons white-wine vinegar
1 teaspoon Dijon-style mustard
3 tablespoons hazelnut oil or walnut oil
  (available at specialty foods shops)
3 tablespoons olive oil
¼ cup hazelnuts, toasted and skinned
  (procedure on page 156) and chopped

In a bowl combine the *frisée*, the *radicchio*, and the
pears. In a small bowl whisk together the vinegar, the
mustard, and salt and pepper to taste, add the oils in a
stream, whisking, and whisk the dressing until it is
emulsified. Toss the salad with the dressing, divide it
among 8 salad plates, and sprinkle each serving with
some of the hazelnuts. Serves 8.

Grape, Arugula, Endive, and Roquefort Salad

¼ cup red-wine vinegar
1 teaspoon Dijon-style mustard
¾ cup olive oil
1 bunch of *arugula*, stems discarded, washed
  well, and spun dry
1 Belgian endive, trimmed and cut lengthwise
  into julienne strips
1 bunch of watercress, coarse stems
  discarded, rinsed, and spun dry
½ pound large black grapes, halved and
  seeded
¼ pound Roquefort, crumbled

In a small bowl whisk together the vinegar and the
mustard and add salt and pepper to taste. Add the oil in a
stream, whisking, and whisk the dressing until it is
emulsified. Divide the *arugula* among 4 salad plates,
top it with the endive and the watercress, and arrange
the grapes and the Roquefort over the greens. Drizzle
the dressing over the salads. Serves 4.

Mixed Green Salad

12 cups bite-size pieces of assorted greens,
    such as *arugula*, watercress, and red- and
    green-leafed lettuces, rinsed and spun dry
1 cup flat-leafed parsley leaves
5 tablespoons extra-virgin olive oil
coarse kosher salt to taste
freshly ground black pepper to taste
2 teaspoons fresh lemon juice

In a salad bowl toss the greens with the parsley, drizzle the salad with the oil, and toss it well. Sprinkle the salad with the salt, the pepper, and the lemon juice and toss it well. Serves 8.

Mixed Greens and Tomatoes with Anchovy Dressing

4 slices of homemade-type white bread, crusts
    discarded and the rest cut into ½-inch cubes
3 tablespoons unsalted butter
4 flat anchovy fillets, rinsed and patted dry
2 tablespoons red-wine vinegar
½ cup olive oil
16 cups mixed baby lettuces, such as
    Lollo Rosso, red oak leaf, and *frisée*,
    rinsed and spun dry
1 pint cherry tomatoes, halved

Let the bread cubes stand, uncovered, overnight. In a skillet melt the butter over moderately high heat and in it sauté the bread cubes, stirring, until they are golden. Transfer the croutons to a bowl, season them with salt and pepper, and let them cool. *The croutons may be made 1 day in advance and kept in an airtight container.*
In a blender purée the anchovies with the vinegar and salt and pepper to taste and with the motor running add the oil in a stream, blending until the dressing is emulsified. In a large serving bowl toss the lettuces, the tomatoes, and the croutons with the dressing. Serves 6.

PHOTO ON PAGE 55

Radicchio and Watercress Salad with Parmesan Curls

2 tablespoons white-wine vinegar
½ teaspoon Dijon-style mustard
2 teaspoons finely chopped fresh
    parsley leaves
⅓ cup extra-virgin olive oil
2 bunches of watercress, trimmed,
    washed well, spun dry, and separated
    into small sprigs
2 small heads of *radicchio*, shredded finely,
    washed well, and spun dry
3 scallions, sliced
6 ounces Parmesan at room temperature,
    shaved into curls with a vegetable peeler

In a small bowl whisk together the vinegar, the mustard, the parsley, and salt and pepper to taste, add the oil in a stream, whisking, and whisk the dressing until it is emulsified. In a large bowl toss together the watercress, the *radicchio*, and the scallions, pour the dressing over the salad greens, and toss the mixture well. Transfer the salad to a serving bowl and arrange the Parmesan curls on top. Serves 8.

Radish, Mushroom, and Endive Salad

½ teaspoon Dijon-style mustard
1 tablespoon red-wine vinegar
2 tablespoons extra-virgin olive oil
2 cups torn soft-leafed lettuce, rinsed
    and spun dry
3 radishes, trimmed and sliced thin
2 mushrooms, sliced thin
1 large Belgian endive, trimmed and cut
    crosswise into ¼-inch slices
1 tablespoon minced fresh parsley leaves

In a large bowl whisk together the mustard, the vinegar, and salt to taste, add the oil, a little at a time, whisking, and whisk the dressing until it is emulsified. Add the lettuce, the radishes, the mushrooms, the endive, the parsley, and pepper to taste and toss the salad to coat it with the dressing. Serves 2.

Lauren Jarrett

*Watercress, Endive, and Apple Salad
with Cider Dressing*

1 tablespoon apple cider
1 tablespoon cider vinegar
2 teaspoons fresh lemon juice
1 teaspoon Dijon-style mustard
1 tablespoon minced shallot
½ teaspoon Worcestershire sauce
⅛ teaspoon dried thyme, crumbled
¼ cup vegetable oil
1½ Red Delicious apples
2 Belgian endives, 2 inches cut from the tips
    and reserved for garnish and the remainder
    cut crosswise into ½-inch-thick slices
6 cups loosely packed watercress sprigs,
    rinsed and spun dry
3 tablespoons sliced almonds, crumbled

In a bowl whisk together the cider, the vinegar, the lemon juice, the mustard, the shallot, the Worcestershire sauce, the thyme, and salt and pepper to taste, add the oil in a stream, whisking, and whisk the dressing until it is emulsified. Let the dressing stand at room temperature for 30 minutes to let the flavors develop. In another bowl toss the apples, cored and cut into ½-inch pieces, with 2 tablespoons of the dressing. In a large bowl toss together the endive slices and the watercress with the remaining dressing and divide the watercress mixture among 6 salad plates. Top the watercress mixture with the apples and the almonds and garnish the plates with the reserved endive tips. Serves 6.

PHOTO ON PAGE 21

Yuletide Tossed Salad

two 1-pound jars whole beets, drained
3 tablespoons red-wine vinegar
2 tablespoons balsamic vinegar
1 teaspoon Pernod
½ cup olive oil
9 cups loosely packed torn red-leaf lettuce,
    rinsed and spun dry
9 cups loosely packed torn chicory (curly
    endive) leaves, rinsed and spun dry

With a small melon-ball cutter scoop the beets into balls. In a small bowl combine the beets with 1 tablespoon of the red-wine vinegar, 1 tablespoon of the balsamic vinegar, the Pernod, and salt and pepper to

taste and let them marinate for at least 1 hour or overnight. With a slotted spoon transfer the beets to a large serving bowl. To the liquid remaining in the small bowl add the remaining 2 tablespoons red-wine vinegar and 1 tablespoon balsamic vinegar, add the oil in a stream, whisking, and whisk the dressing until it is emulsified. To the beets add the lettuce and the chicory, add the dressing, and toss the salad. Serves 12.

PHOTO ON PAGE 81

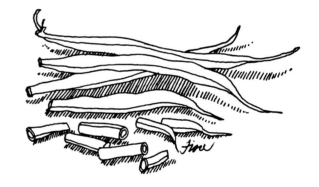

VEGETABLE SALADS
AND SLAWS

*Green Bean, Yellow Pepper, and Bacon Salad with
Orégano Vinaigrette*

1½ pounds green beans, trimmed
1 tablespoon red-wine vinegar
1 teaspoon Dijon-style mustard
½ teaspoon dried orégano, crumbled
¼ cup extra-virgin olive oil
1 small yellow bell pepper, cut into
    paper-thin strips
6 slices of lean bacon, cooked until crisp
    and drained

In a kettle of boiling water cook the beans for 2 to 4 minutes, or until they are crisp-tender, drain them, and refresh them in a bowl of ice and cold water. In a large bowl whisk together the vinegar, the mustard, and the orégano and add the oil in a stream, whisking until the vinaigrette is emulsified. To the vinaigrette add the beans, drained well, the yellow pepper, and the bacon, crumbled, toss the salad, and season it with salt and black pepper. *The salad may be made 8 hours in advance.* Serves 8 to 10.

PHOTO ON PAGE 49

Black Beans, Corn, and Tomatoes Vinaigrette

1 pound dried black beans, picked over, soaked overnight in cold water to cover, and drained
1½ cups cooked fresh corn kernels (cut from about 3 ears of corn) or thawed frozen
1½ cups chopped seeded tomato
¾ cup thinly sliced scallion
⅓ cup minced fresh coriander plus coriander sprigs for garnish
½ cup olive oil
½ cup fresh lemon juice (1 to 2 lemons)
2 teaspoons salt

In a large saucepan combine the black beans and enough cold water to cover them by 2 inches, bring the water to a boil, and simmer the beans for 45 minutes to 1 hour, or until they are just tender but not mushy. Drain the beans and in a bowl combine them with the corn, the tomato, the scallion, and the minced coriander. In a small bowl whisk together the oil, the lemon juice, and the salt, pour the dressing over the vegetables while the beans are still warm, and let the salad cool, stirring occasionally, until the beans are room temperature. *The salad may be made 1 day in advance and kept covered and chilled.* Serve the salad, garnished with the coriander sprigs, at room temperature or chilled slightly. Serves 8.

Thai-Style Cabbage Salad

1 tablespoon fresh lemon juice
1 teaspoon sugar
¾ teaspoon salt

3 cups finely shredded cabbage
½ small red onion, sliced thin (about ⅓ cup)
⅓ cup grated carrot
2 tablespoons finely chopped fresh mint leaves or ¾ teaspoon dried, crumbled
2 tablespoons chopped fresh coriander
1 tablespoon vegetable oil

In a bowl stir together the lemon juice, the sugar, and the salt until the sugar and salt are dissolved, add the cabbage, the onion, the carrot, the mint, the coriander, and the oil, and toss the salad well. Serves 2.

Raw Carrot and Onion Salad

2 large carrots, grated coarse (about 2 cups)
2 tablespoons finely chopped small white onion
1 tablespoon olive oil
½ teaspoon freshly grated lemon zest
½ teaspoon fresh lemon juice

In a bowl toss together the carrots, the onion, the oil, the zest, the lemon juice, and salt and pepper to taste until the salad is combined well. Serves 2.

Tsatsiki
(Greek Cucumber and Yogurt Salad)

4 cups plain yogurt
2 pounds cucumbers (about 3), peeled and chopped fine
1 large garlic clove, minced and mashed to a paste with ½ teaspoon salt
¼ cup fresh mint, chopped fine
2 tablespoons extra-virgin olive oil
quartered pita loaves as an accompaniment

In a sieve set over a bowl and lined with a triple thickness of rinsed and squeezed cheesecloth let the yogurt drain, covered and chilled, for 8 hours or overnight. Put the cucumbers in a sieve and press out as much excess liquid as possible. In a bowl stir together the drained yogurt and the garlic paste, add the cucumbers, the mint, the oil, and salt and pepper to taste, and combine the mixture well. *The tsatsiki may be made 1 day in advance and kept covered and chilled.* Serve the tsatsiki with the pita. Makes about 5 cups.

PHOTO ON PAGE 49

Grilled Eggplant Antipasto

For the garlic and herb oil
2 garlic cloves, minced
2 tablespoons minced fresh parsley leaves
2 tablespoons coarsely chopped fresh
   basil leaves
2 tablespoons minced fresh mint leaves
6 tablespoons extra-virgin olive oil
   (available at specialty foods shops and
   many supermarkets)

1 eggplant (about 1 pound), unpeeled
1½ teaspoons salt
about ¼ cup olive oil for brushing
   the eggplant
fresh mint sprigs for garnish
Italian or French bread, sliced and toasted, as
   an accompaniment

Make the garlic and herb oil: In a small bowl combine the garlic, the parsley, the basil, and the mint, stir in the oil, and let the mixture stand for 1 hour.

While the oil is standing, cut the eggplant crosswise into ⅜-inch-thick slices, arrange the slices in one layer on a large rack set over a tray, and sprinkle them evenly with ¾ teaspoon of the salt. Turn the slices, sprinkle them with the remaining ¾ teaspoon salt, and let them drain, turning them after 30 minutes, for 1 hour.

Pat the slices dry very thoroughly with several changes of paper towels. Brush one side of as many slices as will fit on an oiled rack with some of the oil and grill the slices, oiled sides down, on the rack set 3 to 4 inches over glowing coals for 3 minutes. Brush the slices with some of the remaining oil, turn them, and grill them for 3 to 4 minutes more, or until they are tender. Grill the remaining slices in the same manner. (Alternatively, the eggplant may be grilled on top of the stove in a ridged grill pan over moderately high heat.) Transfer one third of the eggplant slices to a shallow dish just large enough to hold all of them in three layers. Stir the garlic and herb oil, drizzle about 2 tablespoons of it over the slices in the dish, and sprinkle the slices with pepper to taste. Layer the remaining slices in the same manner, adding 2 tablespoons of the garlic and herb oil to each layer, and chill the mixture, covered, turning the slices once, for at least 4 hours or overnight. Transfer the eggplant slices to a platter, garnish them with the mint sprigs, and serve them cold or at room temperature with the bread. Serves 4.

Herbed Green Olive Salad

2 cups firmly packed drained pimiento-stuffed
   green olives, sliced crosswise
4 ribs of celery, chopped
1 red bell pepper, chopped
1 small red onion, chopped
1 garlic clove, minced and mashed to a paste
   with ¼ teaspoon salt
1 carrot, quartered lengthwise and sliced
   thin crosswise
3 tablespoons minced fresh parsley leaves
2 teaspoons dried orégano, crumbled
¼ teaspoon dried hot red pepper flakes
¼ cup olive oil
2 tablespoons white-wine vinegar, or to taste

In a bowl toss together the olives, the celery, the bell pepper, the onion, the garlic paste, the carrot, the parsley, the orégano, and the red pepper flakes, add the oil and the vinegar, and combine the mixture well. Serve the salad as part of an antipasto or as an accompaniment to cheese, salami, and crusty bread. Makes about 4 cups.

Pea Salad

4 cups cooked peas (4 pounds unshelled fresh
   peas, shelled, or two 10-ounce packages
   frozen peas)
¾ cup finely chopped scallion
½ cup finely chopped radish
1½ tablespoons minced fresh tarragon leaves
   or ¾ teaspoon dried, crumbled
3 tablespoons olive oil
1½ tablespoons white-wine vinegar,
   or to taste

In a bowl toss together the peas, the scallion, the radish, the tarragon, the oil, the vinegar, and salt and pepper to taste until the salad is combined well. Serves 8.

Snow Pea and Green Bean Salad

1 tablespoon white-wine vinegar
3 tablespoons olive oil
½ pound green beans, trimmed
¼ pound snow peas, trimmed and strings
   discarded
2 tablespoons shelled sunflower seeds,
   toasted lightly

In a small bowl whisk together the vinegar, the oil, and salt and pepper to taste. In a large saucepan of boiling salted water cook the green beans for 4 minutes, add the snow peas, and cook the vegetables for 30 seconds. Drain the vegetables, transfer them to a bowl of ice and cold water to stop the cooking, and drain them. Pat the vegetables dry between several thicknesses of paper towels and in a bowl toss them with the sunflower seeds and the dressing. Serves 2.

Potato Salad with Cherry Tomatoes, Bacon, and Avocado

¾ pound small red potatoes
2 slices of lean bacon, cooked and crumbled
1 cup cherry tomatoes, quartered
1 small avocado (preferably California)
2 scallions, sliced thin
2 tablespoons finely chopped fresh basil
  leaves, or to taste
1 tablespoon red-wine vinegar
2 tablespoons olive oil

In a steamer set over boiling water steam the potatoes, cut into 1-inch pieces, covered, for 8 to 10 minutes, or until they are tender, and let them cool. In a serving bowl combine the potatoes, the bacon, the tomatoes, the avocado, peeled, pitted, and cut into ½-inch cubes, the scallions, and the basil. In a small bowl whisk together the vinegar, the oil, and salt and pepper to taste, pour the dressing over the potato mixture, and toss the salad until it is combined well. Serves 2.

Potato Salad with Tofu "Mayonnaise"

1 pound (about 7) small red potatoes,
  scrubbed
3 ounces soft tofu
1 tablespoon fresh lemon juice
⅛ teaspoon dried tarragon
2 tablespoons olive oil (preferably extra-
  virgin)
½ small red onion, sliced thin
¼ cup minced fresh parsley leaves

In a large saucepan combine the potatoes with enough water to cover them by 1 inch, bring the water to a boil, and boil the potatoes for 15 to 20 minutes, or until they are tender. While the potatoes are cooking, in a

blender blend the tofu, the lemon juice, the tarragon, and 2 tablespoons water until the mixture is just combined, with the motor running add the oil in a stream, and blend the "mayonnaise" until it is emulsified. Drain the potatoes, quarter them, and in a bowl toss them with the onion, the parsley, the mayonnaise, and salt and pepper to taste. Serves 2.

German Potato Salad

3 pounds (about 6) large boiling potatoes
½ pound lean bacon (about 8 slices), cut
  crosswise into ½-inch pieces
1 cup finely chopped onion
1 cup thinly sliced celery
1 tablespoon sugar
2 tablespoons all-purpose flour
1 teaspoon celery seeds
1 tablespoon Dijon-style mustard
6 tablespoons cider vinegar
3 hard-boiled large eggs, chopped
⅓ cup chopped dill pickles
½ cup thinly sliced scallion greens

Quarter the potatoes lengthwise and cut them crosswise into ½-inch pieces. In a vegetable steamer set over boiling water steam the potatoes, covered, for 10 to 15 minutes, or until they are tender, and transfer them to a large bowl. In a large heavy skillet cook the bacon over moderate heat, stirring, until it is crisp and transfer it to paper towels to drain. Pour off all but 4 tablespoons of the fat, to the skillet add the onion and the celery, and cook the mixture over moderately low heat, stirring, until the onion is softened. Add the sugar, the flour, and the celery seeds and cook the mixture, stirring, for 30 seconds. Stir in the mustard, the vinegar, and ½ cup water, bring the mixture to a boil, stirring, and simmer it for 2 minutes, or until it is thickened. Season the dressing with salt and pepper, pour it over the potatoes, and stir in the eggs, the pickles, the bacon, and the scallion greens. Serve the salad warm. Serves 6.

Spaghetti Squash with Tomatoes, Basil, and Parmesan

a 3-pound spaghetti squash, halved
    lengthwise, reserving one half for another
    use, and the seeds discarded
2 tablespoons olive oil
¼ cup shredded fresh basil leaves plus
    additional for garnish
¼ teaspoon dried orégano
3 tablespoons freshly grated Parmesan
1 cup thinly sliced cherry tomatoes

In a glass baking dish arrange the squash half, cut side down, pour ¼ cup water around it, and cover the dish tightly with microwave-safe plastic wrap. Microwave the squash at high power (100%) for 12 minutes, or until it is soft when pressed, and let it stand, covered, for 3 minutes. In a large bowl whisk together the oil, ¼ cup of the basil, the orégano, and 2 tablespoons of the Parmesan, stir in the tomatoes, and season the mixture with salt and pepper. While the squash is still warm scrape it with a fork to form strands, add the strands to the tomato mixture, and toss the mixture until it is combined. Divide the mixture between 2 bowls, sprinkle the remaining 1 tablespoon Parmesan over it, and garnish it with the additional basil. Serves 2.

Tomato, Mint, and Red Onion Salad

1 pound (about 3) tomatoes
¼ teaspoon sugar
¼ teaspoon salt
1 tablespoon olive oil
1 teaspoon red-wine vinegar
8 fresh mint leaves, sliced thin
1 small red onion, sliced thin and soaked in
    ice water for 30 minutes

Cut the tomatoes into ¼-inch-thick slices and arrange half the slices in one layer in a shallow serving dish. In a small bowl combine the sugar and the salt and sprinkle the layer of tomatoes with half the mixture. Arrange the remaining tomato slices on top and sprinkle them with the remaining sugar mixture. Drizzle the tomatoes with the oil and the vinegar and let the salad stand at room temperature for 30 minutes. Sprinkle the salad with the mint and arrange the onion, drained and separated into rings, on top. Serves 4.

PHOTO ON PAGE 51

Marinated Vegetable Salad

2½ tablespoons red-wine vinegar
1 tablespoon balsamic vinegar (available at
    specialty foods shops and some supermarkets)
2 teaspoons Dijon-style mustard
dried hot red pepper flakes to taste
½ cup olive oil
½ pound pearl onions, blanched in boiling
    water for 1 minute, drained, and peeled
1 pound carrots, cut crosswise into ¼-inch-
    thick slices (about 2½ cups)
1 pound broccoli, cut into flowerets
    (about 5 cups)
2 red bell peppers, cut into thin strips
    (about 1½ cups)
½ cup small brine-cured black olives
    (preferably Niçoise, available at specialty
    foods shops)

In a small bowl whisk together the vinegars, the mustard, the red pepper flakes, and salt and black pepper to taste, add the oil in a stream, whisking, and whisk the dressing until it is emulsified. In a steamer set over boiling water steam the onions, covered, for 2 minutes, add the carrots and the broccoli, and steam the vegetables for 3 minutes, or until they are crisp-tender. Transfer the vegetables to a colander and let them cool. In a bowl combine the steamed vegetables, the bell peppers, and the olives, toss the mixture with the dressing, and chill the salad, covered, for at least 4 hours or overnight. Serves 6.

PHOTO ON PAGE 27

Napa Coleslaw with Dill

3 cups thinly sliced Napa cabbage (about
    ¾ pound)
1 carrot, grated
1 tablespoon minced fresh dill
¼ teaspoon sugar
¼ teaspoon salt
2 tablespoons olive oil
2 teaspoons red-wine vinegar, or to taste

In a bowl combine the cabbage, the carrot, and the dill. Sprinkle the mixture with the sugar, the salt, and the oil, tossing it to combine it well, and sprinkle the coleslaw with the vinegar, tossing it to combine it well. Serves 2.

Cabbage and Apple Slaw

½ cup plain yogurt
¼ cup sour cream
2 teaspoons honey
2 cups coarsely shredded red cabbage
1 Granny Smith apple, peeled and
   chopped fine
3 tablespoons minced onion
¼ cup minced fresh parsley leaves

In a bowl stir together the yogurt, the sour cream, and the honey, add the cabbage, the apple, the onion, the parsley, and salt and pepper to taste, and stir the salad until it is combined well. Serves 2.

GRAIN SALADS

Herbed Corn and Couscous

1 cup fresh corn kernels (cut from about 2 ears
   of corn) or thawed frozen
1 tablespoon unsalted butter
¾ cup chicken broth
½ cup couscous
2 tablespoons minced fresh chives

In a small heavy saucepan cook the corn in the butter over moderately high heat, stirring, for 1 minute, add the broth, and bring the liquid to a boil. Stir in the cous-cous, remove the pan from the heat, and let the mixture stand, covered, for 5 minutes. Stir in the chives and salt and pepper to taste. Serves 2.

Lemon Rice Salad with Peanuts

3 teaspoons salt
1½ cups unconverted long-grain rice
¾ teaspoon freshly grated lemon zest
3 tablespoons fresh lemon juice
6 tablespoons olive oil
½ cup minced fresh parsley leaves
3 scallions, sliced thin
½ cup unsalted dry-roasted peanuts,
   chopped coarse

In a large saucepan bring 4 quarts water to a boil with the salt. Sprinkle in the rice, stirring until the water returns to a boil, and boil it for 10 minutes. In a large colander drain the rice and rinse it. Set the colander over another large saucepan of boiling water and steam the rice, covered with a kitchen towel and the lid, for 15 minutes, or until it is fluffy and dry.

In a small bowl whisk together the zest, the lemon juice, the oil, and salt and pepper to taste. In a serving bowl combine well the rice, the parsley, the scallions, the peanuts, and the lemon dressing. *The rice salad may be made 3 hours in advance and kept covered and chilled.* Serve the salad chilled or at room temperature. Serves 6.

PHOTO ON PAGE 56

JEANNE

SALAD TOPPINGS

Spiced Bacon Bits

2 tablespoons Worcestershire sauce
1 tablespoon firmly packed brown sugar
⅛ teaspoon ground allspice
¼ teaspoon cayenne, or to taste
1 pound lean bacon, cut into
  ½-inch pieces

In a bowl stir together the Worcestershire sauce, the brown sugar, the allspice, the cayenne, and black pepper to taste, add the bacon, and toss the mixture until the bacon is coated well. In a large heavy skillet cook the bacon mixture in 2 batches over moderately low heat, stirring frequently, until the bacon is crisp, transfer the bacon bits with a slotted spoon to paper towels to drain, and sprinkle them with salt to taste. Serve the bacon bits as a topping for tomato or spinach salad. Makes about 1 cup.

Herbed Garlic and Parmesan Croutons

2 large garlic cloves, sliced thin
  lengthwise
1 teaspoon dried orégano, crumbled
1 teaspoon dried basil, crumbled
1 teaspoon dried thyme, crumbled
½ teaspoon salt plus additional to taste
½ teaspoon pepper
½ cup olive oil
1 loaf of Italian bread, cut into ¾-inch cubes
  (about 7 cups)
¼ cup finely grated fresh Parmesan

In a small saucepan combine the garlic, the orégano, the basil, the thyme, ½ teaspoon of the salt, the pepper, and the oil and simmer the mixture for 5 minutes. Remove the pan from the heat, let the mixture stand for 15 minutes, and discard the garlic. In a bowl toss the bread cubes with the oil mixture, spread them in a jelly-roll pan, and bake them in the middle of a preheated 350° F. oven for 8 minutes. Sprinkle the croutons with the Parmesan and bake them for 7 minutes more, or until they are golden. Sprinkle the croutons with the additional salt and let them cool. The croutons keep in an airtight container for 1 week. Serve the croutons as a topping for tossed green salad. Makes about 5 cups.

Peppered Goat Cheese and Walnut "Croutons"

½ cup walnuts, toasted lightly and cooled
2 teaspoons freshly ground black pepper
1 teaspoon salt
½ pound firm mild goat cheese, chilled well
  and cut into ¼-inch cubes

In a food processor grind fine the walnuts with the pepper and the salt and transfer the mixture to a shallow bowl. Working in small batches, roll the cheese cubes in the walnut mixture, coating them completely, and transfer them to a tray. The "croutons" keep, covered and chilled, for 3 days. Serve the "croutons" as a topping for tossed green or tomato salad. Makes about 2 cups.

JEANNE

Coconut Almond Granola

3 tablespoons firmly packed light brown sugar
3 tablespoons unsalted butter
½ teaspoon cinnamon
½ teaspoon vanilla
½ teaspoon salt
1 teaspoon freshly grated orange zest
½ cup sweetened flaked coconut
½ cup sliced almonds
1 cup old-fashioned rolled oats
¼ cup wheat germ

In a small saucepan combine the brown sugar, the butter, the cinnamon, the vanilla, the salt, and the zest and cook the mixture over moderately low heat, stirring, until the brown sugar is dissolved. In a bowl stir together the coconut, the almonds, the oats, and the wheat germ, add the brown sugar mixture, and toss the mixture until it is combined well. Spread the granola in a jelly-roll pan, bake it in the middle of a preheated 350° F. oven, stirring every 5 minutes, for 10 to 15 minutes, or until it is golden, and let it cool. The granola keeps in an airtight container for 1 week. Serve the granola as a topping for fruit salad. Makes about 2 cups.

Crisp-Fried Onions

3 large onions, sliced thin and separated into
   rings (about 5 cups)
vegetable oil for deep-frying

Pat the onions dry between layers of paper towels and in a deep kettle or deep fryer fry them in small batches in 1½ inches of 375° F. oil, stirring, for 1 to 2 minutes, or until they are golden. Transfer the fried onions with a slotted spoon to paper towels to drain and sprinkle them with salt to taste. The fried onions keep, uncovered, for 2 days. Serve the fried onions as a topping for spinach, potato, or tossed green salad. Makes about 2½ cups.

Sesame Cumin Pita Crisps

6 tablespoons Oriental sesame oil
1½ teaspoons ground cumin plus additional
   to taste
three 5- to 6-inch *pita* loaves

In a small bowl stir together the oil, 1½ teaspoons of the cumin, and salt to taste. Halve the *pita* loaves horizontally to form 6 rounds and brush the rough sides of the rounds with the oil mixture. Cut each round into ¾-inch triangles or squares, spread the triangles in a jelly-roll pan, and bake them in the middle of a preheated 350° F. oven, shaking the pan every 3 to 4 minutes, for 10 to 12 minutes, or until they are golden. Toss the crisps with the additional cumin and salt to taste and let them cool. The crisps keep in an airtight container for 1 week. Serve the crisps as a topping for vegetable or tossed green salad. Makes about 3 cups.

SAUCES

SAVORY BUTTERS

Anchovy Butter

1½ sticks (¾ cup) unsalted butter, softened
4 teaspoons minced drained bottled capers
3 flat anchovy fillets, minced and mashed
   to a paste
1 garlic clove, minced and mashed to a paste
2 teaspoons fresh lemon juice

In a small bowl cream together the butter, the capers, the anchovy paste, the garlic paste, the lemon juice, and salt and pepper to taste. Let the butter stand, covered, in a cool place for 1 hour to allow the flavors to develop. Serve the butter with veal or seafood.

Chocolate Almond Butter

1 ounce semisweet chocolate, chopped
1 teaspoon sugar
1 tablespoon Amaretto
1½ sticks (¾ cup) unsalted butter, softened
¼ cup blanched almonds, toasted lightly
   and chopped

In a small metal bowl set over a pan of barely simmering water melt the chocolate with the sugar and the Amaretto, stirring, and let the mixture cool to room temperature. In another bowl cream together the butter, the chocolate mixture, and the almonds. Let the butter stand, covered, in a cool place for 1 hour to allow the flavors to develop. Serve the butter with croissants or toast.

Herb Butter

1½ sticks (¾ cup) unsalted butter, softened
2 tablespoons minced fresh chives
2 tablespoons minced fresh parsley leaves
1 tablespoon minced fresh tarragon leaves
1 teaspoon Dijon-style mustard

In a small bowl cream together the butter, the chives, the parsley, the tarragon, the mustard, and salt and pepper to taste. Let the butter stand, covered, in a cool place for 1 hour to allow the flavors to develop. Serve the butter with seafood, chicken, or meat.

Horseradish Chive Butter

1½ sticks (¾ cup) unsalted butter, softened
2 tablespoons drained bottled horseradish
2 tablespoons minced fresh chives

In a small bowl cream together the butter, the horseradish, the chives, and salt and pepper to taste. Let the butter stand, covered, in a cool place for 1 hour to allow the flavors to develop. Serve the butter with grilled meat.

Lemon Basil Butter

1 cup loosely packed fresh basil leaves
1 stick (½ cup) unsalted butter, softened
1 teaspoon freshly grated lemon zest,
  or to taste

In a saucepan of boiling water blanch the basil for 2 seconds. Drain the basil well, pat it dry, and in a food processor blend it with the butter, the zest, and salt to taste until the mixture is smooth. Let the basil butter stand, covered tightly with plastic wrap, in a cool place for 1 hour or, chilled, overnight. Serve the lemon basil butter with steamed vegetables or grilled meats and fish. Makes about ⅔ cup.

Roasted Red Pepper Butter

2 red bell peppers, roasted (procedure on
  page 135), patted dry, and chopped
1½ sticks (¾ cup) unsalted butter, softened
1 teaspoon fresh lemon juice, or to taste

In a food processor purée the roasted peppers, add the butter, the lemon juice, and salt and black pepper to taste, and blend the mixture until it is smooth. Serve the butter with grilled vegetables or grilled chicken.

Saffron and Leek Butter

½ teaspoon crumbled saffron threads
2 tablespoons dry white wine
½ cup chopped white part of leek, washed
  well and drained
1¾ sticks (14 tablespoons) unsalted butter,
  softened
2 teaspoons fresh lemon juice

In a small saucepan heat the saffron with the wine over moderately low heat until it dissolves. In a small skillet cook the leek in 2 tablespoons of the butter over moderately low heat, stirring, until it is softened, add the saffron mixture, and cook the mixture, stirring, for

1 minute. Let the leek mixture cool to room temperature. In a small bowl cream together the remaining 1½ sticks butter, the leek mixture, the lemon juice, and salt and pepper to taste. Let the butter stand, covered, in a cool place for 1 hour to allow the flavors to develop. Serve the butter with seafood or vegetables.

Shallot and Garlic Butter

6 unpeeled garlic cloves
¼ cup vegetable oil
½ cup thinly sliced shallot
1½ sticks (¾ cup) unsalted butter, softened

In a small saucepan of boiling water boil the garlic cloves for 6 minutes, drain them, and peel them. In a small heavy skillet heat the oil over moderately high heat until it is hot but not smoking and in it fry the shallot for 3 to 5 minutes, or until it is golden. Transfer the fried shallot to paper towels to drain. In a small bowl mash the garlic to a paste, add the fried shallot, the butter, and salt and pepper to taste, and cream the mixture. Let the butter stand, covered, in a cool place for 1 hour to allow the flavors to develop. Serve the butter with meat, poultry, seafood, or vegetables.

Strawberry Honey Butter

1 pint strawberries, hulled
3 tablespoons honey
2 teaspoons fresh lemon juice, or to taste
1½ sticks (¾ cup) unsalted butter, softened

In a food processor purée the strawberries and force the purée through a fine sieve into a saucepan. Add the honey and the lemon juice and boil the mixture, stirring, for 3 minutes, or until it is thickened. Let the strawberry mixture cool to room temperature. In a bowl cream together the butter and the strawberry mixture. Let the butter stand, covered, in a cool place for 1 hour to allow the flavors to develop. Serve the butter with croissants or toast.

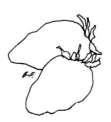

SAVORY SAUCES

Quick Anchovy Mayonnaise

1 large egg at room temperature
5 teaspoons fresh lemon juice
1 teaspoon Dijon-style mustard
3 flat anchovy fillets, rinsed, drained,
    and patted dry
¼ teaspoon salt
¼ teaspoon white pepper
¾ cup olive oil, vegetable oil, or a
    combination of both

In a blender or food processor blend the egg, the lemon juice, the mustard, the anchovies, the salt, and the white pepper and with the motor running add the oil in a stream. Thin the mayonnaise with water if desired and serve it over asparagus. Makes about 1 cup.

Basil Vinaigrette

1 garlic clove
½ teaspoon Dijon-style mustard
¼ cup opal basil vinegar (recipe follows)
    or tarragon vinegar
⅔ cup basil olive oil (recipe follows)
    or other olive oil
1 cup loosely packed fresh basil leaves, rinsed
    and spun dry

In a blender blend the garlic, the mustard, the vinegar, and salt to taste, add the oil and the basil, and blend the mixture until it is emulsified. Serve the vinaigrette over sliced tomatoes or with grilled scallops or other seafood. Makes about 1 cup.

Opal Basil Vinegar

For the first steeping
enough fresh opal basil sprigs, including the
    blossoms but not the woody stems, to fill a
    1½-quart jar two-thirds full loosely
4 cups rice vinegar (available at Oriental
    markets and specialty foods stores)
For the second steeping
3 fresh opal basil sprigs, or to taste
1 cup dry white wine

Prepare the first steeping: Rinse the basil, shake off any excess water, and bruise the basil lightly with a wooden spoon. Pack the basil loosely into a 1½-quart glass jar with a non-metallic lid, add the vinegar, and let the mixture stand, covered, in a cool dark place for 2 days. Stir the mixture with a wooden spoon, tamp down the basil, and let the mixture stand, covered, in a cool dark place for 12 days. Strain the vinegar into a glass pitcher, discarding the basil.

Prepare the second steeping: Rinse the basil, shake off any excess water, and pat the basil dry. Bruise the basil lightly with a wooden spoon and pack it loosely into the 1½-quart jar. Add the wine and the strained vinegar and let the mixture stand in a cool dark place for 2 days. Stir the mixture with a wooden spoon, tamp down the basil, and let the mixture stand, covered, in a cool dark place for 12 days. Strain the basil vinegar through a fine sieve lined with a dampened paper towel into a glass pitcher, pour it into glass jars, and seal the jars with their lids. The basil vinegar keeps in a cool dark place for 6 months. Makes about 5 cups.

Basil Olive Oil

enough fresh green basil sprigs, including the
    blossoms but not the woody stems, to fill a
    1-quart jar two-thirds full loosely
4 cups olive oil

Rinse the basil, shake off any excess water, and pat the basil dry. Bruise the basil lightly with a wooden spoon and pack it loosely into a 1-quart glass jar with a non-metallic lid. Add the oil and let the mixture stand, covered, in a cool dark place for 1 month. Strain the oil into a glass pitcher, pour it into glass jars, and seal the jars with their lids. The oil keeps in a cool dark place for about 6 months. Makes about 4 cups.

Oriental Black Bean and Garlic Sauce

2 teaspoons vegetable oil
1 tablespoon minced garlic
1 tablespoon grated peeled fresh gingerroot
⅓ cup minced red bell pepper
2 tablespoons fermented black beans
    (available at Oriental markets and specialty
    foods shops), rinsed, drained well, and
    crushed slightly
1½ tablespoons medium-dry Sherry

1 tablespoon soy sauce
¼ teaspoon sugar
1½ cups chicken broth
2 teaspoons cornstarch

In a skillet heat the oil over moderately high heat and in it stir-fry the garlic, the gingerroot, and the red bell pepper until the pepper is softened. Add the beans and stir-fry the mixture for 2 minutes. Add the Sherry and boil the mixture for 1 minute. Stir in the soy sauce, the sugar, and the broth and simmer the mixture, stirring occasionally, for 10 minutes. In a small bowl dissolve the cornstarch in 2 teaspoons cold water, whisk it into the mixture, and simmer the sauce until it is thickened slightly. Add pepper to taste and serve the sauce over asparagus. Makes about 1¼ cups.

Cranberry Sauce with Pearl Onions and Golden Raisins

1 cup sugar
10 ounces pearl onions, blanched in boiling water for 3 minutes, drained, and peeled
½ cup golden raisins
a 1-pound bag of cranberries, picked over

In a dry large deep heavy skillet cook the sugar over moderately high heat, stirring constantly with a fork, until it is melted completely and a deep golden caramel. Remove the skillet from the heat, into the side of the skillet carefully pour 1 cup hot water, a little at a time, and cook the mixture over moderate heat, stirring, until the caramel is dissolved. Add the onions, the raisins, and the cranberries and simmer the mixture, stirring occasionally, for 10 minutes, or until the cranberries are tender. Remove the skillet from the heat, let the cranberry sauce mixture cool, and transfer it to a serving dish. Makes about 4 cups.

PHOTO ON PAGE 73

Ham, Gruyère, and Parmesan Sauce

1 tablespoon minced onion
1½ tablespoons unsalted butter
2 tablespoons all-purpose flour
1½ cups milk
¼ cup grated Gruyère
¼ cup freshly grated Parmesan, or to taste
⅓ cup finely chopped cooked ham

In a saucepan cook the onion in the butter over moderately low heat, stirring, until it is softened, stir in the flour, and cook the *roux*, stirring, for 3 minutes. Remove the pan from the heat and add the milk, scalded, in a stream, whisking until the mixture is thick and smooth. Simmer the sauce for 10 to 15 minutes, or until it is thickened to the desired consistency. Strain the sauce through a fine sieve into a bowl, add the Gruyère, the Parmesan, and salt and pepper to taste, and stir the mixture until the cheeses are melted. Stir in the ham and serve the sauce over asparagus. (Alternatively, arrange the asparagus stalks in 4 to 6 individual gratin dishes, ladle the sauce over them, and broil the gratins under a preheated broiler about 4 inches from the heat until the topping is golden.) Makes about 2 cups.

Maltaise Sauce

2 large egg yolks
1 tablespoon fresh lemon juice
a pinch of freshly ground white pepper
1 stick (½ cup) unsalted butter, melted and cooled
1 teaspoon grated orange zest (preferably from a blood orange, available seasonally at specialty produce markets)
1 tablespoon plus 1 teaspoon fresh orange juice (preferably from a blood orange)

In a blender or food processor put the egg yolks, the lemon juice, a pinch of salt, and the white pepper and with the motor running add the butter in a stream. Add the zest and the orange juice and blend the mixture well. Force the mixture through a fine sieve set over a small bowl and keep it warm, its surface covered with a buttered round of wax paper, set in a pan of warm water. Serve the sauce over asparagus. Makes about 1 cup.

Creamy Mustard Vinaigrette

3 tablespoons heavy cream
¼ cup white-wine vinegar
1 tablespoon Dijon-style mustard, or to taste
1 tablespoon minced shallot
a pinch of sugar
2 teaspoons fresh lemon juice, or to taste
¾ cup olive oil

In a blender or food processor blend the cream, the vinegar, the mustard, the shallot, the sugar, and the lemon juice until the mixture is combined well, with the motor running add the oil in a stream, and blend the vinaigrette until it is emulsified. Add salt and pepper to taste and serve the vinaigrette over asparagus. Makes about 1⅓ cups.

Basil Sunflower Seed Pesto

4 cups coarsely chopped fresh basil leaves
1 cup unhulled raw sunflower seeds (available at natural foods stores and some supermarkets)
½ cup olive oil
1 cup freshly grated Parmesan
2 tablespoons unsalted butter, softened
2 garlic cloves, crushed

In a blender in batches or in a food processor purée the basil with the sunflower seeds, the oil, the Parmesan, the butter, the garlic, and salt to taste. Transfer the *pesto* to a small bowl and lay plastic wrap directly on the surface to prevent discoloration. The *pesto* keeps, covered and chilled, for 2 weeks. Makes about 1½ cups.

To use the *pesto*: For every pound of dried pasta cooking in a kettle of boiling salted water, stir together in a heated serving bowl ¾ cup *pesto* and ⅔ cup hot pasta cooking water. When the pasta is *al dente*, drain it in a colander, add it to the *pesto* mixture, and toss the mixture with lemon juice, salt, and pepper to taste.

Green Olive Pesto

1 cup firmly packed drained pimiento-stuffed green olives, rinsed well and patted dry
⅓ cup pine nuts
1 garlic clove, minced and mashed to a paste with ¼ teaspoon salt
1 cup finely chopped fresh parsley leaves
¼ cup extra-virgin olive oil
2 tablespoons freshly grated Parmesan

In a food processor purée the olives with the pine nuts, the garlic paste, and the parsley, with the motor running add the oil in a stream and the Parmesan, and blend the mixture well. Serve the *pesto* with 1 pound pasta, cooked and drained, reserving ¾ cup of the pasta liquid to thin the *pesto*. Or serve the *pesto* as a spread with crackers. Makes about 1½ cups.

Polonaise Topping

5 tablespoons unsalted butter
⅓ cup fresh bread crumbs, toasted lightly
2 hard-boiled large eggs, chopped fine
2 tablespoons finely chopped fresh parsley leaves

In a large skillet heat the butter over moderately high heat until the foam subsides and in it sauté the bread crumbs until they are golden brown. Stir in the egg, the parsley, and salt and pepper to taste and serve the topping over asparagus. Makes about ⅔ cup.

CONDIMENTS

Apple Ginger Chutney

4 large Granny Smith apples, peeled, cored, and chopped
2 cups minced onion
1½ cups cider vinegar
1½ cups firmly packed dark brown sugar
1 cup golden raisins
¼ cup minced peeled fresh gingerroot
1 red bell pepper, minced
¾ teaspoon dry mustard
¾ teaspoon salt
½ teaspoon dried hot red pepper flakes

In a large saucepan combine the apples, the onion, the vinegar, the brown sugar, the raisins, the gingerroot, the bell pepper, the mustard, the salt, and the red pepper flakes, bring the mixture to a boil, stirring, and cook it over moderate heat, stirring occasionally, for 40 minutes, or until it is thickened. Spoon the chutney into glass jars with tight-fitting lids. The chutney keeps, covered and chilled, for 2 weeks. Makes about 6 cups.

Basil Avocado Chutney

2 cups packed basil leaves, rinsed
    and spun dry
⅓ cup blanched almonds
1 garlic clove
2 teaspoons fresh lemon juice, or to taste
1 avocado (preferably California), peeled
    and pitted

In a food processor blend together the basil, the almonds, the garlic, and the lemon juice, pulsing the motor once or twice, until the almonds are ground fine. Add the avocado, cut into chunks, and salt to taste and blend the mixture until it is combined well. Serve the chutney with grilled fish and meats. Makes about 1½ cups.

Red Onion, Apple, and Raisin Chutney

3 tablespoons cider vinegar
2 tablespoons honey
½ cup golden raisins
⅛ teaspoon dried mint
a pinch of ground cloves
2 pounds red onions, quartered lengthwise
    and sliced thin crosswise (about 4 cups)
3 tablespoons vegetable oil
2 tablespoons unsalted butter
1 Granny Smith apple

In a small bowl combine well ⅔ cup warm water, the vinegar, the honey, the raisins, the mint, and the cloves and let the mixture stand while cooking the onions. In a large skillet cook the onions in the oil and the butter, covered, over moderately low heat, stirring occasional- ly, for 15 minutes, remove the lid, and continue to cook the onions, stirring, for 30 minutes, or until they are very soft. Stir in the raisin mixture and the apple, peeled and cut into fine dice, cook the mixture over moderate heat, stirring, until the liquid is almost evaporated and the apple is tender, and season the chutney with salt and pepper. *The chutney may be made 3 days in advance, cooled, and kept covered and chilled.* Serve the chutney at room temperature. Makes about 2½ cups.

PHOTO ON PAGE 24

Tomato Chutney

2 cups sugar
3 cups cider vinegar
2 tablespoons minced peeled fresh gingerroot
2½ teaspoons salt
1½ teaspoons coriander seeds, crushed lightly
½ teaspoon dried hot red pepper flakes
3 pounds plum tomatoes, peeled, seeded,
    and quartered
3 onions, chopped
1 cup golden raisins

In a heavy saucepan combine the sugar, the vinegar, the gingerroot, the salt, the coriander seeds, and the red pepper flakes and bring the mixture to a boil, stirring un- til the sugar is dissolved. Add the tomatoes, the onions, and the raisins and simmer the mixture, stirring occa- sionally, for 1 to 1¼ hours, or until it is thickened. Let the chutney cool and transfer it to a bowl or jars. The chutney keeps, covered and chilled, for 3 weeks. Makes about 3½ cups.

PHOTO ON PAGE 61

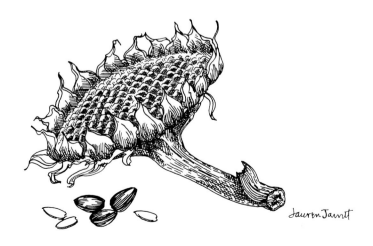

Lauren Jarrett

Rosemary Mint Wine Jelly

2½ cups firmly packed fresh mint leaves
¼ cup fresh rosemary leaves
2 cups dry white wine
¼ cup fresh lemon juice plus additional
   if needed
3½ cups sugar
a 3-ounce pouch liquid pectin

In a food processor or blender blend together the mint, the rosemary, and 1 cup of the wine until the herbs are chopped fine and transfer the mixture to a bowl. In a small saucepan bring the remaining 1 cup wine to a boil, add it to the herb mixture, and let the herb mixture stand, covered, for 45 minutes. Strain the herb mixture through a sieve lined with several layers of rinsed and squeezed cheesecloth set over a large measuring cup, pressing hard on the solids, and add ¼ cup of the lemon juice. (There should be exactly 2 cups liquid; if there is less add enough of the additional lemon juice to measure 2 cups liquid.) Transfer the liquid to a kettle, stir in the sugar, stirring until the mixture is combined well, and bring the mixture to a rolling boil over high heat, stirring constantly. Stir in the pectin quickly, bring the mixture again to a full rolling boil, stirring constantly, and boil it, stirring constantly, for 1 minute. Remove the kettle from the heat, skim off any foam with a large spoon, and ladle the mixture immediately into 4 sterilized (procedure follows) ½-pint Mason-type jars, filling the jars to within ⅛ inch of the tops. Wipe the rims with a dampened cloth and seal the jars with the lids. Invert the jars for 5 minutes and turn them upright. (Instead of being inverted, the jars may be put in a water bath canner or on a rack set in a deep kettle. Add enough hot water to the canner or kettle to cover the jars by 1 to 2 inches and bring it to a boil. Process the jars, covered, for 5 minutes, transfer them with tongs to a rack, and let them cool completely.) Store the jars in a cool, dark place. Makes four ½-pint jars.

PHOTO ON PAGE 30

To Sterilize Jars and Glasses
for Pickling and Preserving

Wash the jars in hot suds and rinse them in scalding water. Put the jars in a kettle and cover them with hot water. Bring the water to a boil, covered, and boil the jars for 15 minutes from the time that steam emerges from the kettle. Turn off the heat and let the jars stand in the hot water. Just before they are to be filled invert the jars onto a kitchen towel to dry. (The jars should be filled while they are still hot.) Sterilize the jar lids for 5 minutes, or according to the manufacturer's instructions.

Lemon-Rosemary-Marinated Ripe Olives

½ lemon, sliced thin
¼ cup fresh lemon juice
3 large shallots, sliced thin
3 tablespoons chopped fresh rosemary
   or 1 tablespoon dried, crumbled
1 teaspoon dried hot red pepper flakes
two 6-ounce cans ripe olives, drained
   (about 3 cups)
about 1½ cups olive oil

In a 1-quart glass jar with a tight-fitting lid combine the sliced lemon, the lemon juice, the shallots, the rosemary, and the red pepper flakes. In a saucepan of boiling water blanch the olives for 1 minute, drain them well in a colander, and add them to the jar while they are still warm. Add enough oil to the jar to just cover the olives. Seal the jar with the lid and shake it several times to combine and distribute the ingredients. Let the olives stand in a cool, dark place, shaking them daily, for 3 days. The olives keep, covered and chilled, indefinitely. Makes about 3 cups.

Quick Cabbage and Carrot Pickle

3 cups thinly sliced cabbage
1 carrot, cut into julienne strips
1 tablespoon salt
½ cup distilled white vinegar
2 tablespoons sugar

In a 9-inch-square microwave-safe baking dish combine the cabbage, the carrot, 2 teaspoons of the salt, and 4 cups water, cover the mixture with microwave-safe plastic wrap, leaving one corner uncovered, and microwave it at high power (100%) for 5 minutes. Drain the vegetables and transfer them to a bowl of ice and cold water to stop the cooking. Drain the vegetables, pat them dry between several thicknesses of paper towels, and transfer them to a bowl. In a small bowl stir together the vinegar, the remaining 1 teaspoon salt, and the sugar until the sugar is dissolved, pour the liquid over the vegetables, and chill the mixture, stirring occasionally, for 20 minutes. Serve the pickled vegetables with fried chicken or grilled meats. Makes about 4 cups.

DESSERT SAUCES

Gingered Cherry Sauce

1 cup (about ¼ pound) dried pitted red tart
   cherries (available at specialty foods shops)
¼ cup sugar
1 teaspoon ground ginger
1¼ teaspoons cornstarch dissolved in
   1 tablespoon cold water
3 tablespoons brandy
ice cream as an accompaniment

In a saucepan combine the cherries, the sugar, the ginger, and 1½ cups water and simmer the mixture for 8 to 10 minutes, or until the liquid is reduced to about 1 cup. Stir the cornstarch mixture, add it to the cherry mixture, and simmer the mixture, stirring, for 2 minutes. Remove the pan from the heat. Heat the brandy in a small saucepan over moderate heat, ignite it carefully, and pour it over the cherry sauce. Let the flame subside, shaking the pan, and serve the sauce warm over the ice cream. Makes about 2 cups.

Honey, Almond, and Date Ice-Cream Sauce

¼ cup chopped almonds
1 tablespoon unsalted butter
¼ cup honey
¼ cup chopped pitted dates
2 tablespoons heavy cream
½ teaspoon fresh lemon juice
⅛ teaspoon almond extract
⅛ teaspoon salt

In a small saucepan cook the almonds in the butter over moderate heat, stirring, for 5 minutes, or until the almonds begin to color, add the honey, and bring the liquid to a boil. Stir in the dates, the cream, the lemon juice, the almond extract, and the salt and stir the mixture until it is combined well. Serve the sauce warm over ice cream. The sauce can be kept, covered and chilled, for 1 month. Makes about ¾ cup.

DESSERTS

CAKES

Apple Ginger Upside-Down Cake

½ stick (¼ cup) unsalted butter, melted
¼ cup firmly packed light brown sugar
2 tablespoons finely chopped crystallized
    ginger plus additional for garnish
2 tablespoons currants or raisins
1 large McIntosh or Granny Smith apple,
    peeled, cored, and sliced thin
1 tablespoon fresh lemon juice
½ cup all-purpose flour
½ teaspoon double-acting baking powder
¼ teaspoon salt
½ teaspoon cinnamon
2 large eggs
¼ cup plus 2 tablespoons granulated sugar
½ teaspoon vanilla
whipped cream or vanilla ice cream as an
    accompaniment

Into an 8-inch round cake pan pour the butter, swirling the pan, and sprinkle it with the brown sugar, 2 tablespoons of the ginger, and the currants. In a small bowl toss the apple slices with the lemon juice and arrange them evenly over the currants. Into another small bowl sift together the flour, the baking powder, the salt, and the cinnamon. In a bowl with an electric mixer beat the eggs with the granulated sugar and the vanilla for 3 to 5 minutes, or until the mixture is thick and pale and forms a ribbon when the beaters are lifted. Fold in the flour mixture gently but thoroughly, pour the batter over the apple slices, and bake the cake in the middle of a preheated 400° F. oven for 20 to 25 minutes, or until a tester comes out clean. Run a sharp knife around the edge of the pan, invert the cake onto a serving plate, and serve it warm with the whipped cream, sprinkled with the additional ginger.

Applesauce Cake with Penuche Frosting

For the cake
1 stick (½ cup) unsalted butter, softened
½ cup granulated sugar
½ cup firmly packed light brown sugar
1¾ cups pink applesauce (recipe follows) or
    bottled applesauce
1 large egg
2 cups all-purpose flour
2 teaspoons baking soda
1 teaspoon cinnamon
½ teaspoon freshly grated nutmeg
¼ teaspoon ground cloves
1 teaspoon vanilla
¼ cup old-fashioned rolled oats
¾ cup raisins, chopped and tossed
    in all-purpose flour to coat them
For the frosting
3 cups firmly packed light brown sugar
1½ sticks (¾ cup) unsalted butter
¾ cup milk

Make the cake: In a large bowl with an electric mixer cream the butter, add the sugars, a little at a time, and beat the mixture until it is light and fluffy. Beat in the applesauce and the egg. Into the butter mixture sift together the flour, the baking soda, the cinnamon, the nutmeg, and the cloves, stir the mixture until it is combined, and add the vanilla, the oats, and the coated raisins. Stir the batter until it is combined well, divide it between 2 well-buttered 8-inch round cake pans, and bake the cake layers in the middle of a preheated 350° F. oven for 25 to 30 minutes, or until a tester comes out clean. Turn the layers out onto racks and let them cool completely.

Make the frosting: In a heavy saucepan combine the brown sugar, the butter, the milk, and a pinch of salt, bring the mixture to a boil over moderate heat, stirring until the sugar is dissolved, and cook it, undisturbed, until it registers 234° F. on a candy thermometer. Let the mixture cool to room temperature. Whisk the mixture until it is thickened, lightened in color, and beginning to lose its sheen.

Working quickly, before the frosting begins to harden and crystallize, frost the top of 1 of the cake layers, top it with the other layer, and frost the top and sides of the cake. (If the frosting becomes too hard to spread, reheat it over low heat, stirring, until it is of spreading consistency and let it cool.)

Pink Applesauce

3 pounds McIntosh apples (about 8), cored and quartered
½ cup fresh lemon juice
½ cup sugar

In a large heavy saucepan combine the apples, ½ cup water, the lemon juice, and the sugar, bring the liquid to a boil, and simmer the mixture, stirring occasionally, for 25 minutes, or until the apples are very tender. Force the mixture through a food mill fitted with the fine disk into a bowl. Serve the applesauce warm or chilled. Makes about 4 cups.

Blueberry Lemon Pound Cake

For the cake
⅓ cup milk
6 large eggs
1½ tablespoons vanilla
2⅔ cups all-purpose flour
1 teaspoon double-acting baking powder
1¼ teaspoons salt
3 sticks (1½ cups) unsalted butter, softened
½ cup granulated sugar
¾ cup firmly packed light brown sugar
¼ cup freshly grated lemon zest
3 cups picked over blueberries, tossed with 1½ tablespoons flour
For the syrup
⅓ cup fresh lemon juice
½ cup granulated sugar

Make the cake: In a small bowl whisk together the milk, the eggs, and the vanilla. Into a bowl sift together the flour, the baking powder, and the salt. In a large bowl with an electric mixer cream the butter with the granulated sugar, the brown sugar, and the zest until the

mixture is light and fluffy, add the flour mixture alternately with the egg mixture, beginning and ending with the flour mixture and beating the batter after each addition until it is just combined, and fold in 1½ cups of the blueberries. Spoon one third of the batter into a greased and floured 10-inch (3-quart) bundt pan, spreading it evenly, and sprinkle ½ cup of the remaining blueberries over it. Spoon half the remaining batter into the pan, spreading it evenly, and sprinkle ½ cup of the remaining blueberries over it. Spoon the remaining batter into the pan, spreading it evenly, sprinkle the remaining blueberries over it, and bake the cake in the middle of a preheated 350° F. oven for 1 hour to 1 hour and 10 minutes, or until it is golden and a tester comes out clean.

Make the syrup while the cake is baking: In a small saucepan combine the lemon juice and the sugar, bring the mixture to a boil, stirring until the sugar is dissolved, and remove the pan from the heat.

Remove the cake from the oven, poke the top immediately all over with a wooden skewer, and brush it with half the syrup. Let the cake cool in the pan on a rack for 10 minutes, invert it onto the rack, and poke it all over with the skewer. Brush the cake with the remaining syrup and let it cool completely.

Brownie Torte

1 cup (6 ounces) semisweet chocolate chips
2½ tablespoons unsalted butter, cut into bits
1 large egg
¼ cup sugar
½ teaspoon vanilla
2 tablespoons all-purpose flour
½ cup chopped walnuts
coffee ice cream as an accompaniment

Butter and flour an 8-inch round cake pan. In a small metal bowl set over barely simmering water melt ¾ cup of the chocolate chips and the butter, stirring until the mixture is smooth. In a bowl whisk together the egg, the sugar, and the vanilla until the mixture is foamy, whisk in the chocolate mixture and a pinch of salt, whisking until the mixture is smooth, and fold in the flour, the remaining ¼ cup chocolate chips, and the walnuts. Spoon the batter into the pan, spreading it evenly, and bake the torte in the middle of a preheated 350° F. oven for 15 to 20 minutes, or until a tester comes out clean. Transfer the torte to a rack, let it cool for 10 minutes, and serve it warm, cut into wedges, with the ice cream.

Iced Cappuccino Cream Cake

1 pound ground fresh coffee
For the crust
1 cup chocolate wafer crumbs
¼ cup blanched almonds, toasted lightly,
    cooled completely, and ground fine
½ stick (¼ cup) unsalted butter, melted
    and cooled
¼ cup sugar

1 envelope of unflavored gelatin
4 large eggs, separated, the whites
    at room temperature
¾ cup plus 1 teaspoon sugar
¼ cup heavy cream
1 teaspoon vanilla
½ teaspoon ground cinnamon
For the topping
1 cup heavy cream
1 tablespoon Kahlúa
3 tablespoons sugar

ground cinnamon for sprinkling the cake

In a large bowl combine the coffee grounds with 4 cups cold water and let them soak overnight. Pour the mixture into a sieve, lined with a paper towel or a paper coffee filter and set over a bowl, and let it drain, pressing hard on the grounds, for 2 hours. (There should be about ¾ cup coffee concentrate.) Add enough water to measure 1¼ cups total.

Make the crust: In a bowl combine well the crumbs, the almonds, the butter, and the sugar, press the mixture onto the bottom and about 1 inch up the side of an 8½-inch springform pan, and bake the crust in the middle of a preheated 350° F. oven for 10 to 12 minutes, or until it is just set. Let the crust cool in the pan on a rack.

In a saucepan sprinkle the gelatin over the coffee mixture, let it soften for 1 minute, and heat the mixture over low heat, stirring, until the gelatin is dissolved. In a bowl beat the yolks with ½ cup of the sugar until the mixture is thick and pale, add half the coffee mixture in a stream, whisking, and whisk the mixture into the remaining coffee mixture. Cook the mixture over moderate heat, whisking, until it is thickened and registers 175° F on a candy thermometer. Transfer the mixture to a metal bowl set in a larger bowl of ice and cold water, whisk in the cream and the vanilla, and let the mixture cool, stirring frequently, until it is just cool to the touch

and is the consistency of raw egg whites. Remove the metal bowl from the larger bowl. In another bowl beat the egg whites until they hold soft peaks, add ¼ cup of the remaining sugar, 1 tablespoon at a time, beating, and beat the meringue until it holds stiff peaks. Stir one fourth of the meringue into the coffee mixture and fold in the remaining meringue gently but thoroughly. Pour the filling into the crust. In a small bowl combine the remaining 1 teaspoon sugar and the cinnamon, sprinkle the mixture over the filling, and chill the filling for at least 6 hours or overnight.

Make the topping just before serving the cake: In a chilled bowl with chilled beaters beat the cream until it holds soft peaks, add the Kahlúa and the sugar, a little at a time, beating, and beat the topping until it holds stiff peaks.

Transfer the topping to a pastry bag fitted with a decorative tip, pipe it decoratively over the coffee mixture, and sprinkle it with the cinnamon. Chill the cake for 2 hours. Run a thin knife around the edge of the pan, remove the side carefully, and transfer the cake to a serving plate.

PHOTO ON PAGE 37

Carrot Raisin Cake with Irish Cream Frosting

2½ cups all-purpose flour
1½ tablespoons double-acting baking powder
½ teaspoon salt
2 teaspoons cinnamon
⅛ teaspoon freshly grated nutmeg
¼ teaspoon allspice
2 sticks (1 cup) unsalted butter, softened
1 cup firmly packed brown sugar
4 large eggs
2½ cups finely grated carrot
½ cup raisins
2 teaspoons freshly grated orange zest
¼ cup fresh orange juice
For the frosting
2 sticks (1 cup) unsalted butter, softened
2¼ cups confectioners' sugar
½ teaspoon salt
¼ cup Irish cream liqueur or heavy cream

confectioners' sugar for sifting over the cake

In a bowl combine well the flour, the baking powder, the salt, the cinnamon, the nutmeg, and the allspice. In another bowl with an electric mixer cream the butter with the brown sugar until the mixture is light and fluffy, beat in the eggs, 1 at a time, beating well after each addition, and beat the mixture until it is smooth. Add the carrot, the raisins, and the zest and combine the mixture well. Stir in the flour mixture alternately with the orange juice in 2 batches and stir the batter until it is combined well. Divide the batter between 2 buttered and floured 8-inch round cake pans, spreading it evenly, and bake the layers in the middle of a preheated 350° F. oven for 40 to 45 minutes, or until a tester comes out clean and the edges begin to pull away from the sides of the pans. Let the layers cool in the pans for 20 minutes, invert them onto racks, and let them cool completely. *The cake layers may be made 1 day in advance and kept, wrapped well, at room temperature.*

Make the frosting: In a bowl with an electric mixer cream the butter until it is smooth, beat in the confectioners' sugar gradually, and beat in the salt and the Irish cream. Beat the frosting until it is light and fluffy.

Invert one of the cake layers onto a plate, spread one third of the frosting on top, and top it with the second layer. Spread three fourths of the remaining frosting on the side of the cake decoratively and reserve the remaining frosting in a pastry bag fitted with a star tip. Put a paper doily on top of the cake and sift the confectioners' sugar over it. Remove the doily carefully. Pipe the reserved frosting around the edge of the cake.

PHOTO ON PAGE 25

Chocolate Chestnut Torte

For the torte
¾ pound (about 2 cups) canned or vacuum-packed whole chestnuts, rinsed, drained well, and patted dry if using canned
1 stick (½ cup) unsalted butter, softened
4 tablespoons dark rum
10 ounces fine-quality bittersweet chocolate, chopped and melted
6 large eggs, separated
¼ teaspoon salt
½ cup sugar
For the glaze and garnish
6 ounces fine-quality bittersweet chocolate, chopped fine
½ cup heavy cream
1 tablespoon dark rum

8 *marrons glacés* (candied chestnuts, available at specialty foods shops)
For the whipped cream
1 cup well-chilled heavy cream
1 tablespoon sugar, or to taste
1 tablespoon dark rum if desired
¾ cup chopped *marrons glacés*

Make the torte: Line the bottom of a greased 9-inch springform pan with wax paper, grease the paper, and dust the pan with flour, knocking out the excess. In a food processor purée the chestnuts with the butter and the rum, scraping down the sides, until the mixture is smooth. Add the chocolate and blend the mixture until it is combined well. With the motor running, add the yolks, 1 at a time, and transfer the mixture to a large bowl. In a bowl with an electric mixer beat the whites with the salt until they hold soft peaks, add the sugar, a little at a time, beating, and beat the meringue until it holds stiff peaks. Whisk about one fourth of the meringue into the chocolate mixture to lighten it and fold in the remaining meringue gently but thoroughly. Pour the batter into the prepared pan, smooth the top, and bake the torte in the middle of a preheated 350° F. oven for 45 to 55 minutes, or until a tester comes out with crumbs adhering to it and the top is cracked. Let the torte cool in the pan on a rack for 5 minutes, remove the side of the pan, and invert the torte onto another rack. Remove the bottom of the pan, reinvert the torte onto a rack, and let it cool completely. (The torte will fall as it cools.)

Make the glaze and garnish: Put the chocolate in a small bowl, in a saucepan bring the cream to a boil, and pour it over the chocolate. Stir the mixture until the chocolate is melted and the glaze is smooth and stir in the rum. Dip each candied chestnut halfway into the glaze to coat it partially, transfer the chestnuts to a foil-covered tray, and let them set.

Invert the torte onto a rack set on wax paper, pour the glaze over it, smoothing the glaze with a spatula and letting the excess drip down the side. Let the torte stand for 2 hours, or until the glaze is set. Transfer the torte carefully to a plate and garnish it with the coated chestnuts.

Make the whipped cream just before serving the torte: In a chilled bowl with chilled beaters beat the cream until it holds soft peaks, beat in the sugar and the rum, and beat the mixture until it holds stiff peaks. Fold in the chopped candied chestnuts.

Serve the torte with the whipped cream.

PHOTO ON PAGE 67

Chocolate Coconut Rum Cake

1 cup sweetened flaked coconut
4 ounces semisweet chocolate, broken
    into pieces
5 tablespoons unsalted butter
3 tablespoons light or
    golden rum
4 large eggs, separated
¼ cup sugar
2 tablespoons all-purpose flour
¼ teaspoon salt
For the frosting
½ stick (¼ cup) unsalted butter,
    softened
1 tablespoon light or golden rum
¼ teaspoon salt
⅔ cup confectioners' sugar

In a baking dish toast ⅔ cup of the coconut in the middle of a preheated 350° F. oven until it just begins to color, transfer it to a small bowl, and let it cool.

In a metal bowl set over a saucepan of simmering water melt the chocolate and the butter with the rum, stirring, until the mixture is smooth and remove the bowl from the heat. In a bowl whisk together the yolks, 2 tablespoons of the sugar, the flour, and the salt until the mixture is smooth and whisk in the chocolate mixture and the remaining (untoasted) ⅓ cup coconut. In another bowl with an electric mixer beat the whites until they hold soft peaks and beat in the remaining 2 tablespoons sugar until the whites just hold stiff peaks. Stir half the whites into the chocolate mixture and fold in the remaining whites gently but thoroughly. Pour the mixture into a buttered 7- or 8-inch springform pan, bake the cake in the middle of a preheated 350° F. oven for 40 to 45 minutes, or until it is set and the top is puffed and cracked, and let it cool in the pan on a rack. (The cake will fall as it cools.)

Make the frosting while the cake is cooling: In a bowl with an electric mixer cream the butter, add the rum, the salt, and the confectioners' sugar, and beat the frosting until it is light and fluffy. Remove the side of the pan from the cake and spread the frosting on the side of the cake. Holding the cake in one hand over the bowl of toasted coconut, with the other hand press the coconut onto the frosting, letting the excess fall back into the bowl. *The cake may be made 1 day in advance and kept covered loosely and chilled.*

PHOTO ON PAGE 47

Microwave Chocolate Orange Raisin Cakes with Chocolate Glaze

For the cake
2 tablespoons raisins, chopped
1 tablespoon Grand Marnier or other orange-
    flavored liqueur
¼ cup firmly packed light brown sugar
3 tablespoons vegetable oil
1 large egg, beaten lightly
2 tablespoons milk
¼ cup all-purpose flour
2 tablespoons unsweetened cocoa powder
¼ teaspoon cinnamon
½ teaspoon baking soda
⅛ teaspoon salt
For the glaze
⅓ cup heavy cream
1 tablespoon unsalted butter, cut into bits
2 ounces semisweet chocolate, cut into bits

Make the cake: Line the bottoms of two 1-cup microwave-safe ramekins with wax paper and fasten a wax paper collar 2 inches high around each ramekin. In a microwave-safe measuring cup stir together the raisins and the Grand Marnier and microwave the mixture at high power (100%) for 1 minute. In a bowl whisk together the brown sugar and the oil and whisk in the egg, the milk, the flour, the cocoa powder, the cinnamon, the baking soda, and the salt. Stir in the raisin mixture, combine the batter well, and divide it between the ramekins. Microwave the cakes at medium power (50%) for 2 minutes, switch their positions, and microwave them at high power (100%) for 2 minutes. Let the cakes stand on a rack for 5 minutes. Run a thin knife around the edges of the ramekins, invert the cakes onto the rack, removing the wax paper carefully, and let them cool slightly.

Make the glaze: In a 1-pint microwave-safe glass measure combine the cream, the butter, the chocolate, and a pinch of salt, microwave the mixture at high power (100%) for 1 minute, or until the cream comes to a boil, and stir it until it is smooth.

Set the rack with the cakes over the baking sheet and pour the glaze over the cakes, spreading it as necessary to coat the tops and sides. Serves 2.

Raspberry White Chocolate Mousse Cake

For the white chocolate mousse
4 large egg yolks
⅓ cup sugar
3 tablespoons cornstarch
1½ cups milk
2 teaspoons vanilla
3 tablespoons unsalted butter,
    softened
9 ounces white chocolate, chopped
1 cup heavy cream

white chocolate *génoise* (page 226), cut
    horizontally into 3 layers
¼ cup framboise for brushing the cake layers
For the raspberry mousse
two 10-ounce packages frozen raspberries in
    light syrup, thawed and drained, reserving
    ⅓ cup of the syrup
1 envelope of unflavored gelatin
3 tablespoons framboise
½ cup heavy cream

2½ cups fresh raspberries
For the garnish
fresh raspberries
white chocolate, at room temperature, shaved
    into curls, covered and chilled
fresh mint sprigs

Make the white chocolate mousse: In a bowl whisk together well the yolks, the sugar, and a pinch of salt, add the cornstarch, sifted, and whisk the mixture until it is just combined. Add the milk, scalded, in a stream, whisking, transfer the mixture to a heavy saucepan, and boil it, whisking, for 1 minute, or until it is very thick and smooth. Strain the pastry cream through a fine sieve into a bowl, stir in the vanilla and the butter, and chill the pastry cream, its surface covered with plastic wrap, until it is cooled completely. In a metal bowl set over barely simmering water melt the white chocolate, stirring occasionally, and let it cool to lukewarm. In a large bowl whisk together the white chocolate and 1 cup of the pastry cream, reserving the remaining pastry cream for the raspberry mousse, until the mixture is combined well. In a bowl with an electric mixer beat the heavy cream until it holds soft peaks, whisk one fourth of it into the white chocolate mixture, and fold in the remaining whipped cream gently but thoroughly.

Line the sides of an oiled 9½-inch springform pan as smoothly as possible with pieces of plastic wrap (the plastic wrap prevents the filling from discoloring and makes unmolding the cake easier), letting the excess hang over the side, and put an 8-inch cardboard round in the bottom of the pan. Invert the top layer of the *génoise* onto the round, brush the cake with some of the framboise, and spread it evenly with half the white chocolate mousse (about 2 cups). Invert the middle layer of the *génoise* onto the mousse, brush it with some of the remaining framboise, and chill the cake and the remaining white chocolate mousse while preparing the raspberry mousse.

Make the raspberry mousse: In a blender or food processor purée the raspberries with the reserved syrup and strain the purée through a fine sieve set over a metal bowl, pressing hard on the solids. In a small saucepan sprinkle the gelatin over the framboise and let it soften for 1 minute. Heat the mixture over moderately low heat, stirring, until the gelatin is dissolved and whisk it into the purée. Whisk the reserved pastry cream into the raspberry mixture, whisking until it is smooth, set the bowl in a larger bowl of ice and cold water, and whisk the mixture until it is the consistency of raw egg white. Remove the bowl from the ice water and in a bowl with an electric mixer beat the heavy cream until it holds soft peaks. Whisk one fourth of the whipped cream into the raspberry mixture and fold in the remaining whipped cream gently but thoroughly.

Spread about 1 cup of the raspberry mousse evenly over the middle layer of *génoise* in the pan, arrange some of the raspberries neatly around the edge of the pan, and continue to arrange the raspberries in concentric circles until the surface of the mousse is covered. Spread the remaining raspberry mousse over the raspberries, invert the third layer of *génoise* onto the mousse, and brush it with the remaining framboise. Spread the remaining white chocolate mousse over the *génoise* (the pan will be completely full) and chill the cake, its surface covered with a sheet of wax paper, for at least 6 hours or overnight. Remove the side of the pan, peel the plastic wrap carefully from the side of the cake, and transfer the cake with a spatula to a plate.

Garnish the cake: Arrange some of the raspberries around the top edge of the cake, mound the chocolate curls in the center of the cake, and garnish the bottom edge of the cake with the remaining raspberries and the mint sprigs.

PHOTO ON PAGE 31

White Chocolate Génoise

3 ounces fine-quality white chocolate,
  chopped
2 tablespoons unsalted butter,
  cut into bits
½ teaspoon vanilla
½ cup cake flour (not self-rising)
¼ teaspoon salt
3 large eggs at room
  temperature
⅓ cup sugar

Line the bottom of a greased 8½-inch springform pan with wax paper, grease the paper, and dust the pan with flour, knocking out the excess. In a metal bowl set over a pan of barely simmering water melt the white chocolate with the butter, the vanilla, and 3 tablespoons water, stirring until the mixture is smooth. Remove the bowl from the heat and let the mixture cool. Into a bowl sift together the flour and the salt. In a large bowl with an electric mixer beat the eggs with the sugar on high speed for 5 minutes, or until the mixture is triple in volume and forms a ribbon when the beaters are lifted. Fold the flour mixture into the egg mixture until the batter is just combined and fold in the white chocolate mixture gently but thoroughly. Pour the batter into the pan, smoothing the top, and bake the cake in the middle of a preheated 350° F. oven for 25 minutes, or until a tester comes out clean. Transfer the cake to a rack, run a sharp knife around the edge, and remove the side of the pan. Invert the cake onto another rack and remove the wax paper. Reinvert the cake onto the rack and let it cool completely.

Cinnamon Roulade with Apple Raisin Filling

For the filling
1 Granny Smith apple
1 McIntosh apple
¼ cup firmly packed brown sugar
2 tablespoons unsalted butter
½ cup raisins
1 teaspoon cornstarch
2 tablespoons dark rum
For the cake
5 large eggs, separated, the whites at room
  temperature
¼ cup granulated sugar

1 teaspoon vanilla
½ teaspoon salt
⅓ cup cornstarch
⅓ cup all-purpose flour
2 teaspoons cinnamon
confectioners' sugar for dusting the towel

1 cup well-chilled heavy cream
1 teaspoon cinnamon

Make the filling: In a saucepan combine the apples, peeled, cored, and chopped fine, the brown sugar, the butter, and ¾ cup water, simmer the mixture, stirring occasionally, for 8 to 10 minutes, or until the apples are tender, and stir in the raisins. In a small bowl dissolve the cornstarch in ¼ cup cold water, add the mixture to the apple mixture, and boil the mixture for 1 minute. Stir in the rum, boil the filling for 1 minute, and let it cool. *The filling may be made 1 day in advance and kept covered and chilled.*

Make the cake: Line the bottom of a buttered jelly-roll pan, 15½ by 10½ by 1 inches, with wax paper, butter the paper, and dust it with flour, knocking out the excess. In a bowl with an electric mixer beat the yolks, the granulated sugar, and the vanilla until the mixture is thick and pale and forms a ribbon when the beaters are lifted. In another bowl with the beaters, cleaned, beat the whites with the salt until they just hold stiff peaks, stir one third of them into the yolk mixture, and fold in the remaining whites gently but thoroughly. Sift the cornstarch, the flour, and the cinnamon over the egg mixture, fold the mixture in until the batter is just combined, and spread the batter evenly in the prepared pan. Bake the cake in the middle of a preheated 350° F. oven for 6 to 8 minutes, or until the top is golden and a tester comes out clean. Dust a kitchen towel generously with the confectioners' sugar, invert the cake onto it, and peel off the wax paper carefully. Roll up the cake gently in the towel, starting with a long side, and let it cool completely on a rack.

Assemble the *roulade*: Unroll the cake, spread it with the filling, leaving a 1-inch border on the long sides, and re-roll it gently. Transfer the *roulade*, seam side down, to a platter and trim the ends diagonally. In a bowl beat the cream until it holds soft peaks, sift the cinnamon over it, and beat the mixture until it holds stiff peaks. Transfer the cinnamon cream to a pastry bag fitted with a decorative tip and pipe it decoratively onto and around the *roulade*.

Date Pecan Pumpkin Squares

2½ cups all-purpose flour
1½ teaspoons double-acting baking powder
¾ teaspoon cinnamon
½ teaspoon freshly grated nutmeg
½ teaspoon ground cloves
½ teaspoon salt
2 sticks (1 cup) plus 2 tablespoons unsalted
 butter, softened
2 cups firmly packed light brown sugar
2 large eggs
1 cup solid-pack (canned) pumpkin
1 teaspoon vanilla
1 pound pitted dried dates, cut into thirds
 (about 2 cups)
1½ cups chopped pecans
nutmeg ice cream and bourbon burnt sugar
 sauce (recipes follow) as accompaniments

Into a bowl sift together the flour, the baking powder, the cinnamon, the nutmeg, the cloves, and the salt. In another bowl with an electric mixer cream the butter and the sugar, add the eggs, 1 at a time, beating, and beat in the pumpkin, the vanilla, and ¼ cup water. In a small bowl toss the dates with ¼ cup of the flour mixture until they are coated well. Gradually add the remaining flour mixture to the pumpkin mixture, beating slowly, and stir in the date mixture and the pecans, stirring until the batter is combined well. Pour the batter into a greased baking pan, 13 by 9 by 2 inches, and bake the cake in the middle of a preheated 350° F. oven for 1 hour, or until a tester comes out clean. Let the cake cool on a rack, cut it into 12 squares, and serve it with the nutmeg ice cream and the bourbon burnt sugar sauce.

Nutmeg Ice Cream

1½ cups milk
1½ cups heavy cream
3 large eggs
¾ cup sugar
1 teaspoon freshly grated nutmeg
⅛ teaspoon salt
¼ teaspoon vanilla

In a saucepan bring the milk and the cream just to a boil. In a bowl whisk together the eggs, the sugar, the nutmeg, the salt, and the vanilla, whisk ½ cup of the milk mixture into the egg mixture, and whisk the mix-

ture into the remaining milk mixture. Cook the custard over moderate heat, stirring constantly with a wooden spatula, until it registers 175° F. on a candy thermometer. Transfer the custard to a metal bowl set in a larger bowl of ice and cold water and stir it until it is cold. Freeze the custard in an ice-cream freezer according to the manufacturer's instructions. Makes about 1 quart.

Bourbon Burnt Sugar Sauce

1½ cups sugar
⅓ cup bourbon

In a dry large deep heavy skillet cook the sugar over moderately high heat, stirring constantly with a fork, until it is melted completely and a deep golden caramel. Remove the skillet from the heat, into the side of the skillet carefully pour ½ cup hot water, a little at a time, and cook the mixture over moderate heat, stirring, until the caramel is dissolved. Add the bourbon and simmer the sauce for 2 minutes. Remove the skillet from the heat, let the sauce cool slightly, and pour it into a heat-proof pitcher. The sauce will thicken as it cools. To return the sauce to a liquid state set the pitcher in a saucepan of barely simmering water and stir the sauce until it reaches the desired consistency. Serve the sauce warm over ice cream. Makes about 1½ cups.

Gingerbread Cupcakes with
Lemon Cream-Cheese Frosting

1¼ cups all-purpose flour
1½ teaspoons ground ginger
1 teaspoon cinnamon
¼ teaspoon ground cloves
½ teaspoon allspice
¼ teaspoon salt
½ stick plus 2 tablespoons unsalted butter
½ cup granulated sugar
½ cup unsulfured molasses
1 large egg, beaten lightly
1 teaspoon baking soda
8 ounces cream cheese, softened
1½ cups confectioners' sugar
½ teaspoon vanilla
1 teaspoon freshly grated lemon zest
2 teaspoons fresh lemon juice
1 tablespoon thinly sliced crystallized ginger

Into a bowl sift together the flour, the ground ginger, the cinnamon, the cloves, the allspice, and the salt. In another bowl cream ½ stick of the butter, add the granulated sugar, and beat the mixture until it is fluffy. Beat in the molasses and the egg, beating until the mixture is smooth. In a measuring cup combine the baking soda with ½ cup boiling water and stir the mixture to dissolve the baking soda. Stir the mixture into the molasses mixture (the mixture will appear curdled) and stir the molasses mixture into the flour mixture, stirring to combine the ingredients well. Line twelve ½-cup muffin tins with paper liners and spoon the batter into the liners, filling them halfway. Bake the cupcakes in the middle of a preheated 350° F. oven for 20 minutes, or until a tester comes out clean. (The cupcakes will be flat or slightly indented on top.) Transfer the cupcakes to a rack and let them cool.

In a bowl cream together the cream cheese and the remaining 2 tablespoons butter, add the confectioners' sugar and the vanilla, and beat the mixture until it is fluffy and smooth. Beat in the zest and the lemon juice and chill the frosting for 30 minutes. Frost the cupcakes and top each with some ginger. Makes 12 cupcakes.

PHOTO ON PAGE 14

Pumpkin Cheesecake with
Bourbon Sour Cream Topping

For the crust
¾ cup graham cracker crumbs
½ cup finely chopped pecans
¼ cup firmly packed light brown sugar
¼ cup granulated sugar
½ stick unsalted butter, melted and cooled
For the filling
1½ cups solid pack pumpkin
3 large eggs
1½ teaspoons cinnamon
½ teaspoon freshly grated nutmeg
½ teaspoon ground ginger
½ teaspoon salt
½ cup firmly packed light brown sugar
three 8-ounce packages cream cheese,
    cut into bits and softened
½ cup granulated sugar
2 tablespoons heavy cream
1 tablespoon cornstarch
1 teaspoon vanilla
1 tablespoon bourbon liqueur or
    bourbon if desired
For the topping
2 cups sour cream
2 tablespoons granulated sugar
1 tablespoon bourbon liqueur or bourbon
16 pecan halves for garnish

Make the crust: Combine the cracker crumbs, the pecans, and the sugars, stir in the butter, and press the mixture into the bottom and ½ inch up the side of a buttered 9-inch springform pan. Chill for 1 hour.

Make the filling: In a bowl whisk together the pumpkin, the eggs, the cinnamon, the nutmeg, the ginger, the salt, and the brown sugar. In a large bowl with an electric mixer cream together the cream cheese and the granulated sugar, beat in the cream, the cornstarch, the vanilla, the bourbon liqueur, and the pumpkin mixture, and beat the filling until it is smooth.

Pour the filling into the crust, bake the cheesecake in the middle of a preheated 350° F. oven for 50 to 55 minutes, or until the center is just set, and let it cool in the pan on a rack for 5 minutes.

Make the topping: In a bowl whisk together the sour cream, the sugar, and the bourbon liqueur.

Spread the sour cream mixture over the top of the cheesecake and bake the cheesecake for 5 minutes more. Let the cheesecake cool in the pan on a rack and chill it, covered, overnight. Remove the side of the pan and garnish the top of the cheesecake with the pecans.

PHOTO ON PAGE 74

Strawberry Lemon Roulade

For the candied lemon zest

¼ cup sugar

the zest of 1 lemon cut into julienne strips

For the strawberry purée

a 10-ounce package frozen strawberries in
    syrup, thawed

2 teaspoons cornstarch

For the cake

5 large eggs, separated, the whites at room
    temperature

¼ cup granulated sugar

1 teaspoon vanilla

½ teaspoon salt

⅓ cup cornstarch

⅓ cup all-purpose flour

confectioners' sugar for dusting the towel

For the lemon filling

⅓ cup fresh lemon juice

½ cup sugar

⅛ teaspoon salt

3 large egg yolks

2 teaspoons unflavored gelatin

⅓ cup well-chilled heavy cream

a 10-ounce package frozen strawberries in
    syrup, thawed, as an accompaniment

Make the candied lemon zest: In a small saucepan combine the sugar and 2 tablespoons water, cook the mixture over low heat, stirring and washing down any sugar crystals clinging to the side of the pan with a brush dipped in cold water, until the sugar is dissolved completely, and cook the syrup over moderately high heat, without stirring, until a candy thermometer registers 260° F. Add the strips of lemon zest, stirring to coat them with the syrup, and transfer them with a fork to wax paper to cool.

Make the strawberry purée: In a saucepan combine the strawberries and all but 1 tablespoon of their syrup and bring the mixture to a boil. In a small bowl dissolve the cornstarch in the remaining 1 tablespoon syrup, add the mixture to the strawberries, and boil the mixture, stirring, for 2 minutes. In a blender purée the mixture,

force the purée through a fine sieve into a bowl, and chill it, covered.

Make the cake: Line the bottom of a buttered jelly-roll pan, 15½ by 10½ by 1 inches, with wax paper, butter the paper, and dust it with flour, knocking out the excess. In a bowl with an electric mixer beat the yolks, the granulated sugar, and the vanilla until the mixture is thick and pale and forms a ribbon when the beaters are lifted. In a large bowl with the beaters, cleaned, beat the whites with the salt until they just hold stiff peaks, stir one third of the whites into the yolk mixture, and fold in the remaining whites gently but thoroughly. Sift the cornstarch and the flour over the egg mixture, fold the mixture in until the batter is just combined, and spread the batter evenly in the prepared pan. Bake the cake in the middle of a preheated 350° F. oven for 6 to 8 minutes, or until the top is golden and a tester comes out clean. Dust a kitchen towel generously with the confectioners' sugar, invert the cake onto it, and peel off the wax paper carefully. Roll up the cake gently in the towel, starting with a long side, and let it cool completely on a rack.

Make the lemon filling: In a saucepan combine the lemon juice, the sugar, the salt, and 3 tablespoons water and bring the liquid to a boil, stirring until the sugar is dissolved. In a bowl whisk the yolks, whisk in ½ cup of the lemon mixture, and whisk the yolk mixture into the remaining lemon mixture. Cook the lemon mixture over moderately low heat, stirring, until a candy thermometer registers 175° F., but do not let it boil. In a small saucepan sprinkle the gelatin over 3 tablespoons water, let it soften for 1 minute, and heat the mixture over moderate heat, stirring, until the gelatin is dissolved. Stir the gelatin mixture into the lemon mixture and let the lemon mixture cool to room temperature. In a bowl beat the cream until it just holds stiff peaks, add the cream to the lemon mixture, beating, and chill the filling in the saucepan in a large bowl of ice water, stirring occasionally, until it is the consistency of raw egg white.

Assemble the *roulade*: Unroll the cake gently, spread it with two thirds of the strawberry purée, leaving a 1-inch border on the long sides, and spread the lemon filling over the layer of purée. Reroll the cake gently, transfer the *roulade*, seam side down, to a platter, and trim the ends diagonally. Brush the *roulade* with the remaining strawberry purée and arrange the candied lemon zest down the center. In a blender purée the strawberries with their syrup and serve the strawberry purée with the *roulade*.

Whipped Cream Cakes with Peaches and Raspberries

1 large whole egg
1 large egg yolk
½ teaspoon vanilla
½ cup granulated sugar
⅔ cup well-chilled heavy cream
¾ cup cake flour (not self-rising)
1 teaspoon double-acting baking powder
¼ teaspoon salt
confectioners' sugar for dusting the cakes
fresh peaches, peeled and sliced, for garnish
fresh raspberries for garnish

In a bowl with an electric mixer beat together the whole egg, the yolk, the vanilla, and ¼ cup of the granulated sugar until the mixture is thick and pale. In a bowl beat the cream with cleaned beaters, adding the remaining ¼ cup granulated sugar, until the mixture holds soft peaks. Fold the egg mixture into the whipped cream mixture. Into another bowl sift together the flour, the baking powder, and the salt and fold the flour mixture into the cream mixture.

Divide the batter among 6 buttered and floured ½-cup muffin tins and bake the cakes in the middle of a preheated 350° F. oven for 18 to 20 minutes, or until they are golden. (The batter will flow over the rims slightly.) Let the cakes cool in the tins on a rack for 10 minutes and turn them out onto the rack, leaving them upside down. Dust the cakes with the confectioners' sugar and serve them with the peaches and the raspberries. Makes 6 cakes, serving 2.

COOKIES

Almond Ginger Sand Tarts

½ stick (¼ cup) unsalted butter, softened
¼ cup vegetable shortening
⅓ cup confectioners' sugar
1 teaspoon vanilla
1 cup all-purpose flour
2 teaspoons ground ginger
½ teaspoon salt
¼ teaspoon double-acting baking powder
½ cup whole almonds, ground fine in a food
  processor or blender, plus about 25 almond
  slices for garnish
1 large egg white, beaten lightly

In a bowl with an electric mixer cream together the butter, the shortening, and the confectioners' sugar until the mixture is combined well and beat in the vanilla. Into the bowl sift together the flour, the ginger, the salt, and the baking powder and combine the dough well. Add the ground almonds, blend the dough well, and chill it, wrapped in plastic wrap, for at least 1 hour or overnight.

Roll out the dough ¼ inch thick between sheets of wax paper, with a 2-inch round cutter cut out rounds, and arrange them 2 inches apart on greased baking sheets. (If the dough becomes too soft, chill it on a baking sheet until it is firm enough to work with.) Brush the tops of the rounds with some of the egg white, put 1 of the almond slices on each round, and brush the almonds with more of the egg white. Gather the scraps, reroll the dough, and make more almond-topped rounds in the same manner. Bake the cookies in the middle of a preheated 325° F. oven for 15 to 20 minutes, or until the tops are pale golden. Let the cookies cool on the sheets for 2 minutes, transfer them with a metal spatula to racks, and let them cool completely. *The cookies may be made 4 days in advance and kept in an airtight container.* Makes about 25 cookies.

PHOTO ON PAGE 57

Chewy Almond Macaroons

¼ pound (¾ cup) blanched whole almonds
  plus ⅓ cup sliced
½ cup sugar
¼ teaspoon almond extract
¼ teaspoon salt
2 large egg whites

In a food processor grind fine the whole almonds with the sugar, the almond extract, and the salt. In a bowl beat the whites until they are foamy (just before they hold soft peaks) and fold in the almond mixture gently but thoroughly. Line a large baking sheet with parchment paper and butter the parchment. Transfer the batter to a pastry bag fitted with a ½-inch plain tip, pipe 1-inch mounds onto the parchment, 2 inches apart, and sprinkle them with the sliced almonds. Bake the macaroons in the middle of a preheated 300° F. oven for 15 to 20 minutes, or until they are golden around the edges, and let them cool on the parchment. Peel the macaroons from the parchment and store them in an airtight container. Makes about 40 macaroons.

PHOTO ON PAGE 47

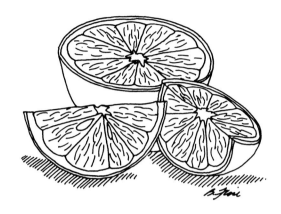

Apricot Butter Cookies

¾ cup (about ¼ pound) dried apricots
¾ cup granulated sugar
1 tablespoon dark rum
2½ cups all-purpose flour
1 teaspoon double-acting baking powder
2 sticks (1 cup) unsalted butter, softened
¼ cup firmly packed brown sugar
1 teaspoon vanilla
1 large egg
1 cup confectioners' sugar
2 teaspoons fresh lemon juice

In a small saucepan combine the apricots, ¼ cup of the granulated sugar, and ⅔ cup water, simmer the mixture for 15 to 18 minutes, or until the liquid is reduced by half, and add the rum. Let the mixture cool slightly and in a blender or food processor purée it.

In a bowl whisk together the flour, the baking powder, and a pinch of salt. In a large bowl with an electric mixer beat together the butter, the remaining ½ cup granulated sugar, and the brown sugar until the mixture is light and fluffy, beat in the vanilla and the egg, and beat the mixture until it is combined well. Add the flour mixture and beat the dough until it is just combined. Form the dough into a log, chill it for 1 hour, and divide it into 8 pieces.

Working with 1 piece of dough at a time, on a sheet of plastic wrap form the pieces into 8-inch ropes, wrap-ping the plastic wrap around the ropes to keep the dough from sticking, and on 2 baking sheets pat the ropes into 8- by 1½-inch rectangles. Make a canal down the center of each rectangle with your finger and spread the apricot purée in the canals. Bake the rectangles in 2 batches in the middle of a preheated 350° F. oven for 18 to 20 minutes, or until the edges are golden, transfer them to racks, and let them cool. In a small bowl whisk together the confectioners' sugar, the lemon juice, and enough water to make a thick but pourable icing. Drizzle it over the rectangles, and cut the rectangles diagonally into 1-inch strips. The cookies keep in an airtight container for 1 week. Makes about 32 cookies.

Chocolate-Dipped Orange Cookies

¾ cup all-purpose flour
2 tablespoons cornstarch
⅛ teaspoon double-acting baking powder
1 stick (½ cup) unsalted butter, softened
⅓ cup confectioners' sugar
1 large egg, separated, the white at
    room temperature
2 tablespoons freshly grated orange zest
¼ teaspoon vanilla
1 tablespoon fresh orange juice
granulated sugar for sprinkling the cookies
2 ounces bittersweet or semisweet chocolate,
    melted and cooled slightly

Into a large bowl sift together the flour, the cornstarch, the baking powder, and a pinch of salt. In a bowl with an electric mixer cream together the butter and the confectioners' sugar until the mixture is light and fluffy, beat in the yolk, the zest, the vanilla, and the orange juice, and stir in the flour mixture, combining the mixture well. In a bowl beat the white until it forms soft peaks and fold it gently but thoroughly into the mixture. (The batter will have the consistency of a soft dough.) Transfer the batter to a pastry bag fitted with a decorative ribbon tip and onto buttered baking sheets pipe 1½-inch lengths 1 inch apart. Sprinkle the lengths with the granulated sugar and bake the cookies in the middle of a preheated 350° F. oven for 10 to 12 minutes, or until the edges are golden. Transfer the cookies to racks and let them cool until they can be handled. Dip 1 end of each cookie into the chocolate and let the cookies dry completely on the racks. Makes about 36 cookies.

PHOTO ON PAGE 13

Coconut Tuiles

2 tablespoons unsalted butter, softened
3 tablespoons sugar
1 large egg white at room temperature
¼ teaspoon vanilla
2 tablespoons all-purpose flour
½ cup sweetened flaked coconut

In a bowl cream together the butter and the sugar until the mixture is light and fluffy, add the egg white and the vanilla, and beat the mixture until it is just combined. Sift the flour over the mixture, fold it in, and fold in the coconut. Working in batches drop the batter by rounded teaspoons 4 inches apart onto well-buttered baking sheets and pat it into 3-inch rounds with the back of a fork dipped in water. Bake the cookies in batches in the middle of a preheated 425° F. oven for 4 to 5 minutes, or until the edges are golden. Working quickly loosen the cookies carefully with a metal spatula, transfer them to a rolling pin, pressing gently to curl them around the pin, and let them cool completely on the pin. (If the cookies become too firm to remove from the baking sheet, return them to the oven for a few seconds to soften.) *The tuiles may be made 1 day in advance and kept in an airtight container.* Makes about 14 *tuiles*.

Lemon Thins

½ cup vegetable shortening at room
   temperature
2 tablespoons unsalted butter, softened
1 cup sugar
½ teaspoon vanilla
½ teaspoon lemon extract
1½ tablespoons freshly grated lemon zest
¼ cup fresh lemon juice (about 1 lemon)
1½ cups all-purpose flour
1½ teaspoons double-acting baking powder
½ teaspoon baking soda
¼ teaspoon salt
confectioners' sugar for dusting the cookies

In a bowl with an electric mixer cream together the shortening, the butter, and the sugar, add the vanilla, the lemon extract, the zest, and the juice, beating, and beat the mixture until it is smooth. Into the bowl sift together the flour, the baking powder, the baking soda, and the salt and blend the dough well. On a piece of wax paper form the dough into a log 1½ inches in diameter.

Chill the log, wrapped in the wax paper and foil, for 2 hours. *The dough may be made up to 3 months in advance and kept wrapped well and frozen.*

Cut the log into ⅛-inch slices with a sharp knife and bake the cookies 2 inches apart on ungreased baking sheets in the middle of a preheated 350° F. oven for 8 to 10 minutes, or until the edges are just golden. Transfer the cookies immediately with a metal spatula to racks, let them cool, and sift the confectioners' sugar lightly over the lemon thins. Makes about 50 cookies.

S'Mores Bars

2 cups graham cracker crumbs
⅓ cup sugar
¼ teaspoon salt
1 stick (½ cup) unsalted butter, melted
1 pound milk chocolate
4 cups mini-marshmallows

In a bowl combine well the crumbs, the sugar, the salt, and the butter and, reserving 1 cup of the mixture, press the remaining mixture into the bottom of a flameproof baking dish, 13 by 9 by 2 inches. Bake the crust in a preheated 350° F. oven for 12 minutes, or until it is golden, and let it cool in the dish on a rack. In a metal bowl set over a saucepan of barely simmering water melt the chocolate, stirring, pour it over the crust, spreading it evenly, and sprinkle it with the marshmallows, pressing them lightly, and the reserved crumb mixture. Broil the dessert under a preheated broiler about 2 inches from the heat for 30 seconds, or until the marshmallows are golden, let it cool completely, and cut it into squares. Makes about 24 bars.

Walnut Cigarette Cookies

½ stick (¼ cup) unsalted butter, softened
½ cup sugar
2 large egg whites
¼ teaspoon salt
¼ cup cake flour (not self-rising)
⅓ cup walnuts, toasted lightly and minced

In a bowl with an electric mixer cream the butter with the sugar until the mixture is light and fluffy, add the egg whites and the salt, and beat the mixture for 10 seconds, or until it is combined well but not frothy. Sift the flour over the mixture and fold it in with the walnuts.

Drop level teaspoons of the batter 4 inches apart onto buttered baking sheets and spread the batter into 2-inch rounds. Bake the cookies in batches in the middle of a preheated 375° F. oven for 6 to 8 minutes, or until they are just firm enough to remove from the baking sheet. Working quickly with 1 cookie at a time, loosen the cookies from the sheet with a metal spatula and roll them quickly, rough sides out, around the handle of a wooden spoon or chopstick to form a thin cylinder, transferring them as they are rolled to a rack to cool. (If the cookies become too brittle to roll, return them to the oven for 20 to 30 seconds to soften them.) The cookies keep in an airtight container for 3 days. Makes about 28 cookies.

PIES, TARTS, AND PASTRIES

Key Lime Pie with Almond Crumb Crust

For the crust
1 cup zwieback crumbs or graham cracker crumbs
⅔ cup blanched almonds, toasted lightly, cooled completely, and ground fine in a food processor
½ stick (¼ cup) unsalted butter, melted and cooled
¼ cup sugar

3 large eggs, separated, the whites at room temperature
a 14-ounce can sweetened condensed milk
½ cup Key lime juice (available bottled at specialty foods shops) or fresh lime juice (about 3 limes)
⅓ cup sugar

Make the crust: In a bowl combine well the crumbs, the almonds, the butter, and the sugar, press the mixture onto the bottom and side of a 10-inch pie plate, and bake the shell in the middle of a preheated 350° F. oven for 10 minutes, or until it is browned lightly. Let the shell cool on a rack.

In a large bowl beat the yolks with the condensed milk and stir in the lime juice, a little at a time, stirring to combine the filling well. Spoon the filling into the shell and chill the pie for 1 hour. In a bowl beat the egg whites with a pinch of salt until they hold soft peaks, add the

sugar, beating, 1 tablespoon at a time, and beat the meringue until it holds stiff peaks. Spread the meringue over the filling and bake the pie in the middle of a preheated 350° F. oven for 15 minutes, or until the meringue is just golden. Chill the pie for 2 hours.

J. Oliver

Alsatian-Style Apple and Cream Tart

1 recipe *pâte brisée* (page 120)
raw rice for weighting the shell
4 Granny Smith apples (about 2 pounds)
2 tablespoons fresh lemon juice
6 tablespoons sugar
3 large egg yolks
1 cup heavy cream
1 teaspoon vanilla
⅓ cup golden raisins
a pinch of cinnamon

Roll out the dough ⅛ inch thick on a lightly floured surface and fit it into a 9-inch tart pan with a removable fluted rim. Prick the shell with a fork and chill it for at least 30 minutes or, covered, overnight. Line the shell with foil, fill the foil with the rice, and bake the shell in the lower third of a preheated 425° F. oven for 15 minutes. Remove the foil and the rice carefully, bake the shell for 10 minutes more, or until it is pale golden, and let it cool in the pan on a rack.

In a bowl stir together the apples, peeled, cored, and cut into eighths, the lemon juice, and 2 tablespoons of the sugar and toss the mixture until the apples are coated well. In a large bowl whisk together the yolks, the cream, 2½ tablespoons of the remaining sugar, a pinch of salt, and the vanilla and stir in the raisins. Arrange the apples decoratively in the shell, pour the cream mixture over them, and sprinkle the remaining 1½ tablespoons sugar and the cinnamon over it. Bake the tart in the middle of a preheated 375° F. oven for 1 hour and 10 minutes, or until the apples are tender when pierced with a cake tester, let it cool in the pan on a rack, and remove the rim.

Blueberry Buttermilk Tart

For the shell

1⅓ cups all-purpose flour

¼ cup sugar

¼ teaspoon salt

1 stick (½ cup) cold unsalted butter,
　cut into bits

1 large egg yolk, beaten with 2 tablespoons
　ice water

raw rice for weighting the shell

For the filling

1 cup buttermilk

3 large egg yolks

½ cup granulated sugar

1 tablespoon freshly grated lemon zest

1 tablespoon fresh lemon juice

½ stick (¼ cup) unsalted butter, melted
　and cooled

1 teaspoon vanilla

½ teaspoon salt

2 tablespoons all-purpose flour

2 cups picked over blueberries

confectioners' sugar for sprinkling the tart

blueberry ice cream (recipe follows) as an
　accompaniment if desired

Make the shell: In a bowl stir together the flour, the sugar, and the salt, add the butter, and blend the mixture until it resembles coarse meal. Add the yolk mixture, toss the mixture until the liquid is incorporated, and form the dough into a ball. Dust the dough with flour and chill it, wrapped in plastic wrap, for 1 hour. Roll out the dough ⅛ inch thick on a floured surface, fit it into a 10-inch tart pan with a removable fluted rim, and chill the shell for at least 30 minutes or, covered, overnight. Line the shell with foil, fill the foil with the rice, and bake the shell in the middle of a preheated 350° F. oven for 25 minutes. Remove the foil and rice carefully, bake the shell for 5 to 10 minutes more, or until it is pale golden, and let it cool in the pan on a rack.

Make the filling: In a blender or food processor blend together the buttermilk, the yolks, the granulated sugar, the zest, the lemon juice, the butter, the vanilla, the salt, and the flour until the mixture is smooth, spread the blueberries evenly over the bottom of the shell, and pour the buttermilk mixture over them. Bake the tart in the middle of a preheated 350° F. oven for 30 to 35 minutes, or until the filling is just set.

Let the tart cool completely in the pan on the rack, sprinkle it with the confectioners' sugar, sifted, and serve it at room temperature or chilled with the ice cream.

Blueberry Ice Cream

4 cups picked over blueberries

1 cup sugar

the zest of 1 navel orange, removed in strips
　with a vegetable peeler

2 tablespoons Grand Marnier, or other
　orange-flavored liqueur

3 tablespoons fresh lemon juice

½ teaspoon vanilla

⅛ teaspoon salt

2 cups heavy cream

1 cup half-and-half

In a large saucepan combine the blueberries, the sugar, the zest, and ¼ cup water, boil the mixture, covered, for 5 minutes, stirring occasionally, and simmer it, uncovered, for 5 minutes. Discard the zest and purée the mixture in batches in a blender or food processor. Transfer the pureé to a bowl and whisk in the Grand Marnier, the lemon juice, the vanilla, the salt, the heavy cream, and the half-and-half. Force the mixture through a very fine sieve set over another bowl and chill it, covered, for 1 hour, or until it is cold. Freeze the mixture in an ice-cream freezer according to the manufacturer's instructions. Makes about 1½ quarts.

Peach Raspberry Kuchen

For the shell

1 stick (½ cup) unsalted butter

⅓ cup granulated sugar

2 tablespoons light brown sugar

1 large egg

½ teaspoon vanilla

¼ teaspoon almond extract
1½ cups all-purpose flour
1 teaspoon double-acting baking powder
¾ teaspoon salt
2 firm-ripe peaches
2 tablespoons sugar
½ pint raspberries
¼ cup currant jelly, melted and cooled

Make the shell: In a small saucepan cook the butter over moderate heat until it is golden brown, being careful not to let it burn, let it cool, and chill it just until it is no longer liquid. *The butter may be browned 1 day in advance and kept covered and chilled. Let the butter soften at room temperature before using.* In a bowl cream together the browned butter, the granulated sugar, and the brown sugar and beat in the egg, the vanilla, and the almond extract. Into the bowl sift the flour, the baking powder, and the salt and beat the dough until it is just combined. Chill the dough for 30 minutes and press it onto the bottom and side of a 9-inch tart pan with a removable fluted rim.

In a saucepan of boiling water blanch the peaches for 1 minute, drain them, and refresh them under cold water. Peel the peaches, halve them, and cut 3 of the halves into ⅛-inch-thick slices, reserving the remaining half for another use. Arrange the slices decoratively, overlapping them slightly, in the shell, sprinkle them with the sugar, and bake the kuchen in the lower third of a preheated 375° F. for 20 minutes. Arrange the raspberries decoratively over the peaches and bake the kuchen for 10 minutes more. Transfer the kuchen to a rack, brush the fruit with the jelly, and let the kuchen cool for 15 minutes. Remove the rim of the pan and serve the kuchen warm or at room temperature.

PHOTO ON PAGE 50

Strawberry and Banana Tartlets in Coconut Pastry Shells

For the shells
¾ cup all-purpose flour
3 tablespoons cold unsalted butter,
    cut into bits
1 tablespoon cold vegetable shortening
⅓ cup sweetened flaked coconut, toasted
    lightly
For the filling
⅓ cup milk

3 tablespoons sugar
1 large egg yolk
¼ teaspoon vanilla
1 small ripe banana
2 tablespoons all-purpose flour
½ tablespoon unsalted butter
¼ cup heavy cream

16 small strawberries, hulled
2 tablespoons strawberry jelly
2 teaspoons fresh lemon juice
toasted sweetened flaked coconut for garnish

Make the shells: In a large bowl blend together the flour, the butter, the shortening, the coconut, and a pinch of salt until the mixture resembles meal. Add 1½ tablespoons ice water, toss the mixture until the water is incorporated, and form the dough into a ball. Flatten the dough slightly, dust it with flour, and chill it, wrapped in wax paper, for 1 hour. Divide the dough in half and roll out each half ⅛ inch thick on a lightly floured surface. Fit each half into a 4¼-inch tartlet pan and roll a rolling pin over the pan edges to trim the excess dough. Prick the shells with the fork and bake them in a preheated 425° F. oven for 5 minutes. Reduce the heat to 375° F. and bake the shells for 12 to 15 minutes more, or until they are golden. Transfer the shells to a rack and let them cool. *The shells may be made 1 day in advance and kept in an airtight container.*

Make the filling: In a saucepan combine the milk and 2 tablespoons of the sugar and bring the mixture just to a boil over moderate heat. In a bowl whisk together the yolk, the vanilla, the banana, mashed, the remaining 1 tablespoon sugar, the flour, and a pinch of salt. Add half the milk mixture in a stream, whisking, pour the egg mixture into the pan, and bring the mixture to a boil, whisking constantly. Simmer the custard for 1 minute, remove the pan from the heat, and whisk in the butter. Force the custard through a fine sieve set over a bowl, cover its surface with plastic wrap, and chill the custard for 2 hours. *The custard may be made 8 hours in advance and kept covered and chilled.* In a bowl beat the cream until it holds soft peaks and fold it gently but thoroughly into the custard.

Divide the filling between the shells and arrange the strawberries decoratively on it. In a small saucepan melt the jelly with the lemon juice over moderate heat and brush the strawberries with the glaze. Sprinkle the tartlets with the toasted coconut. Makes 2 tartlets.

It is very important that the following recipe be prepared in a cool or air-conditioned kitchen, so that the butter used in making the Danish pastry remains firm.

Blueberry Cheese Danish Pastries

For the Danish pastry
two ¼-ounce packages (5 teaspoons)
    active dry yeast
⅔ cup sugar
1 teaspoon salt
3 large egg yolks
2 teaspoons vanilla
⅔ cup milk
3¾ cups all-purpose flour
3 sticks (1½ cups) cold unsalted butter,
    cut into bits
For the filling
8 ounces cream cheese, softened
¼ cup granulated sugar
1 large egg yolk
1 teaspoon vanilla
¼ teaspoon salt
2 teaspoons freshly grated orange zest
1 teaspoon freshly grated lemon zest
2 tablespoons all-purpose flour

1½ cups picked over blueberries
an egg wash made by beating 1 large egg with
    1 teaspoon water
For the glaze
1¼ cups confectioners' sugar
2 to 3 tablespoons fresh lemon juice

Make the Danish pastry: In a large bowl proof the yeast with ¼ cup warm water for 5 minutes, or until it is foamy, and stir in the sugar, the salt, the yolks, the vanilla, and the milk. Add 3¼ cups of the flour, stirring until the dough is combined well (it will be soft and slightly sticky), and chill the dough, covered, for 1 hour. On a cool surface (preferably marble) beat the butter with a rolling pin until it is smooth but still cold, add the remaining ½ cup flour, and blend the mixture quickly until it is smooth. Working quickly, form the butter mixture into a 6-inch square and chill it, wrapped in plastic wrap, for 15 to 30 minutes, or until it is firmer but still malleable. On a well-floured surface roll the dough into a 12-inch square, lay the butter diagonally in the center of the square, and fold the corners of the

dough tightly over the butter like an envelope, enclosing the butter completely. Brush off any excess flour and pinch the edges of the dough together to seal them. With the rolling pin flatten the dough gently with uniform impressions and roll it from the center away from you to within ½ inch of the end. Turn the strip 180° and roll the dough again from the center away from you to within ½ inch of the end. Continue to roll the dough in this manner until it forms an 18- by 8-inch rectangle. (It is important not to roll over the ends in this first rolling to help the later formation of even layers of butter and dough.) Brush off any excess flour from the dough, fold the top quarter of the rectangle down to the center of the strip, and fold the bottom quarter of the rectangle up to the center, leaving about ½ inch between the 2 ends. Fold the top half of the dough over the bottom to close the dough like a book. Turn the dough 90° so a short side faces you, roll it again into an 18- by 8-inch rectangle, and fold it in the same manner. This completes 2 ''turns.'' Chill the dough, wrapped in plastic wrap, for 1 hour. Make 2 more turns in the same manner, always beginning with a short side facing you and chilling the dough, wrapped in plastic wrap, for 1 hour between each turn. Chill the dough, wrapped in plastic wrap, for at least 4 hours or overnight.

Make the filling: In a bowl beat together the cream cheese, the sugar, the yolk, the vanilla, the salt, the zests, and the flour until the mixture is smooth and chill the filling, covered, for at least 1 hour and up to 24 hours.

Roll half the dough into a 16- by 8-inch rectangle, trim the edges evenly, and cut the rectangle into eight 4-inch squares. Stretch 2 opposite corners of each square slightly to lengthen the dough and form flaps that will enclose the filling. Roll out, cut, and stretch the remaining dough in the same manner. Spoon 1 tablespoon of the filling onto the center of each square of dough, sprinkle about 1½ tablespoons of the blueberries over it, and brush the flaps with some of the egg wash. Fold 1 of the flaps across the berries, fold the other flap across the berries in the opposite direction, overlapping the first flap, and tuck the second flap under the Danish. Brush the Danish pastries with the egg wash, arrange them about 3 inches apart on lightly buttered baking sheets, and let them stand for 1 hour. Bake the Danish pastries in the middle of a preheated 350° F. oven for 30 to 35 minutes, or until they are crisp and golden.

Make the glaze while the Danish pastries are baking: In a bowl whisk together the confectioners' sugar, sifted, and enough of the lemon juice to make a thick but pourable glaze.

Transfer the Danish pastries to a rack and drizzle some of the glaze over each pastry. *The Danish pastries may be cooled to room temperature, wrapped in plastic wrap and foil, and frozen for 1 month. Transfer the Danish pastries to a baking sheet and bake them in the middle of a preheated 400° F. oven for 5 minutes, or until they are heated through.* Makes 16 Danish pastries.

CUSTARDS, MOUSSES, AND PUDDINGS

Lemon Lime Curd

2 large eggs, beaten lightly
1 stick (½ cup) unsalted butter, cut into bits
½ cup sugar
1 tablespoon freshly grated lemon zest
1 tablespoon freshly grated lime zest
2 tablespoons fresh lemon juice
2 tablespoons fresh lime juice

In a saucepan combine the eggs, the butter, the sugar, the zests, and the juices and cook the mixture over moderately low heat, whisking constantly, for 1 to 2 minutes, or until the curd is thick enough to hold the mark of the whisk and the first bubble appears on the surface. Transfer the curd to a small bowl, cover its surface with plastic wrap, and let the curd cool. Chill the curd, covered with the plastic wrap, for 1 hour and serve it with biscuits or scones or as a filling for tartlets. Makes about 1 cup.

Lemon Meringue Custards

For the custard
¾ cup sugar
the zest of 3 lemons, removed with a
    vegetable peeler (being careful to include
    none of the white pith)
2½ cups milk
1½ cups heavy cream
¼ teaspoon salt
5 large egg yolks
4 large whole eggs

¼ cup fresh lemon juice
For the meringue
1¼ cups sugar
4 large egg whites
¼ cup fresh lemon juice

silver dragées for garnish

Make the custard: In a food processor grind the sugar and the zest until the zest is chopped fine and transfer the mixture to a large saucepan. Add ¼ cup water, bring the mixture to a boil over moderate heat, stirring until the sugar is dissolved, and boil the syrup for 5 minutes. Stir in the milk, the cream, and the salt and cook the mixture until it is hot, but do not let it boil. In a bowl whisk together the yolks and the whole eggs, add the hot milk mixture in a stream, whisking, and stir in the lemon juice. Strain the custard through a fine sieve into twelve ⅔-cup ramekins set in a large baking pan, add enough hot water to the pan to reach halfway up the sides of the ramekins, and bake the custards in the middle of a preheated 325° F. oven for 40 minutes, or until they are just set. (Alternatively, the custard can be baked in the same manner in a 1½-quart shallow baking dish for 1 hour, or until it is just set.) Remove the ramekins from the pan, let the custards cool completely, and chill them, covered loosely with wax paper, for at least 3 hours. *The custards may be made 1 day in advance and kept covered and chilled.*

Make the meringue: In a small saucepan combine the sugar with ⅓ cup water and bring the mixture to a boil, stirring until the sugar is dissolved. Boil the syrup until it registers 248° F. on a candy thermometer and remove the pan from the heat. While the syrup is boiling, in a bowl with an electric mixer beat the whites with a pinch of salt until they hold soft peaks. With the mixer running add the hot syrup in a stream, beat the meringue on medium speed until it is cool, and beat in the lemon juice.

Transfer the meringue to a pastry bag fitted with a star tip, blot the top of the custard dry with paper towels, and pipe the meringue decoratively onto it. Sprinkle the meringue with the dragées, transfer the custards to a large baking pan filled with ice, and bake them in the top third of a preheated 450° F. oven for 3 to 4 minutes, or until the meringue is golden. *The lemon meringue custards may be made 3 hours in advance and kept in the large baking pan filled with more ice.* Serves 12.

PHOTO ON PAGE 80

Passion Fruit Mousses with Raspberry Swirl

a 10-ounce package frozen raspberries in light
    syrup, thawed
2 teaspoons cornstarch dissolved in
    1 tablespoon cold water
8 passion fruit (available seasonally at
    specialty produce markets)
2½ teaspoons unflavored gelatin
½ cup sugar
3 or 4 drops of yellow food coloring if desired
¾ cup well-chilled heavy cream
12 raspberries for garnish

In a blender purée the frozen raspberries with the syrup, strain the purée through a fine sieve into a saucepan, and stir in the cornstarch mixture. Bring the mixture to a boil over moderate heat, stirring, boil it, stirring, for 1 minute, and chill it, covered partially, until it is cold.

Halve the passion fruit over a sieve set over a bowl to catch any juices and scoop the seeds and pulp into the sieve. Scrape the seeds with a spatula until the juice and most of the pulp have been extracted and reserve ½ cup of the juice. In a small saucepan sprinkle the gelatin over ⅓ cup cold water, let it soften for 1 minute, and heat the mixture over moderate heat, stirring, until the gelatin is dissolved completely. Add ⅓ cup water and the sugar, heat the mixture, stirring, until the sugar is dissolved, and in a metal bowl combine well the gelatin mixture, the reserved passion fruit juice, and the food coloring.

In a bowl beat the cream until it holds soft peaks and reserve it. Chill the passion fruit mixture set in a larger bowl of ice and cold water, stirring, until it is the consistency of raw egg white and fold in the reserved whipped cream. Spoon the passion fruit mousse and the raspberry swirl mixture decoratively into four 1½-cup goblets, chill the mousses, covered, for at least 1 hour or overnight, and garnish them with the raspberries. Serves 4.

PHOTO ON PAGE 19

Rum Lime Mousses

1 envelope (about 1 tablespoon) of
    unflavored gelatin
¼ cup light rum
⅓ cup fresh lime juice (about 2 limes)
1 tablespoon fresh lemon juice
1 tablespoon freshly grated lime zest
3 large eggs, separated, the whites at room
    temperature
½ cup sugar
¾ cup heavy cream
1 drop of green food coloring if desired
twists of lime zest for garnish

In a small heavy saucepan sprinkle the gelatin over the rum and let it soften for 1 minute. Stir in the lime juice, the lemon juice, the zest, the yolks, and ¼ cup of the sugar, cook the mixture over moderately low heat, stirring constantly, until it is thickened slightly and a candy thermometer registers 175° F., and transfer it to a metal bowl set in a larger bowl of ice and cold water. Let the mixture cool, stirring occasionally, until it is cold and has the consistency of raw egg white, but do not let it set.

In a bowl beat the egg whites with a pinch of salt until they hold soft peaks, beat in the remaining ¼ cup sugar, 1 tablespoon at a time, and beat the whites until they just hold stiff peaks. Stir one fourth of the whites into the lime mixture and fold in the remaining whites gently but thoroughly.

In another bowl beat the cream until it just holds stiff peaks and fold it into the lime mixture with the food coloring. Spoon the mousse into dessert glasses and chill it, covered loosely with plastic wrap, for at least 1 hour and up to 24 hours. Garnish the desserts with the lime twists. Serves 6.

Lauren Jarrett

Toblerone Mousse Fondues with Meringues and Fruit

about 7 ounces (two 3.52-ounce bars)
    Toblerone bittersweet chocolate
⅓ cup heavy cream
3 large egg whites
⅓ cup sugar
Accompaniments
strawberries
carambolas (star fruit, available seasonally at
    specialty produce markets), sliced
seedless red and green grapes
dried apricots

In a metal bowl set over a saucepan of barely simmering water melt the chocolate with the cream, stirring, remove the bowl from the pan, and let the mixture cool while making the meringue. In another metal bowl combine the whites and the sugar, set the bowl over a saucepan of hot but not simmering water, and stir the mixture until the sugar is dissolved. With a hand-held electric mixer beat the meringue for 5 minutes, or until it holds glossy stiff peaks and is warm to the touch. Remove the bowl from the pan and continue beating the meringue until it is cool. Transfer 1 cup of the meringue to a pastry bag fitted with a small decorative tip, fold the remaining meringue into the chocolate mixture gently but thoroughly, and divide the mousse among 6 small dishes. *The mousse may be made 4 hours in advance and kept covered at room temperature or it may be made 1 day in advance, kept covered and chilled, and allowed to come to room temperature.*

On a baking sheet lined with parchment paper or foil pipe the remaining meringue into 2-inch strips and bake the strips in the middle of a preheated 300° F. oven for 15 minutes, or until they are lightly golden. Let the meringues cool on the baking sheet and peel them from the paper. *The meringues may be made 2 days in advance and kept in an airtight container.* Serve the meringues and fruit for dipping into the mousse fondues. Serves 6.

PHOTO ON PAGE 20

Chocolate Raisin Bread Pudding

3 slices of cinnamon-raisin bread
1½ tablespoons unsalted butter, softened
1 ounce unsweetened chocolate, chopped fine
1¼ cups milk
1 large egg
¼ cup sugar

½ teaspoon vanilla
vanilla ice cream as an accompaniment

Spread one side of each slice of bread with the butter and cut the bread into ½-inch pieces. In a small saucepan melt the chocolate in the milk over moderate heat, whisking until it is smooth. In a bowl whisk the egg with the sugar, add the hot milk mixture in a stream, whisking, and stir in the vanilla and the bread. Transfer the mixture to a buttered loaf pan, 9 by 5 by 3 inches, let it stand for 5 minutes, and bake it in the middle of a preheated 375° F. oven for 25 to 30 minutes, or until a knife inserted in the center comes out clean. Serve the bread pudding warm with the ice cream. Serves 2.

Fruitcake Trifle

10 large egg yolks
¾ cup sugar
2¾ cups milk
¾ teaspoon freshly grated lemon zest
¾ cup heavy cream
1½ teaspoons vanilla
½ cup sour cream
5 teaspoons unflavored gelatin
thirty-six 2-inch-square slices of fruitcake,
    each about ⅜ inch thick

In a bowl whisk together the yolks and the sugar and add the milk, scalded with the zest, in a slow stream, whisking. In a heavy saucepan combine the yolk mixture and the heavy cream and cook the custard over moderately low heat, stirring constantly with a wooden spoon, to 175° F. on a candy thermometer. Pour the custard into a metal bowl and whisk in the vanilla and the sour cream.

In a small saucepan sprinkle the gelatin over ¼ cup cold water, let it soften for 1 minute, and heat the mixture over moderate heat, stirring, until the gelatin is dissolved. Stir the gelatin mixture into the custard, stirring until the mixture is combined well, set the bowl in a larger bowl of ice and cold water, and chill the custard, stirring occasionally, until it is the consistency of raw egg white.

Line the bottom of a 1½-quart glass bowl with some of the fruitcake slices, pour in the custard, and push the remaining fruitcake slices decoratively into the custard. Chill the trifle, covered, for at least 2 hours or overnight. Serves 6 to 8.

FROZEN DESSERTS

Frozen Lemon Cream Meringue Cake
For the meringue layers
4 large egg whites at room temperature
1 cup sugar

3 cups lemon cream (recipe follows)
For the icing
1½ teaspoons unflavored gelatin
3 tablespoons orange-flavored liqueur
1½ cups heavy cream

lemon slices and unsprayed lemon leaves for
    garnish

Make the meringue layers: Line a buttered baking sheet with parchment paper or foil and on it trace 2 squares, using the top and bottom of a 9-inch-square pan as a guide (one square will be slightly larger than the other). In a large bowl with an electric mixer beat the whites with a pinch of salt until they hold soft peaks, add the sugar, 1 tablespoon at a time, beating, and beat the whites until they hold stiff, glossy peaks. Transfer the meringue to a pastry bag fitted with a ½-inch plain tip, pipe it to fill in the squares, and smooth the tops. Bake the meringues in the middle of a preheated 275° F. oven for 1 hour, or until they are firm when touched lightly and very pale golden. Remove the meringues with the parchment from the baking sheets, let them cool, and peel off the parchment carefully. With a serrated knife trim the meringue layers so that the smaller one will just fit inside the bottom of the pan and the larger will just fit inside the top of the pan. Reserve the trimmings.

Oil the pan with vegetable oil and line it with plastic wrap, leaving about a 5-inch overhang all around. Put the smaller meringue layer, smooth side down, in the lined pan. Stir the reserved meringue trimmings, crumbled, into the lemon cream, pour the filling into the pan, smoothing it, and top it with the remaining meringue layer, smooth side up, pressing gently. Fold the plastic-wrap overhang over the top to enclose the cake. Freeze the cake, wrapped well, overnight, or until the cake is frozen solid.

Make the icing: In a small saucepan sprinkle the gelatin over the orange-flavored liqueur, let it soften for 1 minute, and heat the mixture over low heat, stirring, until the gelatin is dissolved. In another bowl beat the

cream until it just holds stiff peaks, add the gelatin mixture in a stream, beating, and beat the icing until it holds stiff peaks.

Unwrap the cake and unmold it onto a serving plate, discarding the plastic wrap. Spread a thin layer of the icing on the top and sides of the cake. Transfer the remaining icing to a pastry bag fitted with a decorative tip (such as a basketwork one) and pipe it over the cake. Chill the cake for no more than 1½ hours, decorate it with the lemon slices and leaves, and cut it into squares with a serrated knife.

Lemon Cream
1 stick (½ cup) unsalted butter
¾ cup sugar
½ teaspoon cornstarch
½ cup fresh lemon juice (about 2 lemons)
1 tablespoon freshly grated lemon zest
1 whole large egg plus 6 large egg yolks
1 cup plain yogurt

In a heavy saucepan melt the butter with the sugar, the cornstarch, the lemon juice, and the zest over moderately low heat, stirring until the sugar is dissolved. In a bowl whisk together lightly the whole egg and the yolks and add the butter mixture in a stream, whisking. Transfer the mixture to the pan and cook it over moderately low heat, whisking constantly, for 3 to 5 minutes, or until the curd is thick enough to hold the mark of the whisk and the first bubble appears on the surface. Transfer the curd immediately to a bowl, cover its surface with plastic wrap, and let the curd cool. Chill the curd, covered with the plastic wrap, for 1 hour, or until it is cold. Whisk the yogurt into the curd, chill the lemon cream, and serve it with berries or as a filling for frozen lemon cream meringue cake. Makes about 3 cups.

Espresso Granita
¼ cup sugar
three 3- by ¾-inch strips of lemon zest
3 tablespoons instant espresso powder
softly whipped cream as an accompaniment

In a saucepan combine the sugar, the zest, and 1½ cups water and bring the mixture to a boil, stirring until the sugar is dissolved. Remove the pan from the heat, stir in the espresso powder, and let the mixture cool. Discard the zest, transfer the mixture to a metal ice-cube tray without the dividers or to a shallow metal pan, and freeze it, stirring and crushing the lumps with a fork every 30 minutes, for 2 to 3 hours, or until it is firm but not frozen hard. *The granita may be made 2 days in advance and kept frozen, covered. Let the granita soften slightly before continuing with the recipe.* Scrape the granita with a fork to lighten the texture, divide it among 4 chilled dessert dishes, and top each serving with some of the whipped cream. Serves 4.

Red Grape Granita

¼ cup dry red wine
¼ cup sugar
¾ pound red seedless grapes
1 tablespoon fresh lemon juice, or to taste

In a saucepan combine the wine, the sugar, and 1 cup water and bring the mixture to a boil, stirring until the sugar is dissolved. Simmer the syrup for 5 minutes and let it cool. In a blender or food processor purée the grapes with the syrup and strain the purée through a fine sieve into a bowl, pressing hard on the solids. Stir in 1 cup cold water and the lemon juice and chill the mixture, covered, until it is cold. Stir the mixture, transfer it to 2 metal ice cube trays without dividers or a shallow metal bowl, and freeze it, stirring with a fork every 20 to 30 minutes and crushing the large frozen clumps, for 2 to 3 hours, or until it is firm but not frozen solid. Scrape the granita with a fork to lighten the texture and serve it in chilled bowls. Makes about 1 quart.

*Candied Chestnut and Vanilla
Ice Cream with Hot Fudge Sauce*

1 quart vanilla ice cream, softened
1 cup (about 8) finely chopped *marrons glacés* (candied chestnuts, available at specialty foods shops)
1⅓ cups heavy cream
⅓ cup firmly packed dark brown sugar

6 ounces fine-quality bittersweet chocolate, chopped fine
1 ounce unsweetened chocolate, chopped fine
2 tablespoons unsalted butter
2 tablespoons Cognac, or to taste

In a bowl stir together well the ice cream and the *marrons glacés* and freeze the mixture, its surface covered with plastic wrap, for 2 to 3 hours, or until it is firm. In a heavy saucepan boil the cream, stirring occasionally, until it is reduced to about 1 cup, whisk in the brown sugar, and simmer the mixture, whisking, until the sugar is dissolved. Remove the pan from the heat, whisk in the chocolates, whisking the mixture until it is smooth, and whisk in the butter and the Cognac. Serve the sauce warm over the ice cream. Serves 4 to 6.

Chocolate Prune Armagnac Ice Cream

1 cup (about 6 ounces) pitted prunes
⅓ cup Armagnac
1 cup sugar
1 tablespoon cornstarch
3 large egg yolks
1½ cups milk
1 teaspoon vanilla
6 ounces fine-quality bittersweet chocolate, chopped coarse
1½ cups well-chilled heavy cream

In a saucepan combine the prunes and ⅓ cup water and simmer the mixture for 5 to 7 minutes, or until almost all of the liquid is evaporated. Remove the pan from the heat, add the Armagnac, and let the prunes macerate for 3 hours. Drain the prunes in a sieve set over a bowl, reserving the liquid, and chop them coarse.

In a bowl whisk together the sugar, the cornstarch, the yolks, and a pinch of salt, add the milk, scalded, in a stream, whisking, and in a heavy saucepan bring the mixture to a boil over moderate heat, stirring constantly with a wooden spoon. Boil the custard, stirring constantly, for 2 minutes, add the vanilla and the chocolate, and whisk the mixture until the chocolate is melted. Transfer the custard mixture to a metal bowl set in a larger bowl of ice and cold water and let it cool, stirring. Stir in the cream and the prunes with the reserved liquid and freeze the mixture in an ice-cream freezer according to the manufacturer's instructions. Makes about 1½ quarts.

Lemon and Toasted Coconut Ice Cream

3 large eggs
1½ cups sugar
2½ cups half-and-half
1 cup fresh lemon juice (3 to 4 lemons)
1 tablespoon freshly grated lemon zest
1 cup sweetened flaked coconut, toasted
 lightly and cooled

In a bowl with an electric mixer beat the eggs with the sugar and a pinch of salt until the mixture is thick and pale. Beat in the half-and-half, the lemon juice, and the zest. Freeze the mixture in an ice-cream freezer according to the manufacturer's instructions, adding the coconut during the last 10 minutes of freezing. Makes about 1½ quarts.

Prune Sherry Ice Cream with Burnt Sugar Sauce

6 ounces (about 1 cup) pitted prunes
¼ cup dry Sherry
1⅔ cups sugar
1 tablespoon cornstarch
1 whole large egg
3 large egg yolks
2 cups milk
1½ cups heavy cream
½ cup sliced almonds, toasted lightly

In a saucepan combine the prunes and 1 cup water, bring the water to a boil, and simmer the prunes for 15 to 20 minutes, or until they are very soft. Add the Sherry, simmer the mixture for 1 minute, and let it cool. In a food processor purée the mixture coarse.

In a bowl whisk together ⅔ cup of the sugar, the cornstarch, the whole egg, and the yolks and add the milk, scalded, in a stream, whisking. In a heavy saucepan bring the mixture to a boil over moderate heat, whisking, and boil it, whisking constantly, for 2 minutes. Strain the custard through a fine sieve into a metal bowl set in a larger bowl of ice and cold water and add the prune mixture and the cream. Stir the custard mixture until it is cold and freeze it in an ice-cream freezer according to the manufacturer's instructions. Line a metal loaf pan, 9 by 5 by 3 inches, with plastic wrap, spoon the ice cream into it, and freeze the ice cream, the top smoothed and the surface covered with plastic wrap, for at least 8 hours or overnight. *The ice cream may be made 1 week in advance.*

In a dry large deep heavy skillet cook the remaining 1 cup sugar over moderately low heat, undisturbed, until it is melted, increase the heat to moderate, and cook the sugar, swirling the skillet occasionally, until it turns a deep caramel. Remove the skillet from the heat, pour 1 cup hot water carefully into the side of the skillet, and boil the burnt sugar sauce, stirring, until it is syrupy and reduced to about ¾ cup. *The sauce may be made 1 week in advance and kept covered and chilled.*

Unmold the ice cream and serve it, sliced, with the sauce, warm or at room temperature, and sprinkled with the almonds. Serves 6 to 8.

PHOTO ON PAGE 68

Gingered Rhubarb with Vanilla Ice Cream

1¼ pounds rhubarb, trimmed and cut
 into ¾-inch pieces (about 3 cups)
1 tablespoon fresh orange juice
1 tablespoon minced peeled fresh gingerroot
⅓ cup sugar, or to taste
1 tablespoon unsalted butter
vanilla ice cream as an accompaniment
fresh mint sprigs for garnish

In a microwave-safe 2-quart dish combine the rhubarb, the orange juice, the gingerroot, the sugar, and the butter, cover the dish with microwave-safe plastic wrap, leaving one corner uncovered, and microwave the mixture at high power (100%) for 5 minutes. Stir the mixture and microwave it, covered partially, for 2 minutes, or until the rhubarb is tender. Let the mixture cool slightly, serve it with the ice cream, and garnish it with the mint. (The gingered rhubarb may also be served as a compote.) Makes about 2 cups.

Macadamia Nut and Bittersweet Chocolate Ice-Cream Bombe with Macadamia Nut Praline

For the macadamia nut ice cream
¾ stick (6 tablespoons) unsalted butter
1½ cups (a 7-ounce jar) salted macadamia
 nuts, chopped fine
2 large eggs, beaten until foamy
½ cup granulated sugar
¼ cup firmly packed light brown sugar
2 cups heavy cream
1 cup milk
¼ teaspoon salt

For the ganache

3½ ounces fine-quality bittersweet
   chocolate, chopped
3 tablespoons heavy cream
2½ tablespoons Kahlúa or other
   coffee-flavored liqueur

For the bittersweet chocolate ice cream

½ pound fine-quality bittersweet
   chocolate, chopped
2 cups heavy cream
1 cup milk
2 large eggs, beaten until foamy
¼ cup sugar
1 teaspoon vanilla

For the macadamia nut praline

2 cups sugar
1½ cups (a 7-ounce jar) salted macadamia
   nuts, chopped

2 cups sugar for garnish if desired

Make the macadamia nut ice cream: In a heavy skillet melt the butter over moderate heat and in it cook the macadamia nuts, stirring, until they are light golden. Transfer the nuts with a slotted spoon to a small bowl, reserving the butter, and let them cool. In a large metal bowl whisk together the eggs, the sugars, the cream, the milk, the salt, and the reserved melted butter, transfer the mixture to a large saucepan, and cook it over moderately low heat, stirring until it registers 175° F. on a candy thermometer. Return the mixture to the metal bowl and chill it until it is cold. Freeze the mixture in an ice-cream freezer according to the manufacturer's instructions, adding the macadamia nuts, patted dry, when it is frozen partially. Makes about 1 quart.

Make the *ganache*: In a saucepan combine the chocolate and the cream, bring the cream just to a boil, stirring, and remove the pan from the heat. Stir the mixture until it is smooth and stir in the Kahlúa. Transfer the *ganache* to a bowl and let it cool to room temperature.

Make the bittersweet chocolate ice cream: In a small bowl set over a saucepan of simmering water melt the chocolate, stirring, until it is smooth. In a large saucepan whisk together the melted chocolate, the cream, the milk, the eggs, the sugar, and a pinch of salt and cook the mixture over moderately low heat, stirring, until it registers 175° F. on a candy thermometer. Stir in the vanilla and stir the mixture until it is combined well. Chill the mixture, its surface covered with plastic wrap, until

it is cold. Freeze the mixture in an ice-cream freezer according to the manufacturer's instructions. Makes about 1 quart.

Make the macadamia nut praline: In a heavy saucepan combine the sugar with ⅓ cup water, bring the mixture to a boil over moderately high heat, stirring and washing down any sugar crystals clinging to the side of the pan with a brush dipped in cold water until the sugar is dissolved. Cook the syrup, swirling the pan gently, until it turns pale golden. Stir in the nuts, return the syrup to a boil, and boil the mixture until the syrup is golden. Pour the praline immediately onto an oiled baking sheet and let it cool completely. Break the praline into pieces and in a food processor grind it fine in batches.

Line a lightly oiled 2-quart steamed-pudding mold, including the center stem, or a 2-quart metal bowl with plastic wrap, into it pack the macadamia nut ice cream, and spread the *ganache* over the top. Freeze the mold for 5 minutes, or until the *ganache* is set. Pack the bittersweet chocolate ice cream into the mold, cover the mold with the lid or plastic wrap, and freeze the *bombe* for at least 8 hours and up to 3 days.

In a heavy saucepan combine the sugar with ⅓ cup water, bring the mixture to a boil over moderately high heat, stirring and washing down any sugar crystals clinging to the side of the pan with a brush dipped in cold water until the sugar is dissolved. Cook the syrup, swirling the pan gently, until it turns pale golden. Pour the mixture immediately onto an oiled baking sheet and let it cool completely. Break the sugar candy into small pieces.

To unmold the *bombe*, dip the mold several times into a bowl of warm water, run a long thin knife around the outer rim of the mold and the rim of the center stem, and invert the *bombe* onto a platter. Coat the *bombe* with the ground macadamia nut praline. *The bombe may be made 3 hours in advance and kept frozen.* Garnish the top of the *bombe* and the platter with the sugar candy. Serves 8.

PHOTO ON PAGE 79

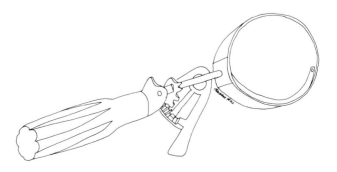

Brownie Ice-Cream Sandwiches with Caramel Sauce

1 ounce (1 square) unsweetened chocolate,
   chopped
½ stick (¼ cup) unsalted butter,
   cut into pieces
1 large egg
½ cup firmly packed brown sugar
½ teaspoon vanilla
½ cup all-purpose flour
¼ teaspoon cinnamon
¼ teaspoon salt
1 pint coffee ice cream
caramel sauce (recipe follows) as an
   accompaniment

In a heatproof bowl set over a pan of simmering water melt the chocolate and the butter, stirring until the mixture is smooth, and let the mixture cool. Beat in the egg, the brown sugar, and the vanilla and stir in the flour, the cinnamon, and the salt. Divide the mixture into 16 mounds, about 3 inches apart, on buttered baking sheets and bake the brownies in the middle of a preheated 350° F. oven for 8 to 10 minutes, or until they are just firm. (They will flatten into disks.) Transfer the brownies with a spatula to racks to cool and freeze them for 30 minutes, or until they are very firm.

Divide the ice cream, softened, among the flat sides of 8 of the brownies, spreading it smooth, and top the ice cream with the remaining brownies, flat sides down. Freeze the ice-cream sandwiches, covered, for at least 1 hour, or overnight. Serve the ice-cream sandwiches drizzled with the caramel sauce. Serves 4.

Caramel Sauce

½ cup sugar
¼ cup heavy cream

In a heavy skillet cook the sugar over moderately high heat, stirring constantly with a fork, until it is melted completely and a deep golden caramel. Remove the skillet from the heat, stir the caramel to prevent further darkening, and pour the cream into the side of the skillet carefully (the caramel will harden when the cream is added). Add 2 tablespoons water and cook the caramel mixture over moderate heat, stirring, until the caramel is dissolved. Let the sauce cool to warm. Makes about ½ cup.

Cranberry Ice-Cream Squares with Chocolate-Cookie Crust

1 pound Oreo cookies (about 42)
1 quart vanilla ice cream
1½ cups whole-cranberry sauce
1 tablespoon Grand Marnier, or other
   orange-flavored liqueur, if desired

In a food processor grind the cookies fine and pat half the cookie crumbs firmly into the bottom of a 9-inch-square baking pan lined with plastic wrap. In the large bowl of an electric mixer beat the ice cream with the paddle attachment until it is softened, add the cranberry sauce and the Grand Marnier, and beat the mixture until it is just combined. Spread the ice-cream mixture over the crust, sprinkle the top with the remaining cookie crumbs, and pat the cookie crumbs to make them adhere. Freeze the mixture, covered, for 6 hours, or until it is firm, invert a platter over the pan, and invert the pan onto the platter. Unmold the dessert onto the platter, discarding the plastic wrap, and cut it into squares with a serrated knife.

Fruitcake Coffee Ice-Cream Terrine

2 cups finely chopped fruitcake
1½ quarts coffee ice cream, softened slightly

Line a metal loaf pan, 9 by 5 by 3 inches, with plastic wrap, leaving a 3-inch overhang on all sides. In a bowl stir together the fruitcake and the ice cream, spread the mixture into the loaf pan, and fold the plastic wrap overhang over the top. Freeze the ice-cream mixture for at least 8 hours, or overnight. Unmold the terrine onto a serving dish and serve it sliced. Serves 8.

Frozen Nectarine Mousse with Blackberry Swirl

3 cups picked-over blackberries plus dditional
   picked-over berries for garnish, rinsed and
   drained well
¼ cup light corn syrup
¼ cup brandy
1½ teaspoons cornstarch, dissolved
   in 1 tablespoon cold water
¾ pound nectarines, pitted and chopped
2 teaspoons fresh lemon juice
1 cup sugar
4 large eggs

1 cup well-chilled heavy cream
mint sprigs for garnish
flowers for garnish if desired

In a blender or food processor purée 3 cups of the blackberries with the corn syrup. Strain the purée through a fine sieve into a heavy saucepan and simmer it, stirring occasionally, for 10 minutes, or until it is reduced to about 1½ cups. Stir in the brandy and the cornstarch mixture, boil the mixture, stirring constantly, for 1 minute, and let it cool to room temperature. *The blackberry mixture may be made 3 days in advance and kept covered and chilled.*

In a heavy saucepan combine the nectarines, the lemon juice, ¼ cup of the sugar, and ½ cup water, simmer the mixture, stirring occasionally, for 10 to 15 minutes, or until the liquid is reduced to about ¼ cup and the nectarines are very soft, and in a blender or food processor purée it. Let the nectarine purée cool. *The purée may be made 1 day in advance and kept covered and chilled.*

In a large metal bowl set over simmering water whisk the eggs with the remaining ¾ cup sugar until the mixture quadruples in volume and registers 160° F. on a candy thermometer and let the mixture cool. In a bowl whisk the cream until it just holds stiff peaks and fold it into the egg mixture. Fold in the nectarine purée gently but thoroughly, pour the mousse into an 8½-inch springform pan, and freeze it for 45 minutes, or until it is thickened. Spoon the blackberry mixture decoratively over the mousse, especially around the edge (some of it will sink into the mousse). Draw a skewer or knife through the mousse, forming decorative swirls, and freeze the mousse, its surface covered with plastic wrap, for at least 8 hours and up to 3 days.

Just before serving, wrap a dampened kitchen towel around the side of the pan, remove the side, and transfer the mousse to a serving plate. Arrange the additional blackberries, the mint sprigs, and the flowers decoratively around the mousse.

Blackberry Sorbet

½ cup sugar
2 cups fresh blackberries
2 tablespoons dry red wine

In a small saucepan combine the sugar and 1 cup water, bring the mixture to a boil, stirring until the sugar is dissolved, and transfer the syrup to a blender or food processor. Add the blackberries and the wine, purée the mixture, and strain the purée through a fine sieve into a bowl, pressing hard on the solids. Chill the purée until it is cold, or quick-chill it by setting the bowl in a larger bowl of ice and cold water, stirring the purée until it is cold. Freeze the mixture in an ice-cream maker according to the manufacturer's instructions. Makes about 1 pint.

PHOTO ON FRONT JACKET

Champagne Orange Sorbet

¾ cup sugar
1 cup chilled Champagne
2 tablespoons strained fresh orange juice
¼ teaspoon orange-flower water (available at specialty foods shops) if desired
1 large egg white

In a small saucepan combine the sugar and ¾ cup water, bring the mixture to a simmer over moderate heat, stirring until the sugar is dissolved, and simmer the syrup for 10 minutes. Let the syrup cool and chill it, covered, for 2 hours, or until it is cold.

In a bowl stir together 1 cup of the chilled syrup, the Champagne, the orange juice, and the orange-flower water and freeze the mixture in an ice-cream freezer according to the manufacturer's instructions until it is frozen but still soft. In a bowl beat the white until it is frothy, add it to the *sorbet*, and freeze the *sorbet* in the freezer until it is firm. Makes about 1 pint.

PHOTO ON PAGE 13

Lime Sorbet

1 cup sugar
⅓ cup fresh lime juice
2 teaspoons freshly grated lime zest

In a small saucepan combine the sugar and 1½ cups water, bring the mixture to a boil, stirring until the sugar is dissolved, and stir in the lime juice, the zest, and a pinch of salt. Chill the mixture until it is cold, or quick-chill it by setting it in a larger bowl of ice and cold water, stirring the mixture until it is cold. Freeze the mixture in an ice-cream maker according to the manufacturer's instructions. Makes about 1 pint.

PHOTO ON FRONT JACKET

Lime Mint Sorbet

1¼ cups sugar
⅓ cup firmly packed fresh mint
3 cups fresh lime juice (about 18 limes)

In a small saucepan combine the sugar and 1 cup water, bring the mixture to a boil, stirring until the sugar is dissolved, and remove the pan from the heat. Let the syrup cool. In a blender purée the mint with the syrup, stir in the lime juice, and in a bowl chill the mixture, covered, for 1 hour, or until it is cold. Freeze the mixture in an ice-cream freezer according to the manufacturer's instructions. Makes about 1 quart.

Mango Sorbet

½ cup sugar
2 small mangoes (about 3 cups), peeled, pitted, and cut into pieces
1 tablespoon fresh lime juice

In a small saucepan combine the sugar and 1½ cups water, bring the mixture to a boil, stirring until the sugar is dissolved, and transfer the syrup to a blender or food processor. Add the mangoes and the lime juice, purée the mixture, and strain it through a fine sieve into a bowl, pressing hard on the solids. Chill the purée until it is cold, or quick-chill it by setting the bowl in a larger bowl of ice and cold water, stirring the purée until it is cold. Freeze the mango mixture in an ice-cream maker according to the manufacturer's instructions. Makes about 1½ pints.

PHOTO ON FRONT JACKET

Raspberry Sorbet

½ cup sugar
2 cups fresh raspberries, picked over
1 tablespoon fresh lemon juice

In a small saucepan combine the sugar and 1 cup water, bring the mixture to a boil, stirring until the sugar is dissolved, and transfer the syrup to a blender or food processor. Add the raspberries and the lemon juice, purée the mixture, and strain the purée through a fine sieve into a bowl, pressing hard on the solids. Chill the purée until it is cold, or quick-chill it by setting the bowl in a larger bowl of ice and cold water, stirring the purée until it is cold. Freeze the raspberry mixture in an ice-

cream maker according to the manufacturer's instructions. Makes about 1 pint.

PHOTO ON FRONT JACKET

FRUIT FINALES

Apple Walnut Crisp

1 cup all-purpose flour
¾ cup old-fashioned rolled oats
¾ cup firmly packed light brown sugar
1 teaspoon cinnamon
½ teaspoon salt
1 stick (½ cup) unsalted butter, cut into bits and softened
1 cup walnuts, toasted lightly, cooled, and chopped
3 pounds McIntosh apples, peeled and sliced ⅓ inch thick (about 8 cups)
2 tablespoons fresh lemon juice
3 tablespoons granulated sugar, or to taste
whipped cream or vanilla ice cream as an accompaniment

In a bowl stir together well the flour, the oats, the brown sugar, the cinnamon, and the salt. Add the butter, blend the mixture until it resembles coarse meal, and stir in the walnuts. In a large bowl toss the apples with the lemon juice and the granulated sugar and transfer the mixture to a buttered 10-inch (2-quart) pie plate. Crumble the topping evenly over the apple mixture and bake the crisp in the middle of a preheated 375° F. oven for 25 to 30 minutes, or until the apples are cooked through and the top is golden. Let the crisp stand for 10 minutes and serve it warm with the whipped cream. Serves 6.

PHOTO ON PAGE 26

Beer-Batter-Fried Apple Rings

1 cup all-purpose flour
1 cup beer (not dark)
1 teaspoon salt
½ cup fresh lemon juice
2 tablespoons firmly packed light brown sugar plus additional for sprinkling the rings
4 Granny Smith or Golden Delicious apples
vegetable oil for deep-frying

In a bowl whisk together the flour, the beer, and the salt until the batter is smooth and let the batter stand, covered, at room temperature for 1 hour. In another bowl combine the lemon juice and 2 tablespoons of the brown sugar, on a baking sheet or a shallow tray arrange the apples, peeled, cored, and cut into ¼-inch-thick rings, in one layer, and pour the lemon juice mixture over them. Let the apple rings stand, covered, at room temperature, turning them once, for 1 hour and pat them dry.

In a deep fryer or large heavy skillet heat 1½ inches of the oil to 375° F., dip each apple ring in the batter, coating it well and letting the excess batter drip off, and in the oil fry the rings in batches, turning them once, for 4 minutes. Transfer the rings to paper towels, let them drain well, and sprinkle them with the additional brown sugar. Makes about 24 fried apple rings, serving 6 to 8.

Blueberry Cobbler

3 tablespoons cornstarch
½ cup granulated sugar
6 cups picked over blueberries
2 tablespoons fresh lemon juice
1½ cups all-purpose flour
½ cup firmly packed light brown sugar
1½ teaspoons double-acting baking powder
¾ teaspoon salt
1 teaspoon cinnamon
1 stick (½ cup) cold unsalted butter,
  cut into bits
vanilla ice cream or whipped cream as an
  accompaniment

In a large bowl stir together the cornstarch, sifted, and the granulated sugar and add the blueberries and the lemon juice. Toss the mixture until it is combined well and transfer it to a buttered 10-inch (6-cup) deep-dish pie plate. In a bowl combine well the flour, the brown sugar, forced through a sieve, the baking powder, the salt, and the cinnamon, add the butter, and blend the mixture until it resembles coarse meal. Add ¼ cup plus 2 tablespoons boiling water and stir the mixture until it just forms a dough. Drop ¼ cupfuls of the dough over the blueberry mixture and bake the cobbler on a baking sheet in the middle of a preheated 400° F. oven for 30 to 40 minutes, or until the topping is golden and cooked through. Serve the cobbler warm with the ice cream. Serves 6.

Citrus and Pineapple Compote

1 pink grapefruit, the rind and pith cut away
  with a serrated knife, the grapefruit cut into
  sections, and the juice reserved
1 navel orange, the rind and pith cut away
  with a serrated knife, the orange sliced
  crosswise, and the juice reserved
½ pineapple, peeled, cored, cut into 1-inch
  chunks, and the juice reserved
3 tablespoons medium-dry Sherry
2 tablespoons honey

In a bowl combine the grapefruit sections, the orange slices, and the pineapple chunks. In a small saucepan combine the reserved juices, the Sherry, the honey, and a pinch of salt and simmer the mixture, stirring, for 1 minute. Pour the mixture over the fruit and toss the compote gently. Makes about 2 cups, serving 2.

Cranberry Apple Cobbler

1½ cups cranberries, picked over
1 Granny Smith apple, peeled and sliced thin
1 tablespoon freshly grated orange zest
½ cup firmly packed light brown sugar
¼ teaspoon cinnamon
a pinch of ground cloves
½ cup plus 1 tablespoon all-purpose flour
1 tablespoon unsalted butter, cut into bits
½ teaspoon double-acting baking powder
¼ teaspoon salt
2 tablespoons vegetable shortening
⅓ cup plain yogurt
½ teaspoon granulated sugar
vanilla ice cream as an accompaniment
  if desired

In a shallow 2-cup baking dish toss together the cranberries, the apple, the zest, the brown sugar, the cinnamon, the cloves, and 1 tablespoon of the flour and dot the top with the butter. In a bowl stir together the remaining ½ cup flour, the baking powder, and the salt. Add the shortening, blend the mixture until it resembles coarse meal, and stir in the yogurt. (The dough will be sticky.) Drop the dough by spoonfuls onto the cranberry mixture, sprinkle it with the granulated sugar, and bake the cobbler in the middle of a preheated 400° F. oven for 30 minutes, or until the top is golden. Serve the cobbler with the ice cream. Serves 2.

Fruitcake Soufflés

3 tablespoons granulated sugar plus additional
  for sprinkling the ramekins
1½ cups crumbled fruitcake
¾ cup crumbled homemade-type white bread
½ cup milk
3 large eggs, separated
2 tablespoons confectioners' sugar

Butter eight 1-cup ramekins and sprinkle them with the additional granulated sugar. In a small bowl combine well the fruitcake, the bread, and the milk and let the mixture stand, covered, at room temperature for 15 minutes. In a metal bowl with a portable electric mixer beat the yolks and the remaining 3 tablespoons granulated sugar until the mixture is combined well, set the bowl over a saucepan of simmering water, and beat the mixture until it is thick and pale. Remove the bowl from the pan and beat in the fruitcake mixture.

In a bowl beat the whites until they are frothy, beat in the confectioners' sugar, sifted, and beat the whites until they just hold stiff peaks. Fold the meringue into the fruitcake mixture gently but thoroughly and divide the batter among the ramekins. Bake the soufflés in the middle of a preheated 375° F. oven for 12 to 15 minutes, or until they are golden and a knife inserted in the centers comes out clean. Serves 8.

JEANNE

Fruitcake with Ginger Cream Cheese

a 3-ounce package cream cheese, softened
1 tablespoon minced peeled fresh gingerroot
thin slices of fruitcake

In a bowl stir together the cream cheese and the gingerroot and chill the mixture for 30 minutes. Spread the ginger cream cheese on the fruitcake. Makes about ½ cup ginger cream cheese.

Grape, Blueberry, and Apricot Compote

¼ cup white grape juice
¼ cup dry white wine
1 tablespoon honey
1 vanilla bean, split lengthwise
⅛ teaspoon freshly grated nutmeg
¾ cup picked over blueberries
⅓ cup dried apricots, sliced thin
1 cup green seedless grapes, halved
1 tablespoon fresh lime juice, or to taste
1 teaspoon freshly grated lime zest

In a saucepan combine the grape juice, the wine, ¼ cup water, the honey, the vanilla bean, and the nutmeg and boil the mixture for 2 minutes. Add the blueberries and the apricots and simmer the mixture for 1 minute. Add the grapes and simmer the mixture for 2 minutes. Transfer the fruit with a slotted spoon to a bowl. Remove the vanilla bean, scrape the seeds into the syrup, and boil the syrup for 2 to 3 minutes, or until it is thickened slightly. Stir in the lime juice and the lime zest and pour the syrup over the fruit. Chill the compote, covered, for at least 3 hours or overnight and serve it with ice cream if desired. Makes about 2½ cups.

Red and Green Grape Gratin

3 large egg yolks
⅓ cup granulated sugar
2 tablespoons cornstarch
2 tablespoons all-purpose flour
1 cup milk
2 teaspoons grated lemon zest
1 teaspoon vanilla, or to taste
¾ cup red seedless grapes, patted dry
¾ cup green seedless grapes, patted dry
¼ cup slivered almonds, toasted lightly
¼ cup firmly packed dark brown sugar

In a bowl whisk together the yolks until they are combined, add the granulated sugar, a little at a time, beating, and beat the mixture until it is light and lemon colored. Add the cornstarch and the flour, a little at a time, beating, and beat the mixture until it is combined well. Add the milk, scalded, in a stream, beating, and beat the mixture until it is combined well. In a heavy saucepan bring the mixture to a boil, stirring, add the zest, and simmer the mixture, stirring, for 3 minutes. (The mixture will be thick and custardlike.) Remove the pan from the heat and beat in the vanilla. Strain the pastry cream through a fine sieve into a bowl and chill it, its surface covered with a buttered round of wax paper, for 1 hour. Arrange the grapes in the bottom of a 6-cup flameproof gratin dish, spoon the pastry cream over them, spreading it evenly, and sprinkle the almonds over the cream. Sprinkle the brown sugar over the almonds and broil the gratin under a preheated broiler about 4 inches from the heat for 3 to 4 minutes, or until it is bubbly and golden on top. Serves 4 to 6.

Mixed Fruit and Rum Ambrosia

1 cup raspberries
1 small mango, peeled, pitted, and diced
1 cup diced fresh pineapple
1 teaspoon sugar, or to taste
2 tablespoons dark rum, or to taste
¼ cup sweetened flaked coconut, toasted
   lightly and cooled

In a bowl toss together the raspberries, the mango, the pineapple, the sugar, and the rum, chill the mixture, covered, for 25 minutes, and sprinkle it with the coconut. Serves 2.

Baked Pears

8 Bosc pears with stems intact
1 lemon, halved
1½ cups dry white wine
1¼ cups sugar
the zest of 2 navel oranges removed with a
   vegetable peeler
two 3-inch cinnamon sticks
⅓ cup orange-flavored liqueur

Peel the pears, leaving the stems intact and dropping the pears as they are peeled into a bowl of cold water acidulated with the juice of the lemon. In a saucepan combine the wine, 2 cups water, the sugar, the zest, the cinnamon sticks, and the liqueur, bring the liquid to a boil, stirring until the sugar is dissolved, and simmer the syrup for 5 minutes. Arrange the pears, drained, on their sides in a baking dish just large enough to hold them in one layer and pour the syrup over them. Cover the dish tightly with foil and bake the pears in the middle of a preheated 375° F. oven for 30 minutes. Remove the foil, turn the pears over gently, and replace the foil. Bake the pears for 20 to 30 minutes more, or until they are tender. Let the pears cool, transfer them carefully to a deep serving dish, and ladle the cooking syrup with the zest over them. Chill the pears, covered, overnight and serve them with some of the syrup. Serves 8.

FRONTISPIECE

Poached Pineapple in Cinnamon Syrup with Yogurt Cheese

1 cup plain yogurt
¼ cup sugar
⅛ teaspoon cinnamon
1 cup fresh pineapple chunks
1 tablespoon dark rum

In a fine sieve let the yogurt drain, covered and chilled, for 40 minutes. While the yogurt is draining, in a small saucepan combine the sugar, the cinnamon, and ¾ cup water and boil the mixture for 5 minutes. Stir in the pineapple, simmer the mixture, covered, for 8 minutes, and transfer the pineapple with a slotted spoon to a metal bowl. Boil the syrup until it is reduced to about ½ cup, add the rum, and boil the syrup for 1 minute. Pour the syrup over the pineapple and chill the mixture, set in a larger bowl of ice and cold water.

Divide the yogurt cheese between 2 bowls and spoon the pineapple mixture over it. Serves 2.

Plum Oatmeal Crisp

3 plums (½ pound), chopped (about 1¾ cups)
1 teaspoon fresh lemon juice
¼ cup granulated sugar
⅓ cup firmly packed light brown sugar
⅓ cup all-purpose flour
½ cup old-fashioned rolled oats
⅛ teaspoon salt
½ teaspoon cinnamon
¼ teaspoon ground ginger
¼ cup finely chopped walnuts
3 tablespoons cold unsalted butter, cut into bits
vanilla ice cream as an accompaniment
   if desired

In a bowl stir together the plums, the lemon juice, and the granulated sugar and spread the mixture evenly in the bottom of a buttered 8-inch square pan. In another bowl blend the brown sugar, the flour, the oats, the salt, the cinnamon, the ginger, the walnuts, and the butter until the mixture resembles coarse meal. Sprinkle the brown sugar mixture evenly over the plum mixture and bake the dessert in the middle of a preheated 375° F. oven for 30 to 35 minutes, or until it is crisp. (For a crisper topping, after baking the crisp, broil it under a preheated broiler for 2 minutes.) Serve the crisp warm with the vanilla ice cream. Serves 2 with leftovers.

CONFECTIONS

Chocolate-Covered Fruitcake Balls

2 cups crumbled fruitcake
7 ounce fine-quality bittersweet chocolate,
    cut into bits

In a food processor grind the fruitcake until it forms a ball, scoop up rounded teaspoons of it and with dampened hands form them into balls. Let the balls stand, uncovered, in a jelly-roll pan lined with wax paper for 30 minutes. In a small metal bowl set in a saucepan of barely simmering water melt the chocolate, stirring until it is smooth, and remove the bowl from the pan. Balancing the fruitcake balls, 1 at a time, on the tines of a fork, dip them into the chocolate, letting the excess drip off. Transfer them to the wax paper, reserving the remaining chocolate for another use. Chill the balls for 30 minutes, or until the chocolate is hardened. *The fruitcake balls keep, covered and chilled, for 1 week.* Makes about 24 confections.

Chocolate Pecan Bars

For the crust
1½ cups all-purpose flour
⅔ cup sugar
1½ sticks (¾ cup) cold unsalted butter,
    cut into pieces
½ teaspoon salt
1 large egg, beaten lightly
For the filling
1 stick (½ cup) unsalted butter, softened
1 cup firmly packed brown sugar
2 large eggs
¼ cup all-purpose flour
1½ teaspoons vanilla
½ teaspoon salt
3 cups chopped pecans
2 cups semisweet chocolate chips

Make the crust: In a food processor blend together the flour, the sugar, the butter, and the salt, pulsing the motor, until the mixture resembles coarse meal, add the egg, and blend the mixture until it forms a dough. Press the dough evenly with floured hands into the bottom of a buttered 13- by 9-inch baking pan and bake it in the middle of a preheated 350° F. oven for 20 to 25 minutes, or until it is golden.

Make the filling while the crust is baking: In a bowl cream the butter with the brown sugar until the mixture is light and fluffy and add the eggs, 1 at a time, beating well after each addition. Beat in the flour, the vanilla, and the salt. Stir in the pecans and the chocolate chips.

Spread the filling over the crust and bake the confection in the middle of the 350° F. oven for 30 to 35 minutes, or until the top is golden brown. Let the confection cool completely in the pan on a rack and cut it into 24 bars. *The bars may be made 2 days in advance and kept in an airtight container.* Makes 24 bars.

Miniature Tartufi
(Frozen Chocolate Almond Confections)

½ cup sugar
1½ teaspoons cornstarch
1 large whole egg
1 large egg yolk
¾ cup milk
3 ounces unsweetened chocolate,
    chopped fine
1 cup well-chilled heavy cream
6 glacéed cherries, halved
⅓ cup blanched almonds, chopped coarse,
    toasted lightly, and cooled
half of a 3-ounce fine-quality bittersweet
    chocolate bar, shaved with a vegetable
    peeler
twelve 1½-inch foil cups

In a bowl whisk together the sugar, the cornstarch, the whole egg, and the yolk until the mixture is combined well and add the milk, scalded, in a stream, whisking. In a saucepan bring the mixture to a boil over moderate heat, whisking, boil it, whisking, for 2 minutes, and stir in the unsweetened chocolate, stirring until the custard is smooth. Let the custard cool, its surface covered with plastic wrap, and chill it until it is cold. Stir in the cream and freeze the custard in an ice-cream freezer according to the manufacturer's instructions until it is almost firm. Transfer the ice cream to a metal bowl and freeze it until it is firm but not solid.

Scoop out 1 portion with a 1½-inch ice-cream scoop and level it with a knife. Press a cherry half into the center of the scoop and turn out the scoop into an ice-cube tray without the divider or a metal pan, turning it flat side up. Make 11 more cherry-filled scoops in the same manner, turning them out into 2 more ice-cube trays.

Smooth the ice cream remaining in the bowl and freeze it and the prepared ice-cream scoops until the ice cream is firm but not solid. Working with 1 tray of scoops at a time, scoop out 1 portion of the ice cream from the bowl with the scoop, leveling it as before, and press the leveled side against the leveled side of 1 of the cherry-filled scoops. Smooth the edges of the scoops to form a smooth ball and transfer the ball to the tray. Working quickly, make 11 more balls with the remaining ice cream in the same manner and freeze them until they are firm but not solid.

In a bowl combine well the almonds and the bittersweet chocolate, roll the ice-cream balls in the mixture, pressing the coating gently to make it adhere, and transfer the confections to the foil cups. *The confections may be made 5 days in advance and kept covered and frozen.* Makes 12 *tartufi.*

PHOTO ON PAGE 32

Chocolate Chestnut Truffles

¼ cup heavy cream
6 ounces fine-quality bittersweet chocolate, chopped fine
2 tablespoons dark rum
¾ cup (about 6) finely chopped *marrons glacés* (candied chestnuts, available at specialty foods shops)
¼ cup sifted unsweetened cocoa powder for coating the truffles

In a small saucepan bring the cream just to a boil, remove the pan from the heat, and whisk in the choco-late, whisking the mixture until the chocolate is melted completely. Whisk in the rum, whisking until the mixture is smooth, and stir in the *marrons glacés*. Chill the mixture, covered, for 3 hours, or until it is firm. Form the mixture by heaping teaspoons into balls and roll the balls in the cocoa powder. Chill the truffles on a baking sheet lined with wax paper for 1 hour, or until they are firm. The truffles keep in an airtight container, chilled, for 2 weeks. Makes about 25 truffles.

White Chocolate Pecan Truffles

2 tablespoons heavy cream
3 ounces fine-quality white chocolate, chopped fine
1 teaspoon unsalted butter, softened
2 teaspoons brandy
¾ cup pecans, chopped coarse, toasted lightly, and cooled

In a small saucepan bring the cream to a boil, remove the pan from the heat, and add the chocolate, stirring until it is melted completely. Add the butter, stir the mixture until it is smooth, and stir in the brandy and ¼ cup of the pecans. Transfer the mixture to a bowl and chill it, covered, for 4 hours, or until it is firm. Form the mixture by teaspoons into balls and roll the balls in the remaining ½ cup pecans. Chill the truffles in a baking pan for 1 hour, or until they are firm. The truffles keep in an airtight container, covered and chilled, for 1 week. Makes about 16 truffles.

BEVERAGES

Mint Juleps

¾ cup sugar
2 cups chopped fresh mint sprigs plus
   additional whole sprigs for garnish
crushed ice
1½ ounces (1 jigger) bourbon, or to taste,
   per julep

In a saucepan combine the sugar and ¾ cup water and bring the mixture to a boil, stirring until the sugar is dissolved. Remove the pan from the heat, stir in the chopped mint, and let the mixture stand for at least 2 hours and up to 4 hours. Strain the syrup through a fine sieve into a jar or small bowl, pressing hard on the solids, discard the solids, and let the syrup cool. *The syrup may be made 2 weeks in advance and kept covered and chilled.* (The syrup will darken but this will not affect the taste.) Makes about 1¼ cups syrup, or enough for about 10 juleps.

For each julep fill a silver julep cup or 10-ounce glass with some of the ice, add 1 to 2 tablespoons of the mint syrup, or to taste, and 1½ ounces bourbon, and stir the julep or holding the cup at the rim rotate it back and forth very rapidly. (A frost will form on the outside of a silver cup.) Garnish each julep with 1 of the additional mint sprigs.

PHOTO ON PAGE 38

Peach Wine

5 ripe peaches
¼ cup sugar
two 750-ml bottles dry white wine

Pit and slice thin 4 of the peaches. In a large bowl toss the slices with the sugar until the sugar is dissolved and stir in the wine. Chill the mixture, covered, for 5 days.

Strain the peach wine through a fine sieve into a pitcher or bottle and serve it chilled or over ice and garnished with the remaining peach, peeled, pitted, and sliced. The wine keeps, covered and chilled, indefinitely. Makes about 1 quart.

PHOTO ON PAGE 47

Pink Pony

2 ounces (2 ponies) light Tequila
⅓ cup chilled cranberry juice
¼ cup chilled apple juice
chilled club soda or seltzer

In a tall glass filled with ice cubes combine the Tequila, the cranberry juice, and the apple juice and top off the drink with the club soda. Makes 1 drink.

Mango Papaya Smoothies

1 mango (about 1½ pounds), peeled, pitted,
   and chopped coarse
1 papaya, peeled, seeded, and chopped coarse
2 cups plain yogurt
2 tablespoons fresh lime juice plus 4 lime
   slices for garnish
3 tablespoons honey, or to taste
¼ teaspoon almond extract

In a blender blend the mango, the papaya, the yogurt, the lime juice, the honey, the almond extract, and 1 cup ice cubes in batches until the mixture is smooth and blend in another ½ cup ice cubes if desired to thin the smoothie mixture to the desired consistency. Divide the mixture among 4 chilled large glasses and garnish each smoothie with a lime slice. Serves 4.

PHOTO ON PAGE 63

PART THREE

A GOURMET ADDENDUM

MORE BOUNTIFUL GIFTS FROM NATURE:

COOKING WITH HERBS

Fragrant, flavorful, naturally beautiful, and also healthful, herbs awaken the senses and add pleasure to our lives. Last year our Gourmet Addendum 1990 addressed nature's harvests—all that is fresh and good from the garden each season. This year we unearth more goodness and retain the premise that some of the very best meals start with the freshest of nature's gifts— herbs from your own garden. While it is true that not everyone has a garden to grow vegetables, herbs can be kept in small pots on your windowsill. And, if this is not possible, fresh herbs are available at the greengrocers in increasing variety and abundance. The days of heavily

depending on salt and sugars to enliven your diet will end as you discover the natural aromatic flavors of herbs.

"Herbs" are defined by herbalists as fragrant soft-stemmed or succulent plants that may be used — as leaves, stems, flowers, seeds, and sometimes roots—to flavor foods. Often, herbs have served in medicinal preparations as well. This broad definition includes a wide range of plants, some of them vegetables, that are botanically divided into plant "families" sharing characteristics. We present three herbal families that will healthfully inspire your cooking prowess—the Mint family, for its wide assortment of green leaves with heavenly aromas; the Lily family, for its savory onion-flavored bulbs; and the Carrot family, for the flavors and scents of the seeds from its flowering umbels, its feather-like foliage, and its sturdy roots. Within each family we have selected a handful of herbs for you to try. Many of our recipes highlight a single herb to familiarize you with its characteristic flavor; others combine assorted herbs to demonstrate their compatibility. Recipes for starters, entrées, side dishes, desserts, and even beverages are included. Throughout, easy recipes using simple, straightforward procedures demonstrate that fresh herbs make a delightful difference.

One beauty of herbs is that they can be grown by expert or novice gardener alike. Whether you are a city dweller or a country landowner you can enjoy fresh "garden" herbs. Depending on the herb, you can either start out with seeds or, more easily, small plants. A few simple rules apply: Place the plants in a sunny location that is not too hot; make sure they have plenty of air circulation; provide ample space for them to grow; do not overwater; and when you do water herbs, do so in the mornings to prevent fungus from growing on their foliage overnight. Little effort brings big rewards; and you will feel quite proud of yourself as, for example, you snip your very own chives for our scone recipe!

It is important to recognize, however, that established plants from your garden are stronger in flavor than the hothouse herbs that you buy in the supermarket. Our recipes give a fresh herb measurement for hothouse herbs or young herb seedlings, so you may need to alter your measurements accordingly. And, if using dried herbs, be aware that they are even stronger in fla-

vor than any form of fresh herbs. A dried herb equivalent is provided throughout our recipes. The proportion is usually one tablespoon fresh herbs to one teaspoon dried, or a ratio of three to one.

Whenever possible, fresh herbs are the herbs of choice for obvious reasons. After the growing season, though, you will want to dry your herbs. While they will lose some of their color and aroma in drying, you will find that they are generally more flavorful than the bottled supermarket-variety. To dry herbs, pick them on a dry day to avoid moisture and mildew. For long-stemmed herbs, gather them in bunches, tie them with string, and hang them upside down on a drying rack or a ceiling beam in a dry, dimly lit place with good air circulation. When they are completely dry, crumble and store the herbs in airtight containers. To dry individual leaves and petals or whole flowerheads, make a footed drying tray out of netting or nylon screening (even a clean window screen propped up on bricks will work). Leave the herbs in a moisture-free, well-ventilated place until they are completely dry. To keep their potency, dried herbs should be stored in airtight containers and kept away from heat and light. If properly stored, dried herbs should keep their full flavor for about six months. You will want to replace all dried herbs after one year.

Herbs are one of the simple pleasures of life—a true gift from nature that should not be missed. We hope that our herbal recipes will inspire you to explore these little gems of the earth. Go ahead, peruse our recipes, choose those that tempt you, and start your garden with the plants you will need. Delightful surprises, both in the growing and the tasting, await you.

THE MINT FAMILY

Rosemary

Sage

Mint

Thyme

*A*lluring aromas have characterized this herbal family for centuries and have made these herbs natural food enhancers and fragrance products. And what a large family it is! The thymes, marjoram, rosemary, orégano, the mints, sage, basil, and the savories all fall into this botanical grouping. ''The mints'' contain essential vitamins and minerals, and are said to have varied health-giving powers, notably in stomach ailments. But, most importantly, we'd like to introduce you to their food-awakening abilities. With the palate as our guide, we begin our discussion with the blandest and progress to the strongest of the herbs in this family.

Thyme, a sweet-smelling decorative little perennial shrub (12 inches in height) with tiny lilac flowers, has a varied history. With a name meaning ''incense,'' thyme was used by the ancient Greeks as such with other aromatics. Also, its reputed antiseptic properties once made this herb a natural medicine for washing cuts and treating sore throats and other ailments.

Today, most chefs agree that they could not cook without a constant supply of thyme on hand. Its subtle sweetness acts as an enhancer rather than as a mask for food flavors. For an ever-so-tender entrée suffused with the gentle sweetness of this herb, try our Loin of Pork

Braised in Milk with Thyme. Here we rub the pork with thyme and garlic, then slowly braise the meat in the milk-thyme liquid. Lemon thyme, an even milder variety of the herb known for its fruity flavor, stars in our Roast Lemon-Thyme Chicken Breasts recipe, another succulent and delightfully aromatic dish.

Sweet marjoram, as its name implies, is another sweet-tasting mint family member and is more aromatic than the other marjorams: pot marjoram and wild marjoram (orégano). This perennial comes in the form of another small bush (12 inches in height) with small smooth-edged oval leaves, and it can be grown indoors or out. Also, its pearly knotted flower buds can be dried before the tiny pink-lavender flowers open, for a concentrated, spicy-sweet marjoram taste. Our Herbed Tomato, Corn, and Pepper Sauté calls on marjoram and thyme leaves to bring out the natural flavors of these vegetables with a hint of sweetness; and a simple yogurt, garlic, marjoram, and mustard marinade quietly enhances our Marjoram Baked Chicken.

The scent of pine and nutmeg, a very strong aroma, can be found in yet another small herbal shrub—rosemary. Resembling lavender, this attractive woody-stemmed perennial has pale-blue flowers and dark-green needlelike leaves. Our recipe for Butterflied Leg of Lamb with Rosemary and Garlic creates a blissful brew of rosemary, garlic, lemon, and orégano to marinate the meat; the lamb is then grilled over glowing coals for a robust charcoal taste. To prove rosemary's versatility, we also present our easy-to-prepare Gratin of Broccoli with Rosemary, Garlic, and Parmesan. This pretty dish, an excellent accompaniment to any meat or fish entrée, combines the crisp-tender vegetable with the bubbling cheese, while the sweet rosemary and oniony garlic further tease the senses.

To refresh and soothe the palate, we turn to garden mint. Several varieties exist; the only one to avoid is horse mint, a gray-green variety (sometimes sold as garden mint), which has an unpleasant smell. (Beware: If planted near other mints it could hybridize and ruin your mint patch.) To complement any lamb dish (it is ideal with our butterflied lamb recipe) we present an English Mint Sauce—a quick mixture of mint leaves, sugar, and malt or cider vinegar. The result is a refreshingly sharp sweet-and-sour herbal surprise! Mint, replacing the traditional dill, is also featured in our Minted New Potatoes, another simple, must-try combination.

We turn next to sage, a decorative shrub (2 feet in height) with oblong velvety gray-green leaves and pretty violet-blue flowers. Derived from the Latin verb *salvare,* meaning ''to save,'' sage was used as a cure-all by our ancestors and remains a very highly respected healer for everything from a sore throat to fortifying a debilitated nervous system. As a culinary herb, sage has a heavy woodsy taste. We present sage in updated traditional roles: in *Saltimbocca* (Veal Scaloppine with Sage and Prosciutto), where we mince the herb for maximum flavor and put it directly onto the veal, and in Cheddar Cheese-Sage Bites, which combine the stronger minced herb with Cheddar for tiny toasts with zip. When experimenting on your own, remember that sage has a very strong personality and a little of it goes a long way.

And then there is basil! Lovers of this pungently fragrant herb dream of pairing its warm, clove-like sweetness with the first home-grown tomatoes of the season. Basil is a tall annual that could, unfortunately, be mistaken for a weed. Its flowers should not be allowed to develop (leaf development will slow down), and if you nip out the centers the plant will become bushy and lush green. Appearances aside, if you try our Spinach Tortellini with Tomato Basil Sauce you will become a fresh-basil-stalker! Here the tomato-basil combination simmers with garlic and olive oil for a natural classic sure to please both nose and palate.

And finally, we turn to the lesser known savories—summer and winter varieties—for their spicy, peppery, warming effects on a variety of bland dishes. Summer savory (about 18 inches in height) is an annual bush with narrow leaves and tiny pink, blue, or white flowers. It is a tender, spindly plant and will die at the first frost. The stronger flavored winter savory (about 12 inches in height) is a hardy perennial shrub with woody stems that survive the cold.

Traditionally the savories have been used in bean dishes as well as in soups for their warming nature (remember to use a light hand with these potent herbs). In fact, many people use the savories as a salt substitute in dishes that are otherwise bland. We employ the savories in colorful combinations: Our Black-Eyed Pea Salad with Summer Savory teams up with shallot-flavored vinegar and sugar for a piquant dish, while our Carrot, Leek, and Apple Soup with Winter Savory uses the stronger herb to create a winning, warming soup.

*Loin of Pork Braised in Milk
with Thyme*

a 3- to 3½-pound boneless pork loin,
    patted dry
2 garlic cloves, minced
1 tablespoon minced fresh thyme plus 1 sprig
    or 2 teaspoons dried
3 cups milk
1 cup chicken broth
1 bay leaf

Rub the pork all over with the garlic, the 1 tablespoon of thyme, and salt and pepper to taste. Under a preheated broiler about 6 inches from the heat, brown the pork on all sides for about 5 to 7 minutes and transfer it to a small saucepan. Add the milk, the broth, the remaining sprig of thyme, and the bay leaf, bring the milk to a boil, and braise the pork, partially covered, over moderately low heat for 1½ to 2 hours, or until it is tender. Transfer the pork to a heated platter and let it stand, covered loosely, for 15 minutes before carving. Serves 4 to 6.

Roast Lemon Thyme Chicken Breasts

2 whole chicken breasts (about 2½ pounds), split
3 tablespoons unsalted butter, softened
2 large shallots (¼ cup), minced fine
2 teaspoons minced fresh lemon thyme
    or 1 teaspoon dried lemon thyme or thyme
1 to 2 teaspoons Dijon-style mustard, or to taste

Loosen the skin on the chicken breasts and pat the breasts dry. In a bowl combine the butter, the shallots, the thyme, the mustard, and salt and pepper to taste. Divide the butter mixture among the breasts, smoothing it under the skin of each, and arrange the chicken in a shallow roasting pan. Roast the chicken in a preheated 450° F. oven, basting it occasionally, for 20 minutes, or until it is golden brown. Reduce the heat to 325° F. and roast the chicken for 15 to 20 minutes more, or until the juices run clear. Serves 4.

Herbed Tomato, Corn, and Pepper Sauté

1 onion, minced
1 red or green bell pepper, diced
2 tablespoons olive oil
1 to 2 garlic cloves, minced, or to taste
3 large tomatoes (about 1¾ pounds), peeled,
    seeded, and coarsely chopped
1 tablespoon minced fresh marjoram leaves
    or 1 teaspoon dried, crumbled, or to taste
1½ teaspoons fresh thyme leaves
    or ½ teaspoon dried, crumbled
2 cups corn kernels, thawed if frozen
¼ cup minced fresh parsley leaves

In a large skillet cook the onion and the bell pepper with salt and pepper to taste in the oil over moderate heat, stirring occasionally, until the onion is softened. Add the garlic and cook the mixture, stirring, for 1 minute. Add the tomatoes, the marjoram, and the thyme and simmer the mixture, stirring occasionally, for 5 minutes. Add the corn, and salt and pepper to taste and simmer the mixture for 10 minutes, or until the corn is tender and most of the liquid has evaporated. Stir in the parsley. Serves 4.

Marjoram Baked Chicken

6 whole chicken legs
1 cup plain yogurt
2 garlic cloves, minced
2 teaspoons Dijon-style mustard, or to taste
3 tablespoons minced fresh marjoram leaves
    or 2 teaspoons dried, crumbled
1½ cups dry bread crumbs
½ stick (¼ cup) unsalted butter, melted
2 tablespoons olive oil

Remove the skin from the chicken legs and cut the legs into drumsticks and thighs. Arrange the chicken in a shallow baking dish.

In a bowl combine the yogurt, the garlic, the mustard, 1 tablespoon of the marjoram, and salt and pepper to taste. Pour the yogurt mixture over the chicken to coat it completely. Cover the chicken with plastic wrap and chill it, turning the pieces once, for 2 hours or overnight.

In a bowl combine the bread crumbs with the remaining marjoram and salt and pepper to taste. Dredge the chicken in the bread crumb mixture and arrange it on a rack in a baking pan. Drizzle the chicken with the butter and the oil and bake it in a preheated 375° F. oven, turning it once and basting it with the pan juices, for 50 to 60 minutes, or until it is golden brown and the juices run clear when it is pricked with a fork. Serves 4.

Butterflied Leg of Lamb with Rosemary and Garlic

a 5-pound butterflied leg of lamb
3 garlic cloves, minced fine, or to taste
1½ tablespoons minced fresh rosemary leaves
    or 1½ teaspoons dried, crumbled
1 tablespoon minced fresh orégano
    or 1 teaspoon dried, crumbled
the juice of 1 lemon
2 teaspoons freshly grated lemon zest
3 to 4 tablespoons extra virgin olive oil
English mint sauce (recipe follows) as an
    accompaniment if desired

Pat dry the lamb and arrange it on a work surface cut side up. In a small bowl combine the garlic, the rosemary, the orégano, the lemon juice, the lemon zest, and salt and pepper to taste. Rub the herb mixture on the cut side of the meat and sprinkle the lamb with the olive oil. Let the lamb marinate, covered loosely, for 1 hour or chill it, covered, overnight.

Either grill the lamb over glowing coals about 5 inches from the heat for 10 to 12 minutes on each side for medium-rare meat or broil it under a preheated broiler about 4 inches from the heat for 12 to 15 minutes on each side for medium-rare meat. Transfer the lamb to a cutting board and let it stand for 10 minutes before carving. Serve the lamb with the mint sauce, if desired. Serves 8 to 10.

English Mint Sauce

3 cups loosely packed fresh mint leaves, chopped
2 tablespoons sugar, or to taste
½ cup malt vinegar or cider vinegar

In a heatproof bowl combine the mint leaves and the sugar with ½ cup boiling water and stir the mixture until the sugar is dissolved. Stir in the vinegar and let the mixture stand at room temperature for 1 to 2 hours before serving. The mint sauce will keep up to 1 week, covered and chilled. Serve the sauce with the lamb. Makes about 1⅓ cups.

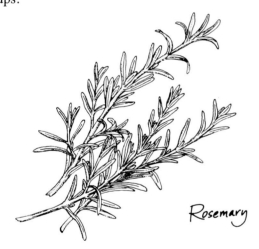

Rosemary

Gratin of Broccoli with Rosemary, Garlic, and Parmesan

1 bunch broccoli (about 1½ pounds), trimmed and separated into medium-size stalks
2 garlic cloves, minced
2 teaspoons minced fresh rosemary leaves or 1 teaspoon dried, crumbled
2 tablespoons unsalted butter
2 tablespoons olive oil
⅓ cup freshly grated Parmesan

In a large saucepan of boiling salted water blanch the broccoli for 4 to 5 minutes, or until it is just tender, drain it, and refresh it under cold water. In a small saucepan

cook the garlic and the rosemary in the butter and the oil over moderately low heat, stirring, for 3 to 4 minutes, or until the garlic is pale golden. Arrange the broccoli in a 1-quart gratin dish, spoon the rosemary mixture over it, and season the broccoli with salt and pepper. Sprinkle the broccoli with the Parmesan. *The dish can be prepared up to 2 hours ahead, covered loosely, or up to 6 hours, covered and chilled. If chilled, bring the dish to room temperature before proceeding.* Bake the gratin in a preheated 400° F. oven for 25 minutes, or until it is bubbling and the top is golden. Serves 4.

Minted New Potatoes

1¼ to 1½ pounds small new potatoes (about 1½-inch in diameter), scrubbed
¼ cup fresh mint leaves or 1 tablespoon dried
For the butter
½ stick (¼ cup) unsalted butter, softened
1 to 2 teaspoons Dijon-style mustard if desired
3 tablespoons minced fresh mint leaves or 1 tablespoon dried, crumbled

In a saucepan combine the potatoes with enough water to cover them by 2 inches, add the mint leaves and salt to taste, and simmer the potatoes, partially covered, for 25 to 30 minutes, or until they are tender. Drain the potatoes, return them to the pan, and steam them, covered, shaking the pan, for 1 minute.

Prepare the butter: In a small bowl whisk together the butter, the mustard, the mint, and salt and pepper to taste.

Transfer the potatoes to a bowl and toss them with the minted butter. Serves 4.

Minted Lemonade

1½ cups fresh lemon juice
½ cup packed fresh mint leaves, or to taste
½ cup sugar, or to taste
1 tablespoon freshly grated lemon zest
fresh mint sprigs for garnish if desired

In a saucepan bring 6 cups water to a boil, stir in the lemon juice, the mint, the sugar, and the lemon zest, and let the mixture cool. Chill the lemonade, covered, for at least 1 hour. Strain the lemonade into tall glasses filled with ice and garnish each glass with a mint sprig. Serves 6.

Herbal Tisane

4 tablespoons minced fresh mint leaves or
    4 teaspoons dried, crumbled
3 tablespoons minced fresh lemon verbena
    or 1 tablespoon dried
1 tablespoon minced fresh sage leaves or
    1 teaspoon dried, crumbled
3 tablespoons honey, or to taste
fresh lemon juice to taste
strips of fresh lemon zest as a garnish if desired

In a heated teapot combine the mint, the lemon verbe-na, and the sage, add 6 cups boiling water, and let the mixture steep for 5 minutes. Stir in the honey and the lemon juice and strain the tisane into cups. Garnish each cup with a strip of lemon zest. Serves 4.

Saltimbocca
(Veal Scaloppine with Sage and Prosciutto)

1 pound veal *scaloppine*, pounded thin (about
    ¼-inch thick) and cut into 4- to 5-inch squares
2 tablespoons minced fresh sage leaves
    or 2 teaspoons dried, crumbled
¼ pound thinly sliced prosciutto
2 tablespoons unsalted butter
1 tablespoon olive oil
½ dry white wine

Sprinkle the *scaloppine* with the sage and arrange a slice of prosciutto on top of each *scaloppina*, trimming the prosciutto to the size of the veal. Secure each ''pack-age'' of veal and prosciutto with toothpicks and season each with salt and pepper.

In a large skillet heat the butter and the oil over mod-erately high heat until the foam subsides. Add the veal, patted dry, and cook it in batches for 1 minute or until it is golden. Turn the veal, reduce the heat to moderate, and cook it for 2 minutes more, or until the veal is gold-en. Transfer the veal to a heated platter and remove the toothpicks. Add the wine to the skillet and boil it over high heat until it is reduced by half. Pour the sauce over the veal and serve it immediately. Serves 4.

Cheddar Cheese-Sage Bites

2 cups (8 ounces) grated sharp Cheddar
1 cup all-purpose flour
½ teaspoon salt

⅛ teaspoon cayenne, or to taste
1 stick (½ cup) unsalted butter, cut into bits
2 tablespoons minced fresh sage leaves
    or 2 teaspoons dried, crumbled

In a food processor combine the Cheddar, the flour, the salt, and the cayenne, and process the mixture until it is combined. Add the butter and the sage and process the mixture until it just forms a ball. Wrap the dough in plastic and chill it for 1 hour.

Form 1-inch balls of the dough, pressing them slight-ly to flatten to about ¼-inch thick, 1 inch apart on parch-ment-lined baking sheets, and bake them in a preheated 375° F. oven for 10 to 12 minutes. Cool the biscuits on a wire rack. Makes about 48 hors d'oeuvres.

Spinach Tortellini with Tomato Basil Sauce

3 garlic cloves, minced
¼ cup olive oil
a 28-ounce can crushed tomatoes including
    the liquid
1½ - 2 cups loosely packed fresh basil leaves,
    chopped
1½ pounds spinach tortellini, cooked
    according to package directions and drained
freshly grated Parmesan to taste

In a saucepan cook the garlic in the olive oil over moderate heat, stirring, until it is pale golden. Add the tomatoes, the basil, salt and pepper to taste, and simmer the sauce, stirring occasionally, for 20 minutes.

Meanwhile cook the tortellini and drain them. In a large bowl toss the tortellini with the sauce and add the Parmesan to taste. Serves 4.

Penne and Shrimp Salad Primavera
with Basil Dressing

1 pound *penne* or similar tubular pasta
½ pound thin asparagus, trimmed and cut into
    pieces 1½ inches long
1 zucchini, trimmed and cut into ½-inch cubes
2 small summer squash, trimmed and
    sliced ¼ inch thick
1 pound (about 16) large shrimp, shelled and
    deveined
1 large red bell pepper, diced
1 red onion, minced

For the dressing
1 cup loosely packed basil leaves
3 garlic cloves
3 tablespoons white-wine vinegar
1 tablespoon Dijon-style mustard
⅔ cup olive oil or a combination of olive oil
   and vegetable oil, or to taste
½ cup toasted pine nuts
½ cup chopped purple or green basil leaves
freshly grated Parmesan to taste

In a large saucepan of boiling salted water cook the *penne* for 7 to 8 minutes, or until it is slightly tender. Add the asparagus, the zucchini, and the summer squash, and cook the mixture, stirring, for 2 minutes. Add the shrimp and cook them, stirring, for 1 minute, or until they are firm. Drain the mixture thoroughly and refresh it under cold water. Drain the mixture thoroughly one more time and in a large bowl combine the pasta mixture with the red pepper and the onion.

Make the dressing: In a blender or food processor combine the basil, the garlic, the vinegar, the mustard, and salt and pepper to taste and blend the mixture, until it is smooth. With the motor running add the oil in a stream and blend the dressing until it is combined well.

Add the dressing to the pasta mixture and toss it gently to combine. Garnish the salad with the pine nuts and the basil and serve it with the Parmesan. Serves 6 to 8.

Black-Eyed Pea Salad with Summer Savory

6 cups cooked black-eyed peas (1 pound dried
   black-eyed peas cooked according to the
   package instructions)
1 red onion, minced
1 red bell pepper, chopped fine
½ cup finely chopped celery
1 tablespoon minced fresh savory
   or 1 teaspoon dried, crumbled
⅓ cup shallot-flavored vinegar
2 to 3 tablespoons sugar, or to taste
⅓ cup vegetable oil

In a large bowl combine the black-eyed peas, the onion, the pepper, the celery, and the savory. In a small bowl whisk together the vinegar and the sugar until the sugar is dissolved, add the oil in a stream, and season the dressing with salt and pepper. Pour the dressing over the salad and toss gently to combine. Chill the salad,

covered, for 2 hours or overnight. Bring the salad to room temperature before serving. Serves 6.

Carrot, Leek, and Apple Soup with Winter Savory

3 tablespoons unsalted butter
1 pound carrots, sliced thin
the white part of 1 leek, chopped and
   washed well
1 green apple, such as Granny Smith, peeled,
   cored, and chopped coarse
4 cups chicken broth
1 tablespoon minced fresh winter savory
   or 1 teaspoon dried, crumbled
sour cream or plain yogurt as an
   accompaniment if desired
minced fresh savory leaves for garnish
   if desired

In a saucepan heat the butter over moderate heat until it is hot, add the carrots, the leek, and salt and pepper, and cook the vegetables, stirring occasionally, until they are softened. Add the apple and cook the mixture, stirring occasionally, for 3 minutes. Add the broth and the savory and simmer the mixture, covered, for 30 minutes, or until the carrots are very soft. In a food processor purée the soup in batches until it is smooth and return it to the saucepan. Heat the soup until it is hot, ladle it into bowls, and garnish each bowl with a dollop of sour cream and the minced savory leaves. Makes 6 cups, serving 4.

Sage

THE LILY FAMILY

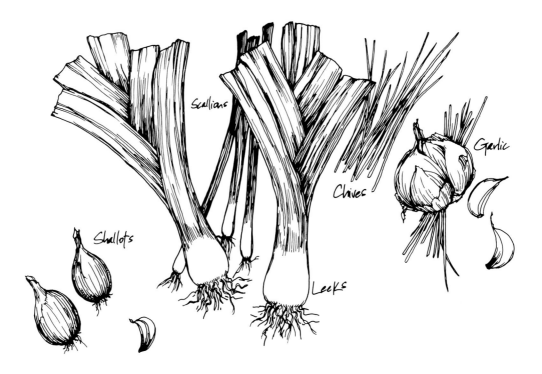

Members of this family fall into two groups: *allium* plants of the onion species, and two lily plants, namely the Madonna Lily and the Lily-of-the-Valley. Since the lily plants are used as medicinal herbs only, we will concentrate instead on five of "the onions"—leeks, chives, shallots, onions, and garlic. As medicinal herbs, these bulbous plants have long been used as fighters of disease. As culinary herbs, they have been enjoyed for centuries for their varying degrees of onion flavor and aroma. Surprisingly, they are quite compatible as culinary condiments; once you know each flavor, you can substitute them for a different taste!

The mildest and sweetest-tasting member of "the onions" are leeks, a hardy biennial with a stout white stalk and very broad flat leaves standing some 24 inches in height. The best parts of a leek are its white bulbous end and the lower green stalk. Not only delectable, tender leeks have a high content of calcium, iron, and vitamin C.

Today the leek is used as both culinary herb and vegetable. Proponents of *nouvelle cuisine* tend to use leeks in julienne strips as a stylish garnish, while other

French chefs and Europeans savor them as a vegetable napped in a cream sauce or a vinaigrette, or in a soup, often with potatoes. Our Leek and Potato Gratin pairs the classic duo in a mild creamy cheese sauce with a hint of mustard and nutmeg. Serve this comforting dish with any entrée willing to play a supporting role. Or serve it alone or with a salad and soup.

Perhaps the most decorative of "the onions" are chives. This perennial herb has slender green rush-like foliage that grows in clumps. Allowed to mature, the plants will reward the gardener in the second season with spectacular pompon flowers that vary from lavender-pink to creamy white depending on the variety. Unlike other *allium* plants, it is the foliage of chives, not the bulb, that is savored for its subtle onion flavor. Nutritionally, chives are rich in calcium, iron, and vitamins A and C; unfortunately, this goodness diminishes with cooking, so it is important to add the herb at the last minute.

Chives make excellent windowsill plants extending the life of their outdoor season. Indoors or out, if you are cooking with chives be sure to give the plant a constant "trim" during growing season to keep the leaves tender and bushy. Our recipe for Cheddar Cheese Scones with Chives combines the flavors of sharp cheese and mild onion with a dash of red pepper for a scone *extraordinaire!* Try these treats with herbed eggs for brunch, or as a flavorful side-kick to soup, or perhaps best of all, by themselves with a glass of wine.

A bit more oniony in flavor than leeks or chives, shallots are now gaining popularity in this country. This perennial has an elongated oval bulb covered with reddish-brown skin at the end of 16-inch flat, fleshy leaves. Like their onion cousins, shallots are known for nutritional value and are high in calcium and vitamin C.

As with leeks, shallots can serve as flavor enhancers as well as vegetables. In our London Broil with Shallots in Red Wine Sauce we put shallots through their paces. Initially they serve as an herb with minced garlic to flavor a red-wine marinade; then, they are broiled alongside the meat to serve as succulent vegetables. The result: steak redolent with a rich, shallot-garlic flavor accompanied by sweet and mild-tasting shallots in an aromatic wine sauce.

More pronounced to the palate than leeks, chives, and shallots are onions. With a name derived from the word "union," which means single, onions have a single bulb consisting of many fleshy layers covered with dry skins, which vary in color according to variety, at the end of a hollow 18-inch stem. Generally, taste varies according to climate, with the juiciest and sweetest versions grown in warmer climes and the stronger smelling, eye-tearing varieties grown elsewhere. The onion has been used throughout history to treat several ailments. It remains a favored folk remedy for colds; and, while it seems a shame to use our Cream of Onion Soup for this purpose, it might well do the trick! We soften sweet Spanish onions, then slowly simmer them in white wine and chicken broth. Processed until smooth, the base then simmers with cream for a warming, aromatic combination. Better yet, try this soup when you are healthy to stay that way; it contains calcium and vitamin C.

And finally we come to the most potent and universal "onion" of all—garlic. Widely used throughout time for its supposed digestive and antiseptic properties, today many European families still give their children a clove of garlic to eat each day as a curative and preventive measure.

Everyone knows about garlic's pungent bulb, but few realize that garlic is a tall plant with broad, flat gray-green foliage. In its raw state, garlic has a very powerful flavor to match its aroma, and it can be overwhelming when combined with delicately flavored ingredients. However, roasting, blanching, or slow sautéeing takes away the hot stinging flavor and aftertaste of the raw garlic cloves. For example, we roast an entire garlic bulb for our Garlic Dip, and the flavor and aroma are remarkably mild. Add raw vegetables and you have a light, refreshing appetizer. For more garlic spark, try our Barbecued Spareribs in Garlic and Hoisin Sauce Marinade, where six minced raw cloves provide a highly charged garlic experience.

Leek and Potato Gratin

2¼ pounds (about 3 large) white and pale
    green parts of leek, well washed and chopped
3 tablespoons unsalted butter
2 tablespoons all-purpose flour
2 cups half-and-half, scalded
¼ cup plus 2 tablespoons grated Parmesan
¼ cup plus 2 tablespoons grated Gruyère
2 teaspoons Dijon-style mustard, or to taste
freshly grated nutmeg to taste
1½ pounds (about 3 medium-large) russet
    (baking) potatoes, peeled and cut into
    1-inch cubes

In a saucepan cook the leeks in 2 tablespoons of the butter over moderate heat, stirring, until they are softened. Add the flour and cook the mixture over low heat, stirring, for 3 minutes. Add the half-and-half, bring the liquid to a boil, and simmer the mixture, stirring occasionally, for 5 minutes. Stir in ¼ cup each of the Parmesan and Gruyère, the mustard, the nutmeg, and salt and pepper to taste.

Meanwhile, in a saucepan combine the potatoes with enough water to cover them by 2 inches, bring the water to a boil, and simmer the potatoes for 1 minute. Drain the potatoes.

Transfer the potatoes to a buttered 1½-quart baking dish. Spoon the leek mixture over the potatoes, sprinkle it with the remaining cheeses, and dot the top with the remaining butter. Bake the gratin in a preheated 400° F. oven for 35 to 40 minutes, or until the potatoes are tender and the top is golden brown. Serves 4.

Cheddar Cheese Scones with Chives

2 cups all-purpose flour
1 tablespoon double-acting baking powder
1 teaspoon salt
⅛ teaspoon cayenne, or to taste
½ stick (¼ cup) unsalted butter, chilled and
  cut into bits
1 cup grated sharp Cheddar
¼ cup snipped fresh chives
⅔ to ¾ cup milk
an egg wash made by beating 1 egg with a
  pinch of salt

Into a bowl sift the flour, the baking powder, the salt, and the cayenne. Add the butter and blend the mixture until it resembles coarse meal. Add the Cheddar and the chives and toss the mixture to combine it. Stir in enough milk to form a dough and gently knead the dough on a lightly floured surface until combined. Pat the dough into a round ¾ inch thick and with a 3-inch round cookie cutter stamp out rounds. Re-form the scraps into dough and stamp out the remaining rounds. Arrange the rounds on a greased baking sheet, brush them with the egg wash, and bake them in a preheated 425° F. oven for 12 to 15 minutes, or until they are golden. Makes about 8 scones.

Shallots

*London Broil with Shallots
in Red-Wine Sauce*

For the marinade
2½ cups beef broth
1 cup dry red wine
⅓ cup minced shallot
2 garlic cloves, minced
1 tablespoon tomato paste

a cheesecloth bag containing 1 sprig of fresh
  thyme or ½ teaspoon dried thyme,
  6 peppercorns, 4 cloves, and 12 sprigs of
  fresh parsley
salt to taste

a 2-pound London broil, about 1½-inches
  thick
For the sauce
3 tablespoons unsalted butter
3 tablespoons all-purpose flour
2 tablespoons red currant jelly if desired

12 whole shallots (about ¾ pound), blanched
  for 2 minutes in boiling water and peeled
1 tablespoon olive oil

Make the marinade: In a shallow baking dish combine all the marinade ingredients.

Add the London Broil to the marinade and turn it to coat. Let the beef marinate, covered and chilled, for at least 2 hours, or overnight. Drain the beef and reserve the marinade. Pat the meat dry and arrange it in an oiled shallow baking pan.

Make the sauce: In a saucepan melt the butter over moderately low heat, add the flour, and cook the *roux*, stirring, for 3 minutes. Add the reserved marinade and simmer the sauce, stirring occasionally, for 20 minutes, or until it is slightly thickened. Add the red currant jelly and salt and pepper to taste and simmer the sauce, stirring, for 2 to 3 minutes more, or until the jelly is melted. Strain the sauce into a sauceboat. *The sauce can be made up to 6 hours ahead, covered and chilled. Reheat over moderate heat before serving.*

In a bowl toss the shallots with the olive oil and scatter them around the London Broil. Broil the beef under a preheated broiler about 4 inches from the heat for 5 minutes on each side for rare meat, turning the shallots occasionally until they are golden brown and tender. (Alternatively, the meat can be grilled on a rack set about 5 inches over glowing coals for 5 minutes on each side for rare meat. The shallots can be put on skewers and grilled with the meat, turning them occasionally until they are golden brown and tender.) Let the meat stand, covered loosely, for 5 minutes. Cut the beef diagonally against the grain into thin slices, arrange it on a platter, and surround it with the shallots. Nap the London Broil and the shallots with some of the sauce and serve the remaining sauce separately. Serves 4 to 6.

Cream of Onion Soup

2 pounds Spanish onions (about 8 cups),
  sliced
2 tablespoons unsalted butter
2 tablespoons olive oil
½ cup dry white wine
6 cups chicken broth
5 tablespoons long-grain rice
1 cup heavy cream or half-and-half
minced fresh chives or scallion top to taste

In a large saucepan cook the onions in the butter and
the oil over moderate heat, covered, stirring occasionally, for 7 to 10 minutes, or until they are softened. Add
the wine and boil the liquid, uncovered, for 1 minute.
Add the chicken broth, the rice, and salt to taste and
simmer the soup, covered, stirring occasionally, for 45
minutes. Transfer the soup in batches to a food processor and process it until it is smooth. Return the soup to
the saucepan, stir in the heavy cream, and simmer the
soup for 5 minutes. Sprinkle the soup with the chives
before serving. Makes about 11 cups, serving 6 to 8.

Roasted Garlic Dip

1 large head of garlic
1 tablespoon olive oil
an 8-ounce package softened cream cheese,
  cut into bits
1 cup sour cream
⅛ teaspoon cayenne, or to taste
fresh lemon juice to taste

Remove the papery outer skin of the head of garlic
without separating the cloves, put it on a piece of alumi-
num foil, and spoon the olive oil over it. Wrap the head
of garlic in the foil and bake it in a preheated 350° F.
oven for 1 hour. Let the garlic cool, peel each clove, and
transfer the cooked garlic pulp to a food processor. Add
the cream cheese, the sour cream, the cayenne, the lemon juice, and salt to taste and purée the mixture until it is
smooth. Transfer the dip to a serving bowl and chill it,
covered, for at least 1 hour. Serve the dip with roasted,
steamed, or raw vegetables. The dip keeps, covered and
chilled, for 3 days. Makes about 2 cups.

Roasted Spareribs in Garlic and Hoisin
Sauce Marinade

For the marinade
6 garlic cloves, minced
⅓ cup Lite Soy Sauce
⅓ cup hoisin sauce*
3 tablespoons honey
2 tablespoons ketchup
2 tablespoons rice vinegar* or cider vinegar
2 tablespoons dry Sherry
1 tablespoon chili oil* or 1 teaspoon red
  pepper flakes
1 tablespoon Oriental sesame oil*

a 3½- to 4-pound rack of spareribs

*available at Oriental food stores and some
  supermarkets

Make the marinade: In a shallow baking dish combine all the marinade ingredients.

Add the spareribs to the marinade and turn them to
coat. Let the ribs marinate, covered and chilled, for 2 to
4 hours. Bake the ribs on a rack in a shallow baking pan,
at 375° F., basting them occasionally with the marinade, for 45 minutes to 1 hour, or until they are tender.
Serves 4 to 6.

Garlic

THE CARROT FAMILY

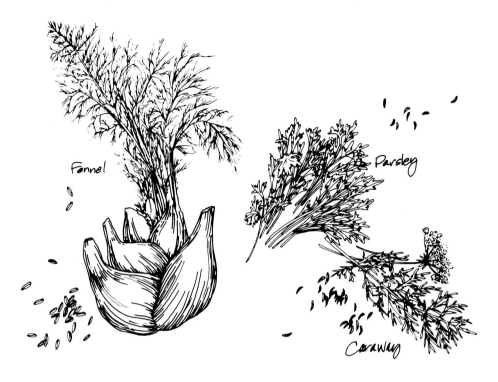

Fennel

Parsley

Caraway

*B*rightly colored flowering umbels and delicate, feathery foliage identify Carrot family members. Known for their pleasant scents and flavors, parsley, chervil, coriander, caraway, dill, fennel, and anise have been chosen to familiarize you with this exceptional herbal group. Some members, such as fennel, are vegetables; and all are used as culinary condiments in the form of foliage, dried flowers seeds, or roots. Most "carrots" have curative powers, although this family is better known for their oils that mask unpleasant tastes and odors in medicinal preparations.

Perhaps the most popular member of this herbal family is parsley, a biennial plant that grows 12 inches high and carries tiny yellow-gold flowers in flat umbels. Containing vitamins C and A, as well as vital minerals and oils, parsley was used by the ancient Greeks in combination with other herbs as a cure for most ailments.

Today many people think of parsley simply as a culinary ornament—and what a shame this is! Several varieties, all faintly celery-like in taste, are readily available. Simply remember to use the curly variety for embellishments, and the stronger-tasting flat varieties for cooking. Our Shrimp in Parsley Sauce showcases parsley's wonderful flavor. An herbal fish stock simmers with many whole parsley sprigs (most of the parsley flavor is in the stalks); this strong parsley essence

permeates the ensuing creamy sauce; and a generous measure of chopped parsley is added at the last minute for a final green touch. Note: To retain its color and flavor, add chopped parsley just before serving.

Chervil is similar in look and size to flat-leafed parsley, but is of little medicinal value. Although chervil is virtually untapped as a food enhancer in American kitchens, the French could not live without this anise-flavored herb. Like parsley, its leaves lose flavor and aroma in cooking and should be chopped and added to a dish at the last moment. We present recipes for two traditional uses of the herb: an Old-Fashioned Potato Salad with Chervil (bowing to the French by using Dijon-style mustard) and an Iced Chervil Pea Soup that is infused with the herb! *Vive la différence de cerfeuil!* It is important to note that we call for only fresh chervil, as it does not dry successfully. Also, if necessary or desired, parsley and chervil can substitute for one another.

Another herb resembling flat-leafed parsley in foliage is coriander. A worldy herb, it is also known as *cilantro* in Spanish, as Indian parsley, or as Chinese parsley! For centuries, coriander has been used as a digestive aid for colic and flatulence. The plant is larger than parsley (growing to about 18 inches), and both its seeds and its leaves have an exciting, minty-fresh flavor. We have paired coriander with sea scallops in a delightfully refreshing *salsa* with lime, with chicken in a fragrant Oriental sesame-ginger sauce, and even coriander seed with apples and cinnamon for a lovely aromatic twist to the classic apple crisp.

Caraway, a lesser-known herb, is also coveted for its reported digestive properties as well as the slight cumin flavor of its strange sickle-shaped seeds. This delicate-looking biennial carries modest white flower umbels and once the seeds are harvested, you can try our Orange Carrot Tea Bread, a simple combination of varied textures and fruity flavor with the unexpected taste of caraway. Serve the bread to unsuspecting guests with a warming brew and enjoy their pleasure!

Dill, a well-established culinary herb, has been thought to have notable curative powers as well. Dill oil is said to cure infantile flatulence, while its seeds may sedate and stave off hunger. The elegant annual stands up to 3 feet high, has feathery bluish-green leaves, and huge bright-yellow flowering umbels. Not surprisingly, dill is often mistaken for fennel; and one should not plant the two next to each other, as they will cross-pollinate and produce hybrids.

The foliage and seeds of dill have a mild, slightly sweet taste with a hint of caraway. We offer an easy recipe for Dilled Cucumber Sauce, a refreshing topping for any fish entrée, and unique unsweetened Buttermilk Corn Muffins with Dill. Guaranteed not to stick to the top of your mouth, these flavorful moist muffins could easily steal the show at your next dinner party.

Another "digestive" herb, the dill look-alike, fennel, also makes a tea once thought to be good for colicky babies. Unlike its more refined cousin, fennel is taller (reaching 4 feet), a biennial, and, if trimmed to 12 inches, even content to grow in a window pot. Fennel is a tougher plant than dill, and it has a stronger anise flavor. Its leaves and seeds make a haunting pairing with fish, while its roots and stems serve as vegetables. Our Seafood Stew with Tomatoes and Fennel combines a variety of vegetables, including fennel bulb, in a heady white-wine fish stock seasoned with fennel seeds, thyme, and orange peel—an excellent example of fennel bulb and seeds working happily together in a meal-in-one.

For true anise flavor you should try our heavenly Anise Snowball Cookies, a combination of anise seed with orange juice and peel in a simple dough. The licorice-orange taste and playful appearance make these unfussy cookies a favorite. Be sure to earmark this festive recipe for holiday giving, although you'll be tempted to make them year round.

Anise, an herb of great antiquity, is a delicate annual with white flowering umbels and two kinds of foliage: feathery leaves on the flower stalks and solid, sharply serrated leaves (unlike other umbellifers) elsewhere. Unfortunately, anise seed rarely ripens in northern climates, so you will have to depend on the imported varieties. If you are able to grow anise in your garden, however, its foliage can be chopped and used in white sauces for its much-loved licorice flavor.

Shrimp in Parsley Sauce

1½ pounds (about 24) large shrimp
2 cups chicken broth
½ cup dry white wine
1 teaspoon fresh thyme leaves or ½ teaspoon
   dried, crumbled
1 bay leaf
6 parsley sprigs
6 peppercorns
5 tablespoons olive oil
1 small onion, minced
2 garlic cloves, minced
2 tablespoons all-purpose flour
1 cup finely chopped fresh parsley leaves

Shell and devein the shrimp, reserving the shells. In a saucepan combine the shrimp shells with the chicken broth over moderate heat and stir in the wine, the thyme, the bay leaf, the parsley, the peppercorns, and salt to taste. Bring the broth to a boil and simmer it for 20 minutes. Strain the broth into a 2-cup measuring cup and if necessary, boil it until it is reduced to 1½ cups.

In a skillet cook the shrimp in 2 tablespoons of the olive oil over moderately high heat, stirring, for 1 to 2 minutes, or until they are just firm. With a slotted spoon transfer the shrimp to a plate.

Add the remaining 3 tablespoons of oil to the skillet and heat it until it is hot. Add the onion and cook it over moderate heat, stirring occasionally, until it is softened. Add the garlic and cook the mixture, stirring, for 1 minute. Add the flour and cook the *roux* over moderately low heat, stirring, for 3 minutes. Add the reserved broth and simmer the sauce, stirring occasionally, for 5 minutes. Stir in the chopped parsley and the shrimp and cook the mixture over moderate heat until the shrimp are heated through. Serves 4.

Tabbouleh
(*Cracked Wheat, Tomato, Parsley, and Mint Salad*)

1 cup bulgur (available at natural foods stores
   and some supermarkets)
3 tomatoes, cored and diced
4 scallions, sliced thin
2 cups minced fresh parsley leaves
1 cup minced fresh mint leaves
For the dressing
⅓ cup fresh lemon juice
2 garlic cloves, minced fine
⅓ cup olive oil, or to taste

In a bowl let the bulgur soak in 2 cups water for 1 hour. Drain the bulgur and squeeze it dry.

In a glass or ceramic bowl combine the bulgur, the tomatoes, the scallions, the parsley, and the mint.

Make the dressing: In a small bowl whisk together the lemon juice, the garlic, and salt and pepper to taste. Whisk in the oil in a stream, whisking until the dressing is combined well.

Add the dressing to the salad and toss it to combine. Let the *tabbouleh* stand, covered and chilled, for at least 1 hour before serving. *The salad may be prepared up to 6 hours ahead, covered and chilled.* Serves 4.

Old-Fashioned Potato Salad with Chervil

2 pounds small red boiling potatoes, scrubbed
½ cup minced celery
⅔ cup minced scallion
¼ cup chopped sweet pickle
2 hard-boiled eggs, chopped, if desired
½ cup mayonnaise
1 tablespoon Dijon-style mustard, or to taste
a pinch of sugar
2 tablespoons minced fresh chervil leaves

In a saucepan combine the potatoes with enough water to cover them by 1½ inches, add salt, and bring the water to a boil over moderately high heat. Simmer the potatoes, covered, for 15 to 20 minutes, or until they are tender. Drain the potatoes and let them cool to room temperature. Peel the potatoes, if desired, and cut them into 1-inch pieces.

In a bowl combine the potatoes, the celery, the scallion, the pickle, and the eggs. In a small bowl whisk together the mayonnaise, the mustard, the sugar, the chervil, and salt and pepper to taste until it is combined well. Add the dressing to the potato salad and combine the salad gently. Serves 4.

Iced Chervil Pea Soup

the white part of 1 leek, minced and washed
   well in a sieve
1 celery stalk, chopped
2 tablespoons unsalted butter
4 cups shelled fresh peas or one 20-ounce
   package frozen peas, thawed
4 cups chicken broth
12 chervil sprigs
1 cup half-and-half or heavy cream
fresh lemon juice to taste
¼ cup minced fresh chervil leaves
sour cream and fresh chervil leaves for
   garnish if desired

In a large saucepan cook the leek and the celery with salt and pepper to taste in the butter over moderate heat, stirring occasionally, until the vegetables are softened. Add the peas and cook them, stirring, for 1 minute. Add the broth, the chervil sprigs, and salt and pepper to taste and bring the liquid to a boil. Simmer the soup, covered, for 10 minutes, or until the peas are tender.

In a food processor or blender purée the soup in batches and force it through the fine disk of a food mill or strain it through a sieve into a bowl. Add the half-and-half, the lemon juice, and salt and pepper to taste and stir in the minced chervil. Chill the soup, covered, for 2 hours, or overnight. Ladle the soup into serving bowls and garnish each bowl with a dollop of sour cream and the chervil leaves. Makes 6 cups, serving 4.

Broiled Sea Scallops with Fresh Coriander Salsa

For the salsa
1½ pounds tomatoes, seeded and coarsely
   chopped
1 small red bell pepper, diced
1 small green bell pepper, diced
6 scallions, minced
1 garlic clove, minced
1 *jalapeño* chili, seeded and minced, or to
   taste (wear rubber gloves)
½ cup finely minced fresh coriander leaves
2 tablespoons fresh lime juice

2 tablespoons olive oil
salt and freshly ground black pepper to taste

1½ pounds sea scallops
2 tablespoons olive oil
2 tablespoons fresh lime juice
2 tablespoons minced fresh coriander leaves
1 garlic clove, minced

Make the *salsa*: In a bowl combine all the ingredients and chill the *salsa*, covered, until it is ready to serve. *The salsa can be made 1 to 2 hours ahead.*

In a bowl toss the scallops with the olive oil, the lime juice, the coriander, the garlic, and salt and pepper to taste and arrange them in one layer in an oiled flame-proof baking dish. Broil the scallops under a preheated broiler about 6 inches from the heat for 7 to 9 minutes, or until they are opaque and firm to the touch. (Alternatively, thread the scallops on skewers and grill them on a rack set about 6 inches over glowing coals, turning them once, for 7 to 9 minutes, or until they are opaque and firm to the touch.) Arrange the scallops on a plate and spoon the *salsa* around them. Serves 4.

Chicken Salad with Coriander, Sesame, and Ginger Dressing

2 pounds skinless boneless chicken breasts
6 coriander sprigs
1 piece of gingerroot (about 1-inch in
    diameter), cut into strips
6 peppercorns
For the dressing
1 cup mayonnaise
½ cup plain yogurt
2 tablespoons Oriental rice vinegar*
2 tablespoons Oriental sesame oil*
1 tablespoon peeled and minced fresh gingerroot
1 teaspoon Dijon-style mustard, or to taste
⅓ cup minced fresh coriander leaves
salt and freshly ground black pepper to taste

½ cup minced scallion
1 small head of red leaf lettuce, separated into
    leaves, rinsed, and spun dry
toasted cashews for garnish if desired

*available at Oriental foods stores and some
    supermarkets

In a saucepan combine the chicken breasts with enough water just to cover them and over moderate heat add the coriander, the gingerroot, the peppercorns, and salt to taste, and simmer the chicken for 7 minutes, or until it is firm but still springy to the touch. Let the chicken cool completely in the liquid. Drain the chicken, cut it into cubes, and transfer it to a large bowl.

Make the dressing: In a bowl whisk together all the dressing ingredients until the dressing is smooth.

Add the dressing to the chicken with the scallion and gently stir the salad until it is combined. To serve arrange the lettuce leaves on a platter, top them with the chicken, and sprinkle the chicken with the cashews. Serves 4.

Apple Pecan Crisp with Coriander

6 Granny Smith apples (about 3 pounds),
    peeled, cored, and sliced
⅓ to ½ cup sugar, or to taste
the grated zest of 1 lemon
the juice of 1 lemon
½ teaspoon cinnamon
For the topping
1 cup firmly packed dark brown sugar
1 cup granulated sugar
⅔ cup all-purpose flour
1 stick (½ cup) cold unsalted butter,
    cut into bits
1 cup chopped pecans
1½ teaspoons crushed coriander seed,
    or to taste

In a bowl toss together the apples, the sugar, the lemon zest, the lemon juice, and the cinnamon. Transfer the mixture to a buttered 12 by 9-inch shallow baking dish.

Make the topping: In another bowl combine the sugars, the flour, and the butter and blend the mixture until it resembles coarse meal. Add the pecans and the coriander seed and stir the mixture to combine it.

Sprinkle the topping over the apples and bake the crisp in a preheated 375° F. oven for 40 to 45 minutes, or until the filling is bubbling and the top is golden. Serves 6.

Orange Carrot Tea Bread with Caraway

2½ cups sifted all-purpose flour
2½ teaspoons double-acting baking powder
½ teaspoon baking soda
½ teaspoon salt
1 cup sugar
2 cups (about 3 large) coarsely grated carrot
1 cup chopped walnuts
1 teaspoon caraway seed
2 large eggs, beaten lightly
1 stick (½ cup) unsalted butter, melted
½ cup fresh orange juice
1 tablespoon freshly grated orange zest

Into a bowl sift the flour, the baking powder, the baking soda, and the salt. Stir in the sugar, the carrot, the walnuts, and the caraway seed. In another bowl beat together the eggs, the butter, the orange juice, and the orange zest. Stir the liquid ingredients into the flour mixture until the mixture is combined. Pour the batter into a well-greased 9 by 5 by 3-inch loaf pan and bake the bread in a preheated 350° F. oven for 50 minutes to 1 hour, or until a cake tester inserted in the center comes out clean. Let the bread cool in the pan on a rack for 5 minutes, invert it onto the rack, and let it cool completely. Makes 1 loaf.

Dilled Cucumber Sauce

1 pound cucumber, peeled, seeded, grated coarse
1 teaspoon salt
1 cup plain yogurt
½ cup minced scallion
½ cup sour cream
fresh lemon juice to taste
salt to taste
cayenne pepper to taste
⅓ cup minced fresh dill

In a colander toss the cucumber with the salt and let it drain for 30 minutes. Squeeze the cucumber dry and transfer it to a bowl.

In a sieve lined with a double thickness of rinsed and squeezed-dry cheesecloth let the yogurt drain for 30 minutes and transfer it to the bowl. Add the remaining ingredients to the bowl, stir the sauce until it is combined well, and chill it, covered, for at least 1 hour before serving. Serve the sauce with poached and grilled seafood. Makes about 2 cups.

Buttermilk Corn Muffins with Dill

1 cup yellow cornmeal (preferably stone-ground)
1 cup all-purpose flour
2½ teaspoons double-acting baking powder
½ teaspoon baking soda
½ teaspoon salt, or to taste
1 cup buttermilk
2 large eggs, beaten lightly
½ stick (¼ cup) unsalted butter, melted
2 tablespoons minced fresh dill or
    2 teaspoons dried

Into a bowl sift together the cornmeal, the flour, the baking powder, the baking soda, and the salt.

In another bowl combine the buttermilk, the eggs, the butter, and the dill, add the mixture to the dry ingredients, and stir the batter until it is just combined. Divide the batter among 12 well-buttered ⅓-cup muffin tins, filling the tins ⅔ full, and bake the muffins in the middle of a preheated 425° F. oven for 15 to 20 minutes, or until the muffins are golden and a tester comes out clean. Turn the muffins out onto racks. Makes 12 muffins.

Seafood Stew with Tomatoes and Fennel

1½ cups (about 2 large) minced and
    well washed leek
1½ cups minced fennel bulb
½ pound mushrooms, sliced
4 garlic cloves, minced
¼ cup olive oil
1 cup dry white wine
5 cups white fish stock or chicken broth
a 28-ounce can crushed tomatoes
1½ teaspoons dried fennel seed,
    crushed
1 tablespoon fresh thyme leaves or
    1 teaspoon dried
2 teaspoons freshly grated orange zest
1 pound mussels, scrubbed well and
    beards removed
1 pound (about 16) large shrimp, shelled and
    deveined
1 pound sea scallops, halved horizontally
    if large
1 pound halibut skinless steak, cut
    into 1½-inch pieces
¼ cup minced fresh parsley leaves

In a large casserole cook the leek, the fennel, the mushrooms, the garlic, and salt and pepper to taste in the olive oil over moderate heat, covered, stirring occasionally, for 5 to 7 minutes, or until the mushrooms begin to give off liquid. Add the wine and boil the mixture for 1 minute. Add the fish stock, the tomatoes, the fennel seed, the thyme, the orange zest, and salt and pepper to taste and simmer the mixture, covered, for 30 minutes.

Bring the liquid in the casserole to a boil, add the mussels, and cook them over moderately high heat, covered, for 5 minutes. Add the shrimp, the scallops, and the halibut and cook the mixture, stirring occasionally, for 8 minutes, or until the mussels have opened and the seafood is firm but still springy to the touch. Stir in the parsley and salt and pepper to taste. Serves 6.

Romaine, Arugula, Radicchio, and Fennel Salad

1 medium head of romaine lettuce, separated
    into leaves, rinsed, and spun dry
1 medium bunch arugula, trimmed, rinsed,
    and spun dry
1 small head of radicchio, rinsed, separated
    into leaves and spun dry
1 fennel bulb

3 tomatoes, cut into wedges
1 small red onion, minced
1 red, yellow, or green bell pepper,
    cut into strips
1 cup oil-cured black olives if desired
For the dressing
2 teaspoons Dijon-style mustard, or to taste
2 tablespoons fresh lemon juice
1 tablespoon white-wine vinegar
⅓ to ½ cup extra-virgin olive oil
2 to 3 tablespoons snipped fresh fennel tops,
    or to taste

Tear the lettuces into bite-size pieces and put them in a salad bowl. Trim the feathery tops from the fennel bulb, reserving several for the dressing, and trim the stalks to the point where they meet the bulb, and discard them. Quarter the bulb, discarding the core, and slice the quarters thin crosswise. Add the fennel and the remaining salad ingredients to the bowl.

Make the dressing: In a large bowl whisk together the mustard, the lemon juice, the vinegar, and salt and pepper to taste. Add the oil in a stream, whisking, and whisk the dressing until it is combined. Stir in the fennel tops.

Drizzle the dressing over the salad and toss the salad until it is combined well. Serves 6.

Parsley

Anise Snowball Cookies

2 sticks (1 cup) unsalted butter, softened
½ cup confectioner's sugar
3 tablespoons fresh orange juice
1 egg yolk
2½ cups sifted all-purpose flour
1 tablespoon freshly grated orange zest,
   or to taste
1 teaspoon crushed aniseseed, or to taste
additional confectioner's sugar for sprinkling

In a bowl beat the butter with an electric mixer until it is pale yellow. Add the sugar, a little at a time, and beat the mixture until it is fluffy. In a small bowl combine the orange juice and the egg yolk and beat it into the butter mixture until it is combined well. In another bowl stir together the flour, the orange zest, and the aniseseed and add the mixture to the butter mixture, a little at a time, beating after each addition, until the mixture is combined. Wrap the dough in plastic and chill it for 1 hour.

Form the dough into 1-inch balls and arrange them 1 inch apart on ungreased baking sheets. Bake the cookies in a preheated 350° F. oven for 12 to 15 minutes, or until they are firm and pale golden around the edges. Let the cookies cool on the sheets for 5 minutes and transfer them to racks to cool completely. Sift the additional confectioner's sugar over the cookies. The cookies will keep in an airtight container at room temperature for 1 week. Makes about 48 cookies.

Spiced Tea

1 large cinnamon stick, cracked
8 cardamom pods
4 whole cloves
1½ teaspoons fennel seed, crushed
3 strips of lemon zest
2 tablespoons Orange Pekoe Tea, or to taste
sugar to taste
fresh lemon juice to taste

In a saucepan combine the cinnamon stick, the cardamom, the cloves, the fennel seed, and the lemon zest with 7 cups water, bring the water to a boil, and simmer the mixture, covered, for 10 minutes. Remove the saucepan from the heat, add the tea, and let it steep, covered, for 5 minutes. Add the sugar and the lemon juice to taste and strain the tea into cups. Serves 6.

Fennel

GUIDES TO THE TEXT

GENERAL INDEX

Page numbers in *italics* indicate color photographs
(M) indicates a microwave recipe

INDEX OF 45-MINUTE RECIPES

*Starred entries can be prepared in 45 minutes or less
but require additional unattended time

Page numbers in *italics* indicate color photographs

(M) indicates a microwave recipe

INDEX OF RECIPE TITLES

Page numbers in *italics* indicate color photographs
(M) indicates a microwave recipe

TABLE SETTING ACKNOWLEDGMENTS

To avoid duplication below of table setting information within the same menu, the editors have listed all such credits for silverware, plates, linen, and the like in its most complete form under "Table Setting."

Any items in the photographs not credited are privately owned.

Front Jacket
Sorbets: Porcelain plate by Laure Japy, Bergdorf Goodman, 754 Fifth Avenue, New York City.

The Menu Collection
Table Setting (page 8): See Table Setting credits for An Autumn Dinner below.

New Year's Eve Dinners For Two
Scallops with Pink Grapefruit Beurre Blanc; Roasted Rosemary Potato Slices; Buttered Snow Peas (page 11): "Ariel" Limoges dinner plate; Lalique "Argos" crystal wineglass—Cardel Ltd., 621 Madison Avenue, New York City. Puiforcat "Chantaco" silver-plate flatware—Puiforcat, 811 Madison Avenue, New York City. Linen napkin— Henri Bendel, Frank McIntosh Shop, 10 West 57th Street, New York City. Nineteenth-century lacquered papier-mâché tray—James II Galleries, Ltd., 15 East 57th Street, New York City.
Veal Chop with Eggplant and Pepper Stuffing and Roasted Red Pepper Sauce; Sautéed Baby Artichokes (page 12): "Ariel" Limoges dinner plate— Cardel Ltd., 621 Madison Avenue, New York City. Lalique "Bourgeuil" crystal wineglass—Lalique, 680 Madison Avenue, New York City. Puiforcat "Cannes" sterling flatware—Puiforcat, 811 Madison Avenue, New York City.
Champagne Orange Sorbet, Chocolate-Dipped Orange Cookies (page 13):

Lalique "Roxane" crystal Champagne glasses—Lalique, 680 Madison Avenue, New York City. Puiforcat "Cannes" sterling teaspoons—Puiforcat, 811 Madison Avenue, New York City. Papier-mâché coasters, circa 1870—James II Galleries, Ltd., 15 East 57th Street, New York City.

A Finger-Food Buffet For Super Bowl Sunday
Dill and Garlic Shrimp Skewers, Herbed Zucchini Spirals, Parmesan Mustard Chicken Wings, Baked Potato Skins, Lettuce Scoops with Coriander Yogurt Cheese (page 15): Fitz & Floyd "wicker" platter and chop plate; Hall hors d'oeuvres plates—Wolfman • Gold & Good Company, 116 Greene Street, New York City. Earthenware serving dish by Barbara Eigen; hand-woven silk shawl—Zona, 97 Greene Street, New York City. Earthenware basket; nineteenth-century French brass bowl—Bob Pryor Antiques, 1023 Lexington Avenue, New York City. Nineteenth-century French console table with marble top—T & K French Antiques, Inc., 120 Wooster Street, New York City. Fabric—Home Textiles, 132-A Spring Street, New York City.

Dinner Florida Style
Table Setting (pages 16 and 17): Taitù porcelain dinner plates—Mayhew, 507 Park Avenue, New York City. Glass soup bowls and plates—Cardel Ltd., 621 Madison Avenue, New York City.

"Tahiti" bamboo and sterling flatware—Buccellati, Inc., 46 East 57th Street, New York City. "Bamboo" crystal wineglasses—Justin Tharaud & Son, 23 Maplewood Avenue, Maplewood, New Jersey 07040. iittala "Erika" glass candle holders—The L • S Collection, 765 Madison Avenue, New York City. Decanter—Bridge Kitchenware Corporation, 214 East 52nd Street, New York City. "Hokokai" cotton fabric (to the trade only)—China Seas Inc., 21 East 4th Street, New York City. Rattan and iron folding chairs— Wolfman • Gold & Good Company, 116 Greene Street, New York City.
Grilled Red Snapper with Thyme; Papaya Coriander Salsa; Grilled Marinated Zucchini; Rice and Tomatoes (page 18): Vanda orchid—Zezé, 398 East 52nd Street, New York City.
Passion Fruit Mousses with Raspberry Swirl (page 19): Val St. Lambert crystal plates—Cardel Ltd., 621 Madison Avenue, New York City.

A Fondue Party
Toblerone Mousse Fondues with Meringues and Fruit (page 20): Handmade "apple" *pot de crème* dishes by Barbara Eigen—Bergdorf Goodman, 754 Fifth Avenue, New York City.
Three-Cheese Fondue with Tomato Onion Chutney; Soft Breadsticks with Fennel Seeds; Roasted Potatoes with Garlic; Assorted Vegetables and Tortellini; Watercress, Endive, and Apple Salad with Cider Dressing (page 21): ANTA ceramic chop plate and dinner plate; Biot wineglass; ANTA cotton

and linen tablecloth—Bergdorf Goodman, 754 Fifth Avenue, New York City. French copper and porcelain fondue pot—Bloomingdale's, 1000 Third Avenue, New York City. Acrylic and stainless-steel fondue forks—Bridge Kitchenware Corporation, 214 East 52nd Street, New York City. Nineteenth-century brass vase, beaker, and telescoping candlesticks—Bob Pryor Antiques, 1023 Lexington Avenue, New York City. Flowers—Zezé, 398 East 52nd Street, New York City.

Dinner Irish Style

Table Setting (pages 22 and 23): Wedgwood creamware dinner plates, circa 1780; cut-glass rummers, circa 1840, and carafes; English mochaware mugs (on table with flowers), circa 1860; "Twig" ceramic cachepots (on mantel), circa 1860; English ebony and pine candlesticks, circa 1830; china pitchers, hen banks, and stoneware squirrels (in cabinet)—Bardith Ltd., 901 Madison Avenue, New York City. "Irish Rib" hand-forged sterling flatware—James Robinson, 15 East 57th Street, New York City. Cotton napkins—Henri Bendel, Frank McIntosh Shop, 10 West 57th Street, New York City. Flowers and votive candles—Zezé, 398 East 52nd Street, New York City. Pine corner cabinet, circa 1890 (one of a pair); pine mantel, circa 1770—Kentshire Galleries, 37 East 12th Street, New York City. Nineteenth-century dummy boards—Yale R. Burge Antiques, 305 East 63rd Street, New York City. Trompe l'oeil fireplace tiles hand-painted by Richard Pellicci, (212) 988-4365. Inlaid satinwood chairs—Newel Art Galleries, Inc., 425 East 53rd Street, New York City. "Cahir" wallpaper from the Cottage Orné collection by Sybil Connolly (available through decorator)—Brunschwig & Fils, Inc., 979 Third Avenue, New York City. Oil painting—Florian Papp Inc., 962 Madison Avenue, New York City.
Fresh Ham with Cracklings and Pan Gravy; Beets with Stout and Sautéed Beet Greens; Mashed Potatoes with Scallion; Red Onion, Apple, and Raisin Chutney (page 24): Wedgwood creamware platter (with ham), circa 1780; Wedgwood platter (with beets), circa 1790; Swansea Pottery comport (with

potatoes) circa 1820—Bardith Ltd., 901 Madison Avenue, New York City. Hand-forged sterling carving knife and fork and sauce ladle—James Robinson, 15 East 57th Street, New York City. Irish silver bowls by Matthew West, Dublin, circa 1775—F. Gorevic & Son, Inc., 635 Madison Avenue, New York City.
Carrot Raisin Cake with Irish Cream Frosting (page 25): Derby cake stand, Wedgwood drabware dessert plates, circa 1820 (from a set of 10)—Bardith Ltd., 901 Madison Avenue, New York City.

An Informal Dinner

Apple Walnut Crisp (page 26): "Athena" crystal bowls—Baccarat, Inc., 625 Madison Avenue, New York City.
Braised Veal Shanks with White Bean Tomato Sauce; Saffron Orzo; Marinated Vegetable Salad; Parmesan Rolls (page 27): Fiestaware dinner plates by Homer Laughlin Co.—Bloomingdale's, 1000 Third Avenue, New York City. International sterling flatware—F. Gorevic & Son, Inc., 635 Madison Avenue, New York City. Wineglasses—Pottery Barn, 117 East 59th Street, New York City. "Athena" crystal salad bowl—Baccarat, Inc., 625 Madison Avenue, New York City. Nineteenth-century oak table—Vito Giallo Antiques, 966 Madison Avenue, New York City. "Fouquet's" rattan and Rilsan side chairs—T & K French Antiques, Inc., 120 Wooster Street, New York City.

Easter Dinner

Table Setting (pages 28 and 29): Céralene "Traviata" porcelain dinner plates—Baccarat, Inc., 625 Madison Avenue, New York City. Robb & Berking "Alta" sterling flatware—The L • S Collection, 765 Madison Avenue, New York City. Water goblets and wineglasses designed by Stephen Smyers; handmade ceramic pitcher and vase by Clarice Cliff, circa 1930—Barneys New York, Seventh Avenue and 17th Street, New York City. Hand-painted linen napkins by Liz Wain—Bergdorf Goodman, 754 Fifth Avenue, New York City. Bougainvillea trees and anemones—Zezé, 398 East 52nd

Street, New York City. Fontana Arte glass table; Viaduct "Queen Bess" metal chairs—Modern Age, 41 East 11th Street, New York City. Hand-stained wood floor by Veva Crozer—Veva Crozer, 19 Rockwood Lane, Greenwich, Connecticut.
Herbed Roast Leg of Lamb with Roasted Onions and Potatoes, Rosemary Mint Wine Jelly, Mixed Spring Vegetables, Minted Pea Purée (page 30): Sterling platter, London, 1834; sterling sauceboat, London 1754—F. Gorevic & Son, Inc., 635 Madison Avenue, New York City. Bone-handled carving knife and fork, circa 1880; silver-plate basket with opaline glass liner, circa 1870; Carey's ironstone plates, circa 1830 (from a set of 12)—James II Galleries, Ltd., 15 East 57th Street, New York City. Céralene "Traviata" porcelain platter—Baccarat, Inc., 625 Madison Avenue, New York City.
Raspberry White Chocolate Mousse Cake (page 31): English nineteenth-century glass cake stand—James II Galleries, Ltd., 15 East 57th Street, New York City.

A Poker Party

Miniature Tartufi (page 32): "T-Square" silver-plate tray designed by Richard Meier for Swid Powell—available at leading department stores.
Chicken Cacciatora with Fusilli; Arugula Salad with Carrot and Yellow Pepper; Breadsticks (page 33): Swid Powell "Eclipse" porcelain plates; silver-plate container designed by Richard Meier for Swid Powell—available at leading department stores.

A Merry May Luncheon

Table Setting (pages 34 and 35): "Parrots of Paradise" porcelain dinner plates by Lynn Chase Designs Inc.—The Naked Zebra, 279 Greenwich Avenue, Greenwich, Connecticut. "Bamboo" sterling dinner forks and knives—Tiffany & Company, 727 Fifth Avenue, New York City. Sterling salad forks, Edinburgh, 1816—S. Wyler & Son, 941 Lexington Avenue, New York City. Blue water goblets and Schott-Zweisel wineglasses—The Pottery Barn, 117 East 59th Street, New York City. "Tourreaux Check" viscose tablecloth (fabric available through decorator)—Cowtan & Tout, 979 Third Avenue, New York City. Hand-painted iron chairs from the Roma Collection for Becara of Spain (available through decorator)—The Syllian Collections, 979 Third Avenue, New York City. French nineteenth-century iron gates—Yale R. Burge, 305 East 63rd Street, New York City.

Roast Fillet of Beef with Chipotle Red Pepper Sauce and Mustard Chive Sauce; Roasted shallot and Sesame Asparagus (page 36): Italian "Wicker" ceramic platter—Tiffany & Company, 727 Fifth Avenue, New York City. English nineteenth-century sauceboats and ladles—James II Galleries, Ltd., 15 East 57th Street, New York City.

Iced Cappuccino Cream Cake (page 37): Gien "Les Tartes" faience cake plate—Baccarat, Inc., 625 Madison Avenue, New York City.

Brunch On Derby Day

Mint Juleps; Corn Cakes; Ham Biscuits; Turkey Hash; Bibb, Watercress, and Mint Salad (pages 38 and 39): Haviland "Louveciennes" porcelain dinner plates; glass salad bowl—Cardel, Ltd., 621 Madison Avenue, New York City. "Salem" sterling flatware; all-purpose crystal wineglasses—Tiffany & Co., 727 Fifth Avenue, New York City. American sterling julep cups, circa 1850; sterling trophies; English silver-plate chafing dish (cover not shown), circa 1870; sterling serving spoons, London, 1794; English silver-plate serving fork and spoon (in salad), circa 1875—S. Wyler, Inc., 941 Lexington Avenue, New York City. Hemstitched linen napkins—Léron, Inc., 750 Madison Avenue, New York City. English burl-wood tray, circa 1880; English *faux-bois* porcelain tray, circa 1840—Burke's Ltd., available from Anne Mullin Interiors, 289 Greenwich Avenue, Greenwich, Connecticut 06830. English mahogany sideboard, circa 1780—Philip Colleck of London Ltd., 830 Broadway, New York City. "Napoleon Trois" cotton fabric (available through decorator)—Brunschwig & Fils, 979 Third Avenue, New York City.

A Cocktail Party

Shrimp Toast with Pickled Ginger (page 41): Cenedese glass serving plate, yellow and blue bottles, and charger (on column)—The L • S Collection, 765 Madison Avenue, New York City. iittala "Marius" glasses and decanter by Markku Salo—iittala, Inc., P.O. Box 463, Elmsford, New York 10523. Hand-painted linen cocktail napkins by Liz Wain—Thaxton & Company, 780 Madison Avenue, New York City. Split-granite triangular nesting tables on casters by Rei Kawakubo—Modern Age, 41 East 11th Street, New York City. Columns hand-painted by Richard Pellicci, (212) 988-4365.

Potato Samosa Tartlets; Thai-Style Chicken Salad on Cumin Quick Bread; Miniature Roquefort Napoleons; Oriental Stuffed Mushrooms; Cod Fritters with Tartar Sauce; Fruit Kebabs with Vanilla Mint Yogurt Sauce (pages 42 and 43): Cenedese gray serving plate; "Trianon" silver-plate tray by Ken Benson; acrylic "Trampoline" by Frieda Bakker—The L • S Collection, 765 Madison Avenue, New York City. "Capitello" gray and white earthenware buffet plate by Renée—Thaxton & Company, 780 Madison Avenue, New York City. Armetale rectangular metal trays by Wilton Armetale; blue-rimmed glass plate—D.F. Sanders & Co., 127 East 57th Street, New York City.

Perennial Garden Luncheons

Pasta with Summer Vegetables, Goat Cheese Toasts (page 44): French faience salad plate—Barneys New York, Seventh Avenue and Seventeenth Street, New York City.

Grilled Chicken Salad with Corn, Peppers, and Tortilla Crisps (page 45): French faience dinner plates—Barneys New York, Seventh Avenue and Seventeenth Street, New York City. Painted rattan table and wicker chairs—J. Garvin Mecking Antiques, 72 East 11th Street, New York City. Perennial garden design—Yard by Yard, (203) 661-2655 (by appointment only).

Summer Picnics

Twilight Dessert Picnic (page 47): "Eugénie de Montijo" porcelain dessert plates and cake plate—Bernardaud, 41 Madison Avenue, New York City. "Chatsworth" metal tray and cotton napkins—Barneys, Seventh Avenue and Seventeenth Street, New York City. Ceramic plate (with macaroons and fruit) and holder; wicker basket—Wolfman • Gold & Good Company, 116 Greene Street, New York City.

Meadow Picnic (pages 48 and 49): Hand-painted ceramic dinner plates and pasta bowl by Fioriware; "Boxwood" flatware by Siècle—Barneys, Seventh Avenue and Seventeenth Street, New York City. Hand-painted nineteenth-century tin box (with wine)—Wolfman • Gold & Good Company, 116 Greene Street, New York City.

Fourth Of July Dinner

Salmon, Scallop, and Pea Terrine; Chive Butter Sauce; Dilled Potatoes Vinaigrette; Tomato, Mint, and Red Onion Salad (page 51): Ceramic plate by Nicola Fasano; wineglass by Laure Japy; etched glass bowl—Bergdorf Goodman, 754 Fifth Avenue, New York City.

A Santa Barbara Barbecue

Table Setting (pages 52 and 53): Earthenware dinner plates by Barbara Eigen—Pierre Lafond, 516 San Ysidro Road, Santa Barbara, California. "Baguette" stainless-steel flatware; "Tuscany" wineglasses—Wolfman • Gold & Good Company, 116 Greene Street, New York City. Cotton napkins—Umbrello, 8607 Melrose Avenue, Los Angeles, California. Earthenware bowls by Barbara Eigen; hand-woven runner by Muffy Young—Zona, 97 Greene Street, New York City. Hand-painted wooden tray (holding vegetables, as centerpiece)—Portico, 379 West Broadway, New York City. Cedar table, circa 1850, and handmade ironwood chairs—Statement on Montana, 1302 Montana Avenue, Santa Monica, California.

Barbecued Spareribs; Southern-Style Tomato Barbecue Sauce; Grilled Corn; Sage Butter; Okra, Squash, and Onion

Kebabs; Mixed Greens and Tomatoes with Anchovy Dressing (pages 54 and 55): Earthenware banana leaf tray by Barbara Eigen—Afton Grove, 1000 Torrey Pines Road, La Jolla, California. Chicken-wire basket—Zona, 97 Greene Street, New York City. Acrylic-handled butter knife—Barneys New York, Seventh Avenue and Seventeenth Street, New York City. Wooden saltshaker and pepper mill—Bridge Kitchenware Corporation, 214 East 52nd Street, New York City. Cotton fabric (under tray of vegetables, on wall)—Umbrello, 8607 Melrose Avenue, Los Angeles, California.

A Beach Picnic

Beach Picnic (page 57): Acrylic plates and flatware—Lee Bailey at Saks Fifth Avenue, 611 Fifth Avenue, New York City. Ovenproof porcelain platters—Bridge Kitchenware Corporation, 214 East 52nd Street, New York City. Napkins made of "Calicut" cotton fabric (available through decorator)—China Seas, 979 Third Avenue, New York City. Table, tray, and baskets hand-painted by Richard Pellicci, (212) 988-4365.

A Late-Summer Dinner

Table Setting (pages 58 and 59): Molin Charolles ceramic plates; "Sand" and "Wind" crystal glasses by Hilton McConnico for Daum, silver-plate salt-shakers and pepper grinders and gold-plate salt and pepper shakers—Bergdorf Goodman, 754 Fifth Avenue, New York City. Bissell & Wilhite stainless-steel flatware—Henri Bendel, Frank McIntosh Shop, 10 West 57th Street, New York City. Cotton napkins—Barneys New York, Seventh Avenue and 17th Street, New York City. Metallic hand-painted wood napkin rings by Chateau X—Wolfman • Gold & Good Company, 116 Greene Street, New York City. Crystal and wire sculpture (on table) and painted metal lanterns (around pool) by Bob Russell—Stubbs Books & Prints, 835 Madison Avenue, New York City. "Astrolabio" frosted glass table on metal base; "Abanica" wicker and iron stackable chairs—Modern Age, 41 East 11th Street, New York City.

Austrian-Style Fried Chicken, Corn and Zucchini Timbales, Tomato Chutney (page 61): Annieglass platter—Bergdorf Goodman, 754 Fifth Avenue, New York City. Gold and pewter bowl and plate—Barneys New York, Seventh Avenue and 17th Street, New York City.

A Rooftop Breakfast

Walnut and Wheat Germ Silver-Dollar Pancakes; Blackberry Syrup; Melted Butter (page 62): Handmade ceramic plates by Barbara Eigen—Zona, 97 Greene Street, New York City. Glass pitchers—Simon Pearce, 385 Bleecker Street, New York City.
A Rooftop Breakfast (page 63): "Wheat" ceramic coffeepot, sugar bowl, creamer, and mugs; cotton napkins; "Twig" furniture—Wolfman • Gold & Good Company, 116 Greene Street, New York City. Footed glass compotes—Zona, 97 Greene Street, New York City. Terrace design—Sadler Lassiter Architectural Design, 218 Madison Avenue, New York City.

An Autumn Dinner

Table Setting (page 65): "Clarendon" bone china chargers by Wedgwood for Ralph Lauren; "Glen Plaid" clear crystal wineglasses by Ralph Lauren; "Woodsman Check" cotton napkins by Ralph Lauren—Polo/Ralph Lauren, 867 Madison Avenue, New York City. Cobalt blue water glasses, circa 1865 (from a set of 6); cabochon garnet and brass candlesticks, circa 1860 (from a desk set); oak and silver-plate cruet set, circa 1870; porcelain playing card cachepot, circa 1845; George II mahogany leather upholstered armchairs, circa 1775 (set of 4); Regency mahogany cabinet with marble top and bookbinding front, circa 1870 (one of a pair); terra-cotta dog, circa 1870; Regency tole planter, circa 1810 (one of a pair); English sporting painting, circa 1780; George I lacquered secretary, circa 1720 (and all items on secretary)—Kentshire Galleries, 37 East 12th Street, New York City. "Kings" hand-forged sterling flatware—James Robinson, 15 East 57th Street, New York City. Scottish tartanware napkin rings, circa 1870 (from a set of 6)—James II

Galleries, Ltd., 15 East 57th Street, New York City. Linen punchwork tablecloth, circa 1910—Ann Lawrence Antiques, 250 West 39th Street, New York City.
Chocolate Chestnut Torte (page 67): Stoneware cheese dish (cover not shown) by George Skey, Wincole Works, Tamworth, 1862-1900; pottery butter dish (lid not shown), circa 1880—Kentshire Galleries, 37 East 12th Street, New York City. "Emma" pressed glass dessert plates by Ralph Lauren; "MacPherson" wool challis table shawl—Polo/Ralph Lauren, 867 Madison Avenue, New York City.

A Spanish Dinner for Columbus Day

Prune Sherry Ice Cream with Burnt Sugar Sauce (page 68): "Brazil" handmade ceramic dessert plates, "Maple Leaf" glazed earthenware jug—Williams-Sonoma, 20 East 60th Street, New York City. Porcelain platter—Bridge Kitchenware Corporation, 214 East 52nd Street, New York City.
Arroz con Pollo, Escarole Salad with Tarragon (page 69): "Brazil" handmade ceramic plates, hand-blown Spanish wine goblets, cotton and linen napkins, terra-cotta *cazuela*—Williams-Sonoma, 20 East 60th Street, New York City.

Thanksgiving Dinner

Table Setting (pages 70 and 71): "Oak Leaf" hand-forged sterling flatware—Old Newbury Crafters, 36 Main Street, Amesbury, Massachusetts. Tel. (800) 343-1388. Royal Worcester porcelain dinner plates and soup bowls, 1879, from a service for 12; English pub glasses, circa 1870, from a set of 13; English amber glass cornucopia vases, circa 1840, and a collection of nineteenth-century amber glass candlesticks; nut dishes from a doll's house dinner service, circa 1870; English sterling napkin rings, circa 1875, from a set of 12; English silver-plate salt cellars and spoons, circa 1875—James II Galleries, Ltd., 15 East 57th Street, New York City. Sterling beakers—James Robinson, Inc., 15 East 57th Street, New York City. "Misty Stitch" handmade linen napkins—Piedad Mantilla, by appointment only. Tel. (718) 458-

5681. Flower arrangements—Zezé, 398 East 52nd Street, New York City. *Roast Turkey with Corn Bread and Kale Stuffing and Paprika Pan Gravy; Cranberry Sauce with Pearl Onions and Golden Raisins; Sherried Sweet Potatoes and Apples; Lemony Creamed Brussels Sprouts and Celery* (pages 72 and 73): Royal Worcester porcelain platters, vegetable dishes, and sauceboat, 1879; English horn-handled carving set, circa 1870; English silver-plate sauce ladle, circa 1880—James II Galleries, Ltd., 15 East 57th Street, New York City. "Oak Leaf" hand-forged serving fork and spoons—Old Newbury Crafters, 36 Main Street, Amesbury, Massachusetts. Tel. (800) 343-1388. English cut-glass decanter, circa 1800, and cut-glass footed bowl, circa 1820—Bardith Ltd., 901 Madison Avenue, New York City. Copper lustre pitcher, circa 1850—Ages Past Antiques, 1030 Lexington Avenue, New York City.

An Elegant Small Thanksgiving

Roast Quail with Cranberry Madeira Sauce; Dauphine Potatoes; Petits Pois (page 75): "Lucia" china dinner plates by Lenox—Lenox Consumer Service, (800) 635-3669. "Lady Hamilton" silver-plate flatware—Oneida Silversmiths, Oneida, New York. "Capri Gold" crystal water goblets and wineglasses—Baccarat, Inc., 625 Madison Avenue, New York City. English china candlesticks, circa 1910 (available through decorator)—Burke's, Ltd., 979 Third Avenue, New York City. Set of six Queen Anne–style walnut chairs, circa 1900 (available through decorator)—Yale R. Burge Antiques, Inc., 305 East 63rd Street, New York City.

Christmas Dinner

Table Setting (pages 76 and 77): Appenzell-embroidered napkins (from a set including a tablecloth and 12 napkins), circa 1910—Ann Lawrence Antiques, 250 West 39th Street, New York City. Baccarat "Massena" crystal candlesticks—Baccarat, Inc., 625 Madison Avenue, New York City. Egyptian cotton tablecloth by Anichini—E. Braun & Co., Inc., 717 Madison Avenue, New York City. Mahogany serving table, circa 1880; majolica urns, circa 1870; majolica coupe (with cherubs), circa 1880; brass repoussé mirror, circa 1850; neoclassical mahogany and ebony armchair with star motif (one of a pair), circa 1820; Charles X cherry side chairs (from a set of 4), circa 1820—Yale R. Burge Antiques, 305 East 63rd Street, New York City. Handmade Bessarabian wool rug, 1919—Coury Rugs, Inc., 515 Madison Avenue, New York City. Flowers and evergreens—Zezé, 398 East 52nd Street, New York City. *Loin of Veal with Shiitake Stuffing; Buttered Haricots Verts* (page 78): Bernardaud "Consulat" porcelain dinner plate—Bernardaud, 777 Madison Avenue, New York City. Christofle "Triade" silver-plate flatware—Pavillon Christofle, 680 Madison Avenue, New York City. Baccarat "Nancy" crystal wineglasses—Baccarat, Inc., 625 Madison Avenue, New York City. Saint Louis "Firmament Blue" crystal water goblets—Bergdorf Goodman, 754 Fifth Avenue, New York City. *Macadamia Nut and Bittersweet Chocolate Ice-Cream Bombe with Macadamia Nut Praline* (page 79): English sterling salver by Crichton, circa 1910; Newhall porcelain dessert plates, circa 1810—S. Wyler, Inc., 941 Lexington Avenue, New York City.

A Christmas Eve Supper

Lemon Meringue Custards (page 80): Hand-painted tole platter—Wolfman • Gold & Good Company, 116 Greene Street, New York City. (The platter is garnished with sugar-coated holly leaves, which are toxic and should not come in contact with food.) *Baked Oysters with Spinach Fennel Purée and Crisp Fried Shallots; Clams Casino; Fillet of Beef on Garlic Croutons with Roasted Onion, Caper, and Tarragon Sauce; Baked Olive and Mozzarella Orzo; Yuletide Tossed Salad* (page 81): English creamware dinner plates; English ceramic platter, circa 1920; green wooden planter (32 inches high, legs not visible), circa 1900—Wolfman • Gold & Good Company, 116 Greene Street, New York City. "Georgian Bead" sterling forks and knives—F. Gorevic & Son, Inc., 635 Madison Avenue, New York City. Cotton napkins—Henri Bendel, Frank McIntosh Shop, 10 West 57th Street, New York City. Eighteenth-century reproduction pewter pitcher—Piccola Cucina, 334 East 11th Street, New York City.

A Recipe Compendium

Rowboat Picnic (page 82): Beacon wool blanket, circa 1930 (one of a kind)—Zona, 97 Greene Street, New York City. Myrtlewood basket—Wolfman • Gold & Good Company, 116 Greene Street, New York City.

Back Jacket

Grilled Chicken and Ziti Salad: See Table Setting credits for Summer Picnics (Meadow Picnic) above.